Migration in the Global Political Economy

Migration in the Global Political Economy

Volume 17 • International Political Economy Yearbook

Edited By Nicola Phillips

Viva Books

New Delhi | Mumbai | Chennai | Kolkata | Bengaluru | Hyderabad | Kochi | Guwahati

First Indian Edition 2012

VIVA BOOKS PRIVATE LIMITED

- 4737/23 Ansari Road, Daryaganj, New Delhi 110 002
  E-mail: vivadelhi@vivagroupindia.net, Tel. 42242200
- 76, Service Industries, Shirvane, Sector 1, Nerul, Navi Mumbai 400 706
  E-mail: vivamumbai@vivagroupindia.net, Tel. 27721273, 27721274
- Jamals Fazal Chambers, 26 Greams Road, Chennai 600 006
  E-mail: vivachennai@vivagroupindia.net, Tel. 28290304, 28294241
- B-103, Jindal Towers, 21/1A/3 Darga Road, Kolkata 700 017
  E-mail: vivakolkata@vivagroupindia.net, Tel. 22836381, 22816713
- 7, Sovereign Park Apartments, 56-58, K. R. Road, Basavanagudi, Bengaluru 560 004
  E-mail: vivabangalore@vivagroupindia.net, Tel. 26607409, 26607410
- 101-102 Mughal Marc Apartments, 3-4-637 to 641, Narayanguda, Hyderabad 500 029
  E-mail: vivahyderabad@vivagroupindia.net, Tel. 27564481, 27564482
- Beevi Towers, First Floor, SRM Road, Kaloor, Kochi 682 018, Kerala
  E-mail: vivakochi@vivagroupindia.net, Tel: 0484-2403055, 2403056
- 232, GNB Road, Beside UCO Bank, Silpukhuri, Guwahati 781 003
  E-mail: vivaguwahati@vivagroupindia.net, Tel: 0361-2666386

www.vivagroupindia.com

Published by arrangement with

Lynne Rienner Publishers, Inc.
1800 30th Street, Suite 314
Boulder, Colorado 80301
USA

ISBN : 978-81-309-2015-3

Published by Vinod Vasishtha for Viva Books Private Limited, 4737/23, Ansari Road, Daryaganj, New Delhi-110 002. Printed and bound by Saku Printers, New Delhi.

Contents

1

Migration in the Global Political Economy

Nicola Phillips

We live, unquestionably, in an "age of migration" (Castles and Miller, 2009). In the middle of the 2000s, widely cited estimates from the United Nations indicated a total number of migrants worldwide of 191 million. But this figure refers only to documented migrants and increases very significantly if we add to it the huge numbers of "undocumented" migrants across the world. Equally, it refers only to migrants moving across international borders, and leaves aside the vast movements of people within countries. The scale and speed of internal migration from rural to urban areas in China, in particular, is without historical precedent. Of course, mobility has underpinned the very history of humanity. But the contemporary era is qualitatively distinct inasmuch as these movements are now genuinely global. Whether as movements of refugees or of workers, contemporary migration shapes all regions and countries of the world. More to the point, it is fundamental to the continuing evolution of the global economy and all its constituent parts. It is not possible to understand the myriad processes we tend to sum up in the term "globalization"—and indeed its many tensions, contradictions, and consequences—without understanding the dynamics of global migration.

It is therefore both striking and curious that the field of international political economy (IPE) should have so neglected the study of global migration. Despite its core agenda of understanding the nature, functioning, and evolution of the global political economy, migration has consistently made only a minor showing in the universe of what is generally classified as IPE scholarship. Even the substantial debates on labor in the global political economy are only rarely enriched by perspectives and approaches drawn from the study of global labor migration. At the same time, the study of migration has too infrequently been approached through the lens of the theoretical constructs and core debates of IPE. More usually, migration has been the preoccupation of social scientists working within such disciplinary fields as sociology or anthropology, as well as the more discrete field of migration studies. Not surprisingly, the most developed theoretical pillars of migration scholarship reflect this profile. The immediate aims of this contribution to the International Political Economy Yearbook series are therefore to do something about this state of affairs—that is, to push further the integration of global migration into the core concerns of IPE and equally to advance the study of the global political economy of migration.

Of course, all these claims constitute rather large generalizations about the state of both IPE and migration studies and overlook a number of very honorable exceptions in each instance, including the work of the authors of the contributions to this volume and that of other scholars acknowledged abundantly in it. Despite their accuracy as generalizations, they also become rather problematic inasmuch as what one has to say about IPE depends on how one defines IPE, and which kind of IPE one engages with. This is not the place to rehearse the vigorous, ongoing debates about what IPE is and should be (Cohen, 2008; Phillips and Weaver, 2010). Rather, it is pertinent simply to point out that "IPE" means many things to many people and that what an IPE perspective on migration would look like is not at all self-evident; it is a question that would attract a huge number of different responses from all sides. I will therefore use this introduction to outline briefly what kind of IPE perspective is being put to work in this volume and how it informs the substance and contribution of the chapters that follow.

The first point to make is that the controversies around IPE take their cue from the wide variety of theoretical and methodological approaches that cluster together, often uncomfortably and at times fractiously, within the field. Yet part of the strength of an IPE approach, as least as it is desirably conceived, is that it opens up much more space than many other approaches do for engagement between diverse perspectives and for a consciously cross- or interdisciplinary mode of inquiry. Admittedly, this potential has not yet been fully realized: one of the perhaps unfortunate characteristics of the field of IPE is that, despite its initial promise to reach across the terrain of the social sciences in the spirit of earlier traditions of political economy, it has in fact remained largely rooted in the discipline of international relations, and its core theoretical, methodological, and empirical concerns reflect this ongoing association. This is particularly the case in the more orthodox strands of IPE associated with what some have called the "American school" of the field (Murphy and Nelson, 2001; Phillips, 2005a; Cohen, 2008; Phillips and Weaver, 2010). But it is to some extent also the case in those parts of IPE that identify themselves with critical scholarship and purport to retain more loyalty to the traditions of political economy. Thus it is fair to say that a good deal of the interdisciplinary openness envisaged for the field at its inception has failed to materialize.

Yet the potential for such openness remains, and we seek to realize it in this study of the global political economy of migration, which in turn reflects what we consider to be the requirements for the effective study of the complex processes and patterns of migration in the contemporary world. Indeed, it has often been noted that migration studies are necessarily interdisciplinary in character; thus framing the key political economy questions about migration in this way pays considerable dividends. The chapters in this volume show that a great deal can be gained in the study of the global political economy of migration by bringing together theoretical, conceptual, and empirical perspectives from geography, sociology, anthropology, economics, political science, and development studies.

Second, our approach is inspired by the core prospectus for what has come to be termed a "new" or "critical" political economy. This hinges on striking a conceptual balance and integration between analysis that concentrates on the nature and influence of "structures," on the one hand, and that which emphasizes the "agency" of key economic, political, and social actors, on the other, in shaping the global political economy (see Cox, 1987; Gamble, 1995; Payne, 1998). IPE and the field of migration studies have often diverged on this terrain. Much of the field of IPE has reflected the structuralist inclination that has always permeated the enterprise of political economy—that is to say, as summarized by Andrew Gamble, that "a proper understanding of the politics [in political economy] requires giving special explanatory weight to economic structures and processes" (1995: 517). The result has often been either to give little attention to agency or to presume that little *intrinsic* interest needs to be afforded to politics and agency in understanding the global political economy (Phillips, 2005b: 254). Conversely, it could reasonably be said that a good part of the field of migration studies has operated on the opposite assumption—that is, it has maintained a focus on agency and politics at the expense of the big political economy picture associated with the functioning of the global economy and the political-economic structures that propel and shape particular kinds of labor migration.

As a corrective, the metatheoretical principle of integrating structure and agency has come to underpin the more critical variants of the contemporary IPE project, and our contention here is that such an approach becomes especially important and instructive in the study of the global political economy of migration. On the one hand, it allows due attention to the structural context within which contemporary migration takes place and in turn to the implications of migration for the evolution of these structures. On the other hand, it calls for appropriate analysis of the forms of agency that constitute and shape migration processes, along with the politics generated by those processes and the manner in which migration is governed at the global, regional, national, and local levels. Specifically, it facilitates an approach to understanding the social foundations of the global political economy, which, as Marcus Taylor astutely observes, have been consistently obscured by the "somewhat fanciful vision of the economy perpetuated in mainstream economics" and replicated in large parts of the field of IPE (2008: 2). This vision essentially defines the "global economy" as the global marketplace in which individuals and firms behave according to the principles of rationality, liberty, stable preferences, and perfect foresight. The result is the concealment of the "everyday power relationships"—that is, the forms of power, politics, and contestation that are inseparable from "everyday material life"—that constitute the social foundations of the global economy (Taylor, 2008: 2). The dynamics of migration and the evolving manner in which migrant labor is embedded in the global political economy represent a pivotal dimension of these social foundations and offer arresting insights into the everyday power relationships to which Taylor refers. For this reason, the neglect of migration dynamics in IPE, even in those analyses concerned with the social foundations of the global economy and issues of labor, is particularly curious and unfortunate.

A focus on migration similarly reinforces a critique of dominant conceptions of agency in IPE and helps to refine our approach to the structure-agency dynamic. It is striking that dominant understandings of agency in IPE, and indeed in other areas of the social sciences, refer in the main to formal, often organized forms of agency with a strong transnational articulation. But, as the chapters in this volume reveal, the relationship between structure and agency looks very different when the focus is on informal, unorganized, and/or disenfranchised actors who have few or no possibilities for influence or participation, face a very different set of political realities, and operate in local and "private" (including domestic) contexts (Phillips, 2005b: 256–257)—characteristics that apply to large parts of the global migrant labor force. A focus on migration thus injects issues of informality forcefully into our analyses of global political economy and invites us fruitfully to reconsider how we understand agency and politics.

The final core dimension of the approach that informs this volume relates to geographical reach. Here again, the perspective is one that draws on the potential of IPE to develop a genuinely global political economy of migration, based on valuable insights into the spatial organization of the global political economy and the ways in which particular spatial dynamics arise from, and in turn condition, particular political economies. Conversely, a much greater focus in IPE on migration offers insights of considerable pertinence into the ways in which we understand and theorize these spatial dynamics: how particular parts of the world are drawn together in complex transnational markets and social networks; how the spatial and the social intersect and mesh with one another; and how increasingly globalized networks of production and trade rest equally on a global labor force, large parts of which are highly mobile. In this spirit, the authors of this volume explore migration as it manifests itself geographically across the structures of the global economy and across the conditions and processes of global development, bringing together perspectives on migration and development in some of the poorer regions of the world with explorations of the political economy of immigration in some of the richer countries. Equally, attention to international and south-north forms of migration is complemented by analysis of migration within countries and regions, including the patterns of south-south migration that are often given rather less attention than those kinds of movement that raise issues of immigration for the core countries of the global political economy.

These three dimensions of our approach—interdisciplinary openness, the integration of structure- and agency-centered analysis, and a wide geographical/spatial reach—inform the ways in which this volume has been organized as well as the substance of its contents.

Part 1: Migration and Global Capitalism

Part 1 addresses dimensions of global migration in the context of the dynamics of global capitalism. It offers four chapters that are linked together by a preoccupation with changing forms of stratification, segmentation, and segregation in global labor markets, and with the complex ways in which the evolution of contemporary labor markets relies on and is facilitated by migration, and in turn shapes the everyday experiences of migrant and nonmigrant workers. The chapters reveal that new and changing forms of labor market segmentation and social stratification operate along a variety of axes relating variously to skill, "cultural capital" (to use Pierre Bourdieu's term), citizenship and migration status, race, ethnicity, and gender.

In Chapter 2, Carl-Ulrik Schierup and Stephen Castles initiate this discussion by focusing on the forms of stratification and polarization that result from what they call "racialized ethnicity." They identify this particular hierarchy as operating alongside the other hierarchies that shape the neoliberalization of contemporary societies, and specifically feed into the ongoing changes in the form of contemporary welfare states in western Europe and the United States—namely those of gender, class, and geography. Concretely, Schierup and Castles argue that the construction of a social hierarchy associated with racialized ethnicity is crucial in the ongoing shift toward the "recommodification" of labor under neoliberalism—that is, a shift away from welfare universalism and social redistribution as a means of (re-)connecting the welfare of people with their value as workers in a supposedly free market for labor. Schierup and Castles' analysis shows that the resulting trend toward "increasingly brutalized approaches to the governance of welfare and race" is most pronounced and furthest advanced in the United States, but is also progressively emulated in Europe. Significantly, migrant workers are among the main victims of the retraction of welfare states and the deregulation of labor markets, and the expansion of migrant labor forces and the dynamics of "racialization" constitute crucial strategies by which labor can be recommodified according to the logic of neoliberalization. Thus we see the dual dynamic by which migrant labor is affected by the restructuring of the global political economy even as it embodies one of the pivotal means by which this restructuring is enabled and entrenched.

Harald Bauder complements this discussion in Chapter 3 by exploring the ways in which forms of legal and cultural regulation act to segment and polarize labor markets. Using the cases of Canada and Germany as the empirical reference points, Bauder echoes Schierup and Castles's emphasis on neoliberalism as the overarching context as he demonstrates how legal and cultural mechanisms of regulation are different in the upper and lower segments of the labor market, producing manifestly different outcomes for migrant workers in each segment. In other words, he is interested in how privileged and underprivileged migrant labor operates in different legal and cultural fields, and explores in each case how their variable attributes of citizenship, cultural capital, and gender act to determine their positioning within labor markets and to entrench the distinctions between these categories. Yet Bauder is quick to highlight the relative nature of this privilege. He cautions against an excessively simplistic view of privileged labor as being able easily to construct what he calls "transnational cultural competences" that ease the conditions of migration and the process of integration into labor markets and societies. Rather, he argues, even in the case of privileged labor, mobility is "risky and typically a problematic and painful accumulation strategy." The difference is that privileged labor is better equipped to navigate the legal and cultural obstacles that affect all migrants' ability to move their various forms of capital—human and cultural—across borders.

In Chapter 4, Nicola Piper takes up the consideration of gender hierarchies in global labor markets, an issue mentioned in both of the preceding chapters, and the forms of social and labor market stratification that emerge along these lines. She takes as her starting point the key process of "feminization" that has characterized both the dynamics of global migration and the nature of global labor markets more broadly as a consequence of the informalization, casualization, and increased precariousness of work across the global economy. She innovatively seeks to draw a link between various dimensions of feminization—namely, the feminizations of work, migration, and poverty—and explores how a focus on global productive and care chains can help us to construct a "gendered political economy of migration." In this way, Piper throws the spotlight onto what she calls "the global division of productive and reproductive labor" which is structured by hierarchies associated with gender alongside social class, ethnicity, and race, thereby picking up on the themes addressed by Schierup and Castles and Bauder. The construction of a more consciously gendered political economy of migration in turn proffers valuable contributions to the development of IPE itself, particularly in highlighting the social foundations of material life, to which we alluded earlier, and the everyday aspects of political economy that are often obscured by the focus on global markets and debates over how they function.

Complementing Bauder's emphasis on citizenship as a key mechanism by which labor markets and societies are stratified and segmented, in Chapter 5 H. Richard Friman throws into the mix a focus on migration status, considering the ways in which informal, illicit, and illegal forms of migration both function within the global political economy and consolidate an axis of differentiation between different groups of (migrant) workers. Friman usefully points out that illegal and informal migration has generally been addressed with reference to the lucrative illegal migration business or industry associated with smuggling and trafficking operations, but that the ways in which structures and politics intersect to shape this industry, and the phenomena to which it responds, have been strikingly underexplored. Friman thus argues both for more attention within IPE to informal and illegal movements of people, and for a more sustained IPE analysis of this dimension of the global political economy of migration. He suggests that this involves analyzing and theorizing the conditioning role of the interplay of states and markets, on the one hand, and the post-Fordist intersection of the licit and illicit global economies, on the other. What emerges very clearly from Friman's chapter is a challenge to conventional and orthodox currents in IPE which, as we noted, focus heavily on the formal markets that make up the global economy. Instead, Friman reveals the very blurred lines between the formal, informal, and illicit criminal economies and invites us to think much more carefully about the social foundations of the global political economy in this light.

Part 2: The Migration-Development Nexus

It is only since the mid-1990s that questions about the relationship between migration and development have found a central place in scholarly and policy debates about both global migration and global development (Skeldon, 2008). In both cases, they have been framed preponderantly in terms of south-north migration, specifically in relation to the potential connections between migration from poorer to richer countries and development in the countries of origin. The chapters collected in Part 2 of the book engage with these established debates, but equally seek to go beyond them by challenging many of the conventional theoretical assumptions about the nature of the relationship between migration and development, and by exploring empirically the diverse forms that the "migration-development nexus" takes in different parts of the world.

Ronald Skeldon sets the tone in Chapter 6 by extending his long-standing argument that development and migration cannot be seen as separate phenomena. Whereas the task as conventionally conceived is to explore how these two processes relate to one another, Skeldon suggests that development and migration are "inextricably linked in a matrix of change." In so doing, he emphasizes the shortcomings of much of the debate—especially in policy circles but also in scholarly ones—about how theoretically we should understand migration and development in the global political economy. The emphasis on understanding a migration-development nexus in this spirit is echoed through the other chapters in this section. Skeldon's second key point is that attempts to identify a single relationship between migration and development are misdirected, inasmuch as the dynamic nature of the migration process, changing as it does across space and time, generates divergent and necessarily fluid interpretations of the migration-development nexus. His third key argument considers the issue of structure and agency, taking issue with the trend in recent discussions of migration and development to shift the responsibility for development (and development failures) away from political-economic structures and toward the individual migrant—that is, to cast the migrant worker as the agent of development. Again, this theme is echoed in the other chapters in Part 2. Skeldon argues that the debate thus suffers from a situation in which, as he puts it pithily, "the migration tail is beginning to wag the development dog," and makes the persuasive case that explanations for development failures are appropriately rooted in broader economic and social structures rather than in the agency of migrant workers.

Chapters 7, 8, and 9 explore some of these debates in the regional contexts of sub-Saharan Africa, Asia, and Latin America and the Caribbean. Here it is interesting to see both the commonalities in the contemporary migration-development nexuses that obtain in each setting and the key differences among the political economies of the three regions. All three chapters combine rich empirical detail with reflections on the core debates about how we should conceive of and theorize the relationship between migration and development. In Chapter 7, Oliver Bakewell picks up on many of the themes introduced by Skeldon and sets out particularly to challenge the prevailing assumption that migration is both a symptom of development failure and a development problem that stands in need of remedy. He highlights the ways in which the notion of development has historically been (and remains) inextricably linked in sub-Saharan Africa to the control of mobility; as he puts it, the assumption driving the debate is that development is a "sedentary" condition in which people would not migrate unless driven by necessity. To the contrary, Bakewell shows that in the sub-Saharan African context migration is at least as much the result of development as the result of development failure, and that the two cannot be separated from one another in understanding the political economy of the region. At the same time, the contradictory attempts to turn migration into a policy lever are misplaced and inappropriate, based as they are on what Bakewell calls the "chimera" and "impossible fantasy" of a virtuous circle in which migration stimulates development processes and in turn reduces migration.

With Ken Young's chapter, we turn our attention to one of the major regional arenas of global migration, Asia. Young captures the complexity of the political economy of migration in this region through a detailed exploration of the varieties and patterns of movement, and he shows—in a manner that intersects nicely with the findings of Bauder and Piper—how the processes and consequences of migration among different groups of people diverge significantly. He also shows clearly how migration is intrinsic to the changing political economy of the region and specifically to the transformation of Asian economies into high-growth centers of the global economy; migration across the region is clearly associated with national growth and the expansion of globalization. Yet Young concurs with other contributors in questioning the extent to which these trends should be seen, let alone celebrated, as unambiguous manifestations of development.

In the chapter that concludes this part of the book, I turn to Latin America and the Caribbean and frame the discussion around the theoretical and conceptual debates about the nature of the migration-development nexus. I argue that our understanding of this nexus is necessarily conditioned by the definition of development that we choose to adopt: the nexus looks very different when approached from a position that emphasizes development as a process of national growth, as opposed to one that rests on a notion of "human" development. In this chapter, I locate migration within the regional political economy of development by exploring the restructuring of labor markets, the dynamics of inequality, and the framing of migration increasingly as a core national development strategy in large parts of the region. On this basis, I go on to explore the divergent perspectives offered by the two approaches to development as a means to understand the political economy of migration both from and within the region. The discussion suggests that many of the debates around the migration-development nexus—and certainly the more optimistic accounts thereof—rest not on notions of human development connected with the material and social conditions in which people (including migrant workers) live, but instead on a conception of development as a national phenomenon associated with the growth of national economies. Thus many of the necessary questions about how migration both arises from and puts in place diverse forms of unequal development are too often obscured from view.

Part 3: The Governance of Migration

The chapters in Part 3 of this volume explore a different dimension of the global political economy of migration, namely the manner in which political actors seek to govern migration processes. The chapters collectively focus on those contexts that are characterized by high levels of immigration, complementing the focus in other parts of the volume on contexts in which the challenges stem primarily from high levels of internal migration and/or out-migration. The chapters offer further interesting insights into the core issue of the relationship between structures and agency in shaping the global political economy of migration.

In Chapter 10, Andrew Geddes takes the European Union (EU) as his focus, inquiring into the role of borders in shaping both the structures and politics that govern migration in this context. He frames the issue insightfully by conceptualizing borders as the sites at which migration "acquires meaning as a distinct social process" and innovatively conceives of borders not just in the conventional sense, as markers of territory, but also as organizational in character, associated with work and welfare, and conceptual, associated with notions of belonging, entitlement, and identity. In so doing, his discussion intersects suggestively with other chapters in Part 1 of the volume, particularly those of Schierup and Castles and Bauder. Geddes argues that EU strategies to control and manage migration, concentrated as they are in efforts to secure and strengthen territorial borders, carry particularly damaging consequences for organizational and conceptual borders, and he explores the political and institutional processes that have propelled the emergence of these strategies.

The emphasis on politics and institutions is carried through by Susan Martin in Chapter 11, where she addresses the dynamics of immigration reform in the United States. Her central objective is to explain the paralysis in immigration reform that has long prevailed in this context, pointing to an intractable contradiction between the structural centrality of migrant labor in the US economy and the continued political and social reaction against large-scale immigration, along with the repeated failures to put in place legislation that could effectively address the problem of illegal movements of workers into the United States. She explores these issues in the context of the most recent attempt at comprehensive immigration reform, which took place during the administration of George W. Bush, and concludes that the contradictions that govern the politics of immigration in the United States, and indeed across the world, remain firmly in place.

In Chapter 12, Jock Collins takes our attention finally to Australia, where again the politics of immigration have been thrown into sharp relief in the form of ethnic tensions and social unrest. Like Martin and Geddes, as well as others in the volume, he starts from the key contradiction between the global economic and labor market structures that shape the place of migrant labor in the Australian economy and the reactions against immigrant workers that are visible in both electoral politics and everyday social life. Collins explores the ways in which both official immigration policy and the societal dynamics of immigration reflect these contradictions and carry significant implications for the welfare and experiences of migrant workers. His conclusions are amplified in the context of the global economic crisis of the late 2000s, whereby, in a "cruel irony," migrant workers shoulder the greatest burden of the recession and are most adversely affected by it even as, across the world, they are made the scapegoats for it.

My concluding chapter picks up where Collins leaves off, offering a tentative perspective on the implications of the global economic crisis for migration and migrants. I seek to reflect on what we now know about these implications and to consider what they indicate for future trends. One thing that is already clear is that both migrant workers and migration patterns have proven far more resilient in the face of the crisis than many expected; dire predictions of mass unemployment and catastrophic reductions in the volumes of remittances flowing to poorer countries and poorer households have not, overall, come to pass. But the uneven geographical and social impact of the crisis has been highly significant across the issues explored in this volume: the dynamics of stratification and polarization that create and perpetuate vulnerability, exclusion, and marginalization; the nexuses between migration and development in different parts of the world; and the often highly tense politics that continue to surround the mobility and movement of human beings.

Part 1

Migration and Global Capitalism

2

Migration, Minorities, and Welfare States

Carl-Ulrik Schierup and Stephen Castles

Our central theme in this chapter is the ways in which immigration and the formation of new minorities have been linked with changes in welfare states. Our focus is on western Europe, although we also pay attention to strong influences from the United States. We argue that European welfare states helped set the conditions under which migration and minority formation took place from the 1950s to the 1970s. From the 1980s, the ascendancy of neoliberalism brought about major changes in welfare states, and migrants and minorities often bore the brunt of such changes. But our argument goes further: the existence of sizable, often marginalized minorities arising from recent immigration was a crucial factor in neoliberal reforms. The differentiation of populations on the basis of ethnicity, origins, and legal status—which we call "racialized ethnicity"—has been crucial in the shift away from welfare universalism and social redistribution. Racialized ethnicity has complemented hierarchies based on gender, class, and location in the neoliberalization (or neo-Americanization) of European societies.

Within Europe, national situations and political approaches vary considerably. In each country, differing historical experiences of class struggle, territorial expansion, and colonialism have shaped welfare ideologies and policies. These differences have been important factors in shaping the ways in which migrants and minorities have become incorporated into societies. Yet all of these approaches are exposed to change through neoliberal practices such as trade liberalization, as well as through trends toward the Europeanization of economic and social policies. The transformation has been accompanied by Islamophobia, populist political movements centered on the "problem of immigration," a growing preoccupation with "terrorism," and the accelerated securitization of migration and asylum policies (Bigo, 2002).

These trends are matched by the increasing radicalism of social and political movements among immigrants and their descendants. Grievances over social exclusion and stigmatization in terms of race, culture, ethnicity, and religion merge in violent urban uprisings, such as those that occurred in northern British towns in 2001, in Paris and across France in 2005 and 2007, and in Copenhagen and elsewhere in Denmark in 2008. These urban rebellions were no less dramatic than the Los Angeles uprising in 1992, which gave momentum to the neoliberal turn in US politics and paved the way for increasingly brutalized approaches to the governance of welfare and race (see Schierup et al., 2006). Deep undercurrents of urban unrest bear witness to an accelerating "Americanization" of Europe (Freeman, 1986; Pierson, 1998) and provide a warning of the imminent consequences of the prevalent politics of citizenship.

These processes of change, differentiation, and convergence create a complex and dynamic field for understanding the relationship between migration and welfare states, creating the need to draw on research on both sides of the Atlantic. In the United States, there is a strong academic tradition of integrating analysis of migration and racial/ethnic relations with political economy, labor, and social policy studies, yet there is little cross-Atlantic comparative research. European comparative sociological theories of welfare states and labor markets provide clues to analyzing the differentiated impact of global changes on nation-states. But they lack frames of reference for understanding the key role of processes of racialization in shaping exclusion and inclusion, labor market segmentation, and access to citizenship and social welfare. It is therefore important to link comparative research on labor and changing welfare regimes with research on international migration and ethnic relations.

In this chapter, we start by presenting a comparative perspective on welfare states in which important groups are excluded from social citizenship and labor protection. Following a brief overview of migration and European labor market dynamics since 1945, we then discuss differing configurations in the United States, the United Kingdom, Italy, and Sweden. Finally, we address the relationship between migration and the welfare state, taking a comparative cross-Atlantic perspective.

This chapter does not deal with the changes resulting from the crisis of the neoliberal model since 2008, which are explored in more detail by Nicola Phillips at the end of this volume. It suffices here to indicate that the governments and employers of labor-importing countries have sought to offload the costs of the economic crisis onto migrants and other vulnerable groups. The mechanisms have included sharper entry restrictions, crackdowns on irregular residents, and schemes to encourage unemployed migrants to return to their homelands. Yet the data available by late 2010 indicate that migration and remittances (the money sent home by migrants to their families and communities) have proven far more resilient than expected. New migration has declined but has not stopped, migrant populations have remained fairly stable, and remittances have not fallen as much as predicted. Migrants are not just economic actors—as neoclassical economists seem to believe—but social beings willing to endure considerable hardships to support their families back home.[1]

Changing Welfare States and the Neoliberal Turn

To develop a critical perspective on the relationship between migration and welfare states, we need an adequate comparative framework for analyzing how different welfare states change in response to the pressures of neoliberal globalization. It is useful to group countries according to Gøsta Esping-Andersen's (1990) idea of "three worlds of welfare":

- the Anglo-American liberal regime, which focuses strongly on the market and a liberal work ethic, and favors private welfare solutions combined with a system of means-tested public welfare transfers targeted at low-income groups and based on a universalism of minimal needs;
- the conservative central and southern European corporate regime, highly influenced by Christian values, which focuses on the conservation of the traditional family and a morally sanctioned social order, and reproduces a particularistic and hierarchic edifice of citizenship; and
- the social-democratic regime, most typical of Scandinavia, which focuses on values of equality and individuality and on safeguarding a high degree of universalism in an extensive and ramified public welfare system, catering to the differentiated needs of even the middle classes.

"Welfare regimes" are understood here as qualitatively different arrangements between state, market, and the family or household, deriving from historically established modes of governance and class relationships. The three welfare regimes differ in terms of historical formation, political foundation, institutional setup, and functional logic. Each of them elaborates institutional arrangements on the basis of its own distinct political rationale, embedded in specific institutional frameworks and based on specific forms of class alliances and modes of consensus making (see Mann, 1987; Turner, 1992).

The chief sources upon which contemporary theorists of the welfare state have built their propositions are, among others, the ideas of Karl Polanyi on the institutional embeddedness of market economies and T. H. Marshall's theory of social citizenship as the foundation of the modern welfare state (Polanyi, 1944; Marshall, 1950). Starting from these premises, Esping-Andersen (1985, 1990) and Claus Offe (1984) developed the notion of the decommodification of labor: a politically contingent and institutionally embedded process that increasingly relieves citizens of the obligation to link their welfare directly to their labor market value (Slavnic, 2010). Relieving citizens of the compulsion of selling their labor at the going labor market prices provides a real freedom to reject the most substandard jobs and working conditions.

The degree to which the decommodification of labor has been established as a social right of citizenship varies greatly from country to country, as do the specific institutional arrangements within which social citizenship has become embedded. In the Nordic countries, the rights of citizenship include universal access to social security and high-grade welfare benefits and services across social classes. In comparison, social security and welfare in the United States and the United Kingdom are based on citizenship only to a limited extent, being more dependent on buying into market-based insurances and services. Similar to the Nordic social democracies, the conservative regimes of central and southern Europe provide a high degree of decommodification. But their welfare provisions are embedded in qualitatively different institutional frameworks that are in turn nested according to professional status groups, and are more dependent on position and performance in the labor market.

However, the actual significance of the decommodification of labor is inadequately explained by most mainstream welfare state research, as Theo Papadopoulos (2005) argues (see also Slavnic, 2010). This is so because of an excessively one-sided focus on social policies that are institutionally anchored outside the labor market and the workplace. Papadopoulos argues that it is essential to analyze policies and institutional frameworks for decommodification both inside and outside the labor market and workplace, as well as to consider their interconnection. His argument is similar to that of David Soskice (1999), who claims that an understanding of the transformation of modern welfare states demands an analysis of their intersection with production regimes—that is, the economic organization of the production of goods and services and the industrial-relations compacts on which this organization is based. The dividing line is between uncoordinated liberal market economies with relatively weak corporatist arrangements in countries like the United States and the United Kingdom and the high degree of corporatist coordination between employers, unions, and the state in countries like Germany and Sweden.

This composite perspective is an important point of departure for a differentiated understanding of ongoing struggles surrounding one of the central political strategies of neoliberal capitalism: the rolling back of the strong welfare state through the recommodification of labor and, consequently, the (re-)connection of the welfare of citizens with the price of their labor on an imagined free market. Recommodification is accomplished by dismantling welfare institutions, breaking compacts between labor and capital, and undermining labor standards and employment protection in deregulated national labor markets. The overall tendency is toward a "work first" society (Ellison, 2006) or a new kind of "workfare regime" (Jessop, 2002). Downward pressure is put on the social wage, which is considered a cost of production rather than a means of redistribution. The ideological maxims are to get people from welfare into work, to create enterprising subjects, and to break a culture of dependency, rather than resort to allegedly unsustainable welfare expenditures.

Migrants and ethnic minorities are among the chief victims of weakened welfare states and deregulated labor markets. But precarious jobs are not simply there, waiting to be taken up by migrants (Bauder, 2006; Castells, 1975). Migrants and ethnic minorities can often be exploited as a "reserve army of labor" due to their exclusion from citizenship and labor rights and their lack of access to established institutions and networks of power. This makes workers available for deregulated sections of the labor market, forcing them to accept substandard wages and conditions (Bauder, 2006; Bauder, Chapter 3 of this volume). Thus migration policy and strategies of racialization can be integral elements of political strategies for the recommodification of labor linked to deregulation of employment and the transformation of citizenship and welfare arrangements (Freeman, 1986).

Migration and European Labor Force Dynamics Since 1945: An Overview

During western Europe's postwar economic boom, migrant workers played a vital part in economic growth, but most were not expected to stay permanently or make welfare claims. After the 1973 oil crisis, however, many so-called guest workers in fact stayed on, and were joined by spouses and children. They began to access social infrastructure (like schools, health services, and housing) and to claim benefits for unemployment, illness, and disability. Then, in the 1990s, Europe experienced new inflows of refugees, asylum seekers, highly skilled personnel, manual workers, and family members. Populations grew more diverse and welfare needs became more differentiated—and more pressing.[2] The relationship between migration and welfare can be understood through an analysis of these phases in the development of European political economy (Schierup et al., 2006: 140–146).

The first phase of the post-1945 accumulation strategy of capital was to concentrate capital investment in the existing core industrial areas and recruit additional labor in order to keep production costs from rising sharply. New labor resources included rural-urban migration, the increasing employment of women, and the recruitment of migrant workers from peripheral areas (including southern Europe, North Africa, and Mexico). This phase was also marked by Keynesian approaches to welfare capitalism. Typical of this model was mass production in large factories where manual workers were concentrated, facilitating strong unions. Trade unions were able to negotiate better wages and conditions, while social-democratic parties could introduce welfare state provisions to protect workers and their families. Many migrant workers were employed in unionized factories and enjoyed the benefits of good wages and strong welfare provisions.

In the 1970s, economic recession and growing competition from new industrial economies led to a second phase in which labor-intensive production was moved to low-wage economies, while migrant-labor recruitment was stopped. The new accumulation strategy was based on the creation of a global labor market, through which specific production stages could be sited wherever they could be carried out at the lowest possible cost. Neoliberal approaches in the old industrial countries included the squeezing out of skilled blue-collar workers, economic deregulation, and reduction of the public sector. The new strategy led to the closure of many rust-belt factories with their strong unions. Domestic economic restructuring was pushed forward by the rightist governments of the Reagan/Thatcher era of the 1980s, leading to a rollback in workers' rights. Many migrant workers were pushed out of regular employment; some got insecure, casualized jobs, while others set up marginal small businesses or became dependent on welfare benefits.

The very success of neoliberal globalization led to a third phase beginning in 1995, in which demand for labor in Europe grew due to a combination of demographic, economic, and social factors (Castles, 2006; CEC, 2004; Münz et al., 2007). At the same time, globalization encouraged the migration of both highly skilled and less skilled workers from less developed areas of Africa, Asia, and Latin America. Migrant workers entered European labor markets at all levels: as highly paid and privileged specialists; as regular workers in manufacturing, building, and services; and as irregular workers in exploitative jobs.

By 2005, foreign-born workers made up 25 percent of the labor force in Switzerland, 20 percent in Austria and Germany, and around 12 percent in other western European countries (OECD, 2007a: 63–66). In Belgium, Luxembourg, Sweden, and Denmark, more than 40 percent of the employed migrants who arrived from 1995 to 2005 had tertiary education. In many cases, migrant workers had higher qualification profiles than local-born workers. Only in southern European countries did low-skilled labor migration predominate (OECD, 2007a: 67–68). Nevertheless, migrants remained important to employers for low-skilled jobs, even in western Europe. Segmentation based on race, ethnicity, gender, and national origin has been a feature of European labor markets ever since the post-1945 reconstruction boom. For workers in general, formal employment within large-scale enterprises has in many cases been replaced by work arrangements that differentiate and separate them. Those who comprise the disadvantaged groups—migrant women, irregular workers, ethnic and racial minorities—end up in the most precarious positions. A labor market based on deprivation of human and workers' rights for vulnerable groups is obviously incompatible with a strong, redistributive welfare state. The new economy is contingent on a new welfare state that disciplines the workforce while legitimating inequality and impoverishment. This has been achieved through the racialization and social stigmatization of difference.

Welfare, Citizenship, and the Challenge of Social Exclusion

Until the early 1970s, labor migrants in the industrial metropolitan countries of western Europe were expected to work and pay taxes but not to make long-term claims on educational systems, welfare institutions and services. However, as already noted, many of these early migrants did stay on to form new minority communities, and they were soon joined by many more migrants from all over the world. Such groups followed similar trajectories of family reunion, settlement, and simultaneous marginalization and minority formation. Welfare planners had to face up to emergent new forms of impoverishment and exclusion as well as their disruptive consequences, such as marginalization, urban polarization, racism, and social conflict.

Colonial migrants in the United Kingdom, France, and the Netherlands were automatically incorporated into national welfare systems, while full social rights were also extended to migrant workers in Scandinavian countries. By contrast, the guest worker-recruiting countries (which included not only Germany, Switzerland, and Austria but also Belgium and the Netherlands for many workers) did not expect migrants to become social citizens. Germany, for instance, set up a special welfare regime based on the subsidization of charities in order to limit migrant use of mainstream benefits and services.

After the recruitment stop of 1973–1974, the ineffectiveness of special welfare approaches became clear. Migrant workers had been concentrated in those parts of the labor market most severely hit by restructuring and unemployment. Now many were unemployed or were forced out of the workforce, often following work-related accidents or illness. Yet the very universalism of most western European welfare regimes meant that immigrants could not, in the long run, be excluded from substantial rights of social citizenship (Guiraudon, 2000; Ryner, 2000). They were gradually incorporated as "denizens"—long-term residents who obtained many of the formal rights associated with citizenship (Hammar, 1985)—or as full citizens. This trend was reinforced by employers' demands for the stabilization of large sections of the migrant labor force who were indispensable in filling the low-grade positions that local workers found unattractive.

Some liberal scholars have suggested that the long-term convergence of citizenship rights for immigrants and natives in Western societies is likely to continue (see Bauböck et al., 1996; Joppke, 1999). This positive expectation appears to be confirmed by the granting of citizenship rights to long-standing immigrants in northwestern Europe. The revised German Citizenship Law, which came into force in 2000, is an important example. However, in the United Kingdom, minorities are political citizens, but this does not necessarily confer social equality. In southern Europe, migrants remain noncitizens; even when they do obtain legal residence status, strong welfare rights are not guaranteed.

Trends toward the inclusion of migrants in the context of formal rights contrast with real economic and social exclusion. Throughout Europe, there are new categories of working poor—that is, people in employment but with wages too low to lift them out of poverty—among immigrants and new ethnic minorities. Multiple modes of racialized exclusion cluster together. Chronic social disadvantage and so-called welfare dependency are potential "incubators" of a workforce whose jobs are "precarious and underpaid and systematically performed by women, immigrants, and disadvantaged minorities" (Mingione, 1996: 382). The growth of low-paid, casual, and precarious jobs, in turn, puts pressure on welfare institutions. This situation can readily be exploited to support political programs for dismantling the function of social citizenship as a sanctuary for the vulnerable from market forces.

Governments strive to meet employers' demands for cheap and flexible labor even as they seek to appease the anti-immigrant populism of some politicians and sections of the media. The resolution of this ambivalence is found in new discriminatory employment practices, ostensibly designed to avoid the errors of earlier labor migration policies that allowed migrants to settle and eventually achieve denizenship or citizenship. Such practices include short-term contract worker systems, "circular" migration, international subcontracting relationships, and irregular labor migration. Highly restrictive refugee and asylum policies are part of the effort to placate anti-immigrant populism. Such measures have forced many refugees to join the most submerged segments of the clandestine labor force in the informal economy. Thus the boundaries between asylum seekers and illegal migrants are becoming increasingly blurred.

This new labor force segmentation further jeopardizes the already fragile relationship between ethnic minorities and the welfare state (Ryner, 2000). Given their particularly vulnerable position in the labor market, stabilized sections of the migrant and ethnic minority populations have had strong reasons to look toward the welfare state as a safety net. But as social citizenship deteriorates, ethnic minorities find themselves in a situation increasingly similar to that of temporary contract workers, clandestine migrants, or new and marginalized refugee groups. Ethnic minorities can no longer rely on the relatively newly acquired rights of social citizenship and are thus forced to watch as their access to the labor market, affected by deregulation and informalization, decreases

(Slavnic, 2010). They become part of the new working poor, as, at one and the same time, victims of the welfare state crisis and agents for the informalization of the labor market and the economy.

North Atlantic Perspectives

In the United States, race, ethnicity, and immigration have played a prominent role in ideological and political battles that have brought about a recommodification of labor and the dismantling of welfare programs. We therefore start our comparison by looking at the case of the United States. This is followed by an examination of three western European cases with contrasting welfare regimes and modes of incorporation for migrants and ethnic minorities: the United Kingdom (the liberal welfare model), Italy (the conservative-corporatist model), and Sweden (the social-democratic model).[3]

The political instrumentalization of migration, ethnic relations, and race as vehicles for the degradation of work and the undermining of social rights is most clearly expressed in the United States. Given that the United States represents the main exponent of the liberal welfare regime according to Esping-Andersen's taxonomy, processes of deregulation and the increasing recommodification of labor in European welfare states have come to be referred to as an "Americanization" of European welfare systems (Leibfried, 1992). The idea of Americanization has also been influential in migration studies (Freeman, 1986; Wacquant, 1996; Cross and Moore, 2002). Yet Robert Kloosterman's (1999) notion of "neo-Americanization" may be more adequate. The US reference points that European researchers focus on—like the so-called African American ghetto poor (Wilson, 1987) or the polarized ethnic division of labor in so-called global cities (Sassen, 2001, 2006a)—do not relate to the heyday of the US welfare state, from the liberal New Deal of the 1930s to Lyndon Johnson's Great Society of the 1960s. They refer to subsequent processes marking a fundamental transformation since the 1980s. These include the downgrading and transformation of US citizenship in general (Sassen, 2006a) and of social citizenship in particular.

The United States

The flexibility of less regulated liberal welfare states has facilitated their fast adaptation to a service-dominated economy (Ellison, 2006). A propensity for market solutions and a low degree of commitment to social citizenship, combined with weak unions and a racially and ethnically fragmented working class, have made the United States particularly disposed toward choosing a "low road" into post-Fordism (Ibid.). A cocktail of neoliberalism, "welfare chauvinism" (Banting, 2000: 21ff.), restriction of migrants' access to social citizenship, and racial discourses have cemented the function of migrants as a flexible reserve army of labor. This trend has been part and parcel of a wider "war against labor" (Fox Piven and Cloward, 1993) integral to the strategies of US capital in the 1980s and 1990s (Pinder, 2007).

In the late twentieth century, a shift to globalized services and information technology produced an "hourglass economy" with two polarized but mutually dependent labor markets (see, e.g., Sassen, 2001): a high-wage sector dominated by financial and information services, corporate management, differentiated product design, and research and development; and a low-wage, precarious, and often informal sector, reliant on outsourced corporate activities and private service providers, as well as on sweatshop manufacturing. The disadvantaged pole of the labor market is mainly staffed by immigrants from Latin America, the Caribbean, Africa, Asia, and Eastern Europe. While experiencing social exclusion along ethnic lines, this disadvantaged group has also undergone "feminization," with increasing employment of women migrant workers in part-time, low-salaried, insecure, and informal jobs, including domestic services.

During the 1990s alone, more than 12 million immigrants settled in the United States. Immigration has continued in the new millennium with a million or more new settlers per year (Martin et al., 2006: 28ff.). Between 1995 and 2005, more than half the net job creation of 16 million involved persons born abroad (OECD, 2007b: 66). A majority of those who arrive legally are the relatives of US citizens or highly educated professionals for whom employers have expressed special needs. Many immigrants hold temporary visas for study or through temporary-worker programs; relatively few arrive as refugees. Since 2000, unskilled nonfarm workers have become the largest category of temporary contract workers, with almost half a million recruited each year. Approximately a further half million undocumented migrant workers are estimated to settle in the United States per year as well; the total undocumented migrant population is about 12 million (Passel, 2006; Hoefer, 2006; Martin et al., 2006; Martin, Chapter 11 of this volume).

The North American Free Trade Agreement (NAFTA), established in 1994, has become a mechanism for the provision of cheap labor vital to the economic restructuring process in the United States (Delgado

Wise and Márquez Covarrubias, 2007a). While most immigrant professionals are recruited from Asian countries, the recruitment of unskilled labor is predominantly targeted at Latin America, especially Mexico. Mexicans make up 60 percent of all undocumented migrants in the United States. They are concentrated in precarious jobs in agriculture, domestic work, menial services, and industrial production. Mexicans work under conditions of outsourcing, informality, and authoritarian management, beyond the protective cover of trade unions and legislation (Gonzales, 2006; Delgado Wise and Márquez Covarrubias, 2007a; Phillips, 2009b). Working conditions have deteriorated since the mid-1980s in terms of hours worked, wage levels, and labor standards (Donato and Massey, 1993).

US migration legislation has contributed to this process of downward development (Donato et al., 2005). The politics of migration became increasingly authoritarian in the 1990s, enhancing the power of clandestine employers and causing a downward trend in wages and working conditions. Negotiations with Mexico since 2001 and prolonged debates in the US Congress on the legalization of undocumented migrants have not succeeded in shifting the status quo (Saucedo and Chretien, 2007). On the contrary, sharpened border controls, deportation measures, and the criminalization of migrants have all acted to increase the insecurity and vulnerability of the undocumented. The situation is worsened by the mushrooming of anti-immigrant organizations and private border guard services, violence perpetrated by far-right groups, and lax policies toward employers regarding the enforcement of labor standards (Smith, 2006).

This situation has led to pessimistic predictions regarding the future of children of migrant working-class parents in a still racist society with a segmented labor market. Such children, argue Alejandro Portes and Rubén Rumbaut (2001), risk "downward assimilation" from their parents' working-class position into a new, ethnically diverse "rainbow underclass" that exists outside the labor market altogether. Others (such as Waldinger et al., 2007) contest this prediction, arguing that, unlike the so-called underclass among African Americans (Wilson, 1987), youths in Mexican and other Latin American immigrant groups can rely on the social capital of ethnic and kinship networks to ensure their integration into the US labor market (albeit at fairly low levels).

There are additional reasons for not expecting a replication of a so-called underclass pattern among working-class immigrant groups and their children. Immigrants have always been excluded from central parts of means-tested welfare, and the Clinton administration's Personal

Responsibility and Work Opportunity Reconciliation Act of 1996 meant further restrictions on the few benefits available to immigrants (Banting, 2000). This powerful welfare-to-workfare act meant a determined move toward making the welfare-dependent underclass an anachronism altogether, and moved the United States in the direction of an authoritarian workfare state (Fox Piven, 1998: 72). It led, among other things, toward the replacement of unionized workers with cheaper workfare labor (Cooper, 1997) and acted to push the African American unemployed and welfare-dependent "ghetto poor" into "a virtually indentured labor force" (Pinder, 2007), bound to compete with poor working-class immigrants.[4]

The United Kingdom

The United Kingdom can be seen as the European society that has most closely followed a neoliberal or "neo-American" path into post-Fordism and globalization. Under Prime Minister Margaret Thatcher, from 1979 to 1996 the United Kingdom pursued radical policies of economic deregulation, privatization, and restructuring of the welfare system. Such practices were continued after 1997 by the Labour governments of Tony Blair and then Gordon Brown. Deregulation was supposed to support two dynamic factors of a "new economy": the growth of small and medium-sized businesses, and the motivation for individuals to become active and responsible stakeholders in their own futures. Until the financial crisis of 2008, British leaders promoted the so-called Anglo-Saxon model of neoliberal growth as an example for the rest of Europe. However, the essence of the neoliberal model was growing inequality, as vast rewards were bestowed on bankers, investors, and property speculators while the gap between the wealthy and the bulk of the population increased.

In a comparative study of what he calls the "illiberal social policy" of liberal regimes in the United States and Britain, Desmond King (1999) demonstrates how an increasing emphasis on the obligations as opposed to the rights of citizenship during the 1980s led to the exclusion of poor population groups from the compact of citizenship in the 1990s. Under New Labour, social exclusion came to be seen as a problem of the underclass, defined, in line with US neoconservative discourse, as a behavioral and moral issue. Workfare-type policies were merged into a general system after 1997 by the Labour government under the labels Jobseeker's Allowance and then the New Deal. The decommodification embodied in the old unemployment benefit system was replaced by individual jobseeker's contracts, which obliged the unemployed, the disabled, and single parents to seek and accept work of any type. If the most vulnerable and exposed were to avoid a future of impoverishment and join the winners, it was their duty to become more flexible, to "get on their bikes" in search of new opportunities, and not to be bothered about wages or health and safety; employment would ensure that the job escalator would take them upward (Jones and Novak, 1999: 71).

Immigration and ethnic minorities have played a crucial role in legitimating the restructuring of the welfare state. In the 1950s and 1960s, immigration from the New Commonwealth (especially the Caribbean and the Indian subcontinent) provided a crucial labor source for manufacturing industries. With Britain's industrial decline in the 1970s and 1980s, many immigrants and their descendants became unemployed and welfare recipients, while others set up often marginal firms. Problems of social exclusion and impoverishment could be largely redefined as issues of race. Thus immigrants were relabeled as ethnic minorities, and welfare measures were linked to their lifestyles and cultures. The race relations approach that emerged in the late 1960s and the 1970s was based on the management of intergroup relations by the state. It meant recognizing the existence of distinct groups, defined primarily on the basis of race. The acceptance of cultural and religious diversity was officially labeled as multiculturalism. The Race Relations Acts of 1965, 1968, and 1976 outlawed discrimination in public places, employment, and housing. A Commission for Racial Equality (CRE) was set up in 1976. However, there was general agreement among political leaders that integration and "good race relations" in Britain were possible only on the basis of a restrictive immigration policy. Thus race relations and antidiscrimination acts have been "inextricably linked" with a series of increasingly restrictive immigration acts (Solomos, 2003: 78).

But the facade of harmonious multiculturalism in the United Kingdom could not hide the reality of racism and social exclusion. Discontent among black youth led to repeated riots in inner-city areas. The government responded with measures to combat youth unemployment, improve education, rehabilitate urban areas, and change police practices. But the Stephen Lawrence Inquiry of 1999, which was set up to analyze the poor police response to the murder of a young black man by a white gang, revealed the continued strength of institutional racism. The situation was further complicated by immigration from new origin areas. Since the mid-1990s, inflows of both asylum seekers and economic migrants have been important both for sustaining economic growth and for developing the perceptions of an external threat that have legitimated the erosion of human rights and the creation of manipulative models of social cohesion.

The general picture in the early twenty-first century is that of a labor force stratified by ethnicity and gender, with a high degree of youth unemployment. On average, people of Indian, Chinese, and Irish background tend to have employment situations as good as or better than those of white British people. By contrast, other groups are worse off, with a descending hierarchy on most indicators of black African, black Caribbean, Pakistani, and, at the very bottom, Bangladeshi groups (Office for National Statistics, 2004). The strong trend toward the casualization of labor has been exacerbated by the deregulation and privatization of public services. Casualization has also extended into producers' services like architecture, banking, and engineering, leading to income polarization within the advanced service sector. Here part-time jobs have proliferated, facilitating the exploitation of a growing pool of female labor in a society with a shortage of public child-care facilities.

Most immigrants in the United Kingdom are British citizens and enjoy full voting rights. Most Commonwealth immigrants already had citizenship when they arrived. It is relatively easy for foreign immigrants to obtain citizenship after five years of legal residence. In the early years of the twenty-first century, the main immigration issue was asylum, while after 2004 concerns about large inflows from new Eastern European member states of the European Union (EU) became prominent. Successive governments introduced five new asylum and immigration laws between 1993 and 2006 that tightened up entry rules and introduced deterrent measures such as detention and restrictions on welfare. Asylum applications declined from 103,000 in 2002 to just 28,000 in 2006. However, by then public attention had shifted to a new issue: the growth of Islam. The London bombings of July 7, 2005, precipitated concern about the loyalty of young Muslims. Government policies shifted to emphasize social cohesion. Citizenship tests for immigrants were introduced, based on ideas of Britishness and core values. A strong contrast remains between the formal equality granted to ethnic minorities and their everyday experience of unemployment, inequality, and social exclusion. The UK experience shows that citizenship and antidiscrimination laws are not necessarily a protection against social disadvantage and racism (Castles and Miller, 2009; Schierup et al., 2006).

Italy

Until the mid-1970s, Italy had a history of large-scale emigration. The combination of rapid economic growth and demographic contraction led to a reversal, as most migrants from non–Organization for Economic Cooperation and Development (OECD) countries entering Italy in the

1980s were undocumented. Since then, several mass legalizations and the tightening of immigration controls related to the Schengen Agreement have modified the situation. Entries of asylum seekers are negligible (reflecting a high rejection rate), while the avenue of family unification, although limited, is on the increase. From 300,000 at the beginning of the 1980s, Italy's legally resident migrant population had increased to more than three million by the mid- to late 2000s. Migrants' residence status is mostly based on temporary labor contracts, so the danger of a (re-)lapse into illegality is constant. The great majority of foreign residents are from Africa, Asia, Latin America, and Central and Eastern Europe. Many have a high educational profile, yet are overwhelmingly employed in "heavy, precarious, dangerous, poorly paid, and demanding" jobs (Triandafyhllidou and Gropas, 2007: 190). Patterns of employment vary between regions: agricultural labor and domestic services predominate in the south, while industrial employment prevails in the north; in addition, many domestic workers are to be found in cities like Rome and Milan.

Most migrants are *extracommunitari* (extracommunitarians), a term that denotes their origin outside the EU. But it also intimates their non-belonging (Petrillo, 1999) and reflects the nation's prevailing, exclusionary and ethnocultural self-definition (Sciortino, 2004). Immigration continues to be regarded as temporary and there is no explicit policy of integration. Before filing an application for citizenship, non–EU citizens must reside in Italy for as long as ten years. Legally resident foreigners have extended social rights. However, the prevailing practices of local authorities continue to obstruct access to welfare provisions and to ensure a discriminatory application of regulations concerning access to permanent residence and citizenship. The political rights of extracommunitarians are limited to involvement in voluntary associations and trade unions. Italy has not ratified EU clauses on immigrants' political rights (Triandafyhllidou and Gropas, 2007: 193). At the same time, by turning merely "unauthorized" status at the beginning of the 1980s into a truly criminalized, "illegal" status, Schengen membership and EU demands have contributed to the increasingly vulnerable social situation of irregular migrants or *clandestini* (see Schierup et al., 2006). A precarious situation in Italian society for regular as well as irregular migrants has been exacerbated by the rise of populist parties within ruling center-right governments and the proliferation of media stereotypes of migrants as criminal outsiders.

Yet immigration has been essential to the development of the Italian economy and society for almost three decades (Ginsborg, 2001;

Schierup et al., 2006). With the increasing exhaustion of the reserves of low-skilled labor in the Italian countryside, labor-intensive strategies for overcoming the Fordist crisis after 1980 have constantly been at loggerheads with the conservative welfare system and an industrial relations compact geared toward strict regulation of the formal sector, leaving no room for flexibility in employment contracts. In this context, immigrants have functioned as a cheap and flexible reserve army of labor. The "second (post-Fordist) economic miracle" is a catchword for Italy's successful reorientation toward flexible industrial specialization of small and medium-sized enterprises, producing high-quality specialized goods for the world market. The exploitation of cheap, most often informal, immigrant labor functioned as a source of "primitive accumulation," important for the takeoff of such enterprises. Today immigrants are an indispensable part of their regular industrial labor force.

Another important area for immigrant labor is domestic service. The educational achievements of a growing number of Italian women and their employment in professional jobs in public and private services has exposed the structural shortcomings of a conservative (male) "breadwinner" welfare model. The virtual absence of publicly organized care has meant that the chief coping strategy for two-career professional households has become the employment of immigrant women as live-in maids and caretakers for elderly family members. Yet, because Italy has the lowest birth rate in Europe, it faces a looming demographic crisis. The industrial relations compact—which until recently outlawed part-time employment and other modes of labor market flexibilization, together with a lack of publicly organized care and an inflexible gender division of labor—has placed professional women in a quandary between career and having children (Andall, 2003; Trifiletti, 1999).

Both labor shortages and the demographic crisis are, however, relative. The female employment rate remains comparatively low and youth unemployment high. Barriers to the formal labor market are high, although young Italians can still afford to be selective in terms of the kind of jobs they will accept. Transfers of high wages or pensions to households and persistent norms of redistribution to family and wider kin still allow Italian youth to reject "immigrant jobs." However, as a response to EU directives and an accord between employers and unions, greater openings for part-time and temporary employment have been created. This has entailed a certain transfer of immigrant employment from informal work to formal, so-called atypical, jobs. Although the conservative welfare system continues to offer Italians alternative sources of sustenance and although Italy is still a far cry from adopting anything like the "work first" imperative in the United States, the current configuration of differential access to decent work may exacerbate the competition between immigrants and Italians in parts of the labor market and fuel an already virulent anti-immigrant populism.

Sweden

The so-called Swedish model has been portrayed as the quintessence of the social-democratic welfare regime (Esping-Andersen, 1990) and its trajectory into post-Fordism. For decades, Sweden has enjoyed a reputation for devising an inclusive migrant-incorporation policy, recognizing the ethnically diverse character of its society, and granting voting rights to foreign citizens. Residence is, alongside birth, an unconditional criterion for access to citizenship, social rights, and the welfare system, as well as equity concerning employment (Sainsbury, 2006)—a criterion devoid of "ethnic" conditions.

By 1972, the labor unions had largely succeeded in blocking Sweden's extensive post–World War II recruitment of migrant labor. They were able to sustain their veto on any attempt to reintroduce import of labor until 2008. Along with family reunion, refugees have long been the main source of immigration. However, a formerly solidaristic refugee policy has become increasingly restrictive following Sweden's participation in the Schengen Agreement in 2001. Yet substantial numbers of applicants (especially Iraqis) still receive asylum for humanitarian reasons at the time of this writing in 2011. Foreign-born residents and their children make up more than a fifth of a Swedish population of 9 million. Given that Sweden offers easy access to citizenship and has one of Europe's highest naturalization rates, most immigrants hold Swedish or dual citizenship. Only a quarter of the foreign-born remain foreign citizens. Until the late 1970s, immigrants from the other Nordic countries (in particular Finland) were still most numerous, but today immigrants from Asia, Africa, and Eastern Europe are the great majority.

The extensive Swedish welfare system, which reached its peak in the late 1970s, remains effective and is supported widely beyond the Social Democratic Party's core constituency. The welfare state's social basis and public legitimacy were strengthened by the incorporation of women into the labor market during the 1960s and 1970s. Women's equitable inclusion in the welfare system and the comprehensive public social service system, which substitutes for domestic care work, are distinctive elements of the Swedish model. During the same period, immigrant workers were incorporated on formally equal terms, but in fact exploited as a reserve army of expendable labor used to manage the peaks and troughs of the economic cycle. Immigrants were to be found in jobs rejected by an upwardly mobile, native working class, and often exposed to discrimination, as an unequal ethnic division of labor emerged (Persson, 1972; Ålund, 1985; Schierup and Paulson, 1994).

Yet immigrants also enjoyed a relatively high degree of social security and material welfare in a society where union power, the equalizing institutions of a large welfare state, and an active labor market policy continued to mitigate the effects of the ethnic division of labor on income differentials, at least until the early 1990s. It was then that the situation changed due to a deep economic recession, during which the ruling Social Democrats sacrificed the full employment regime upon which the postwar Swedish model had rested. Immigrants became the prime victims in terms of their overwhelming overrepresentation among the echelons of the new long-term unemployed. Politically, "welfare dependency" among immigrants and their children became a central concern.

The racialized poverty associated with neoliberal flexibility regimes and the casualization of low-salaried jobs is still much more limited in Sweden than it is in the United Kingdom. Yet substantial groups find themselves not only outside the ordinary labor market but also excluded from unemployment insurance. Given its traditional priorities—the implementation of an active labor market policy and the upgrading of skills—Sweden's welfare regime was simply not geared to cope with large-scale and long-term unemployment. The active labor market policy of the post–World War II Swedish model was the baseline for a decommodification of labor, aimed at eliminating low-wage occupational ghettos. Its increasingly neoliberal character since 1990 has come to underpin a disciplinary adaptation toward a marginalized reserve army exposed to the market discipline of precarious low-wage niches, and increasingly reminiscent of a US-style workfare regime (Junestav, 2004). A growing number of migrants and ethnic-minority Swedes have been pushed from the center to the periphery of the welfare system, into the casualized labor market and a degraded informal sector.

However, in contrast to the experiences of the United States, Italy, and Britain, the exploitation of irregular migrants has, so far, not had a key role in the restructuring of the Swedish labor market. Until 2000, irregular migration to Sweden and undocumented migrant workers were almost unknown. This was due to a still extraordinarily high level of labor unionization, even in small workplaces, which limited employment opportunities for undocumented workers (Hjarnø, 2003). At the end of the 2000s, the number of undocumented workers was estimated at around 50,000—still negligible compared to most other European countries. Strong union insistence on adherence to Swedish collective agreements also continues to limit the potential impact of posted workers from the new low-wage member states of the EU, in terms of wage depression and the deterioration of labor standards.

However, in the late 2000s, the European Court of Justice ruled against established modes of trade union action, thus presenting a serious threat to Swedish labor unions. Moreover, since 2006, the center-right government has dismantled cornerstones of the welfare edifice and squeezed growing numbers of low-wage workers out of the unions. Higher unemployment and health insurance charges are likely to exacerbate these trends. In short, organized labor saw its protective capacities significantly reduced in the 2000s, and migrants as well as other groups outside the core protected labor market are feeling the consequences in the forms of greater insecurity and the deterioration of employment conditions.

Certainly a countertrend to labor depreciation is considerable social mobility among Sweden's ethnic minorities, marked by the ascent of some to leading positions in business, public administration, politics, academia, and the media. Another important trend since the mid-1990s is the defeat of traditional, concerted opposition on the part of employers and unions to antidiscrimination legislation, forms of which have since been adopted following EU directives. Yet these are being implemented alongside the gradual demise of both the protective framework of social citizenship and the unique, active labor market policy that constituted the very linchpin of the univeralist Swedish model and its powerful decommodification of labor.

State of the Union: Europe and the Experience of the United States

In their struggles for recognition and social inclusion, immigrants to the United States have, throughout the nation's history, invoked a professed American Creed founded on the Declaration of Independence and the US Constitution (Myrdal and Bok, 1996; Schierup et al., 2006). It has been the indispensable charter for nation building and political integration in this "nation of immigrants" (Kennedy, 1964). Yet there is an enduring tension in US universalism between "closure and openness, between separateness and inclusion" (Highham, 1993: 198).

Since the Civil Rights movement of the 1960s, important changes have occurred in this, historically, deeply racist society. Policies of equity and antiracism have facilitated elite social mobility among African Americans, Latinos, and other racialized minorities, allowing intermittent ascent to positions of political and economic power. Popular antiracist struggles in the United States have been a source of inspiration across the world. Antidiscrimination policies in the United States and doctrines of "diversity management" have come to exercise a global moral and political hegemony (Bonnett, 2006) and serve as a model for a range of measures included in the directives of the European Commission to the member states of the EU. Incremental unionization among migrants in the United States, including numerous undocumented workers (Milkman, 2006; Petras, 2006), is becoming a model for European trade unions (Sahlström, 2008).

Nevertheless, the United States continues to stand out as the "quintessential case of overt tension where the politics of race have shaped social policy . . . and constrained the capacity of welfare advocates to build stable political coalitions" (Banting, 2000: 19). A liberal inclination to market solutions, fragmented political institutions, and the relative weakness of multicultural consensus-building processes have blocked the formation of broad class alliances and the extension of social citizenship (Carnoy, 1994; Highham, 1993; Wilson, 1999; Banting, 2000). Since the 1980s, the tension between explicit policies of equity and racializing practices, embedded in pragmatic governance and the politics of class, has become increasingly acute.

It has been argued that the weak welfare state in the United States is a result of historical racial divisions, especially between the white majority and the African American minority. Alberto Alesina and his collaborators have claimed that "within the United States, race is the single most important predictor of support for welfare. America's troubled race relations are clearly a major reason for the absence of an American welfare state" (Alesina et al., 2001: 189). They identify other factors as well, such as the historical continuity of political arrangements designed to protect property and Americans' belief in opportunities for upward mobility. However, they emphasize that "racial heterogeneity, both directly and indirectly through political institutions, can explain the bulk of the unexplained portion of the gap between the United States and Europe in welfare spending" (Alesina and Glaeser, 2004: 133). Alesina and his colleagues believe that the majority of the US population is against redistribution because it would mean transferring resources to black people.

The historically weak welfare state has set the scene for a far more heterogeneous US society. Intersecting changes in production, welfare, and migration regimes have generated an unprecedented commodification of labor, with migrants and particular ethnic minorities as the most exposed victims of a consequent social precarity. A restructured migration regime includes masses of undocumented workers who can raise only minimal claims on the welfare system. They are deprived of civil and political rights, and exposed to racialization and threats of harassment and deportation. They function as a wage-depressing "reserve army," putting legal migrants and indigenous blue-collar workers under pressure. The extensive use of short-term contract labor is an intermediate tier with a similar function. The passage of NAFTA, successive illiberal restrictions on rights to family unification, and the exclusionary welfare reforms of the 1990s have all acted to reproduce a cheap, commodified, flexible, replaceable, and unfree labor force. These "new helots" (Cohen, 1987) are largely deprived of even nominal social citizenship and barred from buying into an increasingly expensive and convoluted market for health insurance and other social services.

Access to citizenship via birthright partly releases the second generation from the state of unfree labor. But the neoliberal undermining of public welfare provision for the poor and a disciplinary workfare regime has deprived racialized groups of a platform that used to provide leeway for rejecting the most degraded jobs. This New American Dilemma (to paraphrase Hochschild, 1984), springing from the tension between the ideals of equal opportunity and racial equality and the practices of neoliberalism, is important for Europeans to study. The cases of the United Kingdom, Italy, and Sweden indicate how European countries of immigration are grappling with deepening tensions between market exigency and citizenship. Migration and minorities are now at the center of the politics of economic restructuring and growth, as well as issues of social exclusion and poverty.

Alesina and his colleagues have applied their analysis of the role of racism in weakening the US welfare state to Europe, arguing that "European countries are racially very homogeneous and . . . have a large measure of social spending" (Alesina et al., 2001: 232). The implication is that if European countries became more heterogeneous, support for the welfare state would decline. The Alesina approach has been criticized on methodological grounds (Taylor-Gooby, 2005: 671; Banting and Kymlicka, 2006: 28), but the important question remains whether growing diversity will undermine popular support for welfare measures, as is also claimed by, for instance, Wim van Oorschot (2006) on the basis of his analysis of the 1999–2000 European Values Study, which covered twenty-three countries. However, a study based on large-scale survey data by Markus Crepaz (2006) finds widespread support for multiculturalism among the citizens of developed societies. This research finds no link between the existence of multicultural policies and support for redistributive welfare policies. Interestingly, Crepaz's study shows a positive effect of multicultural policies on trust—a finding that contradicts an increasingly dominant view among European policymakers.

More evidence is provided in a large-scale comparative study of welfare states by Keith Banting and his coauthors in 2006. They found that "there is no systematic pattern of countries that have adopted strong multiculturalism policies seeing erosion in their welfare states relative to countries that have resisted such programmes" (Banting et al., 2006: 83). It appears that although Europe became more diverse as a result of immigration over the course of the latter half of the twentieth century, it has not followed the US example with regard to the welfare state. However, that leaves open a very important question: to what extent could contemporary changes in the economic and social circumstances of European nations transform the configurations of their welfare states—and the position of immigrants and ethnic minorities therein—in the future?

In the United Kingdom, more than half a century of immigration has resulted in a highly diverse population, which is differentiated on the basis of ethnicity, religion, legal status, gender, generation, and class. A policy of state intervention to maintain good race relations and prevent discrimination has been linked to a strict policy of entry control, which categorizes and controls different groups on the basis of complex and opaque criteria. The situation of immigrants and minorities has been closely bound up with the neoliberalization of the economy, and the shift of the welfare state away from social solidarity toward individual case-management of exclusion and impoverishment. Formal possession of British citizenship has never been a guarantee of social inclusion, and the ideological shift from multiculturalism to social cohesion since the mid-2000s indicates that recognition of belonging to the nation remains conditional for people seen as culturally alien by the dominant group.

At the end of the 2000s, as the golden days of its "second economic miracle" were fading, Italy's reliance on disadvantaged, docile, socially excluded, and irregular migrant labor also seemed to be coming to an end. Italy cannot rely solely on a global reserve army of cheap domestic servants to solve its looming demographic crisis. At this critical juncture, where well-worn strategies of informality and clientelism in economic management and governance increasingly prove their inadequacy, the inherent tensions caused by a racialized, dual labor market and exclusivist welfare state and citizenship regime lead to heated public unrest. Nativist populism and racist violence at the street level are increasingly confronted with the mobilization of migrants and new ethnic minorities against harassment and in favor of the latent promises of a liberal constitution.

In most dimensions of the migration-welfare nexus, Sweden is the mirror opposite of Italy. Until the late 1980s, the internationally celebrated Swedish model could boast a promising merger of a powerful and equitable institutional welfare system, a liberal universalist conception of citizenship, a generous asylum policy, and an open, multicultural conception of the nation (Hammar, 1985). The specific labor-capital compact on which the Swedish welfare state rested has, so far, not allowed the use of migration as a key vehicle for wage depreciation and the recommodification of labor, as in the United States, Italy, and Britain.

Yet Swedish policies are loaded with imminent tensions and paradoxes (Ålund and Schierup, 1991). These abruptly came into the open during the economic recession of the early 1990s, which was accompanied by the disruption of the industrial compact geared to the maintenance of full employment through income policies with an indubitable neoliberal twist. These were matched by a gradual shift of the emblematic active labor market policy toward disciplinary neo-US "workfare" practices. However, this crisis also marked the end of the long-term concerted resistance of the social partners to any effective legislation against discrimination. Since the late 1990s, Sweden has introduced new discourses, legislation, and practices of diversity and antidiscrimination that closely match the US matrix on which they are modeled. However, given a parallel neoliberal twist to economics, welfare and labor market regulation, antidiscrimination legislation, and diversity management have come to operate under social circumstances that, step by step, are becoming more similar to structurally grounded forms of poverty and racialized exclusion in liberal welfare states like the United States or the United Kingdom (Schierup et al., 2006).

Our account is not to be read as implying that the road now lies open for the smooth liquidation of the Swedish welfare state or any of the other welfare states in the EU, or, for that matter, that the wholesale importation of the US model is just around the corner. Although there are strong currents of convergence toward overall neoliberal hegemony, the European cases discussed indicate how, compared with the United States, development in the EU's major immigration countries is still highly path-dependent. Europe's historical plurality of policies and regimes of citizenship has not come to an end. Nor has there been an EU-European common voice on the increasingly complex and controversial contemporary issues of social welfare and migration.

Yet an emergent EU regime, which is in many aspects modeled on neo-US policies, represents a common conditionality to which the member states are bound to adapt, and migration is becoming one of the EU's most pertinent policy areas. Following the Amsterdam Treaty of 1997, an impressive EU reform agenda was developed, as shown by a plethora of new initiatives that were often patterned on US models. A manifest antidiscrimination orientation was turned into mandatory directives and programs, which require member states to combat discrimination and social exclusion. Overall, EU policies also seem to be becoming increasingly parallel to those of the United States in terms of propagation of temporary worker schemes, the criminalization of undocumented immigration, the securitization of migration, and the dismantling of formerly humanistic norms and practices concerning asylum (Schierup et al., 2006).

But the US case shows clearly that antidiscrimination, equal opportunities, affirmative action, and diversity management policies are limited in scope, as long as the wider political economy continues to be oriented toward the recommodification of labor. An increasingly unequal ethnic division of labor, discriminatory migration management, and unequal access to civil, political, and social rights are not compatible with measures for the social inclusion of migrants and minorities. This ambiguity also applies to a European Union that continues to pivot uneasily around a central contradiction between economic and political goals (Chamberlayne, 1997; Williams, 1991), and between adjustment to the economic imperatives of global capitalism and the task of generating a new European identity based on a powerful notion of citizenship.

Notes

1. For a collection of texts and links to material about the global economic crisis, see http://www.age-of-migration.com/uk.

2. The history of post-1945 migration cannot be told in detail here, but there is a vast literature on the theme. Apart from our own works (Castles and Kosack, 1973; Castles et al., 1984; Schierup et al., 2006; Castles and Miller, 2009), we recommend among many good books Bade (2003), Lucassen et al. (2006), and Penninx et al. (2006).

3. It would be appropriate to include here a subsection on Germany as an example of the Central European variant of the conservative-corporatist model, but space will not allow.

4. For a critical scrutiny and evaluation of Clinton-Gingrich "welfare reform," see King (1999), the contributions in *Social Justice* (2001), and Handler (2003).

3

The Regulation of Labor Markets Through Migration

Harald Bauder

When privileged and underprivileged workers migrate, they respectively confront very different labor market circumstances in their new countries. Political debate and public discourses reflect these differences. Underprivileged workers are often represented in a negative way. For example, when the editor of a German newspaper published an oped I submitted about migration and the restructuring of labor markets, my original title, "Immigration and Globalization," was replaced with the supposedly more inviting headline, "Immigration Lowers Social Standards" (Bauder, 2005a). Although factually not incorrect, the modified headline suggested that immigrants actively demolish welfare systems and labor standards, whereas the article in fact argued that immigrants are a vulnerable underclass whose exploitation is a structural element in the neoliberal regulation of labor markets. Popular interpretations of the effects of migration into low-skill labor markets often ignore the structural circumstances that act on migrant labor.[1] Conversely, popular debate represents the international mobility of privileged labor in a very different light. Attracting the world's "best and brightest" is supposed to make the national economy internationally more competitive. When immigrants belong to the class of business and economic elites, they are seen as economic assets and valuable human resources (Bauder, 2008a, 2008b).

Important research from a political economy perspective already shows that the top and the bottom of the occupational spectrum are interdependent phenomena. The convergence of managerial and professional functions in global cities attracts not only highly valued and internationally mobile managers and professionals, but also undervalued immigrant workers who provide entertainment to these elites and perform the services necessary to sustain their businesses and lifestyles (Sassen, 2006b). Similarly, Pierre Bourdieu suggests that an immigrant labor force "composed of disposable, temporary, single workers with no families and no social protection (like the French *sans papiers*) [is] ideally suited to providing the overworked executives in the dominant economy with the cheap and largely feminine services they need" (2002a: 40).

The economic elite and the vulnerable and exploitable migrant labor force are thus two sides of the same neoliberal coin.[2] According to such a conceptualization, vulnerable, de-skilled, and sometimes criminalized migrant labor performs the labor-intensive functions at the bottom of the labor market. For example, the increasing employment of de-skilled immigrants in work related to health, welfare, and social reproduction coincides with the retreat of governments from these functions and with pressures to reduce labor costs (Kofman and Raghuram, 2006). At the same time, the global competition for skilled professionals, top-level managers, and innovative entrepreneurs supposedly raises the market value of labor in the upper segments of the market. Neoliberalism supplies an ideology that frames immigrant contributions in both the top and bottom segments of the labor market in terms of personal independence, self-sufficiency, individual responsibility, and property ownership (Jordan and Brown, 2007). Yet despite this singular ideological superstructure, class has an important role in shaping the character of labor mobility and labor valorization. Playing different parts in a system of capital accumulation, the different groups of migrants follow class-particular legal rules and cultural conventions when they negotiate contexts of mobility, transnationality, settlement, and work.

In this chapter, I adopt a critical political economy perspective, as outlined by Nicola Phillips in the introductory chapter, in order to explore how structure and agency interact to produce the social, legal, and cultural foundations of migrants' positions in the labor market. I examine the mobility and valorization practices at the top and bottom ends of the labor market. Although a functional interdependency between the international mobility of labor in the lower and upper segments undeniably exists, my interest lies in the legal and cultural practices associated with migration as they apply to different segments of the labor market. Do legal and cultural practices enable a transnational elite to maintain or increase the value of its labor while they simultaneously devalue labor in the secondary segment? The answer to this question is complex because upper and lower labor market segments define two separate legal and cultural fields; thus the migration of labor belonging to these segments follows different legal and cultural rules. Shedding light on these complex legal and cultural processes is important because it provides a nuanced perspective on the mechanisms that situate migrants in the labor market and rectifies misleading statements that blame migrant workers for eroding wages and labor standards.

I draw on examples from Canada and Germany to illustrate my points. Germany has a relatively high proportion of highly skilled workers among its labor force of non-nationals (Sexton, 2001). Rough calculations based on 2006 data (Statistisches Bundesamt Deutschland, 2006: 89) suggest that about 12.5 percent of all foreigners in Germany then had professional or managerial employment. In Canada, 4.5 percent of all immigrants in 2008 had managerial occupations, 11.8 percent professional occupations, and 6.9 percent skilled and technical occupations (calculation based on Citizenship and Immigration Canada, 2009). Both countries also have large numbers of immigrants who work in the low-skill sector of the labor market. The appeal of using these two countries as examples lies in their similarities as industrialized Group of 8 (G-8) countries as well as their differences in terms of migration history, immigration policy, and national identity (Bauder, forthcoming). This situation places the various legal and cultural practices associated with migration in both countries in a common neoliberal frame of reference.

Culture and Labor Migration

Karl Marx (2001 [1867]) famously observed that a "reserve army of labor" absorbs the fluctuations in labor demand resulting from seasonal and business cycles. Migrants have performed this subordinate role throughout the industrial and postindustrial eras. In the 1970s, Michael Piore (1979) showed that the presence of migrants as shock absorbers serves to secure stable employment for a workforce of nonmigrants. A functional relationship exists between migrants in an unstable secondary labor market segment and nonmigrants in a stable primary segment. Yet when migrant workers are permanently incorporated into the labor market, their position as vulnerable and exploitable labor can initiate destructive competition with nonmigrant labor as they underbid each other with respect to wages and labor standards. In fact, the continuous differential treatment of migrants, the diminishing social and economic benefits they receive, and the increasing criminalization they experience can be interpreted as important forces in the neoliberal restructuring of labor markets.

Yet regulatory processes are not uniform across the labor market. Labor markets in immigrant-receiving industrialized countries have polarized in recent decades, while jobs in the middle segment of the labor market—namely in the well-paying and unionized manufacturing sector—have been in decline. The impact of separated, marginalized, and criminalized migrants does not ripple through the entire labor market but rather applies disproportionately to the secondary segment of the labor market, where it instigates a race to the bottom. The role of migration in the primary segment is different. International competition between top-level managers of multinational corporations has not depressed managerial incomes.

Labor market segmentation theory suggests that individual segments of the labor market operate according to different rules (Peck, 1996). These rules include institutional processes as well as social and cultural practices. These processes and practices tend to devalue the labor of migrants in the secondary segment (Bauder, 2006). However, it would be erroneous to assume that they simply produce the opposite effect (that is, labor valorization) in the upper segments of the labor market. Rather, I suggest that lower and upper segments of the labor market constitute separate legal and cultural fields that operate according to different rules. To Bourdieu (1984), the fields that frame habitus and cultural practices have always been class contingent. I apply this class perspective to the regulation of labor markets through migration.

Leslie Sklair argues that the global capitalist class operates in a transnational field that binds members through common values and capitalist practices, including "values of profit-seeking, corporate expansion and the practice of good public relations," an interest in the "global market," and a shared lifestyle regarding "patterns of higher education (increasingly in business schools) and consumption of luxury goods and services" (Sklair, 2001: 13, 18, 20). In making his argument, Sklair juxtaposes a state-centric notion of class against his idea of a transnational capitalist class. Other research, however, shows that cultural fields are as geographically contingent as that of the state. Aihwa Ong (1999: 17–18) acknowledges that immigrants acquire "a range of symbolic capitals that will facilitate their positioning, economic negotiation and cultural acceptance in different geographical sites." D. John Grove (2007) suggests that national and regional scales continue to define social fields that frame habitus and cultural practices. Although these fields may change in light of global economic development, they maintain a degree of national and regional autonomy. But Grove also believes in the parallel existence of a "global economic field [that] is shaped by the doctrine of neo-liberalism" (2007: 163).

This transnational field is not necessarily the field that applies to migrant labor. Philip Kelly and Tom Lusis argue that "habitus need not be place bound," finding that transnational Filipino migrants who settle in Canada maintain a system of shared social practices and cultural values (2006: 836). Yet their idea of a "transnational habitus" applies to a migrant group whose labor is nevertheless devalued in Canada due to the geographical nontransferability of cultural and other forms of capital (Pratt, 2004). Apparently, this transnational habitus does not enable these migrants to maintain the value of their labor. The thesis that underprivileged labor is locked into national or regional fields and therefore suffers from devaluation when it migrates, whereas privileged labor operates in an "international space" (Grove, 2007: 163–164) that enables it to increase or at least maintain its value with migration, is therefore problematic and probably simplistic. It is more plausible to argue that the fields that frame legal and cultural practices toward migrants are defined by interlocking class and geographical dimensions.

Migrants as Vulnerable Labor

Echoing Marx's aforementioned term for disposable workers during the early industrial period, Pierre Bourdieu associates the underprivileged migrants in our postindustrial economy with a "global reserve army of labour" (2002a: 40). Étienne Balibar similarly calls immigrants "today's proletarians" (2004: 50). Their situation is produced by the devaluation of their labor through migration and settlement in a different, geographically defined legal and cultural field. Legal and cultural processes of distinction play key roles in creating this situation on national and local scales. These mechanisms of labor devaluation interlink to produce well-known outcomes: immigrant labor is devalued and immigrants are used as a low-wage, contingent, and flexible labor force, instigating competition with nonmigrant labor. Below, I discuss the roles of citizenship, cultural capital, and gender in the devaluation of immigrants' labor.

Citizenship

One of the most important legal mechanisms of distinction enacted by the state is citizenship. I treat citizenship as a socially and politically constructed category that constitutes a strategic effort to control access to resources and institutions (see Kratochwil, 1994; Turner, 1997). Despite the strategic nature of citizenship, the notion that the lack of citizenship is a legitimate means of labor market exclusion and subordination is rarely questioned in either political or popular debate. The popular use of the term "illegal immigration" in the media and in daily political discourse indicates that citizenship is perceived as a natural category that endows citizens with legal rights that can be denied to noncitizen immigrants. Even legally admitted noncitizen immigrants can legitimately be subjected to labor market constraints that do not apply to citizens.

In 2008, Canada admitted 192,519 foreign temporary workers (Citizenship and Immigration Canada, 2009). Under the Commonwealth Caribbean and Mexican Seasonal Agricultural Workers Program, a so-called offshore program, 7,247 workers from the Caribbean and 8,475 from Mexico were able to enter Canada in the same year (FARMS, 2010). This program provides an interesting illustration of how the lack of citizenship and the associated denial of social and economic rights renders this workforce vulnerable and exploitable. The program was initiated in 1966, after Canadian farmers and representatives complained about the "poor caliber" of local farm labor (Satzewich, 1991: 151). After an initial agreement with Jamaica, other Caribbean states and Mexico were added to the program. Many of the workers participating in the offshore program have been returning annually, creating a workforce of, as it were, permanent temporary workers (Sharma, 2006). Lacking the benefits and rights associated with formal citizenship, offshore workers are extremely vulnerable and effectively represent a form of unfree labor (Basok, 2002). For example, workers do not possess the right to switch employers.[3] The expression of dissatisfaction by workers may lead to their dismissal from the program and subsequent deportation or to their exclusion from the program in subsequent years. Although they earn the minimum wage, they are expected to work under conditions that Canadian workers would not tolerate, characterized by, for example, long and flexible hours and exposure to pesticides, chemicals, and heat (Basok, 2002). The lack of citizenship and its associated rights and entitlements makes this workforce an attractive reserve army of labor for Canadian agriculture.

Germany maintains a similarly vulnerable labor force of foreign temporary workers. Since labor enjoys virtually unrestricted mobility within much of the European Union (EU), this labor force consists of citizens from countries from outside the EU or from EU countries that are not given full mobility privileges.[4] The vast majority of the 285,217 foreign seasonal workers in 2008 were Poles, who spend up to four months employed mostly in agriculture and forestry. In addition, 16,576 foreign contract workers (*Werkvertragsarbeitnehmer*) were employed in Germany in 2008, mostly from Eastern Europe and the Balkans, and the authorities permit an annual contingent of roughly 11,050 guest workers (*Gastarbeitnehmer*) into the country (Bundesamt für Migration und Flüchtlinge, 2010).[5] Like foreign temporary and seasonal workers in Canada, they are denied free choice of either employer or occupation as well as other social and economic rights that citizens take for granted (Herbert, 2001).

In both Canada and Germany, a lack of formal citizenship provides the conditions in which individuals can be subjected to rigorous assessment procedures for temporary or permanent entry and participation in the labor market. In Canada, noncitizens are permitted to immigrate based on a three-tier system that distinguishes people in humanitarian need from members of Canadian families and from skilled workers, businesspeople, and investors who are deemed useful to the Canadian economy. Only after such an assessment are some selected noncitizens offered permanent residency (or "landed" immigrant status) and access to the Canadian labor market as citizens—with a few exceptions: they are barred from the military, some civil administrative positions, and public office. After living in Canada for at least three of the next four years, immigrants are eligible to apply for citizenship, which eliminates all formal discrimination. Historically, by providing relatively quick access to citizenship through naturalization, Canada has been able to obtain the labor needed for territorial expansion and economic development.

In Germany, citizenship is an even more important ordering mechanism of the labor market, to which workers receive various degrees of access. One immigrant group that has been granted citizenship consists of ethnic German returnees from Eastern Europe and the former Soviet Union who were displaced as a consequence of World War II—the so-called *Aussiedler* and *Spätaussiedler*.[6] They could have been absent from German territory for generations but have immediate access to the labor market upon their return. Other immigrants receive hierarchical access to the labor market based on the passports they possess. EU citizens obtain formal access to most occupations. (As is the case with Canadian landed immigrants, there are exceptions, which include positions in public administration, the police, and the military.) Non-EU citizens must acquire residency and work permits to obtain probationary access to employment. Once immigrants can demonstrate an employment history and show that they have made social insurance contributions, they can claim "postnational" social and economic rights (Soysal, 1994). If they cannot get residency or a work permit, they are relegated to the informal labor market, where abuse is rampant and postnational rights do not accrue, since they make no health, employment, or social insurance contributions (Wilpert, 1998).

Cultural Capital

Cultural capital exists in various forms, including "institutionalized" and "embodied" varieties (Bourdieu, 1986). Institutionalized cultural capital refers to educational credentials, diplomas, and certificates that signify value. A degree from a prestigious institution—say, an MBA from Harvard—is worth more than the pure knowledge that was transmitted in the graduate program; it also symbolizes status and thereby provides access to elite occupations and workplaces.

Migrants often confront the devaluation of the institutionalized cultural capital they possess. Both Canada and Germany have signed international agreements that facilitate the mobility of businesspeople and professionals from more than 140 countries who provide foreign services. The General Agreement on Trade in Services (GATS) of the World Trade Organization (WTO) has also set global education standards for certain professions. In professions such as accounting, institutional cultural capital is defined by the possession of educational credentials that can be applied within the territory of WTO member countries. Nevertheless, the professional associations of the United States and Europe had greater influence in determining the content of these standards, so professionals trained in the Global North tend to benefit from greater international mobility of their institutionalized cultural capital than do professionals trained in the South (Iredale, 2001).

In Canada, the nonrecognition of foreign credentials is a notorious problem for migrants, particularly those from the Global South. Paradoxically, migrants are often admitted to Canada on the basis of their educational and professional credentials. Yet these same credentials are often devalued, deemed either to be irrelevant or to be suited to employment in related occupations but at lower pay scales. In some instances, immigrants whose labor is thus devalued apply their skills in positions below their formal training. Medical doctors work as nurses, nurses as day-care workers, bankers as secretaries, and lawyers as paralegals. This devaluation could be interpreted as a mere organizational mismatch between Citizenship and Immigration Canada—the federal ministry responsible for admitting immigrants—and professional associations that are responsible for the recognition of credentials at the provincial level. However, empirical research suggests that nonrecognition of foreign credentials protects the privileged access of Canadian-trained labor to prestigious professions (Bauder, 2003a; Girard and Bauder, 2007a, 2007b).

In Germany, immigrants confront the same barrier formed by nonrecognition of foreign credentials. The invalidation of credentials relegates highly educated and skilled immigrants to the secondary segment of the German labor market. *Spätaussieder*, who otherwise possess privileged access to the labor market compared to other immigrant groups, suffer particularly from this barrier. Apparently, in situations in which citizenship fails to devalue immigrant labor, nonrecognition of foreign credentials accomplishes the task instead (Bauder, 2006: 125–137). The results in both Canada and Germany are similar: processes of distinction devalue immigrant labor and flood the labor markets of both countries with skilled workers who possess valuable knowledge and experience but who do not receive wages and benefits commensurate with their skill levels.

Another form of cultural capital is embodied cultural capital. Alluding to "techniques of the body" (Bourdieu, 1984: 466), the term signifies certain cultural competences, including the competence to perform a given job. In the absence of more formalized mechanisms of exclusion, such as citizenship or institutionalized cultural capital, these techniques of the body serve as a mechanism of exclusion. While the devaluation of immigrant labor is largely achieved through formal constraints in Germany, labor market exclusion based on the lack of embodied cultural capital poses a significant barrier to immigrants in Canada. In this case, the habitus of an immigrant's place of origin frames his or her system of judgment and interpretation of embodied performances. In short, miscommunication can lead to exclusion from the upper segment of the Canadian labor market. For example, immigrants who seek access to professional employment must demonstrate professionalism according to the dominant culture—for instance, in the ways that they carry themselves during the job interview, which include following dress conventions, greeting with a firm handshake, making eye contact, knowing when to laugh at a joke, and enacting other expected performances. Wearing a turban or a sari, speaking with an accent, and even eating spices that produce distinct body scents can be associated with stereotypical images of incompetence to work in some occupations in the primary segment of the labor market (Bauder, 2003b).

Gender

Gender plays an important role in the regulation of the secondary segments of postindustrial labor markets through migration. Work traditionally performed by women has long been undervalued in Western society. As rising numbers of women are drawn into the waged labor force, domestic work is increasingly performed by paid female labor (Ehrenreich and Hochschild, 2003; England, 1996; Piper, Chapter 4 in this volume). Migrant women provide a supply of exploitable labor to fill the shortage created by "professional households without a wife" (Sassen, 2006b: 178). The cultural perception of so-called female work as inferior and of lesser value goes hand in hand with the feminization of migrant labor in the secondary and informal segments of the labor market.

This trend is particularly apparent in care occupations, including domestic work, health care, and sex work. Saskia Sassen suggests that "the immigrant woman serving the white middle-class professional woman has replaced the traditional image of the black female servant serving the white master" (2006b: 183). As Nicola Piper also indicates in her chapter in this volume, even in regulated care professions such as nursing, skilled female labor suffers disproportionately from de-skilling through the nonrecognition of credentials, racialization, and/or other mechanisms of cultural devaluation (Kofman and Raghuram, 2006). Geraldine Pratt (2004) has exposed colonial histories and processes of racialization that discursively construct migrant women from the Philippines as uncivilized and inferior labor, suitable for work in child care, housekeeping, or home care rather than more prestigious work. The vulnerability of these female migrants is heightened by immigration policies and economic pressures that often leave them with little choice but to comply with their demotion, humiliation, and entrapment at the bottom of the labor market (Preston, 2003).

Men, however, are not always the winners of migration. Women are often more vulnerable and flexible and therefore more attractive to employers than are men. Consequently, traditional gender roles within families often reverse, with the wife performing the role of the breadwinner and the husband that of the child rearer (Bauder, 2005b). Not only do such identity shifts reflect the de-skilling and labor devaluation of the individual, but they also result in the economic downgrading of the entire family. The professionally skilled husband performs unfamiliar household work while the wife, with few educational credentials and little experience in waged work, participates in the lower end of the waged labor market.

Migrants as Privileged Labor

The migration patterns of underprivileged and privileged labor share several characteristics. First, geographical mobility has been increasing in both cases. In the context of privileged labor, "Global capital does not want artificial barriers, and entrepreneurs and corporations have lobbied governments to minimize immigration restrictions and for the right to choose their own employees, independent of outside interference" (Iredale, 2001: 20). Amid international corporate mergers and takeovers as well as the increasing internationalization of corporate structures, the international mobility of privileged labor has become increasingly common (Salt, 1992; Gidden, 2007; Glebe and White, 2001). Second, both privileged and underprivileged labor is legally and culturally regulated. However, the legal and cultural rules of international migration and labor market participation differ widely for the two groups. Third, geographical contingencies exist with respect to the ways in which legal and cultural practices regulate top and bottom segments of the labor market. The following discussion of the migration of privileged labor addresses these commonalities and differences.

Citizenship

Conducting business or performing managerial or high-end professional work internationally usually does not require the acquisition of a particular type of citizenship. Nation-states tend to issue visas or otherwise permit businesspeople and upper-segment labor to be present within its borders. Nevertheless, the acquisition of formal citizenship can be a useful strategy in the wider process of capital accumulation among capitalist elites.

In Canada, privileged migrant labor has relatively easy access to citizenship. Canadian immigration and visa policies provide an avenue for privileged labor to obtain permanent residency and subsequently citizenship. Through the so-called economic class, the Canadian state seeks to provide entry to workers who can benefit Canada's economy based on their human and economic capital. In 2008, 149,072 immigrants were admitted under this class, which represented 63.9 percent of all immigration to Canada.[7] The economic class is further broken down into a points system and a business program.[8] The points system selects immigrants on the basis of education, skills, and experience. In 2008, 103,736 immigrants, or 41.9 percent of all immigration to Canada, were selected under the points system (Citizenship and Immigration Canada, 2009). The vast majority of these were in professional, managerial, and skilled and technical occupations. However, many of these immigrants fail to maintain their privileged labor market status after they settle in Canada, experiencing the devaluation of their institutionalized and embodied cultural capital (Bauder, 2006).[9] More revealing for my argument is the case of business immigrants. This group consists of self-employed artists, athletes, and farm managers; entrepreneurs with a net worth of CAN$300,000 or more who plan to create a business in Canada that employs at least one Canadian worker; and investors with a net worth of at least CAN$800,000 who invest a minimum of CAN $400,000 in Canada.[10] In 2008, 12,107 business immigrants came to Canada, representing 4.8 percent of all immigration (calculation based on Citizenship and Immigration Canada, 2009). Through the business program, a privileged elite—measured by access to economic capital—receives privileged access to permanent residency, which is to say landed immigrant status, along with the option of gaining citizenship after living in Canada for three years.[11] For this elite, lack of citizenship constitutes a barrier to accumulation that can be overcome.

David Ley's research illustrates the different agendas pursued by the Canadian state on the one hand, and by investors and entrepreneurs who migrated to Canada in the 1980s and 1990s on the other (2003, 2010). Rather than coming to Canada to take advantage of local entrepreneurial and business opportunities as intended by the Canadian state, these migrants were primarily motivated by the opportunity to acquire formal citizenship as a form of capital that could be converted into other forms of capital, including such aspects of cultural capital as English language skills and Canadian educational credentials and diplomas for their children. Only later—mostly in the next generation—would this cultural capital be converted into economic capital. Johanna Waters' research shows that business- and entrepreneur-class immigrants from Hong Kong and Taiwan who settled in Vancouver in this period had often planned familial separation prior to migration: the female spouse would manage the household in Canada while her children attended school there, and the male spouse would continue to do business in Hong Kong (2003). The ultimate goal of this strategy was to obtain a Canadian passport (Waters, 2003: 228) while accumulating other forms of capital. On the family level, the acquisition of formal citizenship reflects a particularly lucrative strategy of collective capital accumulation (Ong, 1999).

The German state has recently attempted to follow the North American model of attracting highly skilled labor. The first initiative in this regard was the creation of the so-called German green card program, which began in 2000. Unlike the US green card, which grants permanent residency with the prospect of citizenship, the German version provided a work permit for information technology (IT) experts from outside the EU who had arranged employment with an annual salary of at least €51,000 (51,000 euros), for a duration limited to five years. Although 20,000 green cards were available, only 14,876 were issued. The green card initiative facilitated the mobility of highly skilled labor to small and midsized businesses (Kolb, 2005). More interestingly in the context of this chapter, the green card initiated discussion of a new German immigration law. After fierce debate lasting several years, the law was finally passed in 2004 and took effect in 2005 (Bauder, 2008b). Entrepreneurs who invested €1 million or created ten or more new jobs were now eligible for a work permit and permanent residence after three years and thus able to circumvent citizenship barriers (Bundesministerium des Innern, 2007).[12] Although the Canadian-style points system to attract skilled labor that was included in the original proposal of the law was eventually dropped, the new immigration law permitted highly privileged labor with an annual income of at least €84,000 from outside of the EU to immigrate.[13] In 2008, the German government issued 3,906 corresponding permits to IT specialists, 2,710 permits to workers in academic occupations, and 2,252 permits to top-level managers and specialists (Bundesamt für Migration und Flüchtlinge, 2010). Although there are differences in the procedures and standards to acquire residency status and citizenship, the Canadian and German states have pursued similar goals of making formal citizenship capital available to economic elites.

In addition, Canada and Germany are members of regional associations that facilitate labor mobility. As a member of the North American Free Trade Agreement (NAFTA) and the Canada-Chile Free Trade Agreement (CCFA), Canada offers international mobility to intra-company transferees, traders and investors in supervisory or executive capacity, and workers in 60 selected professions, including engineering, accounting, management consultancy, or computer systems analysis. Lower-segment labor is excluded from these mobility provisions (Citizenship and Immigration Canada, 2007). Germany, as a member of the EU, provides almost complete access to skilled as well as unskilled workers from other EU member countries.[14] The possession of formal citizenship of a member country is an important prerequisite for mobility.

Cultural Capital

Internal labor markets facilitate the transnational migration of privileged labor. Based on the German experience, we may posit that the internal labor markets of multinational corporations provide an institutional infrastructure for the international mobility of labor. However, a uniform migration experience among these transnational workers does not exist. Günther Glebe and Paul White (2001) provide a typology for the migration of skilled labor within internal labor markets. They distinguish between top-level managers, experts and specialists, language educators, and trainees as well as between ethnocentric, polycentric, regional, and global corporate structures. Each of these categories differs in terms of degree of labor mobility, motivation, and expectations of migration.

Moreover, Michael Hartmann (1999) argues that top-level management functions are relatively place bound, having found little evidence of a high degree of mobility among top-level managers across transnational space. This immobility may be interpreted as a "structuring factor for transnational upper classes" to reserve the option of migration rather than actually exercising it (Weiss, 2005: 714). An alternative explanation for the geographical immobility of top-level managers is that the place-particular meanings of cultural capital are not easily transferable to other national and geographical contexts (Weiss, 2005; Bauder, 2005b, 2006). For example, in North America and Great Britain, the educational credentials of top-level managers are valorized within the geographical space framed by national borders (McDowell, 1997). In Germany, where the absence of a system of elite universities limits the accumulation of similar kinds of institutionalized cultural capital, class-particular embodied cultural capital—expressed through the ability to convey confidence, optimism, and business spirit and to observe dress codes and behavioral norms—serves as a location-particular mechanism of inclusion into the business elite (Hartmann, 1999: 135). Foreigners, who may be rich in some forms of capital but lack access to the embodied cultural capital of the German bourgeoisie (*gehobenes Bürgertum*), are denied entry into these elite occupations (Hartmann, 2000). Various geographically defined expressions of cultural capital, on which top-level managers rely, may not be easily transferable from one place to another.

Similar processes of cultural exclusion operate in other upper-segment occupations in Germany. Perfect knowledge of the German language and the "subtleties of native interaction" (Weiss, 2005: 721) are important for migrants who wish to gain access to jobs in the IT sector.[15] The prestige of institutional cultural capital from beyond Germany's borders is rarely recognized within them. For example, German employers may fail to grasp the significance of the achievements of an IT specialist from India who graduated among the top 1 percent of his age cohort and was admitted to the MBA program at the renowned Indian Institute of Technology. Elite students arriving in Germany from other parts of the world, such as Latin America, have similar experiences regarding the nonrecognition of their institutionalized cultural capital (Weiss, 2005: 719–721). Elite migrant labor has to rely on other forms of capital, including monetary capital, to maintain its value.

In Canada, institutionalized cultural capital plays a different role for privileged, transnationally mobile labor. Canada's links with countries of the Pacific Rim provide an interesting perspective in this respect. Next to the internal labor markets of corporations, professional associations and other mesoscale migration channels can facilitate the migration of skilled labor into arranged employment abroad and prevent deskilling (Findlay and Li, 1994, 1998). The prospect of acquiring cosmopolitan identities, cultural competences, and other aspects of cultural capital often provides important personal incentives for young professionals to move abroad (Conradson and Latham, 2007).

In the context of business and entrepreneurial migration from East Asia to Canada, however, the accumulation of transnational cultural capital through migration is often a family-based rather than individual strategy (Ong, 1999).[16] Among "astronaut families" who settle in Canada, the husband—who may continue to do business in Hong Kong or Taipei—accumulates economic capital, the female spouse who maintains the household in Vancouver acquires citizenship capital, and the children who attend Canadian schools obtain institutionalized and embodied cultural capital (Waters, 2003). Based on her empirical research in Vancouver and Hong Kong, Waters (2006: 1063) concludes that "the terrain over which class status is maintained has shifted, through the internationalization of education and an emergent global map of cultural capital, to incorporate transnational space."

Among the East Asian economic elite, the acquisition of institutionalized cultural capital in the form of a North American education is a common strategy for the reproduction of economic privilege (Ong, 1999). After an initial investment of economic capital to send family members abroad,[17] the foreign institutional credentials and the cultural competences gained abroad often become important stepping stones for family members to enter careers in management and professional occupations in multinational corporations. The symbolic value of a Canadian degree encompasses the acquisition of embodied cultural capital. For example, a valuable cultural asset acquired through education in Canada is the ability to communicate in North American English and project an internationally recognized image of professionalism (Iredale, 2001). The attainment of such embodied techniques constitutes an important motivation for transnational mobility.

Yet this transnational mobility is only achieved with considerable personal sacrifices and efforts to overcome existing barriers. Long-distance relationships are particularly hard on spouses and children (Waters, 2003, 2006), and racial and habitual markers present obstacles to full and equal participation in the white settler society for Asian elite families (Ong, 1999: 110–136). These sacrifices and difficulties indicate that transnational mobility, even for the economic elite, comes at a price.

Gender

Complementing the trend toward the feminization of the secondary labor market segment through migration, the primary segment of the labor market has remained inaccessible to many female migrants. Eleonore Kofman and Parvati Raghuram (2006: 296–297) suggest that migrant women often have occupations that are regulated by professional bodies, and are thus exposed to institutionalized processes of de-skilling. An example of such an occupation is nursing (and other reproductive and care work), which has a predominately female labor force and is responsible for a significant migration flow to countries such as Canada. Migrating men, conversely, are more likely to maintain their roles as privileged workers when they assume top-level management and professional functions (such as those in the IT sector), which are regulated not through formal credentials but rather through less tangible forms of capital, including social capital and embodied cultural capital.

The case of Canada illustrates the unequal gender distribution of migrants across labor market segments. Women represent only 34.2 percent of the applicants in the skilled workers program, 15.9 percent of the principal applicants admitted under the business program, and 25.9 percent of the principal applicants under the provincial nominee program (calculations based on Citizenship and Immigration Canada, 2009). Unequal gender distribution also exists across the spectrum of foreign temporary workers in Canada. Among men, 4.6 percent are managers, 19.3 percent professionals, and 21.2 percent technical and skilled workers. Among women, only 2.1 percent are managers, 13.1 percent professionals, and 7.1 percent technical and skilled workers (Citizenship and Immigration Canada, 2009).

This gender difference is linked to the disadvantages women face in accumulating other forms of capital, including economic and institutional capital. For example, the social field of elite workplaces, such as management functions in corporations and banks, operates on the basis of cultural codes of masculinity (McDowell, 1997). For women migrants, the double barrier of gender and cultural exclusion is only heightened as cultural capital and gender roles are defined in a geographically contingent manner (Bauder, 2005b; Preston, 2003).

Conclusion

The regulatory role of the labor market depends to a considerable degree on the legal and cultural contexts that valorize or devalue the labor of migrant workers. These legal and cultural contexts are not uniform for migrants, but rather are class contingent. Privileged and underprivileged migrant labor operates in different legal and cultural fields that produce variable outcomes.

Geography is a crucial dimension that shapes the situation of migrants in the labor market. Underprivileged labor tends to be bound to place-based legal and cultural fields and often suffers from devaluation as it migrates from one place to another. However, the thesis that privileged labor operates in a transnational field and therefore seamlessly overcomes the legal and cultural obstacles of migration from one place to another must be rejected. While transnationally mobile privileged labor may share some consumption patterns and other cultural characteristics, these tend to be embedded in national and regional structural contexts (Weiss, 2006). Based on the literature I reviewed above, the idea that privileged labor constructs cultural competences that are internationally applicable must be questioned. Rather, geography constitutes an obstacle for migrant labor across the class structure. Mobility, even for privileged labor, is typically a problematic and painful accumulation strategy.

The effect of this geographical dimension has a different character and magnitude for privileged and underprivileged migrant labor. Legal barriers are much easier to overcome for privileged labor than for underprivileged labor. In the legal sense, underprivileged labor may indeed be controlled by the state while the transnational capitalist class may increasingly shift to the global scale (Sklair, 2001). Yet cultural obstacles exist across the class spectrum. Place-particular cultural conventions and habitual practices make it difficult for privileged labor to move its various forms of capital from one place to another.

State and other political boundaries are not entirely irrelevant to the formation of place-particular cultural barriers to mobility. Rather, the container logic of the state continues to frame cultural norms and forms of capital, such as institutionalized cultural capital. For example, research by Daniel Hiebert (2006) shows that Canadian immigrants from the United States, Europe, Australia, New Zealand, and South Africa are particularly likely to be in well-paying employment. A probable explanation for the distinct impact of the source country is that cultural capital from these countries—expressed in institutionalized, embodied and other forms—is more easily transferable to Canada than from countries in Asia, Africa, or Latin America.

Cultural capital, which enables the reproduction of privileged elites, is valorized nationally and regionally. While Canada and Germany may constitute distinct national systems of cultural production, both countries are also embedded in regional systems of cultural valorization that operate on the scales of North America, Europe, and the Global North (Iredale, 2001). As a consequence, privileged labor migrating within these regions may be less affected by legal and cultural barriers than are workers who migrate from other countries. The difficulties experienced by students from Hong Kong and Taiwan who migrate to Vancouver in order to acquire region-particular cultural capital illustrate this point (Waters, 2003, 2006).

In addition, an asymmetry exists in the valorization and devaluation of labor that relates to the direction of migration. Skilled workers who migrate from the Global South to the North often suffer from de-skilling and labor devaluation, whereas workers leaving Canada or Germany to work outside Europe and North America can use their cultural capital—such as the ability to judge Western consumer tastes—to increase the value of their labor (see Weiss, 2005). A similar geographical asymmetry applies to the valorization of citizenship and the ability to obtain visas.

The interlocking geographical and class dimensions of the legal and cultural fields are important factors in the regulation of labor markets through migration. These dimensions contribute to the allocation of privileged and underprivileged migrant labor to particular labor market segments. In particular, the vulnerability of underprivileged immigrant workers and the de-skilling of skilled immigrant labor are the results of complex geographies of legal and cultural practices. These practices create a migrant labor force that is unable to compete on a level playing field with local nonmigrant labor, triggering the destructive competition that today characterizes the lower segments of the labor market in Canada and Germany.

To focus only on the outcome of these practices and ignore how structure and agency interconnect in the context of legal and cultural practice—as populist discourses often do—is to paint a misleading image of how migration regulates labor markets. Neither the migration decisions of individual workers and families, nor the abstract notion of immigration, but rather the concrete legal and cultural practices toward migrants regulate labor markets in a manner that supports the neoliberal trend toward eroding labor and social standards and growing socioeconomic disparity in both Canada and Germany. Yet the counternarrative, namely that privileged labor can seamlessly transfer its various forms of capital and apply them in the labor market of a destination country, must equally be rejected.

Notes

I thank Nicola Phillips for her comments and Wolf Gaebe of the Institute of Geography at the University of Stuttgart and the Alexander von Humboldt Foundation for his support.

1. Such interpretations are common not only among the press but also lobbying groups, think tanks, and government. For example, the US-based Center for Immigration Studies has issued a report titled "Immigration Is Hurting the US Worker" (Camarota, 2007). Even the Canadian government reports that "immigration has tended to lower wages in both Canada and the United States" (Statistics Canada, 2007).

2. Unsurprisingly, as I am making the final revisions to this chapter, the EU is announcing plans to increase the mobility of third-country specialists and managers on the one hand and seasonal labor on the other (*Frankfurter Allgemeine Zeitung*, 2010).

3. The program is managed by the nonprofit, private sector–run organization Foreign Agricultural Resource Management Services (FARMS), which oversees the "transfer" of workers between employers. Workers who wish to switch jobs must advise their current employer, who, under certain circumstances and with the approval of the foreign consulate and/or liaison of the worker's country of origin, can place a transfer request with FARMS. The asymmetrical power relationship between workers and employers works in the interests of the latter.

4. Citizens of some of the member states that joined the EU in 2004 have restricted access to the German labor market until 2011, at which point, the restrictions will be lifted.

5. In 2008, however, only 242 guest workers were registered.

6. After the fall of the Iron Curtain, the annual flow of ethnic German returnees increased dramatically, peaking in 1990 at almost 400,000

(Bundesverwaltungsamt, 2003). A toughening of the application procedure reduced this flow to a trickle in subsequent years.

7. Of these, 41.1 percent were principal applicants; the remainder were spouses and dependents (calculation based on Citizenship and Immigration Canada, 2009).

8. Technically, the economic class also includes the provincial nominee program, which consists of immigrants selected by the provinces according to their occupational, educational, and/or entrepreneurial skill sets. This program provided 23,418 immigrants to Canada in 2008 (calculation based on Citizenship and Immigration Canada, 2009). Furthermore, a relatively small but rapidly growing category of the economic class (10,508 entries in 2008) is composed of so-called live-in caregivers, who receive temporary status under the condition that they work as care personnel in a private home. This group suffers from massive deskilling (see Pratt, 2004).

9. However, research suggests that immigrant labor selected by the points system is not devalued to the degree previously thought (Hiebert, 2006). Previous studies used data sets that did not separate the principal applicant, who was evaluated under the points system, from dependents, who were not scrutinized by this system.

10. As of July 2010, the Canadian government proposed to increase the requisite personal net worth of investors to US$1.6 million and the requisite investment to US$800,000.

11. Citizenship not only gives migrants the right to leave and enter Canada at any time but also facilitates, in many instances, travel to and residence in the United States, Europe, and many other places. Moreover, Canada permits naturalized Canadians to maintain their original citizenship(s).

12. Changes to the law in 2007 reduced these requirements.

13. After the new immigration law took effect, the Federal Ministry for the Interior announced that green card holders who reached the five-year limit would obtain an unlimited work permit (Bundesministerium des Innern, 2007).

14. That said, as mentioned in a previous footnote, workers from some Eastern European countries that joined the EU in 2004 remain temporarily excluded. But they will likely obtain access to the German labor market in 2011.

15. Bourdieu's work suggests that in France, too, this embodied cultural capital is increasingly important for maintaining class status in light of the fact that access to other forms of capital is being democratized (Bourdieu and Passeron, 1977; Bourdieu, 1984). Similarly, Linda McDowell (1997) confirmed in a study of banks in London that access to elite banking occupations increasingly depends on the possession of embodied cultural capital in the forms of body image and enactments involving race, gender, weight, and age.

16. To enable and maintain this family-centered accumulation strategy, these families rely on "discursively constructed ideas of the family as a site of morality, purity and tradition" (Yeoh et al., 2005: 309).

17. A significant portion of students "disappear" from the Hong Kong school system at the stage of the Hong Kong Certificate of Education Examination. Apparently, many fail or anticipate failing the examinations, so those whose parents can afford the fees continue their education abroad (Waters, 2006).

4

Toward a Gendered Political Economy of Migration

Nicola Piper

Feminist scholars have long stressed the need for fostering a greater understanding of political economy models as inherently gendered, via their critiques of economistic concepts such as rational choice, the privileging of the public over the private, and the dichotomized treatment of structure and agency (Waylen, 2000). With the renewal of interest in political economy approaches in the 1990s, the argument was advanced for a "gendered political economy" as distinct from a "political economy of gender." The former posits gender as a category for analysis in its own right within the field of political economy, rather than, as the latter implies, simply a subject studied with the conventional tools of political economy (Cook and Roberts, 2000). This mirrors the development of feminist scholarship in the social sciences more broadly, which took the step from merely "adding women in" to a thorough gender analysis based on feminist epistemology. Given the widely acknowledged feminization of migration (UNRISD, 2005; UNFPA, 2006), as well as the fact that the dynamics of international migration involve the crossing of political borders and, therefore, state jurisdictions, the contemporary study of migration requires an approach that not only transcends the analytical and regulatory framework of the nation-state, but also benefits from a serious gendered analysis.

The phenomenon of feminization is not only a recognized feature of international migration but also of work more broadly (Standing, 1989, 1999; Sassen, 2000). Feminization is largely the outcome of the increasing informalization, casualization, and precariousness of work, which negatively affect men's ability to find permanent employment or jobs in traditionally male-dominated sectors. Consequently, feminization has also become a key feature of poverty, especially in the specific definition provided by Sylvia Chant (2008), which refers to the increased burden placed upon women in securing families' livelihoods and economic survival. Establishing a link between the feminization of migration, work, and poverty is the main objective of this chapter. I propose to do so by discussing the three feminizations in relation to the global division of labor and the conceptualization of two "global chains": the global commodity (that is, productive) chain, and the global care (that is, reproductive) chain. In this way, I show how the feminization of migration, work, and poverty is linked to both the transnationalization and the gender segregation of labor markets, the consequences of which have intensified in the wake of the economic crisis of the late 2000s, resulting in a "global jobs crisis" (ILO, 2009).

By adding a further component to the discussion of the feminization of work and international migration—namely, the feminization of poverty—I shall develop a framework of analysis that situates the gendered political economy of migration within the so-called migration-development nexus. The main concerns in this debate—which has recently been revived by global policymakers as well as academics (and indeed constitutes a major focus in this volume)—center on origin countries in the Global South and are related to the structures of socioeconomic inequality that constitute the main push factors for migration. The feminization of poverty and responsibility thus lies at the intersection of specific dynamics linking rich and poorer countries, associated with the effects of structural adjustment policies (SAPs), the demand for labor in feminized jobs in the context of the neoliberal restructuring of economies and welfare states in the North, and the intensification of global commodity and care chains.

The relationship between migration and development has been of renewed interest to global policymakers who aim to turn migration into more a matter of choice than necessity by tackling the slow, at times back-tracking process of socioeconomic development in countries of origin that are typically resource poor (GCIM, 2005; UN, 2006; UNDP, 2009). Countries of origin have themselves placed great emphasis on remittances to spur development, backed by the arguments of some economists that many origin countries would benefit from "exporting" larger numbers of their citizens. But this option is obstructed by the restrictive immigration policies of rich countries, especially vis-à-vis so-called low-skilled migrants, with the effect of turning those migrants into what some have called an "unfree" labor force (Basok, 1999). Given prevailing immigration policies and the inability of origin states to provide public goods and create employment locally, the current focus on remittance-led development carries a strong element of coercion, in that migration comes to be seen as a form of development, or, worse, migration continues without development (Matsas, 2008). By constructing individual migrants, many of whom are women, as "agents" of development, the current phase of the migration-development debate illuminates Chant's argument about the increasing burden now being placed upon women in securing their families' livelihoods and survival.

I begin this chapter by situating the analysis of migration within the emerging global economy and its changing division of labor, highlighting the trend toward the stratification and polarization of migrants with specific gender outcomes. The following section provides a brief discussion of the link between the restrictive migration policies practiced by destination countries and poverty among migrants and left-behind nonmigrants, with specific reference to the example of agricultural and farm work (in its dual role as "push factor" and "pull factor"). The dynamics between destination and origin countries, and the linkages between migration and poverty embedded within a gendered political economy of global production, are connected here to debates on the two aforementioned types of global chains: global commodity/value chains and global care chains. The final section considers the implications of the discussion for pushing scholars of international political economy (IPE) toward making a more profound analytical and conceptual contribution to a gendered political economy of migration.

The Global Division of Labor, Migration, and Gender

As the process of globalization has accelerated, so the spatial division of labor has deepened. Production processes are no longer confined to national economies but involve a complex system of outsourcing, subcontracting, and relocating labor-intensive parts of the manufacturing process to developing countries where the unit costs of labor are substantially lower. These complex processes are well captured by the notions of global commodity chains (GCC) and global value chains (GVC)—to which I will return in more detail—and by arguments that posit a race to the bottom with regard to wages, entitlements, and working conditions for workers positioned at different locations along these chains. Both international flows of workers and internal migration—associated with, for example, export processing zones in Asia and *maquila* (export assembly) industries in parts of Latin America and the Caribbean—are part and parcel of these processes, linking the chain phenomenon to the emergence of transnational labor markets. In the case of international migration, the term "replacement migration" (UN DESA, 2001) describes dynamics that resonate with the metaphor of the race to the bottom. These dynamics can be illustrated by the example of a South African nurse who migrates to the United Kingdom in search of better conditions, perhaps replacing a British nurse who migrates to the United States or Canada; the South African nurse is in turn replaced by a Zimbabwean nurse who, through her own migration, escapes even worse conditions. Another example would be that of a Polish nurse who migrates to Sweden and is replaced by a Moldovan nurse searching for better conditions in Poland. An additional issue relates to in-country locality: rural areas usually fare worse than urban centers with regard to attracting and retaining health personnel.

This division of labor is not only a matter of space. A gender division of labor is customarily one in which women and men occupy different places in the labor market (as Harald Bauder also observes in Chapter 3). Women tend to work in jobs that are less valued, garner less pay, and entail more (or at least differently) difficult working conditions than those dominated by men. In other words, women and men are directed toward certain tasks and/or denied access to others as a result of policies or informal practices that are reflective of specific sociocultural norms or customs.[1] Women are also overrepresented in the informal sector, such as in the petty trading that is often performed by so-called pendular migrants. The term "pendular migration" refers to a process of movement across borders for a very short period of time—usually no more than a week. This is a phenomenon that has been observed in a number of border areas (Dodson, 1998, 2008; Sophal and Sovannarith, 1999) as well as between countries of eastern and western Europe, where pendular migrants are involved in not only petty trading but also other types of work (Morokvasic, 2003).

The gendered division of labor is thus predicated upon gender-segregated labor markets, with men being the dominant workforce in certain sectors and women in others; that is, differentiations exist between sectors. But the division also relates to the differentiation of tasks carried out by workers of different genders within the same sector. In agriculture and manufacturing, for example, women are typically designated to do jobs that require "nimble fingers" (Elson and Pearson, 1981), whereas men usually occupy middle- and upper-managerial positions (Dias and Wanasundera, 2002). In this latter scenario, Melissa Wright (2006) has argued that female labor is being mythically constructed as "disposable." This allows managers to use female workers as skilled labor without changing their unskilled status within the division of labor at production sites, and, as a result, avoiding the necessity of raising women's wages accordingly.

On a global scale, intensified economic integration and changing labor markets have increased both the opportunities for and the pressures on women and men to migrate internationally in larger numbers. Contemporary changes in the economic sphere experienced by many countries of origin, in association with the global trend toward neoliberalism and the aftereffects of SAPs, have resulted in an increasing burden being placed upon women on account of rising male unemployment, the reduction in demand for male labor due to economic slowdowns in certain sectors, and the shift of economic emphasis to the service industries in countries of origin as well as destination. Studies conducted on Latin America and Europe have observed a decline in female economic inactivity in conjunction with a growth in male economic inactivity in the domestic labor market (Farah et al., 2002). This has resulted in a point of convergence between home-state (that is, nonmigrant) and migrant women, as the economic activity of both groups increases to reflect the general feminization of the workforce, albeit one accompanied by a regrowth of inequalities and insecurities as a consequence of the informalization of many sectors (Chaib, 2003). Yet the opposite trend has been observed in the case of women from Eastern Europe: changes during the 1990s led to a loss of local employment for women who had experienced high participation in the labor force during the communist period (Kofman, 2004). This lack of opportunity increased the push for women to migrate. The economic crisis of the late 2000s is bound to add further pressure for emigration but further lessen the possibilities for legal immigration, due to the rise in unemployment in many of the major destination countries.[2]

It has been argued that migrants' labor market positioning and experiences have to be analyzed in relation to gender-segregated labor markets in the countries of destination as well as those of origin (Kofman, 2008; Boyd and Pikkov, 2008; Bauder, Chapter 3 in this volume). In other words, migrants leave and enter already gender-segregated labor markets. In addition, there are qualitative differences between home-state and migrant women at the destination. The significant increases in the labor force participation of home-state women across the Organization for Economic Cooperation and Development (OECD) countries, as well as in certain destination countries in Southeast and East Asia (such as Hong Kong, Singapore, and Taiwan) and Latin America (such as Costa Rica and Argentina), have created a need for social and care-related services, especially where mothers of young children work full time. Many migrant women thus tend to be concentrated to a greater extent than their home-state peers in less skilled personal and domestic service work.

Globally, most migrants generate income through poorly paid jobs that are considered unskilled; they are increasingly regulated via temporary-migration schemes or carried out in an undocumented manner, and often performed in the domestic/private domain or related to the expansion of the service industry and construction projects. That is, these migrants are employed in jobs that tend to be looked down upon socially and/or devalued economically by home-state workers.[3] Across the world, most women who migrate in the less skilled category work in the domestic or care fields. In France, for instance, over 50 percent of migrant women are believed to be engaged in domestic work; in Italy, the great majority of the 600,000 registered domestic workers are non–European Union nationals (ILO, 2003: 11; IRENE and IUF, 2008). In Spain, domestic service is the main—indeed, almost obligatory—gateway for 63 percent of non-EU foreign women (Colectivo Ioé, 2003; IRENE and IUF, 2008); the situation is not so different in Canada, with its live-in caregiver program (McKay, 2003; Hankivsky, 2009; Bauder, Chapter 3 in this volume).[4] Domestic work is also the single most important category of employment among women migrants to the Gulf states, as well as Lebanon and Jordan (Esim and Smith, 2004). Christine Chin's (1998) study of foreign domestic work has situated the "import" of such workers within the politics of development of Malaysia, where the expansion of the middle class has ushered more educated women into the labor market, leaving a care gap to be filled. In the absence of state provision of such services, this gap has been filled by foreign domestic workers (see also Teo and Piper, 2009, on Singapore; Onuki, 2009, on Japan). In this regard, Chin's work echoes that of other social scientists who have linked foreign domestic worker issues to larger questions of global economic restructuring and the feminization of labor migration (Sassen, 1988).

Less skilled male migrants are employed predominantly in construction and mining, on the one hand (as in South Africa, for example), and agriculture and agrofood production on the other (Garcia et al., 2002)—two sectors of the three in which work is deemed most precarious by the International Labour Organization (ILO) (ILO, 2003).[5] The third is domestic work, dominated by women. Male migrant workers now constitute up to 80 percent of the agricultural labor force in some countries or regions (IUF, 2008). Men dominate in agriculture in North America but not in southern Europe, where this sector is female dominated (Kahmann, 2002). Migrant workers from Mozambique, Zimbabwe, and

Lesotho are hired for work in commercial agriculture in South Africa; the Mozambicans are almost exclusively male and young. In the immediate border areas, however, both men and women are said to migrate for farm work, in which tasks tend to be highly gendered, with women concentrated in harvesting and picking (Crush, 2000). In fact, although agriculture remains highly dominated by male workers in many destination countries, including the United States, Canada, and Malaysia (Martin, 1998, 2006; Basok, 1999), an increasing number of employers in agriculture and related food industries are employing women rather than men.

Notably, some 70 percent of all child labor in the world takes place in agriculture. As more women migrate, more children travel with them and become part of the workforce. In Africa, children from Mali and Burkina Faso work in Côte d'Ivoire, a country that produces about 40 percent of the world's cocoa. In the United States, more than 300,000 children work as hired laborers on commercial farms; nearly three quarters of them are Hispanic, many from Mexico. Employers use and abuse the labor of children rather than pay a decent wage to adult workers (IUF, 2008). In this regard, child migration and child migrant labor are important side effects of the feminization of migration.

Although the majority of international migrants fill less skilled jobs upon entry, they are not absent from the ranks of the skilled. Skilled migration is heterogeneous with respect to its gender divisions, occupations, and working conditions (Iredale, 2004). Men overwhelmingly form the majority of those moving within transnational corporations and in the information technology (IT) and scientific sectors, upon which notions of the highly skilled worker and the knowledge society have been predicated (OECD, 2002).[6] Other professions dominated by male migrants are accounting and engineering. Given that men outnumber women in domestic IT sectors, it's not surprising that migrant women are even more inhibited by the demands placed on software specialists for constant physical mobility and flexibility (UNRISD, 2005). Furthermore, gendered demand structures can explain the dominance of one sex over the other in specific migration streams. For example, 88 percent of the green card permits in Germany in 2000 were taken up by men (SOPEMI, 2001), the vast majority being scientists from Eastern Europe where there are almost as many women in the same profession. Thus, the gender imbalance does not necessarily exist in the sending countries (Kofman, 2008).

In global migration patterns, skilled women have tended to go into what can be broadly classified as the welfare and social professions (education, health, social work), which have traditionally been relegated to a largely female workforce. Nursing constitutes the most feminized sector; women make up 90 percent or more of the nursing workforce (Buchan and Calman, 2004). An analysis of UK work permit data for 2000 shows that sectors with high proportions of female staff constituted some of the fastest growing sectors of migrant employment. Between 1998–1999 and 2003–2004, all professional health- and education-related occupations were posted on the Work Permits UK website as priority areas, while IT jobs were demoted (Winkelman-Gleed, 2006).

Recourse to foreign nurses in response to shortages of home-state nurses has become a truly global phenomenon. Health sectors in richer countries have come to be serviced by a global labor market, as is evident in the cases of the United Kingdom, Ireland, Canada, the United States, and countries of the Middle East (Kingma, 2005; Buchan and Calman, 2004). The Philippines supplies the overwhelming number of nurses to overseas destinations, followed by India (Ball, 2004). However, despite being classified as skilled, migrant health workers have been subject to a sustained process in which their work is downgraded and their skills devalued. As Bauder noted in the previous chapter, this raises questions about the accreditation and recognition of skills and their implications for gender, given that so many women work in this highly regulated sector. Similarly, a considerable proportion of the large numbers of foreign women working as domestic helpers worldwide are overqualified but cannot find legal employment in areas of their expertise (Weiss, 2005). This has led to the coinage of the already introduced phrase "de-skilling," also known as "brain waste" (UNFPA, 2006). At the same time, although nurses and other health care workers may be skilled, they are not likely to receive the same quality of benefits that other white-collar workers might expect when working abroad, such as housing, transportation, family relocation, or domestic help (Van Eyck, 2004).[7] The experiences of women migrant health workers from the South are thus often a world away, so to speak, from those of (white) male professional workers from the North.

It has been argued that existing structures of gendered labor division and inequality constrain women's options and relegate to them work roles that reinforce male supremacy and privilege (Chafetz, 1988). The notion of "constrained choice" has also informed gendered analyses of international migration (Cook and Roberts, 2000; Piper, 2000). In the analysis of an evolving hierarchy between highly skilled and less skilled international migrants, Anja Weiss (2005) has argued that the concept of social inequality, that has so far been used only in national contexts, should be applied to the world scale in order to further our understanding of the gendered global division of labor and the place of economic migration therein. What emerges from these accounts is the need for a comprehensive analysis of existing divisions not only between men and women but also between different groups of women. This complex picture is well captured by the notion of stratification.

Our understanding of gendered migration has to be based on the dynamic and changing division of labor (nationally as well as internationally), the selective and changing nature of migration policies in response to the real or perceived needs of origin and destination countries, and an appreciation of the diversity of different migrant groups (Grieco and Boyd, 1998; Kofman, 2004). What we can observe globally, then, is a trend toward greater diversification and polarization of mobility, resulting in a highly stratified pattern of migration. The notion of polarization highlights the distinction between highly skilled or professional and less skilled categories of migrants. Intragroup as well as intergroup differences (as more nationalities enter the migration scene) are captured by the notion of diversification.[8] The shift toward more diversified migration is related to changing political-economic structures (Piper, 2008a).

Geopolitical changes, such as the breakup of the former Soviet Union and the economic reform processes in other formerly socialist countries like Mongolia and Vietnam, have also resulted in the increasing regional integration of labor markets and the opening up of opportunities for migration. As a result, for instance, there are now male and female factory workers from Vietnam working in Korea and Taiwan. The dollarization of the economy in Ecuador in 2001 has made it lucrative for Peruvians to work there (Boccagni, 2008), and relative political stability has attracted migrants to Chile since about 1989 and Argentina since 1983. Increasing overseas investment by Japan, Korea, Taiwan, and more lately China has led migrant workers to opt for migration to East Asia as an alternative to the Middle East or Europe. Katja Hujo and I (2010) suggest that the increasingly restrictive migration policies and high visa fees of Europe, North America, and Australia serve to encourage migrants to remain closer to home. This adds a further layer to the stratification of migration.

The combined effects of gender, ethnicity, legal status, skill level, and mode of entry or exit thus result in complex systems of stratification along new lines of inclusion and exclusion (Castles, 2003). Such a pattern of stratification reflects the ability of skilled workers from countries toward the bottom of the economic hierarchy to move to countries closer to the top, which are experiencing sometimes severe labor shortages and are engaged in the competition for skilled labor in specific sectors. This pattern reveals gender differences along with differences in types and levels of skill: men and women circulate differently in an unevenly globalized economy where significant sectors are heavily regulated by states and corporatist bodies (Kofman, 2004).

In sum, although not a new phenomenon as such, migration has become an issue of increasingly pressing concern for policymakers and politicians around the world, predicated upon the specific interests of and/or pressures exerted upon origin and destination countries. More highly developed countries are pressed into considering how to limit so-called brain drain, produce ethical migration policies, and (rightly or wrongly) foster development through those policies. First and foremost, however, is the pursuit of their own economic and political development, achieved by maximizing the benefits of skilled and less skilled migration and by ensuring the availability of workers in sectors beyond those that comprise the global knowledge economy: care work, domestic work, construction, and agriculture. From the perspective of origin countries, especially less developed countries, access to paid overseas work constitutes an ever more important means of addressing problems of local un- or underemployment. Yet in a highly political environment of restrictive immigration controls that constrain the potential of migration as a livelihood strategy for many, and of oppressive development policies that have obliterated work opportunities in countries of origin, the beneficial outcomes of migration are seriously undermined (Briones, 2009; Phillips, 2009b).

In this stratified system, human capital becomes an important criterion in determining a migrant's experience and socioeconomic condition. Moreover, within specific sectors, there are often further divisions along ethnic and human capital lines—whereby, for instance, English-speaking Filipino domestic workers obtain higher wages and better conditions than their Indonesian and Sri Lankan counterparts (Lan, 2003). Overall, access to movement is highly unequal—and even when it's possible, it can result in de-skilling and thus become a complex issue of social inequality across nation-states (Weiss, 2005). Highly differentiated mobility rights, based on which types of workers a sending state wants to "export" or retain and which types a destination country wants, follow from contemporary modes of managing the circulation of people (Grugel and Piper, 2007; Kalm, 2008).

Managing Migration and Managing Poverty

Since the official halt of immigration in the 1970s, western Europe (and Britain in particular) has begun to reopen channels of economic migration to ameliorate the labor shortages that certain sectors have been experiencing since the 1990s, while southern European countries have begun to serve as destination countries rather than sending countries. Unlike the guest-worker schemes that were practiced in the 1950s and 1960s, contemporary recruitment has taken place under a new discursive framework: that of "management of migration" (Kalm, 2008), whereby recruitment is organized according to categories of skill. This has entailed an increasing bifurcation between the categories of highly skilled and less skilled work in the ease of international migration, as well as access to labor markets and other resources or entitlements. Temporary-contract migration has become a significant feature of the managed migration policy framework in many parts of the world, having experienced a revival in Europe after the official "zero-migration" policies that followed the economic crisis in the early 1970s. In North America and Australia, this policy frame constitutes a new phenomenon, whereas in Asia (including the Gulf countries) it is a well-established feature of migration policies. In this light, the (re-)emergence of temporary and seasonal migration can arguably be described as a globally converging policy.

The difference between the decades following the end of World War II and the early twenty-first century is that not only less skilled but also skilled migrants are now subject to temporary-migration schemes. In Europe and elsewhere, demographic, economic, and labor market-related trends have resulted in the increased demand for skilled foreigners (such as in the health and care sector) and in the revival or intensification of temporary- or guest-worker migration schemes (Castles, 2006; Ruhs, 2006; Piper 2008). Asia contrasts with Europe and traditional immigration countries in that the governments of destination countries in Asia (with a few exceptions) practice only temporary-migration schemes and thus, at least officially, prevent migrants, especially in the less skilled categories, from settling and reuniting with their families in the host country. As a consequence of the absence of integration and family unification policies, the acquisition of permanent residence status, let alone citizenship, is out of reach for most migrants in Asia and, increasingly, those in parts of the Western world also. Thus, despite its signification of migration as an accepted practice to be addressed rather than ignored, the policy of managed migration tends to place greater emphasis on issues of control rather than on the protection of rights (Grugel and Piper, 2007).

Many less skilled migrants end up working in a narrow range of sectors, especially agriculture, construction, and food packaging/processing, as has been well documented in the case of the United Kingdom (Markova and Black, 2007; TLWG, 2007; TUC, 2007). As mentioned, domestic work has proved to be an increasingly important sector all over the world and thus a vital employment opportunity for newly arrived women in Europe, North America, Asia, and elsewhere. Migrant workers' location within specific sectors of the (formal or informal) labor market and the temporary nature of their migration status usually combine to produce a number of legal and economic constraints. Since female-dominated domestic work and male-dominated agricultural work are subject to rigid migration control exercised by both origin and destination countries, both can be said to constitute a form of unfree labor, as has been argued by Tanya Basok (1999) in the context of Mexican agricultural workers in Canada and Leah Briones (2009) in the context of Filipino domestic workers in Asia and Europe.[9]

Foreign agricultural workers are often brought to countries in the North under temporary-migration schemes, largely due to the seasonal, erratic, and low-paid nature of the work, in which home-state workers are reluctant to engage. In Australia, this type of seasonal work is to a large extent performed by young people who take advantage of the working holiday visa the government offers during their "gap year" (time taken out from studying or career development and used for traveling) (Khoo et al., 2008). Philip Martin (1998) explores how agriculture in the United States has been the major side and back door through which unskilled Mexican immigrants have entered the country since the mid-twentieth century. This sector is considered a US economic success story for its ability to provide US residents with low-cost food and generate a consistent trade surplus, although most US farms actually lose money; indeed, government payments account for a quarter of net farm income. The agriculture sector in the United States is thus subsidized in two ways: first through government money, and second through foreign labor, much of which is unauthorized (Martin, 2006).

The subsector of US agriculture most closely associated with Mexican migrants is so-called FVH (fruit and nuts, vegetables, horticulture) agriculture, which is particularly labor intensive. Immigrants comprise almost two thirds of the industry's workforce and nearly all entrants to the seasonal FVH workforce. Many migrants work in this sector for several years (up to a decade) before moving to other job options, which are often in cities. To cope with the labor turnover, farmers lobby (usually successfully) for open borders. In California in particular, the workers typically live in housing that is not provided by employers. Most of them do not speak English and few are high school graduates. Undocumented immigrants who do farm work are usually among the poorest and least sophisticated workers in the United States. The result is an accelerated "transfer of rural poverty from Mexico to the US" (Martin, 1998: 79). Some Mexican workers manage to settle with their families in the United States, trying their luck in urban labor markets. If they do not succeed, then "rural poverty in Mexico becomes rural and eventually urban poverty in the US" (Martin, 1998: 80).

Along with seasonal migrant-worker schemes, poverty enters the picture via Economic Partnership Agreements (EPAs), popular in the EU and Japan, and the effect they have on sending countries. The EU Commission, for instance, is pushing the ACP (African, Caribbean, Pacific) countries into signing such agreements. Women in developing countries are said to be particularly affected by EPAs, as it is "they who mainly work in the agricultural sectors, e.g., as poultry and vegetable farmers, which will be most adversely affected by trade liberalization and the EPAs" (Groth, 2008: 4). Similarly, it has been shown that regional trade agreements like NAFTA have had no effect on reducing the economic hardships that constitute the main push factor for migration from Mexico to the United States (Manning, 2000; Delgado Wise and Márquez Covarrubias, 2007a, 2007b). The effects of such agreements are therefore related to the feminization of poverty insofar as they are linked to the feminization of agriculture that occurs when men are forced to out-migrate to industrial cities or abroad, leaving women behind as the heads of households and the main people working in the fields.

China is a case in point (Solinger, 1999; Jacka, 2008). As part of China's efforts to develop a globalized market economy, increased rural-urban migration has taken place. From the mid-1980s onward, rural incomes began to stagnate and, as a result, rural/urban income inequalities increased markedly, pushing larger numbers of rural people to move to urban centers, where they were welcomed by employers of domestic and foreign-owned companies as cheap, flexible, and unskilled labor. Broken down by gender, roughly two thirds of all rural-to-urban migrants in China are said to be men, but sex ratios vary quite significantly from one region to another. In the Pearl River Delta region, for instance, young rural women are reported to make up 65 to 70 percent of the labor force, being favored by manufacturing companies in the clothing, textile, toy, electronics, and other labor-intensive sectors. Migrant women are more likely to be young and single than men. They also tend to be less educated than rural migrant men, due partly to their lower average age and partly to gender inequalities in education attainment across rural China (Jacka, 2008).

As men pursue new and more desirable forms of nonfarm work, many women are left behind to take care of farms, a trend that has resulted in the feminization of agriculture. Today, across China, a higher proportion of women than men are agricultural laborers. When women are left behind, they typically experience an increased workload, particularly in poor households that cannot afford either to hire labor to help with the farm work or to discontinue farming their land. To cope with labor shortages on the farm, it is commonly girls who are withdrawn from school rather than boys. The reversed form of the gender division of labor, whereby the wife becomes the migrant worker and her husband takes care of farm and domestic work, is rare and considered the very last resort (Jacka, 2008). In Sri Lanka, by contrast, women's participation in agriculture has declined and, as a result, women's out-migration has been on the increase (IOM, 2005). In other words, the burden placed upon many women is increasing whether in the role of principal migrant or that of left-behind household head. Moreover, migration as a route to socioeconomic betterment is also increasingly exposed as a myth, especially in the case of the majority of migrants who are less skilled (Piper, 2008). According to Tamara Jacka (2008), for instance, the 1999 household survey taken in the Chinese provinces of Sichuan and Anhui revealed that 75 percent of returned migrant women and 63 percent of male returnees continued to work primarily in agriculture. The temporary- or seasonal-migration schemes thus have clear limitations with regard to allowing migrants to develop in economic and human capital terms either "here" (in their destination countries) or "there" (in their countries of origin).

Both the socioeconomic changes that result from gendered migration dynamics and the shifts that have occurred in the process of managing poverty have to be analyzed in an integrated manner, by looking at the impacts on origin and destination countries simultaneously or in parallel. The global chain concept is an ideal framework in which to do that, and it is to this concept that I now turn.

Global Chains

Productive Chains

In studies of the changing nature of work and business that have focused on cross-border production and trade networks, many scholars have used the GCC and closely related GVC frameworks, which were developed to map and analyze the internationally dispersed activities involved in the production of specific commodities, goods, and services and thus to illuminate the flows of capital, goods, services, and labor across space (Gereffi, 1996; Gereffi and Kaplinsky, 2001; Gibbon et al., 2008). In other words, global chain analysis provides "key elements for understanding changes in the global economy and the role of developing countries in it" (Ponte and Gibbon, 2005: 1). Within this framework, the example of the garment industry has been particularly amply documented (see, for example, Bonacich and Appelbaum, 2000; Bair and Gereffi, 2003; Esbenshade, 2004; Bulut and Lane, 2011). As I have noted, women constitute the dominant workforce in the textile and garment manufacturing outlets in the Global South, as both internal and international migrants (Pearson, 2004; Prieto and Quinteros, 2004; Bastia, 2007; Hale and Wills, 2007; Dannecker, 2009).

The GCC/GVC concepts have also been applied to horticulture (fresh fruit, vegetables, and cut flowers) and food production in Africa, Asia, and Latin America in their linkages to consumers in the North. It has been argued that in Europe, and particularly in the United Kingdom, large supermarket buyers increasingly dominate the trade in and retailing of fresh produce (Kritzinger et al., 2004; Rogaly, 2008). They do so by working through integrated global value chains, with the result that market conditions govern prices. Because of the intensification and internationalization of the agrofood system, there is a strong downward pressure on price (Kritzinger et al., 2004). The production of food is not only linked to agriculture but also to food processing, two areas in which women and migrants constitute an important workforce.

In response to the formulation of the original GCC approach, it was feminists in particular who argued for and developed the more nuanced GVC approach "to highlight the growing informalization and the links between different sectors along the chain of production" across global supply networks (Waylen, 2004: 563, drawing on Barrientos, 2001, and Pearson, 2003). The main point is that "the design, production, and marketing of many products now involve a chain of activities divided among enterprises located in different places" (McCormick and Schmitz, 2001: 17). This adds another layer to the GCC framework by emphasizing not only the spatial reach of the production process but also the process of creating value. The value added at the design stage (usually in the Global North) is considered higher than that of the final assembly process (in the Global South). The notion of value is thus helpful in elucidating the gendered and ethnic character of production processes as well as the returns to different types of labor (McCormick and Schmitz, 2001).

The value chain concept also highlights that much of the work performed at the "bottom end" takes the form of home-based work (informal, casual, or subcontracted). In the literature on home-based work, it has been argued that

> in developing countries, the broader term "home-based workers" tends to be used in recognition of the fact that the term "home" is not necessarily consistent with a private domestic space and that women often work around or outside their home[s] or travel to and from home in pursuit of different activities. This is particularly the case in activities related to agriculture or food processing. (Pearson, 2004: 138)

Not surprisingly, this type of work is mostly done by women: an estimated 80 percent of home-based workers are female (Pearson, 2004: 136). The dynamics expressed by the chain metaphor thus resonate with the notion of a race to the bottom, in that the workers at the bottom of the chain, who are often women, carry out the least valued tasks.

Reproductive Chains

Both GCC and GVC approaches have a major flaw, namely that they do not provide the full picture of the global division of labor. As feminists have long argued, we have to look beyond the productive sphere to recognize the extent and significance of reproductive labor, which has been and still is carried out overwhelmingly by women. The contention that, in its focus on industrial production by firms, GCC analysis has neglected to consider services and household production is central to feminist critiques (Yeates, 2004). Marilyn Carr and her colleagues (Carr et al., 2000) argue that the GCC analysis fails to recognize the integral role of informalization in the globalization of production in the manufacturing, agriculture and forestry sectors, let alone that of unpaid reproductive labor. Home-based work constitutes a significant source of employment in many parts of the world, but most analyses do not include households as sites of production that are situated within commodity chains (Elson, 1998; Pearson, 2004; Yeates, 2004).

To address these lacunae, the global care chain concept (Hochschild, 2000), while drawing on the GCC framework in its conceptualization, constitutes an important and innovative theoretical tool for the analysis of the relationships between globalization, migration, and care in its paid and unpaid forms. It captures "the significance of transnational care services and the global division of reproductive labor as integral features of the contemporary international economy that are otherwise neglected by globalization studies and also migration studies" (Yeates, 2004: 370). Care work has become one of the most globalized forms of work, forming a complex "series of personal links between people across the globe based on paid or unpaid work of caring" (Hochschild, 2000: 132). But this advance does not come without further flaws. Nicola Yeates argues that it does not directly lend itself to an analysis of the care services sector: "The global care chain concept suffers from its lack of embeddedness in a critical international political economy perspective and from its narrow application to just one group of migrant care workers" (2004: 370).

Yeates' critique is based on a broader understanding of what constitutes the global care economy and the recognition that care, as a key element of social reproduction, involves activities that fall outside market production. What emerges is a "care mix," only part of which can be outsourced because of the distinction between caring *for* (physical care) and caring *about* (emotional care). Hence, there are limits to the commodification of care: aspects such as listening or holding a hand cannot be billed. The main aspect of Yeates' critique, however, revolves around the limited empirical base of the care chain concept. The existing literature on global care chains has focused almost exclusively on domestic work. Also, this literature has not established links to the issue of development. Conversely, the literature on the migration-development nexus has tended to focus almost exclusively on the migration of medical professionals in the form of brain drain or brain gain and neglecting other forms of care work (Piper, 2009). Thus, the important link in the continuum between the (usually female) emigration of unskilled domestic and care workers and skilled health workers from less developed to more developed countries (Hugo, 2009: 189) has not been established—either by academics or policymakers.

Linking the Two Chains

The common element in the global care chain concept and the GCC/GVC concept is that women emerge both as the principal source of labor and as a large bloc of consumers, in their roles as household managers (who employ domestic workers and largely control the family's budget) and targets of the fashion, food, and many other industries. Poorer countries are the main suppliers of the cheap labor demanded by richer countries either "here" (as foreign workers in destination countries) or "there" (at the bottom rank of production or care chains). Hence, what emerges is a global division of both productive and reproductive labor structured by social class, ethnicity, race, and gender (Lycklama, 1994; Anderson, 1997; Wee and Sim, 2005).

This point has also been flagged by Rhacel Salazar Parreñas (2000) in her "three-tier" conceptualization of the global division of reproductive labor. She distinguishes between the following groups of women: (1) middle-class women in receiving countries, (2) migrant domestic workers, and (3) women from the Global South who are too poor to migrate. The migrant domestic worker is thus ranked in the middle of this division of labor, and the care deficit created by her own out-migration may be filled by the poor woman who cannot migrate (in paid form) or by the eldest daughter or another female relative (in unpaid or paid form) (Hochschild, 2000). The notion of the global chain, productive and reproductive, thus elucidates the structures and processes that perpetuate the unequal distribution of resources and reflect the socioeconomic inequalities arising from unequal development.

The Way Forward for a Gendered IPE of Migration

IPE has long focused narrowly on macrostructural issues detached from the real lives of ordinary people. Recently, arguments have been made for a more integrated approach that introduces agency as a focal point (Delgado Wise and Márquez Covarrubias, 2008) and seeks insights into how everyday actions transform the global economy (Hobson and Seabrooke, 2007). The incorporation of "everyday IPE" (EIPE) into mainstream "regulatory IPE" (RIPE), as argued by John Hobson and Leonard Seabrooke (2007), involves bringing in scholarship on social and counterglobalization movements—an approach usually associated with sociology. Thus, the focus is shifted away from "order and regulation" to a focus on "transformation" (Hobson and Seabrooke, 2007: 2). Given that the higher echelons of power tend to be male-dominated spheres (especially in government politics, finance, and trade), the injection of everyday considerations into IPE allows greater inroads for gender perspectives insofar as it helps deprivilege elitist concerns over the nonelitist, the macro over the micro, the public over the private, and the paid over the unpaid.

Related to this neglect of the nonelitist "everyday" within IPE, the study of migration has not been very prominent or developed in the field, as I indicate in the introduction to this volume. The everyday approach, by contrast, allows us to zoom in on the majority of migrant workers who are not part of the highly skilled or professional classes, such as Chinese businesspeople or Indian IT workers whose experiences have been heralded as success stories within the migration-development debate. Instead, we are able to focus on the large numbers of less skilled (male and female) migrants, including farm and care workers whose migration is largely regulated by temporary-contract schemes but whose working conditions are subject to very little regulation. They are often excluded from national labor laws and labor union organizing (Piper, 2008b).

The everyday caring activities by both foreign and home-state household workers and nurses are conceptually linked to the notion of social reproduction. Feminist scholars within IPE have lately revisited this notion in their efforts to broaden the meaning of economics by looking beyond the market to include households and women's unpaid work (Benería, 1979, 2003; Hoskyns and Rai, 2007), namely "work that does not fit into the industrial class framework, the work of women farmers, of the self-employed, domestics, homemakers, and mothers" (Prügl, 2002: 33). Some have pointed to the increasingly marketized and privatized relations involved in social reproduction (Ferguson, 2010). This also highlights the interconnections between neoliberal transformations in the processes of social reproduction and the globalization of commodified care labor (Bakker, 2007). The commodification and marketization of domestic work (turning unpaid care work into paid work) indicate how the constructs of the public and private spheres represent a false dichotomy (Litt and Zimmerman, 2003).

In the mainstream IPE literature, the conceptualization of rights has largely been treated in a top-down fashion as the preserve of international organizations and negotiations among states. Not many attempts have been made to link such analysis to a discussion of political activism and advocacy from within civil society (see Grugel and Piper, 2008). The significance of the feminization of migration and the fact that access to rights and entitlements is stratified highlights the importance and necessity of integrating migrant rights activism and women's rights activism. Interesting in this regard (and a possible starting point for further exploration of women migrants' rights) is Diane Elson and Jasmine Gideon's (2006) study of women's labor activism in Latin America, which considers the ways in which women's organizations employ notions of economic rights to delineate the gender injustices inherent to neoliberal capitalist development. By emphasizing socioeconomic rights, these organizations challenge the liberal association of human rights with civil and political liberties and with the right to private property. The question is whether the migrant-rights movement frames its advocacy in similar terms. Overall, there is still a need for a systematic discussion of the issue of rights and social justice for migrant workers from the perspective of gendered political economy. Useful in this regard is the argument forwarded by Catherine Hoskyns and Shirin Rai (2007) that IPE needs to expand its agenda to include the social, domestic, and household spheres. They suggest that this expansion could lead to a new discipline that might be called International Social and Political Economy (ISPE). The gendered political economy of migration would have a clear place on this discipline's agenda.

Conclusion

The main objective in this chapter has been to situate increasingly stratified and polarized migratory flows within the transnational political economy of gender by bridging the three feminizations—of work, migration, and poverty—that are linked in turn to changes in the gender division of labor and economic restructuring processes on a global scale. These dynamics and interlinkages, as epitomized by the examples of care and agricultural work, constitute issues that are often treated separately in academic analyses, and link up to the broader literature on globalization, especially the combined appreciation of the organizational dimension of globalization (including regulation and governance) and the way it is reshaping the lives of real people around the globe (cf. Coe and Yeung, 2001). Migration constitutes an important component of the direction and shape of these processes.

At the core of these transformations are shifts in gender relations as they are played out at work sites, within households/families/communities, and at the individual level. Thus, the processes and dynamics triggered by international migration require us to go beyond the nation-state as a point of reference and to analyze the complex linkages and interdependencies within (re-)production processes on the global scale. In order to help us understand how exactly these global processes work, IPE has to engage with the social and the everyday, in order to establish connections between political-economic structures and people across places. These varied and complex interconnections also require further research to inform policymakers and advocates. A new vocabulary is required for describing and analyzing these complex interlinkages, beyond that of the North-South divide and beyond the traditional remit of economics, based as it is on human and financial resource flows. The notion of an integrated analysis of productive and reproductive chains, entailing a deliberate blurring of artificial boundaries between the public and the private, might be the first step.

Notes

1. In the context of international migration, this is evident from the various bans imposed by some Asian governments on the out-migration of women in what is classified as unskilled migration (Siddiqui, 2001; Oishi, 2005).

2. One concrete example here is offered by the dynamics between Ecuador and Spain. In 2008, the latter experienced a record high unemployment rate of 17.4 percent (joblessness almost doubled within the space of one year). In response, the Spanish government started to offer so-called return incentives to Ecuadorian and other Latin American migrants in the second half of 2008, when the job crisis began. At the same time, the economic situation in Ecuador has also worsened due to falling oil prices, decreasing tourism, and so on (*The Times*, April 25, 2009).

3. The socioeconomic devaluation of domestic work might be ameliorated by the Domestic Worker Convention that will be drafted and passed at the 2011 ILO congress. At the 2010 congress, the format of new standards were decided upon, namely a full Convention with Recommendations. The exact details will be determined in 2011.

4. This program, which still exists, is explained on a Canadian governmental website as follows: "Live-in caregivers are individuals who are qualified to provide care for children, elderly persons, or persons with disabilities in private homes without supervision. Live-in caregivers must live in the private home where they work in Canada" (http://www.cic.gc.ca/english/work/caregiver/index.asp, accessed June 12, 2009).

5. Also interesting in the cases of agriculture and farming is the difference between countries of origin in the South, where a feminization of agriculture has taken place, especially in Africa (FAO, n.d.) and China (IOM, 2008), where men migrate to urban areas or abroad for work, leaving women behind in charge of farms and rural households.

6. According to the OECD (2007c), there are now more highly skilled migrant women in industrialized countries than previously, and women are overrepresented in the brain drain. But these statistics must be broken down into gender-segregated labor market positioning: most women migrating in the skilled category are health workers.

7. The migration of health workers does not take place only between the developing and developed world but also between developed countries (for instance, Canadian physicians in the United States) and between countries of the South (for instance, Cuban doctors in Ghana) via processes associated with replacement migration.

8. See, for instance, Rojas Wiesner and Angeles (2008) on the greater diversity of Mexicans with regard to skill and place of origin in the United States.

9. Origin countries display a certain control via the imposition of bans, be they total bans on the out-migration of less skilled women or bans on their migration to specific destination countries. Government policies in origin countries are also shaped by elite interests (via the collusion between recruitment agencies and politicians) as well as bilateral agreements, although origin countries typically have a weaker bargaining power than do destination countries.

5

The Illegal "Migration Industry"

H. Richard Friman

The surge in transnational migration since the 1980s has taken place in the context of selective state liberalization and restriction of transnational population flows (Massey et al., 1998). Immigration regulations have been introduced by the governments of both advanced industrial and developing countries to limit the access of less skilled migrants, especially those from developing countries. For an array of economic and political reasons, explored in detail in other chapters in this volume, the supply of less skilled persons seeking to migrate continues to grow. Demand in host countries for such migrants has persisted and in some cases expanded in sectors ranging from agriculture and construction to labor-intensive manufacturing/assembly and services (Cornelius et al., 2004; Väyrynen, 2003). Illegal transnational migration—defined here as cross-border migration in contravention of state regulations—has existed for as long as states have sought to curtail population flows across national borders.[1] Modern immigration regulations and the tightening of border controls through expanded enforcement during the 1990s, and more extensively since 2001, have made it more difficult for migrants to cross into destination countries. The result has been an increased reliance on and expansion of networks of "professional smugglers" (Andreas, 2001: 116). Such reliance is risky, as migrants sometimes find themselves facing exorbitant fees and dangerous conditions during transit, as well as deception and manipulation into horrendous situations of sex trafficking and forced labor (Väyrynen, 2003; Zhang, 2007).

For a growing number of scholars, these networks are best understood as elements of a lucrative, illegal "migration industry." Both a primary contribution and a shortcoming of this literature is its emphasis on the mechanics of illegal migration and the identification, through the use of general frameworks and case-specific illustration, of actors and networks that facilitate the migration process (Väyrynen, 2003: 3). In contrast, broader IPE-based approaches that address the intersection of structural contexts and politics shaping the illegal migration industry have been much less common and are less well developed. This chapter argues for exploring the illegal migration industry as an outgrowth of the "mutually constitutive" relationship of states and markets (Schwartz, 2006: 51–52) and a post-Fordist intersection of the licit and illicit global economies.

Illegal Migration

In 2002, the United Nations Population Division (UNPD) reported that there were 175 million migrants worldwide. By 2005, the UNPD had increased its estimate to 191 million (United Nations, 2002, 2005). Similar figures were offered by the International Organization for Migration (IOM) in its 2005 *World Migration Report*, which estimated a total of 175 million migrants worldwide in 2000 and a likely increase in this figure to between 185 and 192 million persons by early 2005 (IOM, 2005: 379). Whereas the UN claimed these figures covered only documented migrants, the IOM argued, based on census data, that they "did not necessarily exclude" and indeed were likely to "generally include" persons who were "undocumented or unauthorized migrants" (2005: 379). Thus, the IOM report concluded, the figure of 175 million offered a "good basis for estimation of all migrants" (2005: 379). Drawing on the original UN figures as restated in 2004 (United Nations, 2004), Moíses Naím was less cautious, noting in passing that "perhaps half as many again" of the world's 175 million international migrants were in fact undocumented (2005: 89, 239).

While Naím's estimate suggests that there are 87.5 million illegal migrants worldwide, the exact scale of illegal migration is unknown. Due to the clandestine nature of illegal migration, contending definitions of what it entails, and the politicization of the issue by anti-immigration groups and enforcement agencies, the estimates that do exist must be approached with caution (Kyle and Koslowski, 2001: 3; Väyrynen, 2003: 11; Zhang, 2007: 7; Sadiq, 2009). The politics of immigration in advanced industrial countries has also resulted in the use of terminological markers by different sides in public policy debate. For example, opponents of the term "illegal migrant" argue against its negative connotation, whereby the referent is defined by his or her illegality. Conversely, opponents of adjectives like "irregular" and "undocumented" argue that they downplay the fact that the person to whom they apply has broken the law. The literature on the illegal migration industry has tended to devote less attention to this distinction. Since explorations of the industry often provide estimates of illegal migration only as rough indicators of scale, I begin this section by doing the same with the aforementioned caveats in mind.

Global Estimates

Estimates of global illegal migration have tended to focus on the assisted movement of migrants across borders. In downplaying patterns of "self-smuggling," whereby migrants engage in unauthorized entry without the assistance of a professional smuggler (see Andreas, 1998–1999, 1999, 2001), the estimates basically equate the scale of illegal migration with the illegal migration industry. The terms used to describe the assisted movement of migrants have also changed over time. Frank Laczko observes that from the early to the mid-1990s, the term "trafficking" was commonly used in studies to describe migration involving the use of a paid facilitator by persons in their voluntary illegal movement across an international border (2005: 10).

Since the late 1990s, and especially with the formalization of definitions under the trafficking and smuggling protocols to the 2000 United Nations Convention Against Transnational Organized Crime, the use of the term "trafficking" in studies of illegal migration has changed. The earlier description noted by Laczko has come to refer to the practice of "human smuggling," as distinct from the more heinous practices of exploitation encompassed under the definition of "human trafficking." Yet in practice, the line between smuggling and trafficking is often blurry, as migrants move in and out of smuggling and trafficking situations. For example, migrants may seek out professional smugglers for assistance in illegal border crossing only to find themselves in situations of trafficking due to exploitation during the transit process or upon arrival in the destination country (Haque, 2006).

As defined by the UN Protocol Against the Smuggling of Migrants by Land, Sea, and Air, human smuggling is "the procurement, in order to obtain a financial or other material benefit, of the illegal entry of a Person into a State Party of which the person is not a national or a permanent resident" (United Nations, 2000a). Human trafficking is more extensively defined, reflecting in part the controversy over the relationship between trafficking and prostitution (see Friman and Reich, 2007a: 7–9). As defined by the Protocol to Prevent, Suppress, and Punish Trafficking in Persons, Especially Women and Children, human trafficking is

> the recruitment, transportation, transfer, harboring or receipt of persons, by means of the threat or use of force or other forms of coercion, of abduction, of fraud, of deception, of the abuse of power or of a position of vulnerability or of the giving or receiving of payments or benefits to achieve the consent of a person having control over another person, for the purpose of exploitation. Exploitation shall include, at a minimum, the exploitation of the prostitution of others or other forms of sexual exploitation, forced labour or services, slavery or practices similar to slavery, servitude, or the removal of organs. (United Nations, 2000b: 3)

Since both the pre- and postprotocol uses of the terms smuggling and trafficking are found in the discussion of illegal migration, caution is necessary when reviewing the literature on scale. David Kyle and Rey Koslowski, citing a 1997 IOM report on trafficking, note that "it has been estimated that as many as 4 million people are *smuggled* across borders on an annual basis," generating an estimated US$7 billion in revenues (2001: 4; emphasis added). Kyle and Koslowski observe that this figure was an increase from the US$3.5 billion estimated by the United Nations in 1994. John Salt and Jeremy Stein estimate the revenues of the trafficking business (using the preprotocol definition) at between US$5 and US$7 billion during the same period (1997: 472–473). Naím uses the same figure of 4 million persons as Kyle and Koslowski, attributing it to the United Nations rather than IOM but noting that it encompasses both trafficking and human smuggling. He argues further that this "people trade" generates an estimated US$7 to US$10 billion in annual revenue (2005: 88, 293). These and similar revenue figures are problematic at best. Among the methods used to generate such estimates is that of combining estimates of illegal migrants with information from law enforcement officials and/or smuggled migrants regarding the per-person fee paid for smuggling services.

By the late 1990s, the increased international focus on human trafficking—conceptualized in terms of sex trafficking and forced labor—was influencing estimates of illegal migration even further. For example, from 2001 to 2008, the annual *Trafficking in Persons Report (TIPR)* released by the US Department of State included estimates of international human trafficking. These ranged from roughly 600,000 to 900,000 persons annually. Although the broad estimate range changed slightly over the years, in 2007 the *TIPR* settled on 800,000 persons as the official annual estimate based on unidentified US government-supported research conducted in 2006 (USDOS, 2007).[2] In addition to providing these figures, the reports have noted in passing that estimates by other organizations place the annual number of international trafficking victims well into the millions. For example, according to the United Nations Population Fund (UNPF, n.d.), the number of women trafficked across international borders each year ranges from 700,000 to 2 million. Adding men and children to this total would expand the estimates further. The reports also include estimates of the revenues generated by international human trafficking. By the mid-2000s, estimates by the US Federal Bureau of Investigation were the most prominent, positing US$9.5 billion in annual revenues (USDOS, 2005).

The utility of these and similar estimates for gaining insights into the scale of illegal migration, let alone the illegal migration industry, has become more problematic as the line between trafficking as an issue in and of itself and as an issue synonymous with the concept of "modern-day slavery" has blurred in rhetoric and policy practice (see Bales, 1999). Part of the difficulty has been moral entrepreneurs and governments turning to figures that include persons who are not international migrants but are subjected to practices of slavery within their home countries. The result has been the growing prominence of estimates that between 4 and 28 million persons are victims of trafficking/slavery, and that the annual profits of trafficking are reaching upwards of US$40 billion (UNPF, n.d.; UNDOS, 2002; Bales, 2007: 3–4; United Nations, 2008a: 6–7; Kara, 2009: 221–222).

Destination Countries

Along with providing global estimates, discussions of the scale of illegal migration often turn to the situations of select destination countries. Since the 1980s, advanced industrial countries have been among the primary destinations for illegal migration. The United States and the European Union (EU) are commonly used to illustrate the growing impact of the illegal migration industry. For example, in October 2008, the Pew Hispanic Center estimated that 11.9 million persons, over 59 percent of whom had come from Mexico, were living unauthorized in the United States. The figure for 2000 had been 8.4 million persons (Passel and Cohn, 2008a: i). (By way of further comparison, Raimo Väyrynen [2003: 11] notes that official 1992 estimates of the unauthorized population stood at 3.3 million persons.) Drawing on the residual method of subtracting the estimated legal population from the total foreign-born population recorded in census samples, the Pew Hispanic

Center also noted that the unauthorized population was increasing by an estimated average 500,000 persons annually (Passel, 2006; Passel and Cohn, 2008a). By September 2010, in light of the US economic downturn and an increase in immigration enforcement, the Center had decreased its estimate of the unauthorized population to 11.1 million and of annual inflows to 150,000 (Passel and Cohn, 2010: i–ii). Unauthorized migrants in these estimates included both persons who had entered the country illegally and those who had entered legally but had "violated the terms of their admission" by overstaying their visas or in other ways (Passel and Cohn, 2010: i–ii). These figures have played a prominent role in the deadlock over US immigration policy reform, which is detailed in Susan Martin's chapter later in this volume.

For the EU, estimates of annual illegal migration based on data that included border apprehensions, detentions, and illegal trespassing increased from 350,000 in 1993 to about half a million by the late 1990s (Väyrynen, 2003: 11; Chiuri et al., 2005: 3). As argued by the European Migration Network (2007: 5), patterns of illegal migration since the early 2000s have varied across the member states, remaining stable for some countries and decreasing for others. However, by 2007, popular press reports were pointing to an annual entry of 500,000 illegal migrants, contributing to an estimated total illegal immigration population within the EU of up to 8 million persons (e.g., Bilefsky, 2007). By 2010, despite the observed declines stemming from the economic downturn and increased enforcement, estimates of the illegal migrant population ranged from 3 to 8 million, while those of annual entries reached as high as 900,000 (see, for example, Bowcott, 2010; Traynor, 2010).

Illegal migration is prominently cited in the immigration debates of other countries as well. Illegal migration and the threat posed by Chinese smuggling networks have been issues in Japan since the late 1980s (Friman, 2001). Despite these concerns, official Japanese estimates suggest there has been a decline in illegal migration since 2000. Rough comparisons of immigration entry and exit data, which figure prominently in the immigration control debate, reveal that the annual number of visa overstayers peaked in 1993 at 298,646 persons, falling to 113,072 persons by 2008. Deportations for illegal entry and landing have decreased as well, falling from 12,209 in 2004 to 6,389 persons in 2008 (JMOJ, 2009: 37–39). In contrast, estimates of illegal migration in the case of South Africa have been more extensive and the data more problematic. During the mid-1990s, an estimated 2 to 8 million migrants were living in the country illegally (Illegal Immigration, 1995; Solomon, 1996).

Political and economic dislocation in neighboring Zimbabwe during the 2000s accelerated this trend. By the time of the anti-immigrant riots in May 2008, estimates of the number of illegal migrants living in South Africa ranged between 3 and 9 million persons, with annual deportations reaching levels of more than 250,000 per year (Bearak, 2008; CoRMSA, 2008). Deportations of Zimbabweans were suspended in 2009 in light of conditions in the neighboring country. In September 2010, the South African government announced the end of the moratorium, encouraging the estimated 3 million Zimbabweans living in the country illegally to seek legal status paths or face deportation beginning in January 2011 (Kgosana and de Plessis, 2010; South Africa, 2010).

According to the United Nations (2005), Russia and India are primary destinations for the world's documented migrants. In Russia, as in other countries, estimates of illegal migration vary widely; Leonid Rybakovsky and Sergey Ryzantsev (2005) observe that different departments within the Russian government have released estimates ranging from 5 to 10 million persons. By 2007, media reports were positing that the illegal population included most of the country's 10 to 12 million foreigners (*International Herald Tribune,* 2007). By 2009, estimates of the foreign population had decreased to nearly 7 million, of which 4 million were illegal (Mathews, 2009). In India, politics and shifts in governmental control by the country's political parties have led to different official interpretations of the country's illegal immigration problem. Official estimates of illegal (primarily Bangladeshi) migrants by government officials have ranged from 10 million in 1997 to between 12 and 15 million by 2003 (Statement by Indian Home Minister Shri Indrajit Gupta before Parliament on May 6, 1997, noted in Sinha, 1998; see also Nandy, 2005; Sadiq, 2009). By 2007, media reports were noting estimates from experts positing that as many as 20 million Bangladeshis were living in the country illegally (Nandy, 2005; Sullivan, 2007).[3] By 2010, analysts were noting estimates of 6 million illegal Bangladeshi immigrants in the state of Assam alone and pointing to the failure of border fences and citizenship tribunals to address the challenge (see Goswami, 2010; "SC to Govt," 2009).

Clearly, illegal migration is not limited to either advanced industrial countries or the more advanced developing countries. Less developed countries face particular challenges regarding the unauthorized cross-border movement of migrants due to their limited institutional capacity for immigration control and the fact that politicization and corruption related to the provision of documentary proof of national citizenship are common (Sadiq, 2009). But however widespread the practice of illegal migration actually is, it tends to garner greater international attention as a challenge facing developed countries.

Industry Actors and Structures

The failure of advanced industrial country governments to achieve their stated immigration control policy goals has attracted particular attention among scholars (Cornelius et al., 1994; Hollifield, 2000; Cornelius and Tsuda, 2004; Messina and Lahay, 2006). As Stephen Castles and Mark Miller observe, one reason for such failure involves the rise of the so-called migration industry, consisting of "the many people who earn their livelihood by organizing migratory movements" (2009: 201). For Rubén Hernández-León, the migration industry more specifically consists of "private and specialized services offered at specific costs that facilitate people's international mobility" (2005: 8). Research on the migration industry has focused on the ways in which it operates as a loosely defined service sector, moving people from origin to destination points. Less attention has been devoted to the political impact of the industry in shaping the content and implementation of immigration policies.

Castles and Miller view the migration industry as an array of "agents and brokers," including travel agents, labor recruiters, lawyers, interpreters, bankers, and housing agents; other actors, ranging from "shopkeepers, priests, teachers, and other [migrant] community leaders" to opportunistic "police officers or bureaucrats" and "unscrupulous" criminals and human smugglers, also provide assistance (2009: 201–202). The emergence of the migration industry is based on the "special services" it provides to migrants, especially in instances of "spontaneous and illegal movements." The rise of the industry, they argue, is thus an inevitable "aspect of the social networks and the transnational linkages which are part of the migratory process" (2009: 201–202).

Less explicit in Castles and Miller's analysis are the ways in which the need for the industry's services is shaped by the state's regulation of migration. Their passing observation that "a disturbing and increasingly salient element of the migration industry is the rise of organizations devoted to the smuggling and trafficking of migrants" illustrates this omission (Castles and Miller, 2009: 202). The more restrictive the regulation of migration, the less the state serves as a source of infrastructural support, leading migrants to turn elsewhere. Hernández-León comes closer to addressing the impact of state regulation by focusing on the complex relations among "migration entrepreneurs" and their responses to the immigration policies of the state (2005: 8, 12–17, 32). He argues that although social networks play important roles in shaping migration, the infrastructure of the migration industry (especially its for-profit focus) supplements and in some cases replaces these networks. Thus, the industry's rise and structure are "context driven," and anything but inevitable (2005: 8, 12–17, 32; see also Massey et al., 1998; Cornelius et al., 2004).

Although broadly identifying the actors that facilitate migration, Castles and Miller are less helpful in providing insight into how the diverse pieces of the industry fit together, especially in the case of illegal migration. Other scholars have explored these connections in greater detail. For example, Salt and Stein, using the aforementioned terminology of the mid-1990s, define the international trafficking business as "the trading and systematic movement of people as 'commodities'" (1997: 471). Trafficking, the authors note, is best understood as a "system" in which "agents, institutions, and intermediaries" are involved in the "planning of smuggling operations, information gathering, finance and a set of technical and operational tasks" (1997: 471). These activities are carried out by operations of varying degrees of organization ranging from "mom-and-pop" enterprises to large-scale operations (Salt and Stein, 1997: 471, 476–477; also Naím, 2005: 97–98).

Salt and Stein model the trafficking process as consisting of "three consecutive stages" (1997: 477–483). The first is "mobilization," whereby migrants are recruited in their countries of origin. The second stage consists of what takes place "en route": the operations that occur along the array of trafficking paths. The final stage consists of the "insertion and integration" of the migrant into the destination country. In these stages, the line between trafficking and legal migration can blur. Trafficking, they observe, is part of the "system of institutionalized networks" that comprise the broader "migration business" (1997: 468–469). They note that "at origin and destination there are governments, employers, host societies, and migrants (actual and potential). Connecting them are streams of migrants, managed by a string of intermediary institutions designed in whole or in part to encourage and help people move" (1997: 468–469). The identities of these institutions overlap with the aforementioned agents and brokers and include "recruitment and travel agencies, transport operators, legal and advisory firms, and others" (1997: 468–469). The intermediaries, found in various niches of the migration networks, knowingly or unknowingly engage in practices facilitating the trafficking process.

Other scholars since Salt and Stein have sought to develop more detailed explorations of illegal migration. Kyle and Koslowski note the understudied "role of entrepreneurial organizations as actors in undocumented migration flows" as part of the impetus for their edited volume on human smuggling (2001: 11–12). They reveal an array of actors and organizations engaged in evolving practices of smuggling and trafficking—more commonly in loose affiliations than in hierarchical criminal networks—influenced in part by the enforcement practices of the state. With colleagues John Dale (2001) and Christina Siracusa (2005), David Kyle has also sought to place the illegal migration business in the broader context of "historical social relationships involving public and private actors" by exploring the rise and nature of "migrant-exporting" and "slave-importing" schemes (Kyle and Siracusa, 2005: 156).

Sheldon Zhang focuses more explicitly on the business aspects of human smuggling and trafficking. He argues that "human smuggling is essentially an underground travel business that involves arranging and coordinating logistics to transport fee-paying customers to their destinations" (2007: 87). The business of human trafficking adds "elements of coercion and fraud . . . for the purpose of economic or sexual exploitation of immigrants" (2007: 106). Zhang also sees actors in the illegal migration business as more likely to form "groups with loose memberships and limited command structure" than hierarchically or ethnically based organizations (2007: 88). Risk assessment and mitigation—addressing challenges ranging from law enforcement efforts to an "unstable and limited clientele"—are critical components shaping the smugglers' "market environment" (2007: 90-91). Zhang goes on to draw on the experiences of the United States with illegal migration as well as empirical work on Chinese smuggling networks to trace strategies of entry through legal points as well as illegal border crossings. His analysis shows how paths into the United States are distinguished by varying combinations of cost and risk and by a stratified market of services that cater to the needs of migrants with varying financial resources.

Illegality and Diversity

This brief overview of the illegal migration industry portrays a lucrative, multifaceted service sector comprised of diverse brokers and agents linked by highly flexible organizational networks. By turning to the international political economy of illegal migration, we can tease out the forces that shape the industry's rise and structure. Through an IPE lens, we can see that illegal migration is a story of the "mutually constituting" nature of states and markets (Schwartz, 2006: 51–52), and of the intersection of trends toward post-Fordism in the licit and illicit global economies.[4]

Globalization and Regulation

While migration has always taken place, the modern dynamics of economic globalization have influenced the pool of potentially mobile persons, the demand for their labor in destination countries, and the technological means facilitating their transportation (Massey et al., 1998; Mittelman, 2000: 58–73; Koslowski, 2001: 338–339). Douglas Massey and his colleagues explore these dynamics under different approaches, the most IPE-oriented being the rubric of "world systems theory," which they describe as comprising historical structural and world systems arguments that have emerged since the late 1970s to link migration to "the expansion of global capitalism" (Massey et al., 1998: 1–2).

World systems theory emphasizes the "disruptions and dislocations" stemming from the integration of societies into the global market economy (Massey et al., 1998: 18–28, 34–41). In so doing, the theory offers a marked contrast to more mainstream economic approaches in which the focus is on how wage differentials, the cost/benefit calculations of individuals, and the risk management strategies of households shape the decision to migrate. Migration takes place in the context of competitive market pressures that alter patterns of agricultural production, land ownership, and the extraction of raw materials. Inflows of foreign capital develop and distort manufacturing labor markets. These shifts and their associated disruptions to traditional social and economic relations create increasingly mobile populations of men and women who seek opportunity in domestic urban areas and, in some cases, abroad. Migration from developing to more developed countries is influenced by "material and ideological" linkages, including the expansion of "transportation and communication infrastructure" and the diffusion of language and cultural patterns (Massey et al., 1998: 38, 40). Demand for low-wage workers in capitalist centers, especially in the service sectors of global cities, adds to the migratory aspect of capitalist integration.

Although not systematically integrating it into their world systems theory, Massey and his colleagues note the central role of border controls and other regulations on migration imposed by the state (1998: 13–14). As Peter Andreas argues more explicitly, "Through its monopoly to criminalize certain economic sectors, the state defines the boundaries of illegal market activities" (2004: 642; see also Andreas and Nadelmann, 2006: 11). State regulations on international migration, especially measures by advanced industrial countries restricting the flow of low-skilled, low-wage migrants from developing countries, have set the parameters within which the market for illegal migrant labor has emerged.

The existence of this market and the rise of the illegal migration industry that serves it pose a regulatory challenge for the state. In this sense, the issue of illegal migration suggests support for extending prominent theoretical approaches in IPE that emphasize the inherent tensions between states and markets (see Gilpin, 1987; Grieco and Ikenberry, 2003). As argued by Herman Schwartz, however, a more useful approach to IPE involves exploring states and markets as "mutually constitutive" rather than reified, distinct entities (2005: 61). In this light, the illegal migration industry appears more illustrative of Schwartz's conceptualization of a symbiotic relationship whereby the existence of state and market actors "is conditional on the presence of the other" (2005: 61).

Illegal migration and, especially, the rise of identifiable larger-scale actors in the illegal migration industry serve as an impetus for state actors to expand the state's role in regulating transnational flows. Growing concerns with Chinese "snakehead" migrant-smuggling organizations in the aftermath of the 1993 grounding of the *Golden Venture* off the coast of New York (Smith, 1997; Chin, 2001; Zhang, 2007), and the discovery of Russian human trafficking networks during the 1990s in moving "Nastashas" into the EU sex trade (Hughes, 2000; Malarek, 2004) are just two of many examples used by state authorities to introduce new regulations on migration and expand enforcement. Yet, as Andreas and others have argued (Andreas, 2001; Schloenhardt, 2003; Hernández-León, 2005; Andreas and Nadelmann, 2006; Zhang, 2007), these steps have had the unintended effects of widening the defined parameters of illegal activity and encouraging the rise of increasingly large smuggling and trafficking organizations better able to evade the state's enforcement resources. In effect, the cycle repeats itself as market actors expand illegal transnational flows, thereby reinforcing the efforts of state actors to expand the state's regulatory role.

Demand and Diversity

Despite the impact of state measures on patterns of organization and concentration in the illegal migration industry, the diversity of the industry's actors and organizational structures remains a distinguishing feature. I suggest in this section that insights into the persistence of this diversity lie in using the lens of post-Fordism to explore the nature of demand for illegal migrant labor by destination countries, for the services of the illegal migration industry by migrants, and for services within the various components of the industry itself.

Demand in destination countries. The existence of the illegal migration industry requires continued demand in destination countries for foreigners who are unable to gain entry and employment by legal means. For reasons ranging from structural economic shifts to broader concerns of national identity and security, governments in destination countries have imposed restrictions on immigration that privilege the entry of higher-skilled workers over that of low-wage, low-skilled workers from developing countries (Hollifield, 2000; Cornelius et al., 2004). Demand for the latter still exists in destination countries, namely in sectors such as agriculture and food processing, construction, low-skill services, and labor-intensive assembly operations (Mittelman, 2000: 61). In practice, these sectors often blur academic distinctions between formal, informal, and criminal economies (Castells and Portes, 1989: 14–15; Naylor, 2002). For example, some migrants find work in sweatshops and other informal economy operations, defined broadly as the illegal production and distribution of otherwise legal goods and services. Others find themselves in situations of forced prostitution or engaged in the production and distribution of illegal goods and services. These activities in sectors of the formal, informal, and criminal economies can be niche oriented, privileging migrants by attributes such as gender, ethnicity, and national origin as well as skill level (Sassen, 1998; Peterson, 2003; Ahmad, 2008).

According to James Mittelman (2000), patterns of labor demand in destination country markets have been shaped by the transition from Fordist to post-Fordist production structures. Briefly, Fordism's emphasis on mass production and consumption has given way to the post-Fordist focus on specialization through niche production and marketing. This transition has been far from universal. Mittelman notes that the flexible, higher-skilled labor needs of post-Fordist production dominate some sectors in destination countries, while demand for "primarily unskilled and semiskilled workers" continues to exist in "sectors dominated by Fordism" (Mittelman, 2000: 61; see also Friman, 2004). Low wages, limited status, and less attractive working conditions limit the interest of less educated and younger native workers in entering the latter, leading employers in these sectors to look increasingly to migrants as their primary workforce (Massey et al., 1998; see also Sassen, 1998).

The results of this transition are at least twofold. First, to varying degrees, governments in destination countries have responded to clientelist pressures in favor of the presence of foreign workers by selectively tolerating illegal immigration through side and back doors, despite state restrictions on the front-door entry of low-wage, low-skilled migrants (Martin, 1994; Hollifield, 2000; Mittelman, 2000; Koslowski, 2001; Cornelius et al., 2004). The presence of multiple doors shapes the extent to which the resources of larger smuggling organizations are necessary to help migrants gain entry (insofar as their resource needs vary depending on whether they intend to enter as students, company trainees, overstaying tourists, or otherwise) and thus partially offsets the concentration effects of state enforcement noted above. Second, the transition to post-Fordism in destination countries has created uneven pockets of demand for low-wage migrant workers across an array of agricultural, manufacturing, and service sectors by employers of varying degree of scale (Calavita, 2005; Ahmad, 2008). The sheer variety of this demand has helped to shape the organization and concentration of the illegal migration industry in ways that encourage diversity rather than hierarchy and monopoly. To understand why this is the case, we must view the industry itself through a post-Fordist lens.

Fordism entails the mass production of goods and services whose selection is controlled more by producers rather than consumers—a pattern exemplified by the limited model and color choice of automobiles coming off the early Ford Motor Company's assembly lines. Post-Fordism's emphasis on flexible production for niche markets and rapid response to changes in consumer demand represents a shift toward greater consumer influence over the production process (Conti and Perelli, 2005). Consumers of low-wage migrant labor—the aforenoted multiple sectors and employers in destination countries—are one source of demand shaping the illegal migration industry and contributing to its diversity.

Demand by migrants. The consumers of the services provided by the illegal migration industry include the migrants themselves, who seek travel and placement services that will enable them to evade state immigration regulations in the destination country. The financial resources, points of origin, and desired destinations of potential migrants vary considerably. Human smuggling organizations thus require flexibility to be able to respond to variations in demand for their services.

For example, the financial means of potential migrants and their families at home or abroad affects the services they can afford, including passage by land, sea or air and the quality of forged or stolen travel documents (see Salt and Stein, 1997: 479–481; Zhang, 2007: 78, 91). Potential migrants can be found at multiple points of origin (USDOS, 2007). Salt and Stein (1997) focus on Western Europe as the destination for migrants originating in Eastern Europe, the former Soviet Union, North Africa, East Asia and the subcontinent, and the Middle East. Migrants also seek different destinations, their desires often tempered in part by the form of transit they can afford. Although Zhang (2007) primarily explores the smuggling of Chinese migrants into the United States, Chinese migrants have turned to smuggling networks to gain access into an array of destinations, including Japan, Eastern Europe, Southeast Asia, Russia, and the Caucuses (Nyíri and Savelev, 2002).

In order to meet the demand of those seeking to exploit the forced labor or sexual services of trafficked persons, human trafficking organizations must first lure potential migrants into their networks. Instances of kidnapping do occur, but fraud and deception play more critical roles in this process. Promises of employment as well-paid domestic servants or factory workers, offers of travel to exotic destinations, and opportunities for romance are key methods (Malarek, 2004; Friman and Reich, 2007b; Zhang, 2007). As national and international anti-trafficking efforts have expanded awareness campaigns that call attention to such practices (United Nations, 2008b: 437–446), trafficking groups have extended the use of deceptive practices to less informed and more vulnerable rural and ethnic minority populations (Beeks and Amir, 2006).

Demand from within the industry. Finally, the customer base for the illegal migration industry includes actors within the industry itself who rely on the products and services provided by their counterparts in other subsectors. As Zhang observes, control over multiple stages of illegal migration, including "recruitment, travel preparation, departure, transit, arrival, payment collection," is beyond the capacity of most smuggling organizations (2007: 95). Smuggling groups generally work within their own "immediate social network" on those tasks for which they do have the capacity and cooperate with others on those for which they do not (2007: 95). The complexity of the smuggling process requires "working with whoever can provide the needed service for a fee" (2007: 95). This suggests again the importance of flexibility when it comes to the production of products and services that are tailored to the needs of actors at different stages in the movement of migrants from origin to destination. I return to this issue in the concluding section.

Conclusion

As noted in the introduction to this volume, international migration, especially in its illegal form, has been relatively understudied by IPE scholars. This chapter draws on IPE arguments concerning the relationships between states and markets and the dynamics of Fordism and post-Fordism in the intersection of the licit and illicit global economies. States, by their regulation of cross-border flows of people, have played an instrumental role in the creation of illegal immigration. State enforcement of these regulations has facilitated the rise of the illegal migration industry and its patterns of organization and concentration, which have in turn facilitated the efforts of governmental actors to expand the state's regulatory powers. However, these patterns are also shaped by the demand for migrant labor in destination countries, as well as the demands of potential migrants and industry actors operating at various stages of the migration process.

Zhang notes that despite the impact of state controls on the increasing organization of the business of human smuggling, there has been no trend toward "monopoly or consolidation" (2007: 94). Rather, "the enterprise of transnational human smuggling has remained fragmented and dominated by groups of loosely affiliated entrepreneurs" with "multiple layers of operatives" instead of "hierarchical command structures" (2007: 94, 96). Although this chapter has called attention to the dynamics of post-Fordism to explain why the illegal migration industry remains diverse in its organizational structures and patterns of industry consolidation, at least two alternative explanations for this pattern are suggested by the illegal migration industry literature.

One is the aforementioned issue of capacity constraints. Specifically, the processes of migrant smuggling and human trafficking—from point of origin to placement at destination—are so extensive and complex that groups have lacked the capacity to develop more extensive organizational hierarchies and industry consolidation. Yet the dynamics of demand explored in this chapter suggest that even in the absence of capacity constraints, groups might be reluctant to embrace expansion. Post-Fordist trends in the illegal migration industry have privileged market actors who can adapt quickly to changing niche markets for smuggled and trafficked migrants and variations in the services necessary to get them from origin to destination. Further research is necessary to determine the extent to which such flexibility is eroded by the expansion of organizational hierarchies and market concentrations and the extent to which such trade-offs differ from those faced by market actors in more licit post-Fordist industries.

The second explanation in the illegal migration industry literature is that smuggling and trafficking groups choose to remain limited in organizational and operational reach in order to mitigate risk. Zhang points to the concerns of organizations with the mitigation of risk of arrest and asset seizure by state authorities, and notes how these serve as a check on overextension and an impetus for tighter group affiliation (2007: 90–91). Salt and Stein argue that the "separation" and careful definition of "individual and group tasks" are means by which the larger trafficking enterprise can protect itself from "criminal investigations" or "mistakes" that might lead to its discovery (1997: 478). Risk mitigation is a well-established theme in the work of economists and criminologists into the nature and structure of organized crime. So too is profit seeking, however, which suggests that exploring the ways in which human smugglers and traffickers balance considerations of risk and reward in an industry embedded in the dynamic context of global capitalism may yield important insights.

Notes

1. On the relative absence of such restrictions prior to the late nineteenth century, see Williamson (1998) and Frieden (2006: 51–54).
2. The 2009 and 2010 *TIPR* describe the challenge of trafficking in detail but do not include estimates of overall scale (USDOS, 2009, 2010).
3. Nandy indicates that this figure was in circulation as of 2003.
4. The concept of the illicit global economy is discussed in Friman and Andreas (1999).

Part 2

The Migration-Development Nexus

6

Reinterpreting Migration and Development

Ronald Skeldon

It is axiomatic that a relationship between population migration and development exists, but just what that relationship is is difficult to unravel. The movement of people into or out of an area is bound to produce change, demographic and otherwise. Such movement may be a consequence of the introduction of some feature that would typically be thought to construe development, such as the construction of a school or a factory. In short, it is difficult to envisage anything that might be called development without some redistribution of population: equally, it is difficult to envisage the movement of people without some kind of change in local economies and societies. Hence, migration is an integral part of development and is essentially a spatial expression of development through the redistribution of population (Skeldon, 1997). It is impossible to separate one from the other, and it is deceptive to see them as independent phenomena that can be individually manipulated: both are inextricably linked in a matrix of change (Skeldon, 2008a).

"Development" is a highly contested term and has proved very difficult to define. It gives the impression that things are progressing and that the well-being of human populations is improving. The study of development encompasses the factors that bring about social, economic, and political transformations that seem to generate this improvement. Nevertheless, improvements for some may mean that conditions for others deteriorate. We can argue that the massive migration from Europe to the Americas brought about the modern development of the United States and Canada, but we can also argue that it brought about the destruction of the indigenous populations and their ways of life. Hence, the same migration event can have totally different development outcomes for different groups and also for different individuals within those groups. Even more generally, changes in technology that bring improvement for some may have destructive consequences for both physical and social environments that will threaten that improvement over the long term.

Hence, discussions of the migration-development nexus explicitly or (more usually) implicitly evoke the population-environment debate that dates back more than 200 years to the time of Thomas Malthus and still preoccupies us today. The late 1960s and early 1970s saw a rise in neo-Malthusianism, which was perhaps best epitomized in Paul Ehrlich's *The Population Bomb* (1968) and the report commissioned by the Club of Rome entitled *Limits to Growth* (Meadows et al., 1972). As prosperity grew in conjunction with the acceleration of globalization that began in the late 1970s—of which increased international trade and international migration were very much a part—an age of non-Malthusian optimism emerged, coinciding with the so-called Age of Migration (Castles and Miller, 2009). Yet even before the financial crisis began in September 2008, a discernible shift back to more cautious neo-Malthusian approaches had emerged (Diamond, 2005; Rees, 2003; Saul, 2005). The crisis of the late 2000s is likely to have changed patterns of migration as well as our interpretations of migration and development.

Given the difficulty of defining development, a more precise meaning emerged through international policy discussions in the Millennium Development Goals (MDGs), which were billed as representing "a compact among nations to end human poverty" (UNDP, 2003). Through a series of general goals and more specific targets, the most important of which was to "halve, between 1990 and 2015, the proportion of people whose income is less than $1 a day," development took on a more focused and measurable dimension. The MDGs did not address migration—not surprisingly, as it would have been impossible to achieve an international agreement on such a controversial issue (Skeldon, 2005, 2008b). Nevertheless, as with development in general, it is impossible to envisage any progress toward meeting the MDGs in the absence of population migration and redistribution. Governments needed to be made aware of the likely consequences for migration and human mobility if the goals of achieving universal primary education, reducing child and maternal mortality, and providing increased numbers of people with access to drinking water were to be realized.

Such tensions are seldom incorporated into discussions of migration and development, which tend to posit migration as an essentially independent phenomenon that can be managed in some way to achieve particular, and largely positive, development outcomes. To an extent, this viewpoint emerged in response to prior interpretations that saw migration as essentially the result of a failure of development: that is, migration was induced by poverty and the consequences were largely negative for origins, destinations, and the migrants themselves. In these neoclassical interpretations, migration was seen primarily as the result of differences in income-earning opportunities between origins and destinations (see Massey et al., 1993). Hence, it was essentially a lack of development that created the differences in income and wage-earning opportunities in origin countries; if those problems could be eliminated through some sort of development, migration would cease. The elimination of poverty, the first and most important MDG, would go some way toward reducing migration.

Nevertheless, the assumption of such a direct linkage between income differences and migration was shown to have fundamental flaws. It was predicated upon the individual decisionmaker, when migration was so often a group, particularly a household, strategy. It became clear that by migrating, household members could extend their access to resources, seek to minimize risk, and use monies or skills acquired outside their home areas to improve the quality of life at home. Thus migration itself can alleviate poverty and it came to be seen as part of the solution to a lack of development rather than as a problem to be solved. Many, including this author, have subscribed to this more positive point of view. While it is one thing to acknowledge the benefits that accrue through broadening access, it is quite another to conclude that migration can be successfully managed in a way that actively promotes development.

Although development can be facilitated through the movements of people, migration is much more a consequence of development than the other way around. It is true that monies sent back to recipients in origin countries can have a significant impact. However, the effects of migration involve much more than just the transfer of funds: ideas and practices—otherwise known as "social remittances" (Levitt, 1999)—can be transmitted by returning migrants in ways that change behavior in their origin communities, affecting everything from family size and attitudes toward education to agricultural methods. Development has to be thought of more broadly as a system of continuous change in which population migration plays an integral role. Development involves the undermining, even destruction, of certain ways of life as well as the improvement and promotion of others. For example, migration can bring about the depopulation of some villages while contributing to the growth of population in more favored locations. Hence, development encompasses more than the MDGs do, even if the latter are significant for the direction of policy. This chapter will maintain the broader view while critically assessing the contemporary debate on how migration impacts development.

Migration as a Spatial and Temporal Process

The theme of this chapter is that it is the dynamic nature of the migratory process itself that gives rise to divergent interpretations of migration and development. Essentially, our data on migration represent a series of cross-sections through migration systems at different stages of development. The combination of the figures aggregates migration across states and subnational units at one point in time. If migration is conceptualized as a system whose diffusion occurs unevenly through time and across space, a more systematic view of both the causes and consequences of the process can emerge. Knowing that generalizations are very hard to draw for migration, we have come a long way from the so-called laws of migration that Ravenstein (1885) devised more than a century ago. We can see cases, for example, in which males outnumber females in migration flows or flows are dominated by the skilled rather than the unskilled. Perhaps the one generalization that holds true in most cases is that the majority of migrants are young adults. However, we can find exceptions to that and virtually any other statement we can make about migration and its relation to development.

While the search for an all-encompassing model may be a lost cause, it will be argued here that many of the conflicting situations can at least be clarified through the lens of a constantly changing time-space framework. The focus of the discussion will be on areas of origin, which is logical given that the focus of the migration-development debate is how migration can be managed to the benefit of poorer developing countries, as well as improving the lives of the migrants themselves (see, for instance, GCIM, 2005; DfID, 2007; IOM, 2008). Clearly, destination countries also develop as a result of the arrival of migrants, but we will discuss this aspect only indirectly.

Before dealing with the mechanics of the migration process, another fundamental contradiction needs to be addressed, namely the issue of structure and agency. It can be argued that in discussions of migration and development since the late 1990s, the responsibility for development has been shifted toward the migrant and away from the structures in which they operate. In essence, migrants take on the responsibility for development: the monies sent home as remittances should be used productively to bring about development; the skilled migrants in the diaspora should return home to help with the development of their country of origin; and a lack of development at home can be attributed to the exodus of the skilled (Skeldon, 2008a). Rarely is the link between migrant agency and responsibility for development made so explicit, but the individual decisionmaking models supplied by neoclassical theories of migration provide a convenient explanatory framework. Generally, state responsibility for the lack of development in origins and/or the promotion of development in destinations is not explicitly considered a driver of migration.

Yet migration can be managed in an attempt to bring about development (Martin et al., 2006; IOM, 2008). Above all, this might be achieved by encouraging the community of migrants overseas—the diaspora—to leverage their skills by returning or sending remittances home (Kuznetsov, 2006). However, the idea that managing development itself might bring desired changes to migration does not figure prominently in migration policy circles. Promoting circulation, opening broader channels for legal migration, and encouraging certain types of migration, usually on the part of highly skilled workers, while limiting certain other—mainly unskilled—types are among the most common migration policy responses. The migration tail is beginning to wag the development dog, and the focus is firmly on the proximate causes of the movement rather than the indirect causes, which are fundamentally economic and political.

Components of Migration and Development

The discussion of migration and development has revolved around two main concerns: the contribution migrants make to the development of the home areas in terms of remittances and the implications of the loss of migrants, particularly skilled ones, to their countries of origin. These two issues have been brought together in the discussion of the role of the diaspora in contributing to the development of the home country.

Remittances and Localized Origins

Remittances make up one of the largest financial flows from the developed to the developing world. For the purposes of this chapter, remittances need to be placed in the context of the evolution of migration systems, and here the localized areas of origins and destinations of migrant flows are a critical but often unacknowledged part of the process. Migrants in general and international migrants in particular are not randomly drawn from any population: some areas emit migrants more than others. Globally, the number of international migrants was estimated at some 214 million in 2010, which accounted for just under 3 percent of the world's population (United Nations, 2009). Such a figure is not particularly meaningful, as some countries are much more affected by migration than others. About one tenth of the populations of Mexico and the Philippines—countries that might be considered "classic" emigrant societies—reside outside their borders; indeed, these countries rank third and fourth in terms of the volume of remittances received from the developed world—US$22.6 billion and US$21.3 billion, respectively, of the total flow of US$325 billion from the developed to the developing world in 2010 (World Bank, 2011). In both Mexico and the Philippines, distinct areas of outmigration exist. The three western states of Guanajuato, Jalisco, and Michoacán have consistently contributed between 30 and 40 percent of migrants from Mexico (Durand et al., 2001), though they account for only about 15 percent of the total population. Within these states, too, specific loci of concentrated emigration exist (Faret, 2007: 81). In the Philippines, more than two thirds of the labor leaving the country between 1998 and 2002 came from metropolitan Manila and the surrounding regions of Central Luzon and Southern Tagalog (ADB, 2004). Localized migration has also been observed in countries such as Bangladesh, Pakistan, and China (Skeldon, 2008a, 2009a).

Thus, any benefits from migrant remittances are going to be channeled back to very specific parts of countries of origin. However, internal migration also figures into the equation, and the failure to consider it is one of the principal weaknesses in contemporary discussions on migration and development, which have been focused almost entirely on international population movements. Nevertheless, we have no single estimate for the number of internal migrants that can be compared across countries. The number depends entirely upon the size of the spatial unit used to define a "migrant," as well as the length of time that that person has been at a specific destination—and these vary enormously. However, to give the most general of impressions, if we use the standard definition of internal migration to consider China and India alone, we can easily more than double the estimate of 214 million international migrants for 2010. For example, the number of internal migrants in China in 2005 was estimated at 147 million (see Cai and Wang, 2008: 250) and, using the smallest spatial unit to define an internal migrant, some 309 million persons were defined as internal migrants in the 2001 census of India (India, n.d.: 2). The majority of migrants in medium-sized to large countries move internally, and they also send remittances. In one relatively rare study in which remittances from internal as well as international sources were included, it was found that 77.8 percent of households in Guatemala received no remittances, 14.6 percent received remittances from internal sources, and 8.1 percent received remittances from international sources (Adams, 2006: 55).

Thus, in gauging development impact, we must consider that the remittances from international sources flow to a relatively small number of communities in the countries of origin, and these communities may not necessarily be among the poorest. For example, in Peru, more than four-fifths of households that received remittances from overseas were to be found in the more developed coastal region of the country, with some 57 percent in metropolitan Lima alone (OIM, 2008: 55). Only 5 percent of these households were found in the rural sector, which still accounted for 27.4 percent of the population in 2005 (United Nations, 2006: 43) and where fully two-thirds of the population were classified as living in poverty in 2000 (Verdera V., 2007: 116). Data from the Philippines suggests that "roughly half" of the overseas contract workers came from the richest 20 percent of families, with some 80 percent coming from the wealthiest 40 percent of households (Ducanes and Abella, 2008: 5). This pattern is consistent with the distribution of workers' areas of origin observed by the Asian Development Bank (ADB, 2004).

These data should not necessarily be taken to imply that remittances flow only to people who are already relatively wealthy or that migration can have no impact on either the alleviation of poverty or development in a broader sense. However, a certain amount of capital is required to allow people to migrate in the first place. The aforementioned survey of remittances in Guatemala revealed that those households receiving remittances from internal or international sources tended to "have more family members with secondary education, older household heads, fewer children under five, [and] more wealth (value of house) than those households not receiving remittances" (Adams, 2006: 55). Yet it also showed that remittances could help to alleviate poverty, although mainly in terms of severity and depth rather than in terms of absolute numbers of the poor. A robust study of the impact of remittances in Tonga and Fiji found that they could indeed reduce the incidence and depth of poverty (Brown and Jiménez, 2008). However, the impact was much greater in the much smaller Tonga, where benefits could be diffused fairly rapidly throughout the country. However, neither Fiji nor Tonga ranks among the poorest of economies, Tonga being classified within the "high human development" group, Fiji in the "medium human development" band (UNDP, 2008). Further evidence that remittances act to reduce poverty comes from the southern Indian state of Kerala, where they are estimated to have contributed a 12 percent reduction in poverty across the state (Zachariah et al., 2003).

Nevertheless, the available evidence of their impact is often ambiguous. A 2007 assessment of data on remittances to a number of Latin American countries showed that although they "appear[ed] to lower poverty levels in recipient countries," their impact had been "modest" overall and that "the positive development impact of remittances must be qualified" from case to case (Acosta et al., 2007: 96).

More Than Remittances: Broader Linkages

The impact of international migration from any community of origin can reach far beyond the confines of that community. Communities that have seen marked emigration are generally characterized by labor shortages brought about not just by the absence of workers but also by the expectations of locals—increased through experience outside the community as well as improved education—who are unwilling to do the most mundane tasks. Vacant houses and unused land are also available, and migrants from poorer parts of the country are either brought in to undertake menial tasks or attracted by houses and land for rent or sale.

Village communities in rural southern and central Peru that had been typified by out-migration to the cities in the early 1970s became centers of attraction for people from even poorer areas in the early twenty-first century.[1] David Fitzgerald (2009) conducted an important study of long-standing emigration from a community in Jalisco, Mexico, to the United States, showing that workers from Chiapas in southern Mexico have been brought in to undertake the backbreaking work of weeding and tending the agave plants in Jalisco. Fitzgerald also shows that the income difference between Jalisco and Chiapas is slightly greater than that between Jalisco and the United States and that Jalisco has become the Chiapan laborer's Global North. This linkage between internal and international migration is a critical but largely ignored part of the migration-development debate. Patterns similar to those observed in Mexico and Peru have also been observed in Kerala (Nair, 1989), Bangladesh (Gardner, 1995), and northern Pakistan (Ballard, 2003), although the nature of the linkages between internal and international migration can vary (see Skeldon, 2006; King and Skeldon, 2010).

Although the impact of migration on poverty might be contested, its impact on broader development is clear at the local level. In the Jaliscan community studied by Fitzgerald, returned migrants invested in tequila distilleries, which created a demand for agave that turned marginal land into a valuable resource. The state steadily increased in wealth, such that it currently ranks in the top quarter of Mexican states in terms of development and thus constitutes "a model of the economic success that can be achieved by using remittance investment to add value to agricultural products" (Fitzgerald, 2009: 11). According to Richard Adams (1959), migrants from the community of Muquiyauyo in central Peru used the experience they gained working in mining towns in the mid-twentieth century to plan for the construction of a hydroelectric plant back home that could be used to sell power to neighboring towns and enterprises. Although factions within the community that were suspicious of the returnees perhaps militated against the most efficient operation of the project, Adams maintains that it still gave the community an advantage over most in the Andes at that time. However, emigration from both Jalisco and Muquiyauyo continues, and any thought that out-migration will cease by promoting development, even at the local level, seems mistaken.

Migration tends to increase upon development. In favored areas, because of access or the presence of other resources, return or even in-migration may eventually occur, although such reversals are unlikely to occur in more marginal areas. In the more favored areas, local populations may be maintained, although almost certainly through increased in-migration rather than by the cessation of out-migration. Even at the macro level, where economies seem to progress through a transition from net emigration to net immigration (see Abella, 1994) that may parallel a demographic transition, emigration does not cease. The interchange of populations is an essential part of participation in global networks of trade and finance. However, at the macro level, it is neither migration nor the return flow of remittances that serves as sufficient cause for economic development, but rather broader economic and political changes. For example, despite receiving hundreds of millions of dollars in remittances in the 1990s, Kerala did not experience a parallel increase in economic growth, actually declining in state rank by gross domestic product between 1980 and 1998 (Sachs et al., 2001).

Considerable attention has been given to the uses of remittances and the relative expenditure of migrants on productive investment and wasteful consumption. In any event, no clear line can be drawn between the two, as consumption expenditure usually has multiplier effects on local employment and production. In contrast, relatively little attention has been paid to reverse remittances—that is, the use of remittances to fund further migration or support education in another country. An early review (Connell et al., 1976) identified the importance of reverse remittances at the village level, but data are rarely collected at the macro level. However, a 2007 study of internal remittances in South Korea during its period of most rapid urbanization in the 1970s has shown that the net flow was in favor of destination areas in the cities, primarily Seoul (Mobrand, 2007). Remittances may be used to fund further migration, both internally and internationally, and to fund the education of siblings in destination areas. Thus, remittances, which are seen as a source for the development of source areas, may do as much, if not more, to further out-migration, undermine communities of origin, and encourage the types of training that can only be productively employed in cities or overseas. Remittances are a source of development but not in the ways generally assumed; that is, they do not mainly favor the maintenance of local rural communities. They are a significant part of the support of life in, and transition to, an urban society.

Skill Losses and Development

While localized origins have clear implications for the distribution of remittances in countries of origin, so too do they affect the impact of emigration. The exodus of migrants, particularly of skilled migrants, is seen as a loss for the country of origin, a loss that developing countries should not be asked to bear. Among the simplest suggested solutions are that either migration should be discouraged, even stopped, or that appropriate compensation should be given. However, the implications of these solutions are themselves complex and of dubious value and legality. First, the freedom to leave one's country of origin is recognized in the Universal Declaration of Human Rights. Second, when the global flows of the highly skilled are examined, it becomes clear that the origin countries are dominated by developed countries and a relatively small number of middle-income developing countries, including China, India, the Philippines, and Mexico (Docquier and Marfouk, 2006). These countries possess the tertiary institutions that can train the highly skilled. Significant numbers of the skilled are involved in North-South migration, employed not only in transnational corporations but in institutions that provide basic skills. Modern economies are predicated upon the mobility of skills, and the notion that labor and skilled labor in particular should stay where they are seems misguided.

It might be argued that the issue does not concern the absolute numbers of skilled migrants but rather the loss of relatively small numbers from poor economies, which can have a profound impact. Here again, several other factors have to be considered. The highly skilled tend to be from elite families who live in the most developed areas, not where they may be of greatest need—a point that is particularly relevant to the topic of medical personnel. That said, the principal demand in the poorest regions may not be for the highest trained specialists but for those with basic skills. If medical personnel are trained according to global standards, they can be expected to move globally. Even if they do stay in their home countries, there is no guarantee they will move to poor rural areas where needs are great but facilities are lacking. Any attempt to restrict the movement of the skilled is likely to lead to their movement through irregular channels, which will almost certainly mean that they cannot practice their profession openly at destination areas.

The data we have on skilled migration relates country of birth (or citizenship) to country of residence. Rarely is information on the country of training given, but increasing numbers of migrants are students. Their training has increasingly been funded by governments or foundations based in the destination country (Kritz, 2006), or by families themselves, most likely via remittances. The origins of the majority of skilled workers in the developed world and increasingly wealthy developing countries, together with the use of private monies in the funding of training, make the issues of compensation and the management of skilled migration flows even more problematic.

In any event, the actual impact of the emigration of the skilled on the development of countries of origin is exceedingly difficult to demonstrate, even in such a vital service as the health sector. Significantly, an internal exodus from the sector also occurs as practitioners flee poor salaries and working conditions. For example, in South Africa around 2000, some 32,000 vacancies existed for nurses in the public sector, a fact that may be partially attributed to the large number of nurses going abroad, estimated at about 7,000. However, it was also estimated that there remained another 35,000 registered nurses who were inactive or unemployed in South Africa (OECD, 2004: 130). Moreover, many factors other than the number of health personnel account for an increase (or decrease) in mortality and morbidity indicators. It is all too easy to treat the emigration of health professionals as a ready explanation for problems in the health services of a nation or the health of a population (see Skeldon, 2009b).

One seemingly counterintuitive interpretation of the phenomenon of skilled migration is that it is positive for countries of origin. To generalize, potential entrants to tertiary education or further training schemes will opt for desirable careers abroad. However, not all the cohorts in a given skill program will be selected by potential destination countries, and the country of origin will be left with more skilled people at the end of any period than at the beginning (Mountford, 1997; Stark, 2004). Here again, it is difficult to analyze the increase in numbers in skilled categories independent of government policies on tertiary education and other changes occurring in the countries of origin. The emigration of the skilled is only one factor among many affecting economic development, whether negatively or positively, in countries of origin. Any explanation for a lack of development is more likely to be found in broader structures of economy and society than in the pattern of migration.

Diaspora Communities and Hometown Associations

Diaspora communities are seen as an important human resource for the development of countries of origin. The hope is that the diaspora can be "leveraged" for the benefit of the home country in a number of ways (Kuznetsov, 2006). Clearly the community is a source of remittances, as we have discussed, as well as of direct foreign investment. However, it is also a source of skills that may be encouraged to return on a longer- or shorter-term basis. At the national level, however, diasporas can be highly heterogeneous (Skeldon, 2003); not all members will work in the best interests of their home states, and a diaspora can have a "Janus face" (Kapur, 2007). Still, communities of migrants from specific provinces, districts, or villages—known in contemporary literature as "hometown associations"—may indeed play a role in promoting development at the local level.

Perhaps not surprisingly given the schism between studies of internal and international migration, almost no reference is made in the current debate to regional associations of internal migrants in the towns and cities of developing countries and the role they have played in hometown development. Fitzgerald (2009) is one of the few to consider both internally and internationally based associations, although the work on internal associations goes back at least to the 1950s, when pioneering research was done by Kenneth Little (1957) on West Africa and William Mangin (1959) on Peru. Their work emphasized the twofold role of these associations: to assist migrants in adapting to the urban world and to promote hometown development. However, Fred Jongkind (1974) later challenged their interpretation of the effectiveness of these associations by arguing, based on data on hundreds of associations in Lima, that they were principally urban institutions made up of long-term city residents more interested in their own welfare and recreation than in promoting development back home. That is, rather than looking back to the village, migrant associations were more concerned with organizing sports competitions and parties to encourage social interaction. They were also institutions through which rural migrants could gain prestige in urban situations.

I have attempted to seek a synthesis between the two viewpoints (Skeldon, 1976, 1977), arguing that both were correct and that their discrepancies could be understood by placing the roles of the associations within a space-time framework of migration. To simplify, associations will mainly have a recreational role where the migrants from a community are of long standing in the city, the migration is well developed and substantial numbers of migrants from the community can be found. When the community of migrants is more homogeneous and recently established, the association plays a more adaptive and developmental role. Essentially, the role of the association is a function of the relative geographical accessibility of the community and the amount of time that has transpired since the migration from community to city occurred, and these factors change over time. This simple model, the eponymous "Skeldon hypothesis" (Butterworth and Chance, 1981: 139–142), now requires modification, as clearly associations also respond to government policy. In the Peruvian case, many of the associations in Lima at the time of the aforementioned studies were responding to government attempts to establish local organizations for social security that would help migrants in the city if they lost their jobs, experienced a bereavement, or faced other hardships.

While hometown development was an objective, the majority of projects of the Lima-based associations were decorative rather than substantive, the paving of the central square being a favorite. Had government policy been geared more toward village improvement, the results might have been different. For example, in Mexico since 1998, schemes such as the "three-for-one"—in which federal, state, and local governments add one dollar each for every dollar raised by a US-based Mexican association for hometown development—suggest that the role of the association in making improvements can be relatively effective. Nevertheless, as Fitzgerald shows, the fortunes of both internal and international associations wax and wane over time, dependent partly on patterns of migration, partly on the role of institutions such as the church, and partly on the effectiveness of leadership (2009: 103–124). Perhaps more important has been the decentralization of the Mexican government, which effectively reduced the intermediary role that the members of associations could play between village community and central government. In this context, the members of more recent international associations in the United States have not "channel[ed] massive development back home as the [migrants] in Mexico City had in the 1940s" (Fitzgerald, 2009: 124).

As noted earlier, the diaspora can also be leveraged for its skills upon return. Here again, the tension between agency and structure is apparent: the responsibility for development is being placed upon the shoulders of migrants rather than on governments to establish the structures favorable to development. At the most essential level, migrants are not going to return if there is nothing to which to return. That said, migrants can and do act as agents of both revolutionary and less dramatic change. The majority of the great revolutionary leaders in Asia—Ho Chi Minh, Sun Yat Sen, Deng Xiaoping, and Zhou Enlai, as well as Lee Kwan Yew, Jinnah, Ghandi, and Nehru—were all return migrants who played critical roles in the development of their respective countries. The majority were nevertheless building upon the foundations of civilizations with long traditions of centralized and effective government. On a more mundane level, we know that increasing numbers of students do return home over time, for instance to assume government positions (Skeldon, 2008a: 12). Migration may not be the reason that we see shifts toward more effective, even transparent governments, but migrants who return with more democratic values are a means through which governments can evolve to wield more penetrative power and less despotic power (Weiss and Hobson, 1995). The role of migration and political development tends to be overshadowed by its linkages with economic and social development.

Conclusion

In this chapter I have attempted to place migration and development within a dynamic framework. Patterns of migration are constantly changing in terms of direction, duration, and composition. Development, by definition, is constantly changing. Hence, the relationship between migration and development, too, is constantly changing, as well as varying across space. For example, the impact that remittances have in an area where migration is characterized by short-term internal mobility to local towns is going to be different than the impact of remittances to communities characterized mainly by international migration. Other communities may experience both types of migrations simultaneously. Meanwhile, the role played by hometown associations in the evolution of both internal and international population flows also varies through time and across space. To determine how these changes are related to other demographic, economic, and political shifts, further research is required, but they seem to point to the need for some form of transition model that can provide a more systematic understanding of migration and development.

Thus, our interpretations of migration and development need to be both cross-sectional and longitudinal. That is, we will need to look at change in the linkages between migration and development over time and at different points across space. Migration does not have a universal impact across space: some areas will be typified by in-migration, others by depopulation; some areas may be typified by labor migration, others by forced migration. How these scenarios will vary over time depends on their place in a spatial system and on other variables such as agriculture, industry, and, perhaps most important, state structures, which are also changing throughout the system. By mapping changing spatial patterns of migration onto changing agricultural patterns in rural areas and industrial shifts in urban areas within the context of both national and local development policy, we may achieve a much more nuanced approach to the migration-development nexus. At the local level, the objective would be to link sequences of change in migration patterns and other variables that are chosen to represent development across space and through time in an integrated system. While systems approaches are certainly not new in migration studies (Mabogunge, 1970), they are rarely used in relation to a space-time dynamic for specific contexts. Not only will no single path of sequential change exist, but reversals, stasis, and/or other outcomes can be anticipated and accounted for in the same framework. This approach will not provide an all-encompassing explanation for migration but it will, for specific areas, allow the assessment of the impact of the various factors, including policy intervention, over time. Thus, we need to rethink the implications for migration as development diffuses unequally throughout a country.

The implications of such transitional approaches might suggest an inexorable process in a particular direction. Yet many transitional pathways will exist; perhaps the critical issue is the extent to which governments can affect their direction through policy intervention. Generally in the migration field, policies are characterized by a gap or mismatch between objectives and outcomes (Cornelius and Tsuda, 2004). Two types of policymaking impact migration: direct policies that attempt to manage movement, most commonly in the form of immigration policies; and indirect policies, such as road construction, to access a natural resource that might have profound implications for the redistribution of population. The main difficulty for those who attempt to anticipate outcomes is that virtually any development policy can have implications for population movement, but gaps emerge in the implementation of both direct and indirect policies. Thus, issues of migration need to be addressed more fully in development policy, and their likely implications need to be considered in accordance with time and place. As we have noted, the impact of remittances and the degree of hometown influence vary across space and through time.

Thus, migration policies need to be placed more firmly within the context of a nation's overall development policy context so that they are responsive both to development policies and to the evolutionary trajectory of migration itself. Such a strategy is consistent with the World Bank's assessment of the need to "put development in place" (2009: 20). However, any such approach will introduce other complexities. Most migration policy is still about control and regulation. For example, almost three-quarters of the governments of developing countries in 2005 were considering policies to reduce internal migration into urban centers (United Nations, 2006: 24). In the developed world, internal migration policy entails admitting those who can make the best perceived contribution to the economy and society of an immigration country and keeping others out—a perfectly rational response in polities where governments are responsive to their electorates. This tension between migration and development policy well illustrates what James Hollifield calls the "liberal paradox" between economic pressures to import labor to satisfy demand in a context of low or even negative labor force growth and domestic political pressures to keep migrants out (2004: 886). In the poorer countries of the developing world, international migration policies are geared more toward preventing brain drain.

Yet the use of direct migration policies as a means to manage internal migration has largely failed over all but the immediate short term. In the case of international migration, the politically expedient presence of an international border can make management more effective in certain circumstances but can also be counterproductive, leading to increasingly irregular population movements. The most effective strategies are likely to anticipate the impact of development policy on migration and elaborate migration policy accordingly: to plan *for* migration rather than plan migration. The critical question is thus not how to manage migration directly but how particular development outcomes affect migration—specifically, how a development policy is likely to impact on migration in a particular place. Migration policy, like that of development, needs to be put in its place if it is to be effective.

Notes

This chapter is based on work completed at the Global Research Centre for Migration, Globalisation, and Development at the University of Sussex, supported by the UK Department for International Development (DfID).

1. These field observations were made in the departments of Cuzco and Junin in July 2008 on a reconnaissance visit supported by the British Academy.

7

Migration and Development in Sub-Saharan Africa

Oliver Bakewell

Migration in sub-Saharan Africa, as in the rest of the world, has always been an essential element in historical processes of social, political and economic change. Development (however defined) and migration are intertwined in a set of complex, heterogeneous, and changing relationships in which causality is never one way. In short, migration can be seen as both a cause and consequence of development and, equally, development is both a cause and consequence of migration. The analysis of the overlap between the two processes has often been relegated to the margins of development studies. It is only in the 2000s that questions about the extent to which migration can help or hinder development have moved to the center of both academic and policy agendas, including that of the field of political economy.

Studies of African migration have tended to offer a somewhat contradictory picture of movement and its relationship with development on the continent. Two key strands of literature have largely existed in parallel with limited contact. On the one hand, there are many studies that highlight the mobility of the peoples of Africa, which has given rise to a rich diversity of intertwined languages, cultures, and traditions whose historical threads can be traced far across the continent. Migration is presented as a norm of life, one that plays an essential role in sustaining livelihoods—diversifying income sources and diffusing risk—and disseminating goods, skills, and labor across Africa (Bilger and Kraler, 2005; de Bruijn et al., 2001; de Haan and Rogaly, 2002).

On the other hand, a large body of literature tends toward a more negative view (Burawoy, 1976; Murray, 1981; Amin, 1995; Akokpari, 2000; Epstein and Jezeph, 2001). This literature also relates migration to livelihoods, but presents it as the result of structural forces, the failure of individuals to make ends meet where they live, or crises—such as conflict, environmental degradation, and/or natural disasters—that make life intolerable. Moreover, those who move can create new problems in both their areas of origin, such as by reducing agricultural production, and the areas in which they settle, such as increasing pressures on urban infrastructure. Hence migration has been seen as a symptom and cause of exploitation and underdevelopment; either way, it has been treated as a problem that needs to be addressed. It is only in the last decade that the picture of migration as a development problem has come to be routinely challenged, with the "discovery" of remittances and a newfound enthusiasm for identifying policies and approaches that can secure the maximum benefits of migration for countries of origin, countries of destination, and migrants themselves in so-called win-win-win scenarios.

To a large extent, the on-off relationship between development and migration in Africa echoes trends in the rest of the world. For example, enthusiasm for understanding the potential engagement of the diasporas in development in Africa is part of a global interest in such issues (Mohan and Zack-Williams, 2002; Ionescu, 2006; Davies, 2007; Thomas, 2008). These broad debates about the relationship between migration and development and the impact of remittances are discussed by Ronald Skeldon in the previous chapter. Rather than reprising those discussions here, I will instead focus on some of the distinctive features of sub-Saharan Africa that have shaped both the conduct of academic debates and policy responses within the region.

In the next section I argue that the experience of colonialism left an indelible mark on the political economy of Africa, shaping both the patterns of migration and their impact across the continent. The European powers created the boundaries of nearly all the modern sub-Saharan African states, and these borders have had a profound effect on mobility. Moreover, in their attempts to marshal the labor of Africans to serve the colonial enterprises in the profit centers of plantations and mines while maintaining traditional ways of life in the rural areas, the colonialists established migration systems that remain important to this day; examples include the labor migrations to the coast of West Africa and the mines of southern Africa. They also established an ideology of state control of mobility that continued after independence. Another important legacy of the colonial era is the institutionalization of concepts of development, which have tended to cast rural-urban migration as a problem to be addressed. Hence, in many parts of sub-Saharan Africa, the notion of development has become inextricably linked with the control of mobility. I suggest that this "sedentary" bias is echoed in development strategies across the continent today. The subsequent section briefly outlines the changing directions and scale of migration in sub-Saharan Africa. I argue that the dynamics of migration on the continent have been shaped by shifts in political and economic conditions at the national, regional, and global levels. I also highlight the fact that, despite the preoccupation of policymakers and academics in Europe, a large majority (more than 70 percent) of sub-Saharan African migrants move within Africa.

Having set the scene, I then turn to the relationship between migration and development in sub-Saharan Africa. The discussion focuses on four areas that are particularly prominent in the debates on Africa. These are the impact of migration on income and inequality and the contribution of remittances; the emigration of skilled workers and the issues generally summed up in the phrase "the brain drain"; the attempts by development actors to engage African diasporas in their development activities; and the consequences of the protracted displacement of refugees on development progress. The conclusion draws attention to an inherent contradiction in many contemporary discussions about the links between migration and development. On the one hand, migration and the contribution of migrants are being feted for offering new avenues to achieve the elusive goal of development in sub-Saharan Africa. On the other hand, these mainstream conceptions of development, to which they are expected to contribute, have deeply embedded within them sedentary assumptions that cast migration as a symptom of development failure.

It is important to note that although the focus of this chapter is on sub-Saharan Africa, migration patterns cross regional and even continental boundaries. For instance, despite the portrayal of the Sahara as a natural border that separates North Africa from the rest of the continent, the desert has long been crossed by well-established migratory routes. The use of such routes has ebbed and flowed over the decades, but the settlement of sub-Saharan Africans in North Africa is not a new phenomenon. The history of trans-Saharan migration is particularly important to bear in mind in the face of growing European unease about transit migration, which tends to stem from an assumption that all those moving north across the Sahara are migrants en route to Europe.

African Mobility

Africa has long been portrayed as a continent of people on the move (de Bruijn et al., 2001). The myths of origin of many ethnic groups draw on narratives of great migrations—for example, the Bantu expansion of movement from Central Africa, the Hamitic myth of migration from north to south, and even the Voortrekkers' so-called Great Trek in South Africa. While some of these migrations may be little more than legends, they all serve an important function in the (mythic) construction of Africa and its people in the modern world (Bilger and Kraler, 2005).

Across Africa, migration has always played an important role in sustaining and expanding people's livelihoods in many different ways (de Haan, 1999). These include expansion into new areas to gain access to natural resources, such as land, minerals, water, game, and fish; the conquest of neighboring groups to capture both their goods and their labor, either directly through slavery or indirectly through the payment of tribute; and the expansion of networks to gain access to new markets for both goods and labor. Migration has also been driven by conflicts at different levels, ranging from family disputes to wars.

From the early days of their encounters with African populations, European powers sought to control this mobility. Once the brutal transatlantic slave trade had been abandoned, they turned their attention to controlling the movement of Africans within the continent to ensure that labor was available to serve their colonial endeavors. They introduced measures such as forced labor, little removed from slavery, which was practiced in Portuguese colonies until the middle of the twentieth century (Henderson, 1978); the imposition of hut and poll taxes; the expropriation of the best land for settler agriculture; and the provision of services to attract wage laborers. Such policies drew Africans into the cash economy as wage laborers in the mines of southern Africa; in the rubber, cocoa, coffee, and tea plantations of East, Central, and West Africa; and in the colonial administration via armies and police forces across the continent. Thus they stimulated the large-scale movement of people across Africa. Most notably, in West Africa, the colonial period saw widespread labor migration from Benin, Niger, Mali, and Togo to the plantations and mines of Ghana, Nigeria, and Côte d'Ivoire (Schuerkens, 2003). In southern Africa, the mines of South Africa and the Zambian (then Northern Rhodesian) Copperbelt drew in hundreds of thousands of laborers from across the region. These colonial policies established patterns of migration that continue to this day. For example, in South Africa, the recruitment of young men on short-term contracts from Mozambique, Botswana, Lesotho, Swaziland, and Malawi to work in the gold and diamond mines was highly organized. During the apartheid years, "immigration policy was a naked instrument of racial domination"; but, despite attempts to reduce dependence on foreign mine workers since 1994, recruitment has continued at increasing levels (Crush, 2003).

The international borders that divide mainland Africa into 48 separate states are another legacy of the colonial period that has had a profound influence on migration across the continent. Most of these were agreed by European powers in the late nineteenth century. These colonial lines on the map paid little respect to language and cultural boundaries, cutting across traditional chieftainships and separating kinsfolk. Many run over huge distances in very remote areas. Formal crossing points are relatively rare; many of the borders are unmarked and can be crossed with no government control (Griffiths, 1996).

A number of authors have suggested that, lacking legitimacy or enforcement, these borders mean little in the day-to-day lives of African people and thus international migration in Africa should be treated as an informal extension of internal migration (Skeldon, 2006: 19; Adepoju, 2008a), or "cross-border" migration (Deshingkar and Natali, 2008: 180). Although there is certainly a case for breaking down the sharp distinctions between internal and international migration, the significance of African borders may be downplayed too often.[1] Skeldon may be right to claim that sub-Saharan Africa contains more borders imposed by colonial powers "without regard to underlying social and political realities" than does Asia (Skeldon, 2006: 19). However, his contention that the crossing of such borders should be treated as internal migration is less convincing. As he himself argues, when people cross borders, their rights, their relationship with the state, and even their self-identities change (Skeldon, 2006: 19). The colonial borders were created to mark territories for different institutional regimes, for taxation, social policies, military service, the language of education, and so forth. The Europeans defined their power by the territory they controlled, and the borders defined the extent of their authority. This immediately created incentives for Africans to cross to the more favorable side. For example, the introduction of taxes in Zambia by the British stimulated movement into neighboring Angola. The Portuguese practice of forced labor in Angola encouraged people to move the other way into Zambia (Pritchett, 1990; von Oppen, 1995). Crossing borders has also meant finding protection from war for many thousands of refugees across Africa. Hence the establishment of these international borders introduced a new set of constraints and opportunities that have become an important part of African peoples' lives, whether they cross to avoid taxation and violence, gain protection, or find jobs, markets, education, and health care (Nugent and Asiwaju, 1996; Miles, 2005).

A third legacy of the colonial intervention in Africa is a concept of development that is inherently "sedentary" (Bakewell, 2008a). As noted earlier, the functioning (and profitability) of the colonial state required that people move to work. At the same time, the colonial authorities took great care to ensure that these migrants did not settle permanently in the new urban centers (Rakodi, 1997a). Migrant laborers were expected to retain links with their homelands; ideally, when they finished their contract or retired, they would return to the village to make way for new laborers. In order to encourage this circular migration, the colonial authorities encouraged African labor migrants to maintain their village homes and traditional ways of life. In many areas, these were assumed to be largely sedentary, based around stable villages in fixed locations populated by particular (static) tribes. Such views were embedded in the work of structural-functionalist anthropologists. Migration featured very little in their conservative analysis, which portrayed many African societies as homogeneous, largely unchanging, and isolated from other groups (Evans-Pritchard, 1940; Radcliffe-Brown, 1952). Moreover, the colonial systems for the collection of taxes, the imposition of colonial law, and the provision of government services all relied on the knowledge of people's whereabouts. Mobility left the Europeans confused. As James Ferguson remarks,

> colonial rulers were dismayed at the high mobility exhibited by villagers in Northern Province [of Zambia] and could not understand why people did not stay put in "proper villages." They were sure that such behaviour was not "traditional" but the result of recent pathology brought on by industrial development and the "migrant-labour system." Small temporary villages, with people moving about in an undisciplined manner between them, they felt sure, were a sign of the "breakdown" of traditional institutions, a breakdown that government policy would have to check if "detribalization" was to be avoided. (1999: 39)

This concern over migration came to be fixed in the foundations of social and economic development thinking across Africa. Out-migration from rural areas was widely seen as creating economic and social problems, from the decline in agricultural production to the erosion of rural societies. Although the practice of sending remittances from urban areas back to the villages was widespread, these were thought to be used for consumption rather than investment and tended to increase inequality within rural communities (Lipton, 1980). In urban areas, unplanned in-migration was seen as overwhelming the embryonic urban structures and creating enormous social pressures (Rakodi, 1997a).

As African states gained their independence in the second half of the twentieth century, this analysis remained largely unchanged. The new governments dropped many of the colonial restrictions on urban settlement and pursued policies of industrialization and modernization focused on the cities (Rakodi, 1997b), but they were still anxious to control migration. Many development aid programs focused on the improvement of rural areas, which was seen as essential to encourage people to stay in the villages rather than try their luck in the ever-growing cities. There were massive government investments in rural development programs, agricultural extension, and rural infrastructure (such as roads, water supply, health facilities, and schools). Policies such as Tanzania's so-called villagization "arguably reinforced a mindset amongst policy makers that development was best promoted through interventions in rural areas that would reduce the need for migration" (Black et al., 2004: 27).

Such policies have had very limited impact on rural migration; urbanization across Africa has increased regardless (Rakodi, 1997c). Development in the forms of improved incomes, education, and infrastructure has tended to be associated with higher levels of mobility. It may change the conditions of migration (for example, by reducing transport costs) and enable different people to move (as income levels increase, migration becomes a more affordable option), but it does not reduce the scale of migration (de Haan, 1999: 20). Despite this insight, gained over many years, the belief that development progress will be marked by reduced migration—whether rural-urban migration or African-European—is deeply embedded in contemporary approaches to development by donors and African states. Both the European Commission and the African Union have claimed that poverty is the main cause of migration and that creating development opportunities and jobs in Africa will serve to reduce the flow of migrants from the continent:

> Turning to the migration and development agenda, the prime challenge is to tackle the main push factors for migration: poverty and the lack of job opportunities. The EU must recognize that creating jobs in developing countries could significantly reduce migratory pressure from Africa. (CEC, 2006a: 5)

> Migration can be an effective tool for development. . . . However, poverty is one of the main causes of migration. Creating development opportunities in countries of origin would mitigate the main reasons for young people to engage in migration. (African Union, 2006: 4)

Changing Patterns of African Migration

Having forged both the political boundaries of nation-states and an economic system based largely on primary production and resource extraction, colonialism has left an indelible mark on the political economy of sub-Saharan Africa. This is still clearly reflected in the postindependence patterns of migration. For example, the divisions between colonial powers have tended to channel movement within European, especially Anglophone and Francophone, language zones. There have been large population exchanges between Ghana and Nigeria, and many migrants have circulated within the East African Community of Kenya, Uganda, and Tanzania. Francophone migrants have tended to move within Francophone West and central Africa. Nevertheless, such colonial patterns of migration have been reshaped by local, regional, and global shifts in political and economic conditions in the decades since African states gained their independence. In this section, I pick out a few examples to illustrate these changes.

Across the continent, newly independent governments adopted various strategies to enhance the processes of nation building. Many states focused on consolidating the loyalty of citizens to the state via, for example, the philosophies of Ujamaa (African socialism) in Tanzania or Harambee ("All Pull Together") in Kenya. By contrast, in West Africa, the relatively prosperous countries of Ghana and Côte d'Ivoire adopted a strong anticolonial ideology of pan-Africanism, which had a direct impact on migration. In the early years of independence, both countries, especially the latter, welcomed immigrants to work and stay (Anarfi and Kwankye, 2003). They attracted large numbers of people from countries such as Togo and Nigeria (who went mainly to Ghana), Burkina Faso and Guinea (who went mainly to Côte d'Ivoire), and Niger and Mali (who went to both).

However, this ideology was inevitably tempered by economic and political upheavals. In Ghana, a coup in 1966 was followed by increasing repression, a declining economy, and rising unemployment. The immigrant community in Ghana became a scapegoat for the deteriorating situation, and in 1969 the Ghanaian government enacted the Aliens Compliance Order, leading to a mass expulsion of an estimated 155,000 to 213,000 migrants working informally in the cocoa industry, predominantly Nigerians. Ghanaians also started emigrating in large numbers. An estimated 2 million Ghanaian workers left Ghana between 1974 and 1981, their primary destinations being Nigeria and Côte d'Ivoire. Skilled Ghanaians such as teachers, doctors, and administrators migrated to Nigeria, Uganda, Botswana, and Zambia. Since the mid-1980s, Ghanaians have increasingly migrated to a range of destinations in Europe and North America (Van Hear, 1998; Anarfi and Kwankye, 2003; Bump, 2006).

While migration to Côte d'Ivoire continued, oil-rich Nigeria took Ghana's place as West Africa's major migration pole when oil prices rose dramatically in 1973. However, misguided economic policies and a major decline in oil production and prices soon heralded a long period of economic downturn alongside sustained political repression. In 1983 and 1985, Nigeria followed the Ghanaian example and expelled an estimated 2 million low-skilled West African migrants, including more than a million Ghanaians (Arthur, 1991; Bump, 2006). As Ghana had done earlier, Nigeria transformed itself from a net immigration to a net emigration country (Black et al., 2004: 11), although many immigrants (in particular Beninois and Ghanaians) have remained. Toward the end of the 1990s, Côte d'Ivoire's position as West Africa's most important migration destination was reversed as it entered into a civil war and a deep economic crisis, creating a new population of refugees.

At the other end of the continent, the southern African labor migration system had been transformed by the end of apartheid in South Africa. Until 1994, the mines of South Africa drew in migrants from the labor reserve countries of the region, namely Lesotho and Mozambique, but migrants from further afield in Africa were few and far between. With the end of apartheid, the situation has changed dramatically, and over the last fifteen years South Africa has become a major pole for migrants from all over the continent (Crush, 2003).

In east, central, and southern Africa, conflict and violence have played a much larger role in shaping postcolonial migration. Beginning in the 1960s, prolonged liberation wars such as those in Algeria, Eritrea/Ethiopia, Angola, Zimbabwe, Mozambique, and Namibia, as well as civil wars such as those in Sudan and Somalia, forced millions of refugees to flee to neighboring countries (and millions more to become internally displaced persons) over generations. The end of the Cold War in the late 1980s helped bring some of the prolonged conflicts to an end, but during the 1990s new and brutal civil conflicts erupted in West Africa (namely Sierra Leone and Liberia), Rwanda, and the Democratic Republic of Congo, creating more refugees and internal displacement.

The plight of refugees in different regions of Africa has quite rightly been the subject of great concern and policy interest and has stimulated major aid interventions over many years. While highlighting the situation of refugees has been essential with respect to some parts of

Africa—in particular the Horn and East and central Africa (Oucho, 2006)—doing so has cast other forms of migration into the shadows. This focus on refugees epitomizes what can be called the "misery discourse" of migration in sub-Saharan Africa: "In this region, completely grounded in poverty, emigration pressure is compounded by demographic dynamics, unstable politics, endemic ethnoreligious conflicts, persistent economic decline, and environmental deterioration" (Adepoju, 2008b: 21). Such factors have always played an important role in shaping African migration. Farmers and pastoralists have been driven off land by falling yields and crop prices, erratic economic growth has failed to keep step with growing populations, and migration is a strategy widely employed to diversify income streams and reduce household risk (Stark and Levhari, 1982).

In order to understand the evolution of contemporary African migration, it is also necessary to recall the rapidly changing global context in which Africans are moving. Despite its weak position, Africa is embedded within the globalized political economy; hence African migration processes are driven by the same broad forces of globalization that shape migration in the rest of the world. As a result, patterns of African migration share many features with those of the rest of the world in that they are becoming more complex, involving a wider range of people moving to more destinations over longer distances. Like the rest of the world, the real costs of travel in Africa have decreased with the slow expansion of road networks and air routes. Although air travel remains the most exclusive form of transport, fares have come down and it is more affordable for more people. This is helping to expand opportunities for ordinary people across Africa: for example, Ghanaian market traders are now moving between Accra and China (Awumbila et al., 2009).

Africa may lag behind the rest of the world in access to new information technologies, but the latter are still having a profound effect across the continent. Satellite television beaming images of life in other parts of the world can be found even in very remote areas of sub-Saharan Africa, expanding the horizons of potential migrants. Perhaps more important, mobile telephony penetration is growing rapidly, and with the development of community phone schemes, phones reach far beyond individual subscribers.[2] African migrants anywhere in the world are now able to maintain links with families, friends, and business contacts in their countries of origin relatively cheaply. This facilitates the development of sustained transnational relationships over long distances and many years.

Such factors are likely to have contributed to the marked feminization of migration in sub-Saharan Africa (Adepoju, 2006), albeit at a much slower pace than we have seen in parts of Asia (Yamanaka and Piper, 2005). According to empirical research by the Southern African Migration Project, the proportion of women, especially younger single women, among international migrants in the region was increasing in 2008, although a large majority was still male (Dodson et al., 2008).

The impact of globalization can also be seen in the diversification of destinations for African migrants (Zlotnik, 2006: 30). Table 7.1 shows estimates of stocks of migrants by region of origin in Africa and destinations across the world. It is important to note that a large majority—more than 70 percent—still remain within the continent (see also Sander and Maimbo, 2003; Ratha and Shaw, 2007). Even in West Africa, where migration to the industrialized countries is higher than elsewhere in sub-Saharan Africa, regional migration is still at least seven times greater (OECD, 2006). Thus, despite popular views of an invasion of sub-Saharan migrants into the EU, the actual numbers remain very limited compared to those of migrants from Eastern Europe and North Africa (de Haas, 2008).

Table 7.1 Origin and Destination of African Migrants by Continent (in thousands)

	Destination							
Origin	Europe	Western Asia	South and East Asia	Africa	Oceania	North America	Latin America and the Caribbean	Total
East Africa	1,032	231	100	3,091	63	350	11	4,878
Middle Africa	606	36	59	2,243	1	52	10	3,008
Northern Africa	4,367	2,229	172	1,007	45	326	19	8,165
Southern Africa	249	11	18	388	107	113	3	889
West Africa	996	99	168	6,452	6	398	16	8,136
Total	7,250	2,606	517	13,182	223	1,239	59	25,075

Source: Global Migrant Origin Database, v. 4, http://www.migrationdrc.org.

However, it should be no surprise that, with the rapid development of global social, economic, and technological networks, net migration from Africa to wealthier regions of the world has likely grown since 1990. European census data show that 14 percent of the foreign-born people living in the EU were from Africa, forming the second largest group of non-EU immigrants (Katseli et al., 2006). Italy, Spain, and Portugal have reported significant increases in migration from Africa. The overall trend for migration from Africa to the United States has also been upward since the 1990s. The African-born population in the United States grew from 1 percent of the total US population in 1995 to 3 percent in 2005—a four-fold increase in absolute numbers from 270,000 in 1995 to 1.1 million in 2005.[3] Today African migration represents a small but growing segment of the overall migration picture in the United States.[4]

Changes in the global political economy are not only driving increases but also decreases in African migration. As the economy across the world moves into recession and resource prices plummet, the demand for African migrant workers will shrink, both within the continent and beyond. For example, there have been large-scale layoffs in the Zambian Copperbelt; similar retrenchment in the past has led to the return of large numbers of workers to rural areas (Ferguson, 1999; Potts, 2005). The tightening of job markets in Europe, North America, and Asia is likely to reduce the already limited employment opportunities for African graduates in the global labor market. Furthermore, widespread concerns about terrorism across the world have resulted in migration being increasingly linked to security. In both Europe and Africa, national security is commonly cited as a rationale for imposing tighter immigration controls as governments erect ever stronger bureaucratic and physical barriers to limit movement.

The Relationship Between Migration and Development in Africa

This very brief survey of migration patterns illustrates that African migration is strongly related to processes of economic, social, and political change. Development progress may facilitate migration, for instance by providing new transport routes, but may also render it unnecessary by creating new livelihood opportunities in local areas. In very general terms, it is not the poorest people who migrate; wealthier countries have higher levels of out-migration than do the least developed.[5] This suggests that as countries increase their incomes, we may expect to see higher levels of mobility among their populations. In other words, increasing development is likely to be associated with increased migration.

Unfortunately, to date, the levels of development in much of sub-Saharan Africa remain very low. By almost every development indicator, sub-Saharan Africa remains the least developed region of the world. Of the forty-one states in mainland sub-Saharan Africa, twenty-nine are categorized as least developed countries by the United Nations (UN), and thirty are low-income countries according to the World Bank. Sub-Saharan African countries take thirty-one of the bottom thirty-three places in the ranking for the Human Development Index, which is calculated on the basis of income, literacy, and life expectancy (UNDP, 2009). Moreover, it is in sub-Saharan Africa that the least progress has been made toward meeting the Millennium Development Goals (MDGs). Despite countless development interventions in the region absorbing billions of dollars since the middle of the twentieth century, it seems little has been achieved. Indeed, the structural adjustment programs imposed by the International Monetary Fund across the continent in the 1980s, which drastically cut back state subsidies in an effort to introduce competition to stimulate developing economies, succeeded only in entrenching poverty and increasing inequality (Milanovic, 2007).

Given the consistent failure of conventional development programs in sub-Saharan Africa, the recent reassessment of the potential impact of migration on development has offered the tantalizing prospect of a new set of approaches. The turnaround in thinking was foreshadowed by Douglas Massey and his colleagues, who argued that the prevailing view of the impact of migration on economic development was "unduly pessimistic and harsh," based on inadequate theory and data (1998: 272). The World Bank's *Global Development Finance Report 2003* helped to propel the issue up the policy agenda by drawing attention to the massive growth in remittances (Ratha, 2003). As Devesh Kapur has somewhat ironically put it, remittances have become "the new development mantra" (2004).

There is a vast and rapidly growing literature on the links between migration and development (Sørensen et al., 2002; Chamie and Dall'Oglio, 2008; Castles and Delgado Wise, 2008; Naik et al., 2008). Much of the empirical research is based on cases of migration from poorer to wealthier regions of the world, especially Mexico-US migration. Research on the impacts of migration on development and poverty reduction within poor regions such as sub-Saharan Africa has only recently come to the fore (Black et al., 2006; Hujo and Piper, 2007;

Ratha and Shaw, 2007). The emerging literature shows that the specific nature of the relationship appears to be very complex and heterogeneous. As the broad debates are outlined in Chapter 6, my discussion is focused on four themes that are particularly pertinent in the context of sub-Saharan Africa: the impact of migration on income and inequality and the contribution of remittances; the impact on human capital formation, particularly the brain drain; the engagement of the African diaspora in development; and the consequences of protracted displacement on development progress.

Income, Inequality, and Remittances

There are some indications that the extent to which migration enables migrants and their families to improve their livelihoods depends critically on whether or not they stay within the continent. In general, migration within the continent is less remunerative. For instance, studies conducted in Burkina Faso (Hampshire, 2002; Wouterse, 2006) suggest that internal and international migration within the African continent should primarily be seen as means to enhance livelihood security through income diversification and that welfare gains are relatively small. It was mainly migration to Europe that allowed households to accumulate substantially more wealth and stabilize incomes.

It is also important to bear in mind that regional migration is generally less costly and therefore more accessible for the relatively poor than is intercontinental migration. It is therefore not surprising to find that migration to Europe also tends to exacerbate household inequalities, whereas regional migration is associated with a reduction in inequality (Wouterse, 2008). The latter may not enable households to diversify income and spread risks as widely as can longer-distance migration, but even modest income increases can make a huge difference to their livelihoods and substantially reduce poverty levels. In short, it is possible that intra-African migration may have a much greater positive impact on poor communities.

The major mechanism by which migration enhances household incomes is through remittances. According to the most recent estimates posted by the World Bank at the time of writing, migrants' remittances to sub-Saharan Africa through official sources totaled US$21 billion in 2008, having more than doubled since 2005.[6] Whether these numbers are a reflection of real increases in remittance flows or simply improved reporting is not clear.[7] In any case, the actual flow of remittances is likely to be much higher, as many transfers are made informally. For example, the World Bank data suggest that remittances to Ghana were on the order of US$100 million in 2006, whereas Ghana's president, John Kuofor, was reported as claiming they were about US$4 billion (Ratha and Shaw, 2007). The data on the scale or direction of remittances transferred by migrants within Africa are even less reliable. In general, formal channels for sending remittances within the continent are more expensive and harder to access than those for doing so from Europe to Africa. For migrants moving between neighboring countries, reliance on informal channels and the personal delivery of cash and goods is likely to be much easier (Ratha and Shaw, 2007).

That said, recorded remittances in sub-Saharan Africa do appear to be rising more slowly than those in other regions and remain less than official forms of development aid in many countries. They do make a vital contribution to the balance of payments and, of course, to recipient households and communities (Sander and Maimbo, 2003). The highest rates of dependence are found in smaller states, where remittances represent a very significant portion of gross domestic product (GDP): examples include Lesotho (24.5 percent), The Gambia (12.5 percent), and Cape Verde (12.0 percent) (Ratha and Xu, 2008). However, they tend to be highly concentrated in other countries as well. According to the World Bank estimates, remittances to Nigeria account for over half of the recorded remittances to Africa, and 80 percent of total remittances are sent to just six countries (Nigeria, Sudan, Kenya, Senegal, Uganda, and South Africa). Granted, such figures must be treated with caution. If remittances to Ghana did indeed reach US$4 billion in 2006, it would place Ghana second only to Nigeria in the league table of remittance-receiving nations in sub-Saharan Africa.

The debate about the extent to which remittances actually contribute to development is ongoing in Africa, as it is in the rest of the world. This debate is reflected clearly in the discussions in other chapters in this section of the volume. Research from sub-Saharan Africa remains limited (Montclos, 2005; Azam and Gubert, 2006), and the conclusions may reflect particular understandings of development as much as the findings of empirical research. For example, studies of remittances sent by intra-regional migrants from five countries of southern Africa (Botswana, Lesotho, Mozambique, Swaziland, and Zimbabwe) have shown that the vast majority of migrant-sending households receive remittances, mostly in the form of cash, from both male and female migrants (Pendleton et al., 2006; Dodson et al., 2008). A large portion of these remittances are spent on food and there is very little evidence of their being invested in income-generating activities. As Wade Pendleton and his colleagues conclude:

> Clearly migration and poverty are closely related in this region. The migrant-sending households of Southern Africa are generally poor although the degree of poverty does vary. Migration is a livelihood strategy of the poor. Remittances in cash and kind keep poverty at bay but they do not do much else. There is very little evidence, as yet, that remittances in Southern Africa have developmental value, as conventionally defined. Equally, they are critical for poverty alleviation in many households. (2006: 40)

A significant reduction in poverty through remittances does represent a very real improvement in people's well-being. Hence, while these remittances may not have developmental value "as conventionally defined," they do enable people to achieve a better quality of life than they might manage without them. Whether or not they contribute to development depends on one's concept of development.

Human Capital Formation

Although relatively few African migrants leave the continent, those who do travel to Europe and North America include a high proportion of people with tertiary education. Africa is the main sending region of highly skilled migrants to Europe (13.5 percent of all highly skilled foreigners living in the EU are African). In general, the United States attracts more highly skilled migrants than does Europe, including those from Africa (data from Katseli et al., 2006). Migrants of African origin are the best-educated foreigners in the United States, showing higher rates of high school completion (95 percent) than any other immigrant group (Schmidley, 2001: 37).

Due in part to the predominance of highly educated people among African migrants, migration has come to be seen as a major development issue for the continent. Such figures demonstrate the so-called brain drain that deprives many African states of their few highly skilled personnel. In both Ghana and Mozambique, for example, the emigration rate for people with tertiary education is over 40 percent (Ratha and Xu, 2008). These people are commanding large incomes relative to those available in their countries of origin, and they are generating significant flows of remittances. The extent to which their financial contribution outweighs the cost of their training and the loss of their skills has long been at the center of the migration and development debates.

There has been particular concern about the exodus of trained doctors and nurses from various countries in sub-Saharan Africa. In Ghana, one of the worst affected countries, more than half the doctors and a quarter of nurses trained in the country emigrate, according to some estimates (Ratha and Xu, 2008). The exit of health professionals has widely been held responsible for the shortage of trained staff in many clinics across Africa, especially in rural areas. However, recent studies suggest that the evidence to support this causal link is quite limited. Instead, they argue that the parlous condition of the health sector is caused by other issues, such as lack of investment and poor governance. The emigration of staff is a reflection of the very poor working conditions and lack of professional opportunities within the domestic health sector. Moreover, there is little evidence to suggest that even if health workers did remain in Africa, they would actually take up posts in rural areas to meet health needs there (Clemens, 2007; OECD, 2007c).

Engaging the African Diaspora in Development

The recognition of ongoing transnational linkages between migrants (and their descendants) and their countries of origin has spurred a growing interest in the role of diasporas in development, as indicated by Skeldon in the previous chapter. From the perspective of African states, not only do diaspora communities provide resources to their countries of origin in terms of both finance and skills, but they can also be portrayed as members of the nation in a way that is impossible for other donors. Both official and nongovernmental organization (NGO) donors in Europe can communicate with African communities through their migrants, whose knowledge of the language and culture gives them an inside track to understanding development priorities and allows them to bypass or challenge the corrupt institutions of African states. African diasporas are now seen by some as "a potentially exploitable if underdeveloped resource" (Davies, 2007: 64).

Thus, there are increasing efforts in both Africa and Europe to facilitate different ways for diasporas to engage in the mainstream practice of development. Major development NGOs and European development ministries such as the UK Department for International Development and the Dutch Ministry of Foreign Affairs have been looking for ways to collaborate with diaspora organizations through funding and capacity-building initiatives (de Haas, 2006). Maintaining or reestablishing contact with the diaspora has also become an important policy concern for many African governments. For example, in 2001, Ghana changed its citizenship law to allow dual nationality (Akyeampong, 2006: 303). It is also considering introducing a special status for the African-American diasporas to enable them to buy property and invest in the country.

There have also been various schemes to harness the skills and expertise of migrants to support development. For example, the UK-based diaspora organization African Foundation for Development (AFFORD) has established a Diaspora Development Professionals Network with the aim of supporting Africans who are working in development organizations. There have also been multilateral programs to engage the diaspora in development initiatives (Ghosh, 2000). The United Nations Development Programme (UNDP) program for the Transfer of Knowledge Through Expatriate Nationals (TOKTEN), established in 1976, has operated in various African countries with the aim of mitigating the effects of brain drain by assigning migrants with appropriate expertise for short-term consultancies in their countries of origin. In 2001, the International Organization for Migration (IOM) established Migration for Development in Africa (MIDA) as a "capacity-building program, which helps to mobilize competencies acquired by African nationals abroad for the benefit of Africa's development."[8] However, these efforts by development circles to engage African migrants appear to make few concessions to the long-standing practices of so-called hometown associations and other diaspora organizations. These have been providing informal support to their areas of origin for generations (Lampert, 2009; Mazzucato and Kabki, 2009). Such associations are taken seriously only with respect to the potential impact of their political engagement in countries of origin, especially in conflict and postconflict situations, as we shall see (Montclos, 2005; Mohan, 2008).

What is almost completely missing from this picture is any consideration of the African diasporas within Africa, which are likely to include a much larger number of people. The growing body of research and policy initiatives regarding the role of diasporas in the development of Africa is almost exclusively concerned with Africans living beyond the continent (Henry and Mohan, 2003; Sørensen, 2007). As Nauja Kleist points out, in the case of Somalia, "the 'diaspora' refers to Somalis living in the West and the Gulf states and not, it seems, to the hundred thousands of Somali refugees in neighboring countries" (Kleist, 2007: 119). There is virtually no interest in the potential contribution of, say, Congolese living in Nigeria (Bakewell, 2008b).

Protracted Displacement

Finally, we turn briefly to consider the impact of the prolonged displacement of people by conflict on development in sub-Saharan Africa. About 20 percent of the migrants in Africa are refugees; many more people have been internally displaced. Many in these groups have been in exile for long periods, and there is increasing concern about the impact of such protracted displacement on their identities and livelihoods, as well as on the security and stability of the source and host countries. Protracted refugee populations constitute over 70 percent of the world's refugees (Crisp, 2003; UNHCR, 2008). The long-term presence of refugee populations in much of the developing world has come to be seen by many host states as a source of insecurity. In response, they have enacted policies of containment by placing refugees in isolated and insecure camps, preventing the arrival of additional refugees, and, in extreme cases, engaging in forcible repatriation (Loescher and Milner, 2005).

The human consequences of this protracted displacement in Africa include material deprivation, psychosocial and gender issues, social tension, and violence. To cope with their situation, displaced persons resort to various survival strategies, often with adverse consequences for themselves and their hosts; examples include sexual exploitation, exploitative employment, illegal and unsustainable farming, the manipulation and maximization of humanitarian aid, negative coping mechanisms such as theft and substance abuse, reliance upon remittances, and migration (Crisp, 2003).

It is clear that such circumstances are inimical to development. However, it is important to consider forced migrants in a wider context beyond that of humanitarian responses. Refugees are often enmeshed in transnational livelihoods, which may span their countries of origin, multiple African countries of first asylum, and resettlement countries, mainly in Europe, North America, and Australasia. For example, Somalis in the camps of northern Kenya are in close contact with the large and economically active Somali community in Nairobi as well as relatives and friends in Europe, the United States, the Gulf, and Somalia itself (Horst, 2006; Kleist, 2007, 2008; Lindley, 2007). This dense network can provide Somalis with the crucial and to some extent autonomous support that lies largely beyond the power and control of aid agencies and even states. Whether this exercise of freedoms (or at least subversion of unfreedoms) and capabilities in the face of incredible constraints contributes to development may be open to question. However, without it, the situation for many Somalis would likely be considerably worse.

Conclusion

There are many other facets to the relationship between migration and development in sub-Saharan Africa that are not explicitly covered here, such as the transfer of social remittances (Levitt, 1999). However, while

I do not claim it to be comprehensive, I believe the foregoing discussion illustrates some of the contradictions running through the current discourse on migration and development. As I have outlined, there has been a dramatic shift in the analysis of the potential contributions of migration to development in sub-Saharan Africa; there has also been a fundamental reappraisal of the evidence on remittances and the brain drain, which has resulted in a much more positive assessment than the one criticized by Massey and his colleagues (1998).

African migrants are increasingly being regarded as agents of development who may be harnessed to pull the new development bandwagon. However, what is rarely considered is the path on which this wagon is rolling. While migration and migrants are being celebrated for their contribution to development, many policymakers still seem to be concerned with enabling people to stay at home. Activities that do not reflect their initiatives are often marginalized. For instance, the autonomous activities of diaspora hometown associations tend to be regarded as unprofessional. The contributions of migrants living outside the centers of the development industry in Europe are largely ignored. The remittances of regional migrants in southern Africa are seen as merely reducing poverty rather than contributing to development. Moreover, forced migrants who have been effectively trapped in refugee camps and who develop their own diaspora networks of support are seen as a potential threat to security.

Rooted in its colonial origins, the discourse of development in Africa remains resolutely sedentary. It is largely concerned with enabling people to establish better lives where they are. Mobility still confuses the picture. Most development initiatives are framed around interventions in particular geographical locations. The assessment of development progress is based on measurements within national boundaries. The emigration of people is still seen as a symptom of development failure (Bakewell, 2008a). Studies of the colonial and more recent past suggest that attempts to use development policy as a lever to control migration are likely to fail. The attempt to use migration as a policy lever to stimulate development seems equally problematic insofar as the prevailing development paradigm fails to account for people's aspirations, which may well entail increased mobility. In the context of sub-Saharan Africa, the virtuous circle—whereby migration from the region stimulates development processes (through remittances, other transfers, and return migration), resulting in reduced migration—seems likely to remain a chimera. Unfortunately, it appears to be on such a fantasy that many of the current policies on migration and development in Africa are based.

Notes

1. Discussions of the international migration of Africans usually focus on its intercontinental aspects, largely dismissing the implications of intracontinental mobility. A different logic seems to apply elsewhere. Intra-European borders, for instance, are becoming ever more porous, especially in the expanding Schengen zone, but no one suggests that migration between European states is not really international.

2. The International Telecommunications Union (2008) estimates that mobile phone signal coverage reached 40 percent of the population in rural areas of sub-Saharan Africa in 2006.

3. MPI Data Hub, http://www.migrationinformation.org/datahub/index.cfm.

4. Data from the *Yearbook of Immigration Statistics 2005*, http://www.uscis.gov.

5. For example, the emigration rate as a percentage of population is approximately 2.1 percent for low-income countries, compared to 3.6 percent for high-income countries. Based on data from the Global Migrant Origin Database v. 4, updated March 2007, http://www.migrationdrc.org; World Population Prospects 1950–2050 Database, 2006 Revision, Department of Economic and Social Affairs, UN Population Division, New York.

6. World Bank Remittance Data November 2009, http://siteresources.worldbank.org.

7. The World Bank's own *Migration and Remittances Factbook 2008* (Ratha and Xu, 2008) estimated 2007 remittances to sub-Saharan Africa to be US$11 billion, but subsequent revisions have pushed the figure upward.

8. IOM Migration for Development in Africa (MIDA): http://www.iom.int (accessed April 14, 2009).

8

Migration and Development in Asia

Ken Young

Asia is home to more than 60 percent of the world's human population. Its nations exhibit the full spectrum of economic development, extending from postindustrial Japan to impoverished Bangladesh. Economic growth in Asia has for some time been more rapid and sustained than in most of the rest of the world. The economic transformation of China, India, and a number of other large Asian countries has raised the living standards of hundreds of millions of people. These and related economic developments are remaking the entire world economy (Yusuf et al., 2007). Clearly connected to Asia's economic expansion have been patterns of similarly sustained and growing international migration.

According to census data in 2000, in the preceding two decades China and India between them had sent more than 4 million migrants to wealthy countries in other parts of Asia and the rest of the world (OECD, 2007a: 44–45). The rapid urbanization and industrialization taking place in Asia have stimulated the internal movement of hundreds of millions of people from the countryside to the cities in countries like China, India, and Indonesia. The sustained but smaller cross-border flows of emigrants from these countries to other parts of Asia and beyond, while still impressive in scale, are not primarily responses to these domestic developments, but rather capitalize on fairly specific opportunities in certain sectors of the economies of the receiving countries. Although this chapter will show that migration has played an important part in the broader processes of social transformation in Asia, its significance can only be assessed in terms of its differentiated contribution in a limited number of sectors. Contemporary migration has developed in relatively novel ways; it differs from that of earlier periods in, for example, its high proportion of female migrants and the predominant reliance on contract labor among the unskilled.

In the 1990s and 2000s, international migration, both legal and illegal, has been largely directed toward cities, especially the wealthier global cities of Asia and the West. A proportion of migrants go elsewhere, and a minority, like the Indonesian plantation workers in East Malaysia, works in agriculture. Unskilled migration is predominantly circular, flowing toward particular Asian cities; it originates in a limited number of source regions, many of which are rural. These source regions have come to depend, for a variety of structural and historical reasons, on income from impermanent migration, especially limited-term contract migration.

The role of states in regulating migration is at best ambiguous. It also varies considerably across Asia, reflecting, among other things, differences in state structures and the means and objectives of government intervention. The provision of migrant labor is generally seen by governments to work quite advantageously on a bilateral level, yet it can be a source of popular discontent in both sending and receiving countries. One of the major economic aspects of contemporary international migration is the importance of remittances to workers, home communities, and those who profit from the exchange of workers in the migration industry. These remittances are on a very large scale. They are also vitally important to certain Asian states and provincial governments, a number of which have become financially dependent on the continued repatriation of money earned by migrants. There are marked differences in the treatment of unskilled contract workers and skilled and professional migrants, as Harald Bauder noted in Chapter 3. The latter are generally highly valued and move much more freely internationally. States are much more active in regulating the movement of semiskilled and unskilled migrants. Yet their controls are clearly imperfect, since the numbers of undocumented workers are estimated to exceed those of legal migrant workers.

To understand the varied and variable role that migration plays in development strategies in Asia, one must begin with a sketch of the types, sources, and destinations of migrant movements.

Varieties of Migration in Asia

Legal cross-border migrants in the contemporary era can broadly be classified in six major groups: professional and skilled workers; semiskilled and unskilled workers; students; entrepreneurial migrants; illegal migrants (including trafficked persons); and refugees. The sending and receiving countries of Asia vary considerably. A number of Asian nations are, by any measure, already developed—Japan, South Korea, Taiwan, Singapore, Hong Kong, and tiny, oil-rich Brunei—and these have been the main destinations for wage earners and other categories of migrants. The receiving countries are not only wealthier and more developed but also often face labor shortages. In part this is because, having made the development transition, they have experienced sustained declines in fertility. Korea and Taiwan were countries of emigration from the end of World War II until the late 1960s, but, along with other industrialized Asian nations, they moved rapidly to a pattern of low fertility beginning in the 1970s.

The source countries for migration within and beyond Asia have generally been the poorer nations: in East Asia, mainly China; in South Asia, India, Pakistan, Bangladesh, Sri Lanka, and Nepal; and in Southeast Asia, the Philippines, Thailand, Indonesia, Malaysia, Vietnam, Myanmar, Cambodia, and Laos. A number of countries have experienced simultaneous emigration and immigration, the two most important cases in Southeast Asia being Malaysia and Thailand; for instance, Thai workers go to Singapore and Taiwan, and Burmese, Khmer, and Lao migrants move to Thailand.

Most of the semiskilled and unskilled varieties of legal migration involve the supply of workers on a nonpermanent basis. In important respects they are an ideal "reserve army of labor." Workers who cross borders are subject to higher levels of control than are citizens. Numerous issues arise with respect to industrial and personal rights, social service entitlements, visa conditions, access of family members, and so on, mostly to the detriment of workers. Contemporary patterns of migration are achieved through mechanisms that limit the risk of claims to the provision of health, education, and housing. They generally exclude prospects of settlement or citizenship.

Statistics on legal international migration are available both from official national sources and international agencies. The data from official sources are inconsistent and too often of questionable reliability. They do not include undocumented migrants, whose numbers are widely estimated to be at least as large as legal migrants. Transborder migrations are generally of a lesser magnitude than internal population movements, which are principally from villages to urban areas. Intra-Asian migration has grown strongly as an aspect of the growing economic integration of the region underway since the 1970s, which accelerated significantly from the late 1980s onward. In the early post-World War II period, certain extra-Asian destinations had been much more important.

The major destinations beyond Asia have been the traditional countries of immigration in North America, Australasia, Europe, and the Middle East. In the 1970s, the Middle East was a major destination for semi-skilled and unskilled labor from Asia, though that region's relative importance as a destination has declined to some extent. Moreover, any account of major source countries like India, the Philippines, and China that does not address the expanding importance of the movement of professionals and highly skilled migrants is seriously lacking. In this case, the flow of migrants to the United States stands out, though it is also important in most of the Organization for Economic Cooperation and Development (OECD) countries, including those within Asia.

Asian Brain Drain? Professionals and Highly Skilled Workers

There is a worldwide shortage of skilled and highly qualified workers, and the situation is unlikely to improve for some time. The apparently limitless pool of labor in China, for example, has reached the point where the relentlessly expanding demand for skilled labor has stimulated higher wages (Maxton, 2007; *Economist*, 2008). There is a shortage of technical skills across Asia generally, and labor turnover rates are increasing (*Economist*, 2007a).

There are variations between economic sectors and professional fields, but the expanding demand for skilled workers and professionals has contributed to a significant loosening of restraints on their movement internationally. The migratory patterns of these workers are footloose, contrasting with both the traditional patterns of migration for permanent settlement and the circular patterns of unskilled contract workers. Some international movements, of doctors and lawyers for example, may be determined primarily by individual career choices. The movements in other professional groups may more strongly reflect patterns of employment within large transnational corporations. In any case, skilled workers move relatively easily and relatively often, regardless of whether their migration reflects personal career choices or corporate decisionmaking (Xiang, 2004: 164–165; Lakha, 2005: 339). Like the nurses and doctors studied in 2007 by the OECD (2007a), their paths may span a number of countries; place of employment is rarely unambiguously permanent.[1]

Most skilled migrants move from poor to rich countries. More than half of these professionals come from Asia; in the 2000s, the greatest numbers came from India and China (OECD, 2007a: 44–45). Indeed, over the long term, India, China, and the Philippines have contributed the largest numbers of skilled and professional migrants. At the same time, there is a significant reverse flow from advanced economies back to the developing economies in Asia (Thuno, 2001). These returning migrants frequently move as part of the business strategy of their corporate employers. Again, patterns of movement vary, but, in addition to private decisions to migrate—such as might be made by a medical professional—the major motivations of migration tend to be transnational employment and education.

Education is perhaps the least obvious route for the migration of highly qualified people. Yet Asian students are more numerous than fully credentialed professionals. They often approach employment (and residency) with an advantage insofar as they have training and experience in the developed country where they completed their tertiary education (Khadria, 2001). In advanced postgraduate and technical fields, Asian postgraduate and postdoctoral students are quite disproportionately represented in leading universities, notably in the United States. In science and engineering, Asian candidates are the majority in the United States (Hugo, 2004: 89; *Economist*, 2007b: 21). The cost of overseas tertiary education is met in the majority of cases—even that of China (Hugo, 2004: 89–90)—by the students' families, adding to tendencies to regard their training as a private investment.

Recruitment by corporations (particularly transnational corporations) of students either in-country or overseas constitutes another transmission belt of highly skilled people out of Asian societies. Recruiting firms, host governments, and even societies as a whole generally view students and experienced professionals as assets, making positive contributions while exacerbating neither security threats nor welfare burdens. These skilled migrants are prepared to move multiple times rather than settle permanently (Xiang, 2004: 164–165; Lakha, 2005: 339), although family, cultural, and lifestyle considerations also influence their choices. They are also only barely affected by the punitive control mechanisms, legal constraints, and suspicions that confront the large numbers of semiskilled, unskilled, and illegal immigrants.

Historically, many skilled Asians migrated to the West (Skeldon, 1992: 35–37). Contentious arguments have been made that the skills of Indian and Chinese people are otherwise underutilized in their countries of origin (Khadria, 2001). Since the end of the twentieth century, there has been a trend toward return migration, with streams of highly qualified migrants coming home after successful careers elsewhere. A number of governments, such as those of Singapore, South Korea, and Taiwan, have created incentives for skilled members of their diasporas to bring their talents home (OECD, 2007a: 123; see also Low, Toh, and Soon, 1991; Zhang and Li, 2002; Battistella, 2004; Jayaram, 2004). Chinese and Indian firms are actively recruiting nationals living in the United States and elsewhere. Arguments about who gains and who loses on both the individual and social level are complex; assessment of this aspect of migration to, from, and within Asia is hampered by the inadequacy of reliable information on the nature, scale, and consequences of skilled migration (OECD, 2007a: 164).

To illustrate (rather than resolve) these issues, consider a contrast between information technology (IT) and medical professionals. The IT field perhaps presents globalization as its most enthusiastic advocates would like to portray it: capital, labor, skills, finance, information, and profits flow across borders with significant benefits for enterprising firms and individuals in developing countries as well as large productivity gains for firms and government departments in advanced economies. India is not alone in benefiting from these trends, but it stands out as a source of IT skills: "Indian IT firms will soon have a share of nearly 20% of their addressable market's value and almost 40% of its volume" (*Economist*, 2007c: 61–62). The downsides of the outsourced jobs involved are rationalized in familiar ways.

The spectacular growth of this lucrative service industry has been very important for the Indian economy as a whole, creating opportunities both for large numbers of talented professionals and for Indian investors. The industry has grown at close to 30 percent per annum since 2000. Its revenues, around US$50 billion, now contribute 5.4 percent to India's gross domestic product (GDP) (*Economist*, 2007c: 61; see also Guochu and Wenjun, 2002).[2] Reverse flows are no less important. These include the international migration of top Indian professionals to Silicon Valley start-ups and the movement of subsidiaries of already successful Indian IT firms—Tata Consultancy Services (TCS), Wipro, Infosys, and so on—to California and elsewhere. The best of these specialists are highly mobile, and their placement at any given time is more a function of market forces than long-term resettlement plans. The implications for development in India and for skilled Indian professionals—whether they stay or migrate—are surely, on balance, positive.

India is also a major source of medical professionals, including doctors and nurses. Some training institutes, such as those in the Philippines, train nurses with the expectation that they will work abroad on graduation. India, China, and the Philippines are major sources of medical professionals for wealthy countries in both Asia and the West (OECD, 2007a: ch. 2). Along with a wide range of other source countries in Africa, Oceania, Eastern Europe, Latin America, and the Caribbean, Asian countries have contributed a significant proportion of staff in the hospitals and clinics of OECD countries for several decades.

Though this hardly new phenomenon clearly benefits the receiving countries, whose health systems would be in crisis were it not for these migrants, its impact on the developing countries that see their scarce medical professionals leave, frequently for good, is far from clearly beneficial. The absolute number and percentage of foreign-trained doctors has increased significantly in most OECD countries since the 1980s, and "radical upward shifts in the immigration trends have occurred" as of 2005 (OECD, 2007a: 163). The loss of health professionals from the developing world to the wealthy countries of Asia and the West might be justified in terms of individual opportunities, yet health care expertise is obviously more than a private good. It is also a national and international public good. The World Health Organization (WHO) recently estimated that there is a global shortage of 4 million health workers (WHO, 2006a), and the most serious deficits are in developing countries.[3] Moreover, the origins of migration flows are typically heavily concentrated in particular subregions within large countries, so evaluations by country and in the aggregate potentially mask far more intense local impacts.

In general, the migration of professionals and skilled workers does expose at least two sources of tension, if not outright contradiction, between existing patterns of migration and national development priorities. The first is the tension between the rights of professional individuals, namely to mobility and to the development of the full potential of their talents, and their obligations to the home communities that supported them originally, especially if their skills are crucial for social and economic development. The second contradiction arises from the objectives of national development programs, which invariably aim to steer the placement of their most talented people in favor of an optimal contribution to development goals. Against that stands the reality that the deployment of these talents is significantly shaped by international market forces and not infrequently directed by the corporate strategies of transnational firms. The trajectories of many professionals are primarily responsive to these imperatives rather than to development objectives formulated by the state.

Of course, most states recognize this; thus begins the tale of how and why development plans take particular forms in the era of globalization. Where states are concerned, further intriguing contradictions develop, since the orientation of governments to unskilled migrants differs markedly from their treatment of skilled migrants. Sending states value the lucrative flows of remittances from their migrant workers, and receiving states solve targeted labor shortages in particular economic niches without bearing the responsibility of permanent new settlers. In current circumstances, the individual rights of professionals tend to win out. The rights of the unskilled are subject to both market and state imperatives.

Semiskilled and Unskilled Labor Migration

The outstanding features of legal, unskilled Asian migration in the present era are its size, its steady and sustained growth, the predominance of overseas contract workers (OCWs), and the extent of its feminization. There was a generalized acceleration of migration from the 1960s to the late 1970s. From then on, migration grew strongly within Asia itself, so that intra-Asian migration became much more significant than movements to (or from) other parts of the world. Industrialization and urbanization rapidly advanced in most large Asian countries, drawing surplus labor from the countryside. In the early stages of industrialization, labor-intensive industries created a strong demand for low-cost labor of relatively low skill levels. However, much of East Asia moved past this point, and its increasingly urban populations experienced many rapid social and cultural changes, among them a pattern of rapidly declining fertility levels (Castles and Miller, 2009: 74; Hugo, 2004). Following Japan and the so-called newly industrializing countries (NICs), other East and Southeast Asian countries have moved progressively along the same path; some have continued apace while others have faltered to some degree. South Asian countries have not been transformed at the same pace, although India has been gathering momentum on a high-growth path since the 1990s.

Asia therefore presents a mosaic rather than a simple, unified pattern of industrializing trajectories. However, the phases of urban industrial and economic growth in various regions were accompanied at each point by changing demands for labor in general and for certain types of labor in particular. In certain cases, like Taiwan, Singapore, and increasingly, Japan, economic, demographic, and societal transformations have directly stimulated international labor migration. Notably, these developed Asian countries are increasingly faced with aging populations; the attendant challenges already clearly confronting Japan are also likely to be posed in China in the twenty-first century. The nascent labor shortages appearing in China are most obvious among young, skilled workers (*Economist*, 2010: 46–48). The complex composition, quality, and nature of the migration flows stimulated by these multiple developmental trajectories depend on a range of factors. The most common is the flow of migrants from poor, labor-surplus regions into well-defined niches in the advanced regions of urban Asia where skills and labor cannot otherwise be adequately supplied. These movements lead to the tightly regulated provision of those workers who are willing to accept the least attractive and, often, most hazardous jobs of urban society. The numbers of international labor migrants are large, but they in no sense represent an undifferentiated wave of mass migration.

The great stimulus for migration out of Asia after the post–World War II recovery was a response—largely from South Asia but also from the Philippines, Indonesia, Thailand, and Korea—to rapid growth in the oil-producing states of the Gulf and Saudi Arabia that began with the Organization of Petroleum-exporting Countries (OPEC) oil crisis of 1973. By the early 1980s, the annual recruitment of workers to the Middle East ranged between 700,000 and 1 million. India and Pakistan were initially the main participants from South Asia, but Bangladeshi and Sri Lankan migration grew as well, with labor sources diversifying as the patterns of demand changed. India and Pakistan supplied 97 percent of Asian workers in 1975, but their share had declined by the 1990s to less than one-third, while the numbers from Southeast Asia grew to around 50 percent. The early period was one of mostly male migration, largely devoted to the construction sector (Hugo, 2004: 82), but from the 1980s onward there was a pronounced shift to the services sector, with a much higher participation of women workers (Castles and Miller, 2009: 133). Most of these women came from the Philippines, Indonesia, Sri Lanka, and Thailand.

The numbers going to Europe were relatively small; the largest number moving beyond Asia went to North America and Oceania, primarily to the United States. Moreover, by the mid-1990s, around 3 million migrants were resident in other parts of Asia, but an equal number had moved beyond Asia (Martin, Mason, and Nagayama, 1996: 163). By 2000, the number of migrants in Asia and elsewhere from India and China alone exceeded 3 million. Census data from around the year 2000 showed that around 2 million Chinese migrants and 2 million Indians were resident in OECD countries (OECD, 2007a: 44–45).

Very few countries in Asia seek or need to increase their population through immigration.[4] By far the most common pattern in the recent migration of workers—whether male or female, whether employed in industrial, construction, or service work (or occasionally in agriculture)—is that of engagement on a short- to medium-term contract, with limited visa entitlements and little labor market mobility. Most of these jobs provide low status, few industrial entitlements, and poor wages. Some workers take consecutive contracts and others do settle permanently, but in general the expectation is that they will return home once the contract is over. Therefore, many of the issues that have been bound up with migration in other times—those of settlement, labor and personal rights, health and social welfare, citizenship, cultural and religious diversity, family reunification, education, and housing—are not seriously addressed, since it is assumed that the worker will not stay. In extreme cases, the sequestration of the immigrant community can persist through generations, as might be seen in the difficult situation of Koreans in Japan (Okano and Tsuchiya, 1999; Lie, 2000; Sugimoto, 2003).

That, at least, is the situation where legal labor migration is concerned. It is important to remember that there are almost as many undocumented workers as there are officially sanctioned people moving across borders. Their situation is even more precarious than that of OCWs. In general, governments in the region have been slow to address issues of workers' rights. There are a number of reasons why this is so, including sensitivities in some countries to officially sanctioned issues of national identity. But the most consistent is that governments, employers, and broad elements of the public want to be reassured that foreign labor flows are well managed. The restricted legal entitlements of OCWs demonstrate this resolve (Lim and Oishi, 1996; Ball and Piper, 2006). By the end of the twentieth century, the networks of OCW migration had become extensive throughout Asia, with intra-Asian migration eclipsing the earlier movements to destinations like the Middle East. These trends have continued in the early years of the twenty-first century, the main new element being the increasing share of workers from China and India (OECD, 2007a).

Feminization

Legal, low-skilled male migration within Asia in the contemporary era tends to involve work in construction and, to a lesser extent, manufacturing, shipbuilding, and transportation. The early migrations of low-skilled Asian workers to the Middle East involved mainly males from South Asia. Thais and Filipinos later went to the Middle East in significant numbers, and large numbers of Filipinos have always worked in international shipping and maritime industries (Asis, 2005: 22).[5] Male workers going to other Asian destinations tended to be more specialized: Thai and Filipino construction workers go to Singapore (Kong, 2008), Thai factory workers to Taiwan (Loveband, 2006), and so on. Yet for most of the main Asian labor-exporting countries outside of South Asia, the outflow of workers since the mid-1970s has involved a growing and eventually dominant participation by women OCWs. Asian women are well represented in the Middle East, but women outnumber men in the flow of legal workers to the major intra-Asian destinations of Hong Kong, Taiwan, Japan, Singapore, and Malaysia (Amjad, 1996: 346–349; Asis, 2005: 24). These women migrate principally from the Philippines, Indonesia, Thailand, Sri Lanka, and Bangladesh.[6] As Mark Castles and Stephen Miller observe:

> Most migrant women are concentrated in jobs regarded as "typically female": domestic workers, entertainers (often a euphemism for prostitution), restaurant and hotel staff, assembly line workers in clothing and electronics. These jobs are low in pay, conditions, and status and are associated with patriarchal stereotypes of female characteristics, such as docility, obedience, and willingness to give personal service. (2009: 133)

Indeed, there are many notorious cases of mistreatment of vulnerable female workers both in the Middle East and in Asia, such as the hanging of Flor Contemplación in Singapore in 1995 (Hilsdon, 2000; Rahman et al., 2006; Robinson, 1991), but many of these migrants have achieved their economic and personal goals in spite of the risks involved in their contracts (Constable, 1997; Loveband, 2006). The women, particularly the Filipinas, are often well educated, and many have, through their communities and private networks, a good understanding of the foreign work environments they are entering. They are resourceful in successfully negotiating their interests despite asymmetric power relations that are otherwise very unpromising. It is difficult to judge whether their sacrifices are worth the income and the degrees of independence they may gain from working overseas, but it is a mistake to see them simply as passive victims (Parreñas, 2001, 2003; Battistela and Asis, 2003; Huang et al., 2005; Loveband, 2006). Their standing in their households and communities of origin may change too, but the extent to which it does is rarely straightforward. These women are increasingly better educated than those of earlier generations, and their shared communications outside the workplace have greatly improved, both at home and abroad. They are able to control their fertility and they contribute a reliable flow of cash income back home through the remittance of their earnings, which often gives them a crucial economic role in the household (Adams and Dickey, 2000). Migration unquestionably contributes to conditions that could undermine patriarchal dominance (Wolf, 1992; Hilsdon et al., 2000; Hirai, 2002).

Among the Asian middle classes, the increasing proportion of women studying abroad is another indication of the cultural change associated with both migration and development. Similar trends can be seen to arise from the opportunities open to women with skills, especially in health care. Perhaps more than any other country, the Philippines has come to depend on the export of labor and the reverse flow of remittances. Its profile, in terms of destination and occupational distribution, is different from other labor-exporting countries. Table 8.1 shows the percentage of women among the total number of Filipino workers on contract residing in the top ten destination countries in 2002. These figures demonstrate the extent to which female migration dominates contemporary OCW movements from the Philippines.

These workers' incomes are very important for their households, but their collective weight is such that their contracts are also strongly encouraged by their home governments. Before considering the aggre-

Table 8.1 Top Ten Destinations of Filipino OCWs, and Percentage of Females Among Them, 2002

	Country	Deployed Workers	Percentage of Female OCWs	Jobs Commonly Held by Filipina OCWs
1	Saudi Arabia	193,157	24	Domestic work, nursing, health work
2	Hong Kong	105,036	93	Domestic work
3	Japan	77,870	53	Entertainment
4	United Arab Emirates	50,796	56	Domestic work, service, sales
5	Taiwan	46,731	53	Domestic work, care giving, factory work
6	Singapore	27,648	72	Domestic work
7	Kuwait	25,894	74	Domestic work
8	Italy	20,034	63	Domestic work
9	United Kingdom	13,655	50	Nursing, other health work
10	Brunei	11,564	33	Domestic work

Source: Asis (2005: 25).

gate impact of their earnings and the considerable attention given to them by both governments and the private facilitators of the so-called migration industry, it is important once again to note that the migration statistics available to us only register the legal movement of workers. There is a flow of mostly unskilled workers on a scale equivalent to that of legal OCWs that also contributes, through less well-regulated financial channels, to many of the same international destinations.

Undocumented Workers, the "People Trade," and Refugees

Most of the illegal or undocumented migrants within Asia are unskilled and originate from a limited number of migration-intensive regions situated within the great labor reserves of South Asia, China, Indonesia, and the Philippines. A large proportion of South Asian undocumented workers go to North America, Europe, and Australasia rather than to other Asian destinations. In the case of Sri Lanka alone, estimates of those living overseas illegally are as many as 100,000. They are distributed over a number of OECD countries, with perhaps 10,000 in Japan and 20,000 in Italy (Skeldon, 2000: 379). The United States has attracted Chinese migrants for a long time—at least as far back as the Californian gold rushes of the nineteenth century—and Chinese migration to both North and South America is often underestimated (McKeown, 2004). In addition, undocumented Chinese migrants—perhaps as many as 100,000 per annum—move throughout Asia and ultimately find their way to Europe, South America, Russia, and Eastern Europe.

Still, the most significant destination outside of Asia is the United States. Contemporary illegal Chinese migration to the United States illustrates a number of the important features of Asian migration flows in general (Chin, 1999). Characteristically, they rely on personal networks and migration brokers. The movement of workers is tightly controlled within these networks; relatedly, source and destination locations tend to be geographically concentrated. The migrants come from a very limited number of places, and they move within their networks to very specific destinations where they have a degree of security but also heavy obligations to their patrons (Kwong, 1987, 1997). This is succinctly illustrated by Ronald Skeldon (2000: 379–380), who points out that the operation of these Chinese networks and syndicates returns US$100 million annually to the Changle district in Guangdong province alone (see also Castells, 1996; Smith, 1997).

Border controls in Japan and Korea are effective, but in much of the rest of Asia, national boundaries are far from impermeable. In certain zones of Southeast Asia in particular, borders are very porous, and people continue to move along ancient land and maritime routes that predate modern states and colonial boundaries (Asis, 2004; Scott, 2009). There is very significant illegal migration within Asia, where several million workers and their families reside undocumented outside their own countries.

Thailand, both a source and recipient of migration, provides a useful illustration. Burmese, Khmers, Lao, and minority tribal peoples from China live and work in Thailand, numbering close to 1 million. The most populous province in the northeast has a high proportion of people speaking Lao dialects. Most are citizens, but significant numbers are not (Kong, 2008). Many are simply economic migrants, though others, such as Kachin ethnic minorities and other Burmese political refugees, have fled into Thailand from the repressive military regime in Myanmar. Estimates in 1999 put the total number of legal and illegal migrants inside Thailand at 2 million (Srawooth, 2002: 14; Hewison, 2006: 93). At the same time, Thailand sends large numbers of workers abroad through both legal and illegal channels (Samarn, 2000). Thus, although a worker or entertainer in Taiwan, for example, may be considered Thai, his or her origins, ethnicity, and identity may well be far more complex.

Undocumented migration covers a very diverse range of human mobility. At one extreme, these journeys are confident and purposeful. But most migrants are taking risks, usually for economic gain, even along well-worn paths. This majority is managed, with significant profit, by agents, local officials, and others who profit from the migration industry. At the darkest edge, systematic profits are made from the trafficking of people across borders, especially with respect to the flourishing trade in women within and beyond Asia—a phenomenon explored by H. Richard Friman in Chapter 5 of this volume.[7] Many of the women are drawn from poor regions in Myanmar, China, Laos, the Philippines, and Thailand. Their destinations are usually Japan, Taiwan, Malaysia, the United States, and Australia, but they can travel further afield (Pimpawan et al., 2003). The favored destinations reflect the domination of these trafficking rackets by the Japanese yakuza and various Chinese triad societies (Murray, 1994; Seymour, 1996; Smith, 1997; Castells, 1998; Chin, 1999). Like the trade in drugs and other forms of smuggling (gemstones, oil, rainforest timber, and so on), the trafficking of people on a relatively large scale corrupts a spectrum of local institutions, particularly in the poorer source countries (Trocki, 1998). Local units of the military, bureaucracy, and law enforcement have been routinely involved in facilitating the trade (see Barker, 1998; Ryter, 1998; Siegel, 1998; Rafael, 1999). These systematic, if often localized, forms of collaboration between well-organized, illicit economic actors and powerful elements of the state—segments of the military in Thailand, Indonesia, and the Philippines, for example—clearly call into question the tendency of orthodox IPE scholars to largely restrict their focus to the analysis of formal markets and national-level development policies. In this context, one must stress again the arguments made by Friman about the necessity of recognizing and theorizing the intersection between formal, informal, and illicit economies in many parts of the world.

Finally, the contemporary period has been relatively free of political and natural disasters that stimulate refugee flows. Asia is rarely free of typhoons, tsunamis, earthquakes, floods, volcanic eruptions, and man-made disasters. From the 1980s until the early 1990s, Asia produced around two-thirds of the world's refugees, but the numbers declined to 5.12 million by 1995, contributing only 35 percent of the global total (Hugo, 2004: 78). Yet the Southeast Asian tsunami in 2004 and the calamities in Pakistan in the late 2000s—first earthquakes in the north, then the immense floods that devastated the populous Indus River Valley in late 2010—demonstrated how quickly natural disasters can occur and cause huge surges in the numbers of displaced persons and refugees.

Remittances, the State, and Development

The motivations of migrant workers are complex and variable. There is no doubt, however, that the opportunity to earn higher rates of pay more quickly than they otherwise might is a common impetus (Hewison, 2006: 95). It is also plain that, in most cases, the gains that are sought are not merely individual or short term (Weekley, 2006). Over an extended period, OCWs typically make regular financial contributions to their households. In Singapore, Hong Kong, and most other destinations in Asia as well as the West, workers pay the owners of "money shops" in local currency, knowing that matching payments will be made in the local currency at home within 24 hours. This is a widespread and reliable, albeit informal, money-transfer system that avoids the usual fees charged by banks (Richter and Napaporn, 1995; Hewison, 2006). For the most part, the individual transactions it facilitates escape the official record of remittances. Although they are small, in the aggregate they amount to a considerable sum. Thus, the true value of total remittances can only be estimated as being in excess of officially recorded sums.

The scale of contemporary labor migration in Asia means that the issue of remittances extends beyond the concerns of individual households; remittances can significantly influence both national development as a whole and state emigration policies. Asia contributes a major share of total global remittances through its trade in mobile labor, which means that the latter is of intense interest to governments as well as to the agents of the migration industry. Substantial revenues from remittances flow to a number of Asian countries. South Asia, India, Pakistan, Sri Lanka, and Bangladesh all receive important streams of migrant remittances. So do the Philippines, Indonesia, Thailand, Vietnam, and China. Yet within these countries—notably China, India, Pakistan, Indonesia, and Thailand—there are provinces (or states) or smaller regions that encourage labor migration and benefit greatly from it. For example, almost half of India's migrant workers come from a single state, Kerala. Certain communities within Kerala contribute disproportionately to migration and therefore benefit conspicuously from the receipt of remittances (Zachariah et al., 2002). Thus, just as Skeldon presents a more nuanced view of the spatial patterns of migration and remittances in Chapter 6 of this volume, I propose that viewing the movement of Asian workers at the level of cities and regions yields different judgments from those that are superficially suggested by official, national-level data.

At US$356 million, remittances were equivalent to merely 0.9 percent of Indonesia's exports in 1995 but have increased considerably in the decade since. In Thailand in 1995, official remittances were US$1.9 billion, equivalent to 4.2 percent of exports. Yet in the same year, official remittances represented a value equivalent to 37.1 percent (US$4.93 billion) of exports in the Philippines, where they nearly compensated for the trade gap and exceeded inflows of foreign direct investment by three times (Hugo, 2004: 91). By 2003, the value of remittances transferred to the Philippines through official channels reached US$7.2 billion. They accounted for 10 percent of Philippine GDP and were critical to the supply of hard currency, covering the imports of oil and improving the balance of payments. As Rochelle Ball and Nicola Piper observe, "The macroeconomic importance of remittances indicates that the Philippine state and economy [are] more dependent on the earnings of overseas workers than [they are] on foreign investments and foreign loans, emphasizing the high level of economic and political importance of this industry to the Philippine state" (2006: 218).

Other labor-exporting countries occupy an intermediate position. Remittances are important in Pakistan, Bangladesh, and Sri Lanka, but they are not as crucially bound to labor export as is the Philippines. In 1988, the US$2 billion in official remittances received by Pakistan was equivalent to 30 percent of exports (Castles and Miller, 1998: 148). Nepal, though a much smaller country than the Philippines, is in an even more extreme situation. By the late 1990s, Nepal's remittance income represented 25 percent of GDP, and the country was critically dependent on these financial transfers (Seddon et al., 2000; Frost, 2006).

The sheer economic weight of remittances brings to the fore some important issues of migration and development, particularly those linking the state and development. The Philippines is a case where these issues are most starkly posed. There, as elsewhere, the national financial dependency on remittances exposes certain contradictions and complexities in state policy. Is the government primarily concerned with the welfare of its citizens and thus with measuring human development broadly conceived? Or is development to be assessed using the metrics of the national accounts and judged by the conformity of national policy with the guidance of the International Monetary Fund and the broader Washington consensus? To address migration and development policies in this way is to assume that policy formation is primarily a rational process determined at the national level within a state structure capable of devising and implementing such plans. Within the diverse range of Asian state structures, we can find many cases—such as, at the extreme, Afghanistan or Pakistan—where the usual assumptions of modern statehood simply do not hold. Alex de Waal (2010), for instance, shows how Afghanistan is more accurately thought of as a polity in which central power, to the extent that it is exercised at all, emerges from processes of negotiation and contestation (sometimes violent, sometimes not) among warlords, clan leaders, heads of religious and ethnic groups, and other regional elites in a very complex political marketplace.

While Afghanistan and Pakistan are patently difficult cases, they draw attention to the complexity of the territories and populations governed by contemporary Asian states. Other Asian countries, whose governments are clearly stable and successful, also face very challenging internal situations. As an example, consider the vast area of 2.5 million square kilometers of upland territories in mainland Asia, which is examined by James C. Scott in *The Art of Not Being Governed* (2009). This area—extending from southern and western China to northeast India and the upland regions of Burma, Thailand, Laos, Vietnam, and Cambodia—is populated by more than 100 million minority peoples[8] who have, over two millennia, largely escaped the full extension of state power into their territories.[9] Their capacity to hold the state at bay has depended on a number of factors, including the difficult terrain of their homelands and, crucially, their mobility. This mobility may lead to regular movements that cross state boundaries (Scott, 2009), as in the case of the Malay traders of the Indonesian archipelago that I discuss below. Making sense of both development and migration policies thus requires recognition of the complexities of state forms, political systems, and patterns of political patronage that, for the most part, do not conform with the ideal-typical notions of modern, centralized statehood that permeate debates on migration and development.

Entrepreneurial Migration

The patterns of migration examined so far mainly depict labor mobility as a response to relatively attractive opportunities for paid employment overseas. Yet in Asia there are other forms, legal and illegal, of international mobility that do not fit this mold whose economic importance is far reaching. Moreover, they are connected with patterns of mobility and with practices of cooperation, production, and trade that have existed for centuries. Aside from the fact that they usually prefer not to attract official attention, the actors engaged therein are heterogeneous, but they can be distinguished from the migrants already discussed. I will refer to them here as "entrepreneurial migrants." I will concentrate on two East and Southeast Asian examples of people who move or operate networks across national boundaries, and thereby achieve a degree of autonomy from states in the region. They are entrepreneurial, but their motivations are by no means purely economic (see Hefner, 1998).

The characteristic preference of "overseas Chinese"[10] for creating family-based firms whose prevalence and success is on display throughout the zone of Chinese migration in East and Southeast Asia is noteworthy for a number of reasons (Wong, 1985; Chung, 1988; Redding, 1990; Mackie, 1992a, 1992b; Hamilton, 1998). It must first be observed that even though the migrants in question originate overwhelmingly from a few key areas on the coast of southeast China (Pan, 1998), they do not constitute a homogenous group, nor do they act in concert (see Thuno, 2001: 910). Moreover, people of Chinese descent whose forebears migrated out of China several generations ago may not be readily acknowledged as unambiguously Chinese back in China itself (Cushman and Wang, 1988; Guldin, 1997). Their integration into various Southeast Asian societies is variable, but they have generally endured a history of discrimination (Wang, 1992, 2003; Tu, 1994; Skinner, 1996). Moreover, although the potent networks (*siang hwee*) of connections (*guangxi*) through which many of the firms organize much of their business activities are closely knit, the firms themselves and their supporting networks compete vigorously with one another. Loyalty cannot be readily attributed to common ethnicity or language; to refer to the "overseas Chinese" as if these people constitute a coherent collectivity is misleading.

Keeping this complexity in mind, we can observe that these migrants have had an immense impact on the economies of a significant number of noncommunist states of East and Southeast Asia (Mackie, 1992a, 1992b, 1998; McVey, 1992a, 1992b; Hefner, 1998; Ch'ng, 1993). Overseas Chinese, contrary to popular perceptions, can often be found among the poor in Southeast Asia. Yet of all the billionaires in the Western Pacific outside of Japan, Korea, and the People's Republic of China, the clear majority are overseas Chinese. The efficiency and commercial acumen of Chinese family firms are universally acknowledged, although many of their commercial ventures remain relatively small, and many fail. On the other hand, large Chinese conglomerates dominate private business in Southeast Asia. In Indonesia, those residents and citizens identified as "Chinese" encompass only about 6 percent of the population yet control over 70 percent of the private wealth. Comparable concentrations of wealth can be found in Thailand, the Philippines, and most of the major Southeast Asian nations (Ch'ng, 1993; East Asia Analytic Unit, 1995). We must discount misleading mythologies that account for this success in terms of conspiracies, secret societies, ethnic essentialisms, and so on, in favor of serious studies that identify the foundations of this spectacular record of economic migration (Mackie, 1992a, 1998; McVey, 1992). The overseas Chinese have made a remarkable contribution to the nations that received them, and have also contributed a very large share—between 70 and 80 percent (Bolt, 2000)—of the investment that has underpinned the surge of industrialization in China itself.

There is no doubt that overseas Chinese entrepreneurs are very successful in open market conditions. Yet the success of large overseas Chinese conglomerates in Southeast Asia also owes much to the ability of owners of these firms to win preference from the state. The full story is complex and varies from country to country, but repeatedly we find "an increasing intimacy . . . between business and political leadership . . . [with] members of the indigenous power elite [also] . . . playing serious business roles" (McVey, 1992: 22). National business leadership is usually dominated by the domestic Chinese minority, while indigenous entrepreneurs lag as entrepreneurs and managers (Mackie, 1998). This is in a context where the state has historically played a critical role in development and is accused of discrimination in issuing licenses, exclusive importation rights, contracts, subsidized credits, joint ventures with foreign companies, and so on (Mackie, 1998: 165). Much of the conglomerates' success can be traced to their superior skills in winning state preferment, to the extent that these "emigrant entrepreneurs" (Wong, 1988) are a clear vanguard of classical capitalist transformation.

Entrepreneurship is much more likely to flourish in the difficult and less regulated environment of small and medium-sized businesses and even in the informal sector. It is to be found not only where there are large concentrations of capital but also in various hinterlands where economic opportunities have newly emerged (Reid, 1988, 1993). These patterns have been fostered by local conditions as well as historical traditions in archipelagic and mainland Southeast Asia, principally in coastal and riverine settings. This region was the natural meeting place of major waterborne trade routes beginning in China, India, and beyond to Arabia and the Mediterranean. It was convenient for the colonial rulers of these lands to characterize the populations as living in a hinterland of "small, homogenous, stable, subsistence-oriented" peasant villages that owed unquestioned loyalty to their rulers (Kahn, 2006: 43). Yet "the traditional Malay world was also marked by cultural and religious dynamism, movement, commerce, and a certain cosmopolitanism in relation to other racial, religious and cultural groups from the Persian Gulf, southern India, southeastern China and Europe" (Kahn, 2006: 43). Certainly agricultural communities flourished here as well, but they did so away from the great quasi-feudal domains that flourished in the Mekong and Red River deltas, central Java, Ayutthaya, Angkor, and so on. By contrast these groups of entrepreneurial cultivators and traders were generally peripatetic. Such patterns of mobility were common among Malay ethno-linguistic groups, but by no means limited to them (Krastoska, 1985). Land frontiers were open, and rulers were obliged to attempt to settle, control, and tax working populations. It was an environment where mobility could often be a means of evading oppressive rulers, and the burden of taxes on peasant land and labor. Hence, particularly in the coastal Malay domains, the control of trade was often crucial to the economic foundation of states and the prosperity of society in general (Kahn, 2006: 33). Geography was also important across the Asian mainland massif, frequently allowing the populous minorities of highland areas to evade domination by lowland agrarian states (Scott, 2009).

Historically, populations that engaged in agriculture and trade moved freely throughout not only the Indonesian archipelago but also the Philippines and the coastal and riverine expanses of mainland Southeast Asia. European colonial empires laid otherwise questionable boundaries across this terrain while opening up previously unexploited interior regions. As they did so, "they facilitated the movement, commerce, and cultural transnationalism that already characterized these regions" and their inhabitants (Kahn, 2006: 38). Therefore, if in the contemporary era 1 to 2 million people have moved from Indonesia into Malaysia, the phenomenon is less a manifestation of differentials in wages and commercial opportunities (though these are important) than a continuation of the propensity of the people in this region to move wherever economic opportunity takes them. The boundaries of modern states simply complicate the process (Asis, 2004). In other words, these are not simply laborers chasing better wages. Indeed, due to both long-established practices and cultural inclinations, many migrant groups look upon wage labor as a stopgap in the absence of preferred opportunities for small-scale production and trade. These cultures are genuinely entrepreneurial in that sense and others. The ways in which these small-scale Southeast Asian entrepreneurs are linked to the broader society and economy and their propensity to move without conventional attention to national, social, and political boundaries, do not fit into most of the official analyses of interstate migration.

These are two important dynamic patterns of movement and migration that do not clearly reflect the statistically driven classifications of migration policy discussions—but there are others as well in Asia and beyond (see Dobbin, 1996). The groups that forge such patterns do, indeed must, respond to market forces and state policies, but they also have well-entrenched sociocultural aims of their own, which are no less important and may even conflict with official development discourses.

Conclusion

Asian societies are being transformed on a vast scale. To some extent, these transformations are facilitated by international migration, which, except in the periodic case of refugee movements, almost always has an important economic impetus. People are moving from poor labor-surplus regions to more economically advanced, usually urban regions to meet labor shortages in particular occupational niches. Contemporary international migration within and from Asia has several novel qualities, notably the high proportion of women, the predominant circulation of contract workers among the unskilled, and the high degree of transnational mobility among skilled and professional migrants. The international regulation of migration throughout the region is of limited efficacy, and the protection of the rights of foreign workers is generally poor (Oishi, 2005; Ball and Piper, 2006).

Asian migrants contribute to the economic growth of both sending and receiving nations. That growth would be hampered without the relatively free movement of labor. Migration can have more far-reaching consequences in particular source regions such as Kerala, the Visayas, and West Java than at a national level. The productive revolution in agriculture and the immense construction of modern industrial, transportation, residential, and social infrastructure that is driving the sustained growth of much of Asia are occurring on a far more extensive scale than international labor migration. The emergence of Asia in general (and China in particular) as the workshop of the world in the twenty-first century should not be taken lightly. Furthermore, the capacity of well-educated Asians, notably in India and China, to play a much more important and competitive role in knowledge-based industries and services is likely to continue to expand as the center of gravity of the world economy shifts toward Asia.

In almost every case, migration facilitates national growth strategies, the internationalization of labor markets, and the advance of globalization in general. Yet whether these trends deserve to be celebrated as unambiguous manifestations of development remains contestable. It is obvious that Asia presents a variety of trajectories of economic development, and the part that migration contributes to these trajectories is likewise variable. In countries like the Philippines and Nepal, labor migration and wage remittances are crucial to the national economy, and the experience of migration has widespread social and cultural consequences. Yet there are also cases in which migration is nowhere near as important to economic development processes. Annual cross-border movements of 1 to 2 million workers, students, and professionals from China have an impressive impact on global migration flows. Yet they are only one aspect of the colossal socioeconomic transformation taking place in China, where internal movement of people in the next ten to fifteen years will bring around 300 million people from rural areas into the numerous burgeoning cities, many of which already have populations in excess of 5 million. Remarkable as it might seem, China appears to be nearing a point of difficult labor shortages (*Economist*, 2010: 46–48).

Only a few of the nation-states of Asia, notably Japan, are internally homogeneous. For the most part they encompass populous, plural societies inhabiting significant regional centers of political and sociocultural influence. As we have seen, the complex social and cultural influences that contribute to patterns of mass mobility can be obscured by theoretical approaches that make uniform and reductive assumptions about the forces that drive migration. Patterns of mass mobility in Asia vary considerably; the motivations of migrants are complex and rarely separable from their social and cultural contexts.

State policies that attempt to regulate migration and link its outcomes to development objectives are themselves subject to conflicting domestic and international pressures. Governments can be as much motivated by satisfying domestic constituencies and maintaining patronage commitments as by adhering to centrally formulated development objectives. Again, theoretical assumptions about the nature and role of the state in debates about migration and development need to be able to accommodate the diversity of Asian state apparatuses.

Therefore, while Asian migration in recent decades has been based on the provision of skilled and semiskilled migrants with limited entitlements into particular economic niches in advanced economies, the underlying complexities of both sending and receiving countries should discourage any theoretical tendency to reduce these movements of workers to a simple market mechanism. Attention must be given to the political and local realities of Asian states and societies in order to understand all the influences that shape the variety of migration and development policies and the practical functioning of Asian migration systems.

Notes

1. Nevertheless, the OECD study suggests that the path tends ultimately to lead to the United States (OECD, 2007a: 174).

2. The Indian industry's very success has brought it to a turning point. Costs are rising, salaries are increasing at 10 to15 percent annually, and there is a growing talent shortage. Low-cost competitors are emerging elsewhere, such as in Eastern Europe.

3. Fifty-seven countries were identified as having a critical shortage, more than two thirds of these being in Africa. According to the OECD, "The shortage is calculated on a need-based approach which sets at 2.28% health workers (doctors, nurses and midwives) per 1,000 population, the threshold under which, on average, countries fail to achieve an 80% coverage rate for deliveries by skilled birth attendants" (OECD, 2007a: 202, fn. 21).

4. Singapore and Japan are perhaps exceptions, though Singapore is short of land as well as the sort of people it favors (Weiner, 1997; Okano and Tsuchiya, 1999; Lie, 2000; Sugimoto, 2003).

5. These industries often account for around a third of overseas Filipino workers each year; for example, in 2003, 651,938 were land-based workers and 216,031 were sea based. (See Asis, 2005: 22, table 1.1).

6. Variations in the destinations of Asian women workers are influenced by an array of cultural and historical circumstances. For example, Muslim Indonesians and Bangladeshis can adjust more readily to working in Saudi households. Sri Lankans go mostly to the Middle East and Indonesians go mainly to Saudi Arabia and Malaysia, but in recent years growing numbers work in Singapore, Taiwan, and Hong Kong (Asis, 2005; Loveband, 2006).

7. The trade managed by organized crime also extends to trade in children and in body parts (Castells, 1998: 176f).

8. These include ethno-linguistic groups such as the Akha, Chin, Hmong, Kachin, Karen, Khmu, Lahu, Miao, Wa, and Yao.

9. However, modern technologies and logistics have been shifting the balance of power in favor of the state in recent years (Scott, 2009).

10. For the rest of this discussion I will refrain from the use of quotation marks around "overseas Chinese" and "Chinese" so as not to distract the reader. The term encompasses Indonesians, Malaysians, Filipinos, and others who have lived in their dispersed homelands for generations. Many have married into the local populations and speak only national, non-Chinese languages. They think of themselves as Indonesians, Filipinos, and so on, and frequently dislike being labeled "Chinese," especially when that invokes widespread and long-standing forms of anti-Chinese prejudice and discrimination.

9

Migration and Development in Latin America and the Caribbean

Nicola Phillips

The connections between migration and development in Latin America and the Caribbean (LAC), as in the rest of the world, have excited sustained attention and debate in recent years. It has emerged in other chapters of this volume that attempts to nail down the precise nature of the relationship between migration and development, in both theoretical and empirical terms, have been beset by difficulties and the results have been less than satisfactory. Many of the shortcomings of the debate stem from the failure adequately to specify what is meant by the term "development" and on this basis to generate understandings about the intertwining of the political economies of development and migration. The task of this chapter is to do just that, building on the discussions initiated in the preceding chapters to explore the relationships between migration and development that emerge in the LAC context.

The point of departure is the simple contention that our understanding of this relationship depends on the conceptualization of development that we choose to deploy, since different conceptualizations of development lead to differing perspectives on the dynamics of the relationship. Specifically, there is a tension at the heart of the debate between arguments that emerge from an understanding of development as a national (or sometimes regional) process, which focuses on aggregate economic growth, and those that emerge from an emphasis on the dynamics of human development, which entails the material and social conditions in which individuals and groups of people live. The distinctions between these two approaches have formed the basis of ongoing debates in development theory and practice, as perspectives on human development have been developed precisely as a challenge to those conventional theories that defined development essentially as growth and worked on the assumption that what developed were countries (or regions) and national (or regional) economies (Payne and Phillips, 2010). Yet the general failure in debates, especially policy discourses, on migration to distinguish between these two very different understandings of development—not to mention the even more common tendency to conflate them—continues to generate very partial perspectives on how the relationships between migration and development work both in theory and in practice. Our discussion of the LAC context reveals and underlines the resulting complexities in interpretations of the actual and potential relationship between development and migration.

The second core contention of the chapter is that we need to reconsider the customary framing of the relationship between migration and development as a question of how migration "affects" development in various parts of the world. This approach not only conceives of the relationship as unidirectional in nature but also depicts migration as somehow separate from development processes in general. The contention here—as has been recognized in many valuable recent contributions to the debate, including those in this volume—is that we need to think of migration as an intrinsic dimension of global and local development processes, to consider how development shapes both patterns and outcomes of migration, and to develop understandings of a complex and changing nexus between migration and development on this basis.

The chapter is divided into three parts. The first presents a sketch of the contours of migration in and from LAC, and the second locates these patterns in a wider discussion of contemporary development in the region. The third goes on to explore the tensions between what, for convenience, are termed "growth-based" and "human" approaches to development as they manifest themselves within three of the key arenas of the migration-development nexus: labor markets; the financial flows associated with remittances; and the movement of skilled, educated, and professional people.

Patterns of Migration

As in other regions, reliable data on migration trends from and within the LAC region remain scarce, especially given the challenges of accounting for informal and undocumented forms of migration on a large scale. Nevertheless, a number of key trends can be identified in contemporary patterns of LAC migration that both reveal its distinguishing features and reflect commonalities with other regions, including those considered in the preceding chapters.

First, the period since the mid-nineteenth century has been marked by a key change in the migration profile of the region: once dominated by an influx of migrants from Europe and elsewhere, it is now marked by high, and rapidly accelerating, levels of emigration from the region. In the second half of the nineteenth century and the first part of the twentieth century, immigration to the region took both coercive forms—as in the movement of indentured labor from parts of Asia and Africa—and forms associated with the movement of European and other workers to the so-called New World in the pursuit of land and economic opportunities. Significantly, a good part of immigration flows during this period were encouraged by LAC governments in order to generate the labor supply needed for large-scale infrastructural projects—for example, the movement of Japanese workers (the first-generation *nikkeijin*) particularly to Peru and Brazil. Immigration from other LAC countries was also important, as with the movement of Guatemalan workers to the coffee plantations of southern Mexico (J. Smith, 2006).

In the contemporary period, by contrast, emigration has become vastly more important than immigration for the region as a whole. By the latest estimates, immigration accounts for only around 1 percent of the region's total population, even though in some countries, such as Argentina, Costa Rica, and Venezuela, immigrants continue to exceed emigrants as a percentage of the population. The number of immigrants as a proportion of the total population is highest in some of the Caribbean countries, due to the very small populations of these states (ECLAC, 2006: 14). Conversely, the region has seen a rapid acceleration of emigration, particularly from the late 1990s onward. Some indicative estimates measure an increase in the numbers of LAC emigrants from 21 million in 2000 to 25 million in 2005, which would account for around 13 percent of the global stock of migrants in that year and nearly 4 percent of the region's total population (ECLAC, 2006: 14–16). In some countries, particularly the small states of the Caribbean and Central America, levels of emigration account for significant proportions of the national population—in some cases around 20 percent—and even for larger countries the figures are significant, such as an estimated 8 percent for Colombia (Khoudour-Cásteras, 2007). The primary destination of LAC migrants continues to be the United States, but there are significant movements also to Canada, Europe (particularly Spain), and other countries like Japan.

Second, by contrast with the Asian region, levels of intraregional migration in LAC are much less significant than levels of emigration from the region. In the mid-2000s, it was estimated that there were around 3 million intraregional migrants, accounting for some 60 percent of all registered immigrants across the region (ECLAC, 2006: 16). In some cases, intraregional migration is facilitated by provisions for the movement of persons in regional integration blocs such as the Mercosur (see Pérez Vichich, 2005). The primary destinations for intraregional migrants continue to be those with larger economies—Argentina, Brazil, Venezuela, Mexico—but the patterns are considerably more complex than this generalization suggests. In the first place, smaller as well as larger economies are characterized by inward migration, often from neighboring states, as in the cases of migration from Peru to Ecuador (Jokisch, 2007) and from Haiti to the Dominican Republic or the Bahamas (Martin et al., 2002; Davis, 2009). In the second place, the role of what we might call "transit migration" is also of growing importance, whereby migrants move through other countries of the region in order to reach their final destination; such patterns are obscured when the focus is simply on movement from one country to another. In 2006, for example, the International Organization for Migration (IOM) estimated that up to 12,000 new Guatemalan migrants arrived in the United States each year via Mexico and that 60,000 are also deported from Mexico each year (J. Smith, 2006). Similarly, across the Caribbean, governments are confronted with the increasing "island hopping" of desperate Haitian migrants trying initially to reach the United States, but often ending up staying illegally in other Caribbean countries (Lacey, 2007). As many countries become zones of transit migration, much greater attention is being paid to the kinds of immigration policies that need to be developed therein.

The important point here, as with extraregional migration, is that the figures account largely, or indeed solely, for registered immigrants and hence exclude the vast bulk of the migrant population, which is undocumented and informal. Indeed, as is the case in other regions, the size and scale of the informal economy in LAC are pivotal to the nature of the migration-development nexus in this region—a point that is missed in much of the discussion and obscured by official statistics. We will return to it shortly.

Third, in some parts of the region, and particularly in the larger economies, internal migration is also of some significance. This is particularly the case in Brazil, characterized as it is by high levels of migration from the poorer states of the north to the more economically prosperous states of the center and south of the country, driven in particular by rapidly expanding agricultural activities such as sugar cane cultivation. In Mexico and some other countries, internal migration has been stimulated not only by long-standing and accelerating processes of urbanization, themselves partly the result of the transformation and decimation of rural livelihoods, but also by the construction and expansion of export processing zones (EPZs) and *maquila* (export assembly) industries in the border regions (see Sklair, 1989; Kaplinsky, 1993; Dunn, 1999; Willmore, 2000; Heron, 2004; Gereffi, 2006; Milberg, 2007). In some parts of the region, notably Colombia, the issue of forced migration is also significant. In this case, a massive internal displacement of communities has been occasioned by civil conflict that has been conducted largely in the rural regions of the country for decades, with the consequence of large-scale migration to cities and other countries—most notably to Venezuela and Ecuador, as well as to the United States and Spain (see Flórez, 2003; Ardila, 2006). While accurate figures are scarce, available estimates indicate that there may well be up to 3 million Colombians in these two neighboring countries, half of whom were likely displaced by the spread of paramilitary violence (Cárdenas and Mejía, 2006; Jokisch, 2007; Phillips and Prieto, 2011).

Fourth, the aggregate profile of the region has historically been, and remains, dominated by labor migration rather than forced and refugee migration, despite important instances of the latter. Colombia has already been mentioned in connection with processes of forced and refugee migration that have been ongoing for several decades. Cuba is another important instance in which flows of refugees have been occurring since the mid-twentieth century, particularly to the United States, often through Mexico; Cuba and Mexico signed an agreement in October 2008 to try to tackle the movements of these so-called dusty-foot migrants. Other instances feature historical peaks of refugee migration, particularly in the midst of civil conflict in countries such as El Salvador or Guatemala or political upheaval in countries like Chile or Argentina. But it remains the case that migration both from and within LAC is overwhelmingly associated with labor.

At the same time, as in other regions, the profile of migration is characterized by movements both of low-paid, low-skilled workers with low levels of education and of highly educated, highly skilled, and professional workers. Intraregional and internal migration flows are dominated very significantly by the former (Martínez Pizarro, 2009), but emigration from the region is more heterogeneous. At an aggregate level, migration from Mexico and Central America is predominantly undertaken by low-paid, low-skilled workers, whereas in the Caribbean and South America the profile is dominated by high-skilled, educated, professional workers. Only 4 percent of Mexican migrants have tertiary education; the figures for Central American migrants are 7 percent, for the Caribbean 12 percent, for the Andean region 24 percent, and for other South American countries 30 percent (Fjanzylber and López, 2007: 10). Significantly, Mexican and Central American migrants account for around 70 percent of the LAC-born population in the United States (ECLAC, 2006: 18). They consequently dominate the overall education profile of LAC emigrants in a way that sets it in sharp contrast with that of migrants from other parts of the world (Fajnzylber and López, 2007: 10). Meanwhile, more than 80 percent of people born in Haiti, Jamaica, Grenada, and Guyana who have higher education qualifications live and work overseas; the respective figures for Mexico are only around 14 percent, for El Salvador 32 percent, and for the Dominican Republic 22 percent (Fajnzylber and López, 2007: 11; Kapur and Hale, 2005: 18–19). At the same time, it must be emphasized that the profile of LAC immigration in the United States is not simply the result of the dominance of unskilled or less educated Mexican workers. Rather, reflecting worldwide trends among migrant workers, the occupational profile of LAC migrants reveals a concentration in low-skill jobs regardless of level of educational attainment (Phillips, 2009b: 237; Canales, 2007; Bauder, Chapter 3 in this volume; Piper, Chapter 4 in this volume).

Finally, migration from and within LAC shares some of the characteristics of feminization that are discussed extensively by Nicola Piper in her contribution to this volume. While it appears to be less pronounced than in Asia, the available statistics indicate not only a significant growth of migration by women, corresponding with an ongoing change in the gender composition of the region's labor force, but also instances in which women migrants outnumber men. Migration from the region to both Spain and Canada, for instance, has for some time been dominated by female workers, while young male workers are in the preponderance in migration to Japan (ECLAC, 2006: 22–23). Intraregional and internal migration has been characterized by a significant growth in the representation of women, particularly, as in Asia, in connection with domestic service sectors, while sectors such as construction and agriculture tend to be dominated by male migrant workers.

Locating Migration in the Political Economy of Development

The direction of LAC development since the 1980s has been shaped by the consolidation of neoliberalism as the foundation of the global political economy. There is always a risk in generalizing about a region as large and diverse as the one we are considering here, but, in the broadest terms, the development models pursued across the region have conformed with the neoliberal tenets of consolidating markets as the drivers of national and regional economies, fostering enhanced levels of integration into the global economy, and achieving national and regional economic competitiveness on this basis (see Phillips, 2004; Robinson, 2008). In this context, the pertinent dynamics for understanding the migration-development nexus are threefold: first, the evolution of labor markets and the dynamics of what we will call "adverse incorporation" into global and local economies; second, the dynamics of inequality within LAC societies as well as between economies and societies in the global political economy; and third, the evolution of development strategies and state policies around migration.

Labor Markets and the Dynamics of Adverse Incorporation

Of particular centrality to the neoliberal development model is the flexibilization of labor, which has underpinned the means by which the region's economies and societies have been integrated into processes of economic globalization and local economic restructuring. Development strategies and corporate restructuring processes since the 1980s have involved a dismantling of the contracts that previously existed between labor and capital in order to undermine the bargaining power of labor and reduce unit labor costs by making employment more flexible—that is, among other measures, by increasing casual, temporary, seasonal, and part-time labor and enhancing employers' ability to hire and fire workers according to their needs at a given time. The process of flexibilization is thus intrinsic to what Carl-Ulrik Schierup and Stephen Castles termed in Chapter 2 of this volume the "recommodification" of labor under neoliberalism.

Among the results of these processes in LAC has been an arresting expansion of precarious work in the 1990s and 2000s, which is often hidden by the headline news about regional employment trends. The United Nations Economic Commission for Latin America and the

Caribbean (ECLAC) (2008) documented an increase in the average household income in the region from 2002 to 2007, driven predominantly by labor income. In most cases, the increase in labor income was due to a rise in the wages of the employed person(s); in others, the key factor was the net employment rate. Meanwhile, although unemployment rose considerably across the region during the 1990s as a result of neoliberal restructuring, during the 2000s there was evidence of a decline in unemployment in the majority of the major cities. (It should nevertheless be noted that gender disparities are significant.) Yet the point is that the bulk of employment growth—as opposed to economic growth—has been in the low-productivity, low-wage sectors of the informal economy, particularly those associated with enhanced integration into global production networks (GPNs) and global value chains (GVCs) (see Barrientos et al., 2008; Ponte, 2008; Phillips, 2010a). In Latin America in 2006, informal workers accounted for some 45 percent of all workers in urban areas alone (ECLAC, 2008: 7); among them, migrants were visibly represented.[1] The inherent vulnerability and "disposability" of a large, mobile, and informal workforce facilitate flexibility in determining labor costs and rates of employment at any given time, and the continual ability to replace workers who have outlived their utility to employers—a process amply documented by Melissa Wright (2006) in the context of women workers in the Mexican *maquila* industry. Labor is thus treated as a factor of production and informality as a valuable means by which firms can manage the huge commercial pressures on price that are intrinsic to participation in GVCs.

The concept of adverse incorporation, which has recently been developed in interesting ways in the study of chronic poverty (Hickey and du Toit, 2007), offers a framework for understanding these labor market dynamics and their connections with migration. Embedded therein is a critique of the generalized, orthodox argument that the major problems of development are caused by exclusion from labor markets and from the benefits of participation in the global economy (see Milanovic, 2003, and Kaplinsky, 2005, for discussions). The notion of adverse incorporation, by contrast, implies that the principal determinant of poverty and marginalization is not socioeconomic exclusion but rather the terms on which some social groups are included in global and local economic activity. In some circumstances the terms of inclusion may be beneficial for producers and workers; in others, they amount to situations in which poverty, marginalization, and vulnerability are reinforced rather than alleviated (Wood, 2000, 2003; Hickey and du Toit, 2007; Ponte, 2008; Phillips, forthcoming).

The connections between the dynamics of adverse incorporation and migration are very clear, inasmuch as migrant workers in the low-productivity and low-wage informal economy—in LAC as elsewhere—are usually among the most vulnerable to the various forms of adverse incorporation. The poorest in Latin American societies, as elsewhere, do not move, as they lack the resources to do so. But the dynamics that position poor migrant workers as an underclass in both richer and poorer destination countries are well documented (Harriss, 1995; Sassen, 2001; Bauder, 2006 and Chapter 3 in this volume; Phillips, 2009b). While net employment among poor migrant workers is high, it is also extremely precarious, reflecting the frequency of underemployment and high levels of vulnerability in employment conditions. These forms of adverse incorporation in global and local labor markets manifest themselves in both agricultural and manufacturing sectors. The flexibilization of labor, casualization of employment, and downward pressure on wages and working conditions have been well documented in low-cost manufacturing sectors in Mexico, Central America, and the Caribbean, especially in EPZs (see, for instance, Elson and Pearson, 1981; Kaplinsky, 1993; Willmore, 2000). Likewise, the restructuring of labor and working conditions in the sugar cane industry in Brazil, the cut-flowers industry in Colombia and Ecuador, and the fruit industry in Chile, for example, show clearly the varied dynamics of adverse incorporation into national, regional, and global markets (Biofuel Watch Center, 2009; Korovkin and Sanmiguel-Valderrama, 2007; Barrientos et al., 1999). In all these activities, migrant workers are strongly represented. They may be internal migrants, as in the case of Brazilian agriculture, or intraregional migrants. In the case of Costa Rican agriculture, for example, some 90 percent of all workers are from Nicaragua (Martínez Pizarro, 2009: 7); in southern Mexico, migrant agricultural workers from Guatemala continue to be heavily represented; and in the Dominican Republic, 90 percent of seasonal sugar workers and two-thirds of coffee workers are Haitian migrants (Martin et al., 2002: 574).

The final point that needs to be emphasized is that the dynamics of adverse incorporation into GVCs are reflected also in patterns of outward migration from LAC—that is, in the incorporation of migrant workers from the region in sites of production located in other countries. For example, in discussing the global garment industry and the place of both the region and the region's workers and producers therein, we need to take account of both the activities rooted geographically in LAC economies and those that are heavily dominated by Latin American (and other) migrant workers in such places as Los Angeles (Bonacich and Appelbaum, 2000; Rosen, 2002; Esbenshade, 2004).

The Dynamics of Inequality in the Migration-Development Nexus

The countries of LAC are recognized as featuring the highest levels of socioeconomic inequality in the world. ECLAC data from 2008 indicate that average per capita income in the tenth decile of the region's population is about 17 times greater than that of the poorest 40 percent of households; for the richest quintile, it is about 20 times higher than for the poorest one. National variation is also significant: in Colombia, for example, the per capita income of the richest 10 percent is 25 times higher than that of the poorest 40 percent. The crucial characteristic of inequality in the region (and indeed around the globe) is that it is strongly associated with the acceleration and concentration of wealth accumulation in the richest sections of societies, which has been far greater than any increase in the rate of absolute poverty. Hence, in this region, a reasonably significant (although far from uniform) aggregate reduction in poverty in the 2000s has been accompanied by an increase in inequality (ECLAC, 2008; Phillips, 2010a).

Discussions of migration and development often rest on considerations of inequality, but in rather simplistic and problematic ways. As has been noted earlier and in other chapters, the key to migration patterns is not poverty; rather, emphasis is rightly placed on the role of inequalities in shaping migration, even though the assumption that inequalities, particularly wage inequalities, between countries are the drivers of migration is problematic. The conventional argument is that a reduction in the levels of inequality between economies, and particularly a narrowing of wage differentials, will stem the tide of migration by reducing the pressures and incentives for people to migrate. This view was made explicit in discussions about the North American Free Trade Agreement (NAFTA) and is commonly heard in many of the major countries of immigration (see Manning, 2000; Delgado Wise and Márquez Covarrubias, 2007a). In the LAC context, differentials in employment opportunities and wages are unquestionably an important driver of labor migration, both in the form of emigration to the United States, Europe, and elsewhere and in the form of intraregional migration from, say, Paraguay or Bolivia to Argentina or Brazil, Peru to Chile, or Haiti to the Dominican Republic. Between the United States and Mexico, for instance, the income gap is not only significant but has grown since the mid-1990s, when NAFTA was established: in 1994, the per capita gross domestic product (GDP) of the United States was 2.6 times higher than the Mexican equivalent and 2.9 times higher in 2004; for the same years, crucially, manufacturing wages were, respectively, 5.7 and 6.8 times higher in the United States than in Mexico (Delgado Wise and Márquez Covarrubias, 2008: 1370).

However, this depiction of the relationship between migration and inequality is problematic in several ways. The first is fairly simple: it obscures the complexity of patterns and motivations for migration, not all of which are related directly to economic incentives associated with differentials in wages and opportunities. Many scholars have emphasized as well the sociological characteristics of global migration associated with the development of transnational social networks, which in very important ways shape the political economies of migration across the region (see Smith and Guarnizo, 1998; Guarnizo and Díaz, 1999).

The second problem is highlighted by Ronald Skeldon and Oliver Bakewell in their respective chapters in this volume: as Bakewell puts it, such a view expounds a conception of development as inherently "sedentary." In other words, it rests on an assumption that, given the choice, people would rather stay in their places of origin than migrate. Yet a body of research has highlighted a key characteristic of migration that contradicts this assumption—namely, that migration is as much a result of development as it is a result of its lack. Consequently, "development will not stop migration" (de Haas, 2007). Development has always fostered increased levels of migration and continues to do so, as higher levels of education, opportunity, and resources expand people's horizons and aspirations (de Haas, 2007, 2010; Skeldon, 1997, 2008a). A slightly different formulation is offered by Anthony Maingot (1999, cited in Martin et al., 2002: 576), who argues that emigration from the Dominican Republic and Haiti is "structural" and therefore will not slow as a result of trade, aid, or economic growth. He also points out, interestingly, that unskilled Caribbean workers often favor work overseas as they associate manual labor in their home countries with slavery.

The third problem is related to the second—namely, that the relationship between migration and inequality is usually depicted in terms of the migration of low-skilled workers. As discussions in other chapters show clearly, the concern in the United States and other high-immigration countries tends to revolve around unskilled and undocumented forms of migration, whereas migration among highly educated and highly skilled workers is generally seen as more acceptable or even desirable. In these cases, the problems with the "sedentary" assumptions that are embedded in the discussions of the migration/development nexus become even more apparent: the migration of highly skilled, highly paid, and highly educated people is increasing alongside the migration of less skilled and less educated workers from the same region.

Furthermore, the migration of skilled and educated workers puts a different gloss on the relationship between migration and development and the connections with inequality. Indeed, it is possible to make a preliminary observation that the migration-development nexus is characterized by a sort of inequality trap, in which high levels of socioeconomic inequality seem to be associated with a decreased propensity to migrate among the richer, better-educated, and more highly skilled sections of the population. Thus, the incentives offered by emigration to the richest 20 percent of Brazilians, who command a 64 percent share of national income and already enjoy lifestyles similar to that which they would have in a richer destination country, are less than for their counterparts in India, whose income shares are substantially lower (Kapur and McHale, 2005: 80). From this perspective, therefore, inequality does not lead to more outward migration but rather to less, and the potential mobility of individuals at this end of the inequality spectrum constitutes an important obstacle to progressive tax policies. In other words, "Low-income countries might well be caught between a rock and a hard place in that they have to either tolerate much higher levels of income inequality or risk losing their brightest and best" (Kapur and McHale, 2005: 83). The threat of exit by emigration could thus be construed as one of the means by which inequality becomes a stubborn characteristic of LAC societies.

The fourth problem echoes one of the points made in the introduction to this chapter—namely, that the relationship between migration and inequality is depicted in the orthodox construction as unidirectional. That is, the focus is on the ways in which inequalities drive migration rather than on the ways in which migration can reinforce existing patterns of inequality and lead to new forms of unequal development (Phillips, 2009b). Indeed, in much of the more optimistic literature on the migration-development nexus, the relationship is presented as one in which migration helps mitigate inequalities between economies and societies. These kinds of arguments rest predominantly on notions of "diasporic development" whereby migrant workers become "transnational development agents" (Bhagwati, 2003; Faist, 2008). As indicated earlier, our critical assessment of these arguments hinges on our definition of development: if we focus on development as national economic growth, our conclusions about the relationship between migration and unequal development are rather different from those that emerge if we focus on human development. These issues are explored more fully in the third section of this chapter.

Migration as Development Strategy

The final issue that we need briefly to address relates to the role of migration within national and local development strategies. We have already noted the ways in which neoliberal economic restructuring in LAC has rested on the creation or expansion of an ultra-flexible labor force in which migrant workers are strongly represented. But we are also interested in the ways in which governments have approached questions of emigration in the context of their development strategies. In one respect, governments have historically put in place policies to manage processes of emigration. For example, from around 1900 until the 1970s, the strategy in Mexico was one of controlling emigration; from the 1970s until the early 2000s, by contrast, policies of "no policy" were designed to maintain the status quo, prevent an increase in border control, and avoid opening up the idea of shared responsibility (between Mexico and the United States) in managing migration (Rosenblum, 2004; Rozental, 2004; Fitzgerald, 2006, 2009). The Colombian government was also among the first to try to develop a strategy for managing labor migration in the 1970s (Mármora, 1979).

In another, more significant respect, we are now seeing a generalized move among governments to position migration as a development strategy in a number of LAC countries, ostensibly to harness the payoffs of large-scale emigration (see Phillips, 2009b). In LAC as elsewhere, the pivotal issue relates to remittances: debates about migration and development in the region have come to be dominated by a concern with the attraction and use of remittance flows as a form of development financing. Table 9.1 illustrates the importance of remittances in the region at the height of such discourse in the mid-2000s, around which time development strategies were being systematically oriented to harnessing remittances and we were beginning to talk about the advantages and disadvantages of the emerging "remittance economies." Conversely, migration has been positioned as a development strategy in ways that cast the emigration of highly skilled and educated citizens as the key to future growth and prosperity. The government of Chile, for instance, announced its intention in 2008 to create a Bi-Centennial Human Capital Fund of US$6 billion to send 6,500 Chilean students per year to pursue postgraduate studies in the United States, Europe, and Australia.

Table 9.1 Significance of Remittances, Selected Latin American Countries, 2005

	Volumes of Remittances, US$ millions	As a Percentage of GDP[a]	As a Percentage of Exports (goods and services)[a]	Percentage of Imports (goods and services)[a]	As a Percentage of Total Net FDI	As a Percentage of Aid (net official development assistance or official aid)[b]
Argentina	780	0.4	1.7	2.2	21.8	857.1
Bolivia	860	9.2	25.3	28.1	-307.6[c]	112.1
Brazil	6,411	0.8	4.8	6.5	51.1	2249.5
Colombia	4,126	3.4	15.5	15.8	71.7	810.6
Costa Rica	362	1.8	3.7	3.4	40.0	2784.6
Dominican Republic	2,682	7.7	27.5	24.4	262.1	3082.8
Ecuador	2,005	5.5	17.8	17.0	121.8	1253.1
El Salvador	2,830	16.7	61.9	37.0	942.7	1341.2
Guatemala	2,993	9.5	60.1	31.3	1438.9	1372.9
Haiti	1,077	25.9	179.9	63.1	11336.8	443.2
Honduras	1,763	21.1	51.5	34.3	648.4	274.6
Jamaica	1,651	16.7	45.7[b]	32.1[b]	283.9	2201.3
Mexico	20,034	2.6	8.7	8.3	160.7	16557.0
Nicaragua	850	17.3	61.9	30.0	352.5	70.0
Peru	2,495	3.1	12.8	16.4	96.7	512.3
Trinidad and Tobago	97	0.6	1.1	1.5	16.2	-9700.0[d]
Uruguay	110	0.6	2.2	2.4	15.4	500.0
Venezuela	272	0.2	0.5	0.9	19.4	555.1

Sources: Author's own calculations. Primary data on remittances from Inter-American Development Bank, http://www.iadb.org/mif/remittances/; primary data on GDP, exports, imports, FDI and aid from ECLAC, *Statistical Yearbook for Latin America and the Caribbean, 2006* (Santiago: ECLAC); and *World Bank, World Development Indicators 2006* (New York: World Bank).

Notes: a. Shown here at current market prices.

b. Calculated using 2004 figures.

c. Minus percentage arises as the figure for net FDI to Bolivia in 2005 was –279.6 (US$ millions).

d. Minus percentage arises as the figure for aid to Trinidad and Tobago in 2004 was –1 (US$ millions).

"Brain exports" were conceived as "Chile's big bet for the future" (Oppenheimer, 2008).

Of course, the other sense in which migration can be conceived as a development strategy involves a focus not on countries, economies, or societies but on individuals and households. If we adopt an approach to development that centers on its human dimensions—on the social and material conditions in which people live and the strategies they employ to try to manage or improve those conditions—then we become aware that migration in all its forms constitutes a development strategy on the part of migrants and their households.[2] The difficulty is that these two development strategies—the one emphasizing growth, financial flows, and poverty reduction at an aggregate (national/regional) level, the other focused on the human development of migrants and their families—often conflict with one another in practice as well as in theories of the migration-development nexus in LAC and elsewhere. In order to illustrate these complexities and contradictions, we now turn briefly to consider three of the major arenas of the migration-development nexus: the insertion of migrant workers into labor markets and other social contexts; remittances; and the consequences of migration among highly skilled and well-educated parts of the region's population.

Labor Migration, National Development, and Human Development

In debates about the migration-development nexus whereby development is conceived in aggregate national (or regional) growth-based terms, the phenomenon of large-scale out-migration of workers attracts differing interpretations (see Portes, 2009; de Haas, 2010). The "optimists" see these movements as positive for development in the country of origin, emphasizing in particular the significance of remittances to the national economy and local communities, but also the role of migration as a "safety valve" that eases problems of unemployment, poverty, overpopulation, and even crime. Conversely, more "pessimistic" accounts emphasize the costs to sending countries. Among the most notable of these are, first, the depletion of population and the conversion of many localities, particularly in rural areas, into places populated only by the economically inactive (see Pritchett, 2004), and, second, the manner in which migration has been deployed, within the neoliberal development model, to make available to global and local capital a vast "reserve army of labor." Sometimes this argument is also cast in terms of a "new dependency" on the labor markets of rich economies, especially in terms of remittances. Raúl Delgado Wise and Humberto Márquez Covarrubias have been particular exponents of this view in relation to Mexico:

> By losing its labour force to this massive exodus Mexico is losing one of its most valuable resources in the accumulation process. The direct exportation of workers represents a drain on human resources that . . . leads to the abandonment of productive activities, represents a waste of resources spent on the formation of the emigrating labour force and, to an extent, causes the displacement of relatively qualified labour and the consequent weakening of labour sovereignty. . . . The indirect export of labour via the *maquila* and disguised *maquila* industries implies a transfer of net profits to the US economy. This constitutes a new mode of dependency that is even more acute than those examined in the structuralist and dependency theories previously endorsed by the Economic Commission for Latin America and the Caribbean. (2008: 1369)

Clearly, both the optimistic and the pessimistic accounts of the relationship between migration and development focus on the big picture of national development. In both, the migrant workers themselves tend to be rather invisible: migration is conceived as a structural process that brings particular structural and socioeconomic consequences for the country (or region), economy, and society in question. By contrast, a focus on human development invites greater attention to the agency of migrant and nonmigrant workers and also to the integrated nature of migration and development. Optimistic accounts from this perspective consider the enhanced prospects of migrant workers for improving their own material and social conditions and those of their families. That these enhanced prospects might be accompanied by negative consequences for the national or local economy or society, as illustrated above, generates much of the political tension in debates about migration. If the consequences of brain drain are disastrous for a country, should individuals be deprived of the right to mobility? What is the relation between the generation of the kinds of "new dependency" noted earlier and the rights of individual unskilled workers to seek better remuneration in a different geographical location?

Indeed, there are ample reasons to consider a more negative picture of the migration–human development nexus, which are associated with the pronounced vulnerability of migrant workers to exploitation, abuse, marginalization, and discrimination. The labor conditions that prevail for LAC migrant workers in the United States, for instance, are well captured in Chapter 3 in Harald Bauder's general arguments about the devalorization of labor in the secondary segments of the economy. Susan Martin (2003) has drawn attention to what has been called the "Virginia model" of immigration in the United States (Fuchs, 1990), whereby migrant workers are used to cover labor shortages but denied a wide range of welfare benefits and social and legal rights, giving rise to a system of "intensified social stratification" (Phillips, 2009b: 247). Similar kinds of social stratification result from intraregional migration: migrant Colombians, for example, have in turn come to dominate a portion of the unskilled and low-skilled Ecuadorian labor market and have as a consequence suffered growing hostility and widespread discrimination in accessing public and social services (Rodas and Arguello, 2004; Riaño and Villa, 2008; Phillips and Prieto, 2011).

On the grounds that varied forms of exploitation and exclusion are endemic among migrant labor forces, the case can be made that the human-developmental benefits of migration are often not as significant as depicted in the more optimistic accounts of the migration-development nexus. However, without discounting many of the worst forms of abuse and exploitation that are unanticipated by the migrant workers—relating especially to human smuggling and trafficking—it must be recognized that in many cases workers who migrate earn higher wages than they would otherwise be able to earn, and for this reason sometimes make a decision to tolerate difficult conditions of work for a period of time. For instance, research on the cattle and sugar cane sectors in Brazil—which are heavily dominated by seasonal migrant workers from the poor northern states of the country—indicates that migration constitutes a conscious, long-term human-development strategy on the part of the workers, who are often aware of harsh working conditions that are involved (Phillips and Sakamoto, 2010). Similarly, research on the agricultural contract labor program between Mexico and Canada reveals how the narrowing of human-development options available to Mexican workers leads to conscious calculations about the benefits of the program and active decisions "to please their employers and continue in the program" (Binford 2009: 505). This pattern is replicated across migrant workers in many sectors.

However, a recognition of the agency of migrant workers cannot be substituted for a clear critique of the conditions of vulnerability, exploitation, and marginalization that are entrenched by means of the expansion of a large, mobile reserve army of labor that enables capital accumulation on a national, regional, and/or global scale. To this extent, the human-development potential of migration must be recognized as constrained by the enhanced process of social stratification on which contemporary national, regional, and global economies rest.

Remittances

The debate surrounding the developmental potential of remittances has been similarly vexed. On the one hand, as shown in other chapters, flows of money from migrant workers in the early 2000s came to be seen as "remittance gold," and migrant workers themselves were celebrated as heroes. The fact that remittances were countercyclical and growing faster and more stably than other forms of development finance led to the elaboration of national and local development strategies based explicitly on these financial flows. However, by the end of the decade, such optimism was coming under strain, and the global economic crisis appeared to challenge the assumption that remittances were a stable and reliable form of development financing. Table 9.2 shows the trajectory of remittances during the period of the crisis and indicates their fragility as a foundation for development strategies.

It was in this context that more credence started to be given to arguments that stressed the dangers of basing economies and development strategies on the remittances of migrant workers, building on a widespread recognition that the impact of large inflows of remittances was mixed (see Cohen, 2005; Brown, 2006; Fajnzylber and López, 2007), particularly as regards poverty and inequality (Adams and Page, 2005; World Bank, 2005; Acosta et al., 2006). We do not need to rehearse the debate here, but it is worth noting that since the rural poor in LAC, like the poorest people in other societies, tend to be the least mobile and not to migrate internationally, the impact of international remittances on the incomes of the poorest rural households in the region tends to be low (Escobar Latapí, 2008: 84). That said, research on all of these issues has indicated significant variation across countries and regions. It must also be recognized that there is no necessary correlation between levels of outward migration and levels of inflowing remittances. It has been shown, for instance, that Mexico has one of the lowest migration-to-remittance ratios, attributed to the concentration of migrants in low-income jobs, their frequent lack of documentation that leads to less favorable working conditions, and increasing family migration to or reunification in the United States. This picture suggests that migration may well be a net loss to Mexico, unless one considers the migrant population to be economically redundant at home (Escobar Latapí, 2009: 83).

Table 9.2 Remittances to Latin American Countries, 2005–2008

	Percent Growth, 2001–2005	Percent Growth, 2005–2008	Percent Growth, 2007–2008
Mexico	125.2	25.5	4.9
Brazil	146.6	12.3	1.8
Colombia	135.0	17.4	7.1
Guatemala	412.5	44.1	4.5
El Salvador	48.1	33.9	2.5
Dominican Republic	48.4	16.0	-0.3
Peru	168.3	18.6	2.1
Ecuador	40.2	40.7	-8.5
Honduras	283.3	53.2	5.5
Jamaica	70.5	23.1	2.9
Haiti	33.0	73.6	2.2
Bolivia	734.9	27.6	4.5
Nicaragua	28.8	17.6	1.0
Argentina	680.0	22.4	3.8
Costa Rica	352.5	72.4	11.4
Venezuela	100.0	205.9	152.1
Uruguay	161.9[a]	18.2	4.0
Trinidad and Tobago	136.6	34.0	4.0

Source: Data from Inter-American Development Bank, http://www.iadb.org.
Note: a. Indicates percent growth for the years 2003–2005.

If we shift our perspective to one associated with human development, the picture again changes. In the new remittance-led development strategy, migrant workers themselves are positioned as the agents of development, in the place of national and local states and governments. Significantly, the majority of workers sending remittances, for whom the ability to support their families back home was the objective of migration, tend to be low skilled and poorly paid. Highly paid professional workers, by contrast, generally belong to families who are not in need of this kind of financial support and thus tend to remit less money. Thus, an important critique of remittance-based development is that it is precisely poorer workers who come to shoulder the burden of supporting not just families but also development in their countries or places of origin. In other words, "the idea is that some of the most exploited workers in the world can make up for the failure of mainstream development policies" (Castles and Delgado Wise, 2008: 7). This is particularly problematic given that the financial burden of sustaining families through remittances can be extraordinarily heavy for migrants, in some cases to the extent that their social mobility and ability to accumulate capital that would allow for their return to or investment in their home countries is severely limited (Levitt and Sorenson, 2004: 7).

Questions are also raised by recurrent policy proposals, particularly in the United States, to make remitting money more difficult for migrant workers, particularly those who are undocumented. In tandem (and some contradiction) with attempts to ease restrictions on opening bank accounts in order to pull remittances further into the formal banking system, legislation has focused on the requirement of proof of citizenship for the transfer of money through formal channels. This inevitably encourages recourse to illegal or semilegal channels of remitting monies, where charges and commissions are not regulated. More worrying still are widespread proposals to introduce taxation on remittances—that is, to levy taxes on the money sent out of country in the form of remittances, even if the income of the worker in question has already been taxed. If these moves are a sign of things to come, the developmental consequences for migrant individuals and communities within the United States will clearly be significant (Phillips, 2009b: 247–248).

All of these points highlight the extent to which remittances and their prospects for human development are increasingly coopted, even hijacked, based on their potential as an instrument of aggregate development. Ester Hernández and Susan Bibler Coutin (2006) have set out a persuasive critique of the ways in which remittances are envisaged as the return for the export of labor, on the basis that the sending nation can claim to own the labor of its citizenry in a manner that "displaces the sale of labour from the labourer to the nation to whom the labourer is presumably indebted" (Hernández and Coutin, 2006: 189). Similarly, remittances are often treated as a form of overseas aid, which is to say a cost-free form of revenue for the national economy. This interpretation has been echoed in the discourse of the major migrant-receiving countries, including the United States, where congressional proposals have occasionally been made to cut off remittances to particular countries. Again, the insinuation is that remittances are owned by the country in which migrant workers reside.

If remittances are kept "all in the family" (Inter-American Dialogue, 2004) and thus remain immune to these kinds of politicization, including those enacted in the name of development, then their impact on poverty in remittance-receiving households can in many cases be positive. But the number of caveats to this proposition is huge, not least because the poorest sections of LAC societies tend to be characterized by very low levels of international mobility. Furthermore, the social costs for migrant workers as well as their families and communities can be considerable, and much attention has been drawn to the problems associated with fragmented families and the so-called care deficit that is emerging, as Piper notes in her chapter in this volume. To this extent, the dimensions of the migration-development nexus associated with remittances present a complex and contradictory picture that is often obscured by much of the debate on the pros and cons of remittance-led development at national and local levels.

Brain Drain

Earlier we illustrated the scale of emigration of highly skilled, educated, and professional workers from LAC to, especially, the United States, Spain, and other countries of the Organization for Economic Cooperation and Development (OECD). The orthodoxy ascribes these movements to development problems in the countries of origin, echoing the assumption that an enhancement of growth, employment and opportunities for advancement in LAC economies would remedy the "problems" of emigration for sending countries and immigration for receiving countries. Yet the absolute numbers of educated emigrants and the frequently high propensity among the most educated in these societies to emigrate are not in themselves indicative of a significant development problem. Rather, as we noted earlier, conditions of development for these sectors of LAC societies are themselves partly responsible for the propensity to migrate; furthermore, high levels of inequality have actually been associated with a reduced propensity to migrate among those who enjoy relatively privileged positions in their societies of origin. Positing a link between a lack of opportunity and migration of skilled and highly educated citizens is therefore problematic.

The question of the developmental impact of the out-migration of skilled and educated people is also complex and contingent on the conceptualization of development that is deployed. The conventional discourse on brain drain emphasizes the loss to national societies of large parts of the educated and skilled population; it also recognizes the perpetuation and exacerbation of inequalities that could be considered from a North-South perspective—that is, a widening of the conventional territorial contours of inequality whereby LAC economies are characterized by much lower average skill, education, and wage levels than those of the United States, Canada, and the parts of Europe that constitute major destinations for their skilled and educated citizens. The revisionist accounts that emphasize "brain circulation"—that is, the acquisition of skills by emigrants who then return to their countries of origin equipped to make a positive developmental impact—also find much less traction in the LAC context than in that of Asian countries such as India. In the countries most affected by these processes of brain drain, particularly those in the Caribbean, the lack of programs designed to address the associated problems and encourage return migration is striking (Phillips, 2009b).

Yet from a human-development perspective, we see the same normative arguments coming into play, questioning the relationship between the rights of individuals and households to use migration for their material and social advancement, and the obligations that they may or may not be said to hold to their countries of origin and processes of development within them.

Conclusion

My aim in this chapter has not been to try to settle the extensive debates about the migration-development nexus in LAC more broadly, but rather to give a sense of their complexity and to indicate the ways in which so much rides on the theoretical assumptions that are deployed. On the one hand, I have favored an approach that rejects a notion that migration and development are in some way separate from one another, such that the debate revolves around the impact of one on the other. Rather, to echo Skeldon in Chapter 6 of this volume, Hein de Haas reminds us that "migration and development are functionally and reciprocally connected processes" and we need to conceive of migration as intrinsically endogenous to development processes (2010: 253). On the other hand, I have sought to illustrate how different conceptions of development often lead to substantially different perspectives and conclusions on the nature of the migration-development nexus. Much of the debate echoes conventional currents in development theory that emphasize national growth as the indicator of developmental progress and thus obscure the dynamics of human development, which are intrinsic to the dynamics of migration. In other words, the migration-aggregate development nexus, as it were, looks very different from the migration-human development nexus. The argument here is that we need to adopt a much more sustained focus on the latter in our scholarly and policy-based debates.

We have seen how these contentions inform our views of the migration–(human) development nexus in LAC, where many unwarranted assumptions about its nature are clearly exposed. In a region beset by huge problems of both aggregate and human development, the social and normative implications of strategies that seek to use migration as a development tool, cast migrant workers as development agents, and create or expand ultra-flexible (migrant) labor forces as the foundations of competitiveness are of arresting significance. Under these conditions, migration not only is shaped by a well-entrenched regional political economy of unequal development in LAC, but also becomes a crucial means by which it can be reproduced and perpetuated.

Notes

1. In the late 2000s, some evidence emerged to indicate that migrant workers are less strongly represented in the informal economy than are native workers. However, it is unclear how informality is being defined in these studies, and it is recognized that survey data do not adequately account for undocumented migrant workers, who operate in the shadows of both formal and informal economies (see Martínez Pizarro, 2009: 5; Tokman, 2008).

2. For a good discussion of theories conceptualizing migration as a "household livelihood strategy," see de Haas (2010).

Part 3

The Governance of Migration

10

Borders and Migration in the European Union

Andrew Geddes

In this chapter, I analyze the regional governance of migration in the European Union (EU). I show it to have a multilevel dimension in that migration policy decisions are made on subnational, national, and regional levels and involve a wide range of public and private actors. It is also multidimensional in that it encompasses a wide range of migration types (put very broadly, to work, study, seek refuge, and join with family members). Yet this notion of "multiness" does not get us very far in analytical terms; it tends to redescribe the issues rather than offer a deeper understanding of contemporary European migration policy, particularly toward labor migrants. I contend that to understand more fully the dynamics that underpin multilevel and multidimensional migration politics, we must pay close attention to the sites at which migration acquires meaning as a distinct social process—that is, at the borders of states (Zolberg, 1989). The analytical focus is thus on the underlying condition for "multiness," which is identified as changes in the location and impact of Europe's borders as the sites at which meaning is ascribed to international migration.

Going further, I contend that these borders are not just those of territory—the traditional concern of migration studies—but also organizational borders of work and welfare and conceptual borders of belonging, entitlement, and identity. Territorial borders are land, airports, and seaports at which potential migrants present themselves (or in some cases seek to evade). Organizational borders are those sites at which decisions are made about issues such as access to the labor market and entitlement to welfare benefits. Conceptual borders center on the "who are we" questions of identity that seem to drive so much of the debate about immigration and add the issue of "who deserves" to the issue of "who is entitled"—and thus demonstrate the linkage between organizational and conceptual borders. These distinctions allow us to develop the point made by Martin Heisler (1992) that international migration is simultaneously an international and a societal issue and that linkages must be recognized accordingly.

By considering borders in such terms, we can better understand migration's resonance within Europe's contemporary political economy. Such an approach does mean placing the focus on the borders of rich, economically developed European states that are destination countries for migrants from less economically developed parts of the world. But it also recognizes the important linkages between migration and development that resonate with the EU approach (Nyberg-Sørensen et al., 2002; CEC, 2005a; OECD, 2007b). This helps demonstrate the ways in which the regional governance of migration in Europe is linked to a much bigger debate about the nature of the EU as an international organization and the power that it projects both internally and internationally.

My main analytical focus is on labor migration and policy developments within the EU, which consists of 27 member states. Labor migration in this context is highly diverse. For instance, it is strongly sectorally concentrated at both the lower- and higher-skilled ends of the job spectrum, oriented toward shorter- and longer-term work, mediated by agencies and networks operating either formally or informally to recruit and mobilize migrant workers, and located within formal and informal economies. There is elision in public and policy debate between types of migration, such as between labor migration and asylum. The migration policies of the EU also have important effects on states in its neighborhood and bear some comparison with the labor migration policies of other liberal states such as the United States and Australia, the subjects of the next two chapters, although in those contexts the regional dimension of policy responses to migration is clearly much less developed than it is in the EU. Underlying the claims made in this chapter is a point about method, as the argument here is underpinned by an understanding of international migration not as a driver of social, political, and economic change in Europe but as an effect of broader changes in the European and global system—that is, of the location and meaning of the borders that, in turn, give meaning to international migration. This is not to downplay migrant agency; central to any understanding of international migration is the way patterns of movement are embedded within complex networks. But these networks must also be related to the borders of states and the responses to international migration organized around them.

Finally, I focus on states' efforts to regulate migration. I do not address either the moral or the practical justification for such controls, although there are good grounds for questioning their effects on both counts. The basic assumptions, which seem well founded, are that EU states intend to control their borders (however understood and however practical this intention is) and that this objective will remain a prominent feature of European migration politics for some time to come.

I thus raise three specific questions. First, how did we get to the point where we can speak of common migration and asylum policies? Second, what impact has this had on policies toward labor migration? And third, what does this tell us about the place of labor migration in the contemporary political economy of the EU as a unique form of regional governance?

The Meaning of Migration

At the core of the analysis presented in this chapter is an issue of perennial interest to students of international migration—namely, the impact of changed border relationships on understandings of and responses to international migration. As Aristide Zolberg observes, "It is precisely the control which states exercise over borders that defines international migration as a distinctive social process. This arises from their irreducible political element, in that the process entails not only a physical relocation but a change of jurisdiction and membership" (1989: 405–406).

More specifically, attention is directed to the impact of changed border relationships within and between EU member states on understandings of and responses to labor migration. This is an intriguing issue for a number of reasons, not least because the free movement of EU citizens has been integral to the so-called European project (CEC, 1997). Free movement for nationals of EU member states (called "EU citizens" since the Maastricht Treaty came into force in 1993) has long been a core EU objective. Migration and asylum from outside the EU were not central to the initial integration objectives laid out in the 1950s. However, since the 1980s there has been a developing momentum behind action at the EU level, and since the late 1990s talk of common migration and asylum policies has become much more meaningful (Geddes, 2008a).

If the location/meaning/practices of borders change, then, it would seem, so too will the meaning ascribed to international migration in its various forms. This approach to the analysis of borders is explored more fully in the next section. The key border relationships that this chapter will focus on are those of work and welfare—that is, labor markets and welfare states—which, with their associated notions of belonging and entitlement, play a key role in giving meaning to labor migration in Europe (Bommes and Geddes, 2000; Geddes, 2005, 2008a). These types of borders tend to exist within states, but have an external aspect in that they inform strategies of territorial control. It is of course the case that there is significant variation in the organization of systems of work and welfare, but "varieties of capitalism," however broadly understood, will interact with international migration in different ways according to, for example, conditions affecting labor market access, vocational and workplace training systems, and the organization of industrial relations (Boyer and Hollingsworth, 1997; Hall and Soskice, 2001).

My chapter also has a strong empirical focus with the aim of better understanding how the EU has arrived at a point where some aspects of a common migration and asylum policy are currently in place, but not those involving labor migration by non-EU citizens, discussion of which has so far been minimal except among a few member states. That said, this may be about to change. At the EU level and in some member states, a more positive outlook to new migration has been evident, which is focused on three things: the shortages of workers in key economic sectors; the effects of demographic change as Europe's population ages; and a perceived need to compete against traditional immigration countries such as the United States, Canada, Australia, and New Zealand in the international market for highly skilled migrant workers. However, the point is that none of these indicates unambiguously a need for new migrants. In any case, migration alone cannot resolve these concerns, but it is now seen as part of the solution, and considerable expertise has been mobilized to support this view.

The momentum has been evident in policy planning by the European Commission (EC), which has the power to make policy proposals and an implementation role (CEC, 2004, 2005b). In October 2007, the EC made two proposals for new EU legislation on labor migration. The first was a draft Framework Directive on the admission of highly qualified migrants to the EU, which was labeled the blue card proposal, mimicking the US green card system. This would be a fast-track scheme for highly skilled workers with a signed work contract in an EU state offering remuneration at least three times higher than that state's minimum wage. The key objective was to respond to changing demands for highly qualified immigrant workers by facilitating and harmonizing both the admission of such workers to the EU and their movement in the labor market. Blue card holders would be entitled to some socioeconomic rights and more favorable conditions for family reunification. The second proposal was a draft Directive for a single-application procedure whereby non-EU nationals, known as "third-country nationals," could obtain permits to reside and work in the territory of a member state; the proposal also laid out a common set of rights for these legally residing third-country workers.

Such measures concern migration for higher-skilled forms of employment.[1] An obvious missing element is any reference to lower-skilled migration. There is abundant evidence that strongly gendered patterns of migration into lower-skilled, often temporary forms of employment, such as family and domestic care, food processing, agriculture, hospitality, and tourism, have been rapidly growing and that much of this is mediated by employment agencies (European Industrial Relations Observatory, 1999; Forde, 2001; Michon, 2006). There is evidence too of informal economic activity in these sectors, not least the employment of so-called illegal immigrants. EU action on irregular migration has tended to center on the proclaimed fight against illegal immigration, although member state responses have differed. Whereas some countries, such as Spain and Italy, have pursued large-scale regularizations, others, such as the UK, have refused to follow such an approach (CEC, 2002, 2006b, 2006c).[2] There are important relationships between formal and informal employment and legal and illegal immigration. Illegal immigration is defined in mere opposition to the designation of some migration flows as legal and is thus epiphenomenal (Samers, 2004).

Italy, for example, saw the largest growth in the legally resident immigrant population in its history, from 1.3 million in October 2001 to 2.67 million in January 2006. This population included 646,000 people who had their status regularized in 2002 and 2003 (ISTAT, 2006). Yet elements within the governing coalition continued to employ hardline anti-immigration rhetoric and even threaten military action against immigrants (Geddes, 2008b). Moreover, those who were regularized had obviously already entered the country—usually via regular channels—and were often delivering domestic welfare–related services in a welfare system with a strong orientation to family and charitable provision. As Luca Einaudi notes, this fact "drew attention to the dimensions of the substitution of welfare state services by provision of private welfare for families thanks to the work of carers and domestic workers from abroad, above all from eastern Europe" (2007: 371). The

Italian regularization process indicates the ways in which international migration reflects organizational borders and that the nature of this interaction will differ according to the broader constitution of work and welfare systems.

The Borders of Europe

The EU is the world's most developed form of supranational political and economic integration. It can be understood as, first, providing an institutional setting within which debates about migration are played out and, second, a new structure of political opportunity for the actors that populate the migration policy field. Key issues to explore, then, are how the institutions of the EU work, how decisions are made, and which actors and which interests have tended to prevail in migration-related decisionmaking. In so doing, we may see why labor migration has not, thus far at least, been central to EU policymaking—and why security-driven concerns have been.

It is abundantly evident that, since the mid-twentieth century, EU member states have been prepared to cede competence to the EU in important areas of social, economic, and political life. This has had obvious and important effects on the meaning and practice of sovereignty in Europe, as in some areas responsibilities have been shared, sovereignty pooled, and a common set of supranational institutions established with lawmaking powers (Caporaso, 1996; Peterson and Bomberg, 1999; Hix, 2005; Wallace et al., 2005). Migration for EC nationals—that is, movement within the EU—has always been central to this process insofar as the EU's core "market-making" objectives were linked first to the Common Market and then to the Single Market (Guild, 1998).[3] Free movement by EC nationals within the Common Market and, since the 1990s, by EU citizens within the Single Market, has been, is, and will continue to be integrally related to the EU's core purposes. Migration for third-country nationals has only come onto the EU agenda more recently, with particularly significant developments occurring in the 1980s and 1990s. These will be analyzed more fully in the next section.

With regard to extra-EU migration, however, the main focus has been on those forms of migration defined by state policies as "unwanted" (Joppke, 1998). Resulting EU action has focused on assisting member states in halting migration rather than helping in the recruitment of new migrants (Geddes, 2008a). In essence, this has led to a policy focus on stemming flows of migrants who fall into the categories of asylum seeker or refugee, with some evidence of elision between these categories (Morrison and Crosland, 2000). Elision of differing types of migration has also resulted from the expansion of the EU, as transition restrictions (for a period of up to seven years) were imposed by most member states on movement from the so-called A8 states, which joined in May 2004, and from Bulgaria and Romania, which joined in January 2007.

How then to understand the EU's role in migration policymaking, both in areas where it is highly developed (as with asylum, illegal immigration, and border security) and in those where it is not (particularly labor migration)? As already noted, international migration, as distinct from intrastate migration, is defined by the presence and meaning (and changes in the presence and meaning) of state borders. It seems reasonable to assume that European integration has had considerable effects on Europe's border relationships. Three indicators should suffice to affirm this observation. First is the expansion of membership from the original 6 to 27 states to form a distinct, supranational and international organization with the power to make and enforce laws (Sandholtz and Stone Sweet, 1997). Second is the extent to which market-making has become a core component of the EU project, with effects that both remove and reinforce borders and boundaries. And third is the apparent "paradox of European integration," whereby market-making efforts prompt reinforcement of other forms of boundary and border—a dilemma implicit in what James Hollifield calls "the migration state" (2004). European integration means that sovereignty (or the uses to which it is put) has changed rather than ended, because it simultaneously removes, redefines, and creates new boundaries (Bartolini, 1998).

These three indicators provide evidence of the tensions at Europe's borders and in the spaces that are bounded by them. Political geographers have long focused on notions of "bounded space" (Johnston, 2001: 683), identifying states as containers of power, wealth, society and culture that are neither leak-proof nor irrelevant or redundant (Taylor, 1994: 156–157). Territory continues to resonate as the basis for social organization in Europe, while territorial politics centered on "fixed and mutually exclusive enclaves of legitimate domination" continue to be a point of reference (Ruggie, 1993: 151). Although not a replacement for statehood, European integration can be understood as an aspect of what John Gerard Ruggie calls the "unbundling" of territory in favor of a "nonterritorial, functional organization of political authority" (Ruggie, 1993: 151). As a counterpoint, Christopher Ansell suggests that it may be more appropriate to think about the "rebundling" of authority within bounded space that now has a strong supranational dimension

(2004). Rebundled authority may create new possibilities for the development of regional responses to migration centered on the EU, which itself creates alternative forms of bounded space within which states continue to play a key, albeit changing, role in regulating migration. In short, rebundled authority signals neither the "end of territory" nor the "loss of control" (Badie, 1995; Sassen, 1996). As Malcolm Anderson (1998) notes, such cataclysmic "endisms" are highly improbable because there is a highly developed sense of territoriality in Europe. This is not to say that this sense remains fixed on immutable units called nation-states; that would be absurd, as said units are patently not immutable. But it is to say that territoriality as a spatial strategy "to affect, influence, and control" (Sack, 1986: 2) is closely related to the forms of bounded space created in Europe—that is, to the European state system as it has developed and changed since the nineteenth century and as it has structured international migration (Bade, 2003).

The focus on the EU could also shed light on analogous situations in other countries and regions. For example, Mark Purcell and Joseph Nevins (2005) provide a useful spatial dimension to the analysis of the US-Mexico border that resonates with European experience. They highlight concerns on the part of some citizens about a "thinning out" of place that has led to what they characterize as processes of "boundary build-up," whereby liberalization with regard to capital, goods, and services is accompanied by closure with regard to the movement of people (Purcell and Nevins, 2005; see also Cornelius, 2001). They define such build-up in the following terms:

> Complex interchanges between state actors and groups of citizens produced a deep set of concerns about the ethno-cultural, socio-economic and bio-physical security of the nation, all of which are inherently geographical given their inextricable relationship to a particular territory. The boundary build-up was thus a territorial strategy to achieve that security and assuage those concerns. (Purcell and Nevins, 2005: 213)

There are some clear points of convergence with EU actions on migration and asylum, as the borders of member states have moved as a result of EU enlargement to become more pronounced international borders of inequality.

The setting within which these policy orientations occur is also highly relevant and requires specification. EU politics are particularly reliant on the use of technical knowledge and expertise in technocratic settings. Within these relatively shielded forums, issues are discussed in ways that have been characterized as leading to "policy without politics" (Schmidt, 2006). The deployment of technical knowledge and expertise has an important impact on the narratives that develop to make sense of and form an ordered political response to international migration (Boswell et al., 2011). It has been argued that the security narrative has become dominant, deployed by experts drawn from national interior ministries and security agencies. The EU is used in that narrative as an alternative venue for national-level migration control systems in order to, for example, export migration control systems to new member states and neighboring countries (Lavenex, 1999, 2001; Bigo, 2001; Guiraudon, 2001; Lavenex and Uçarer, 2002; Huysmans, 2006).

The main focus of EU action has thus far been on territorial borders—that is, on the borders of EU member states, particularly those in Central, Eastern, and southern Europe that are seen to be more vulnerable to migration flows. The key point here is not just that these borders are those of EU member states but also that the EU has sought to exert control over the borders of non-EU states. The borders of Europe have thus moved (Guild, 1998), although, as Zolberg (2006) observes in his history of US immigration policy, attempts to deploy remote-control measures to stem or solicit migration flows from third countries are probably as old as migration policies themselves. What is new is the EU's role as a unique international organization attempting to exert controls on nonmember states. These controls can take a more direct form for countries, such as those in southeast Europe, that harbor hopes of joining the EU, or those that have close "international migration relations" (Geddes, 2006) with the EU but little prospect of membership, such as Morocco and Libya.

Territorial borders influence the meaning of international migration insofar as an integral element of the politics of migration is the categorization of the complex human material that comprises international migration into the types of migration that occur at those borders. But it is not only along these territorial borders that meaning is given to international migration; borders and boundaries within EU member states play a role as well. These are of course related to territorial borders but cannot be reduced to versions thereof. Through a more fine-grained analysis of borders, we can better explore international migration's domestic and societal resonance.

Organizational borders such as those that determine access to labor markets and welfare states also play an important role in shaping understandings of and responses to international migration (Bommes and Geddes, 2000; Dörr and Faist, 1997; Ferrera, 2005). Immigration has been seen as a challenge to the welfare state, as Carl-Ulrik Schierup and Stephen Castles explore in detail in Chapter 2. Herbert Kitschelt asks whether "the multiculturalization of still by and large homogenous or ethnically stable Western Europe . . . led to a decline of the welfare state" (1995: 270). Gary Freeman argues that immigration has been "a disaster" in the sense that "it has led to the Americanization of European welfare politics" (1986: 61). Susan Martin argues that migration challenges Europe's "relatively structured and rigid labor market and economy" when compared to the United States (2002: 2). Others question the extent of this erosion of welfare provision and contend that welfare states are a changed but still durable and valued aspect of the European political scene, serving as an important source of political legitimacy for national governments (Flora, 1986; Banting, 1995; Rhodes and van Apeldoorn, 1998). Maurizio Ferrera addresses more specifically the changed configuration of welfare systems. He sees European integration and other challenges such as migration as "weakening and tearing apart those spatial demarcations and closure practices that nation states have built to protect themselves" (2005: 2). If the capacity of welfare state boundaries to "cage" actors and resources has diminished, then issues such as European integration and immigration have indeed challenged the identities of welfare states, the territorial basis upon which they are organized, and the symbolic functions of group membership. As a result, they become a basis for political contention (Ferrera, 2005: 20).

The regulation of labor migration raises some significant challenges because of the sheer diversity of movement, much of which occurs in sectors that are themselves difficult to regulate, such as construction, domestic work, and agriculture. One generalization we can make about movement for the purposes of work is that it is very specific. Although we may discuss migration into the nation-state, migrants move to particular places (towns, cities, rural areas) and toward particular types of employment. In short, migration tends to be spatially and sectorally concentrated, as indicated in several other chapters in this volume. Sectors such as health care, construction, agriculture, tourism, and food processing have all become important sites of migrant employment. The fact that some of these migrants are nationals of EU member states with the ability to move freely provides an additional element of complexity (Favell and Hansen, 2002). The EU and its member states have directed their attention toward migration into higher-skilled employment. Yet recruitment agents do not only target regular migrants for formal employment (that is, for firms that are compliant with tax-based and other regulations such as workplace safety). There is also migration by irregular migrants into both the informal economy (where activity is legal but compliance with tax-based and other workplace regulations is mixed) and the illegal economy (where the activity that is undertaken is illegal). An additional element of complexity involves the key role that labor market intermediaries play in the recruitment of migrants. These could be kith- and kinship connections that serve as a basis for migration and then employment, multinational employment agencies that move people into work, or much smaller-scale recruitment agents or so-called gangmasters that recruit temporary labor, particularly into lower-skilled work such as agriculture or construction (European Industrial Relations Observatory, 1999; Geddes et al., 2007; Geddes, 2008c).

In this section I have aimed to demonstrate how it is borders that give meaning to international migration, necessitating a discussion of border types, locations, and effects. European integration clearly implies that border relationships within and between EU member states have changed. I have shown that these changes need to be understood not only in relation to borders of territory—the classic site for much analysis of migration—but also to organizational borders of work and welfare and conceptual borders of belonging, entitlement, and identity. By so doing, we can make connections between the global and domestic aspects of international migration. It is at these points of connection where the sites at which the contestation of particular migration types can be most intense are revealed.

The Regional Governance of Migration in Europe

This section outlines key empirical developments in the regional governance of migration by the EU. It shows the effort that has been made to stem unwanted migration flows and the relative lack of effort to regulate labor migration. Following my earlier conception of the EU as an institutional arena and structure of political opportunity, I argue that the reason for this discrepancy is that the interests that have been most successfully mobilized at the EU level are those related to migration as a security issue. By contrast, responses to labor migration remain national in their orientation because of the extent to which organizational borders of work and welfare resonate in a national context. There is some evidence that this is beginning to change as a result of the broader dynamics of economic integration, including its latest manifestation in the EU's ambitious program for economic reform and liberalization (called the Lisbon Agenda). There is also some realization that efforts to control "unwanted" migration are partly dependent on the EU's management of what it classifies as "wanted" migration and that a coherent policy for the regulation of migration must encompass both types.

A powerful and useful account of European integration is that EU action on migration and asylum has been driven by the interest of member states in finding new ways to resolve domestic problems (Freeman, 1998; Guiraudon, 2001) and that there is consequently a strong state-led, intergovernmental drive to cooperate. However, this is only part of the story; it neglects the networks of transgovernmental action that have developed around issues of migration and asylum for more than thirty years and that have, to some extent, changed the meaning and practice of European migration policy (Wallace, 2005). These networks can be seen as linking formal and informal modes of social and political action and putting a sectoral framework around issues of migration and internal security within the EU's opportunity field for actors from, particularly, national interior ministries. This has been the case especially since the 1990s, when the Maastricht Treaty created a Justice and Home Affairs pillar and the Amsterdam Treaty, which entered into force in 1999, introduced important developments. On this basis it has now become meaningful to talk about a common EU migration and asylum policy, albeit one that covers only some aspects of migration. Asylum and illegal immigration are at the forefront, while labor migration remains a noticeable omission.

The Maastricht Treaty built on developments in the 1980s. The first of these was the Schengen Agreement, which allowed a pioneer group of member states to establish a mini-laboratory outside of the formal Treaty structure, where experimentation with the kinds of internal security measures that would be required if single-market integration were to be realized was conducted (Monar, 2001). This was followed in 1986 by the Single European Act, which sought to formulate a European market within which the free movement of people, services, goods, and capital would be assured. The Maastricht Treaty acknowledged migration and asylum to be matters of common interest but not bases for a common policy. The result was the creation of a security framework that gave meaning to international migration as a European issue and played a key role in constituting the EU migration policy field and the institutions and interests mobilized therein (Favell, 1998).

While Maastricht provided a new base for cooperation, the decision-making processes it entailed, with their reliance on conventions of international law and unanimous agreement, made action almost impossible. Yet there was the will to establish more common EU structures and there was a template from which to draw, in the sense that the Schengen system had been operating as a free-movement laboratory since the 1980s (Monar, 2001). The Amsterdam Treaty of 1997 defined the EU as "an area of freedom, security, and justice," formulated positions on free movement, migration, and asylum, brought Schengen within the Treaty framework, and created a scope for antidiscrimination legislation on the basis of race and ethnic origin. The significance of this was that migration and asylum were taken from the intergovernmental pillar created by Maastricht and placed within the Treaty framework, which meant that common migration and asylum policies could develop based on binding EU laws (as, indeed, to some extent they have). Migration and asylum priorities were established by the member states at a meeting held in Tampere, Finland, in October 1999 (European Council, 1999). Four key elements of a common EU approach to migration and asylum were specified: partnership with countries of origin; a common asylum system; fair treatment for third-country nationals; and management of migration flows. These objectives were renewed and updated by The Hague Programme to be carried out through EU action until 2010 (Council of the European Union, 2004). The Hague Programme included partnership with third countries to improve their asylum systems, tackle illegal immigration, and implement resettlement programs. It also devised a policy to expel and return illegal immigrants to their countries of origin and created a fund for the management of external borders operated by the Warsaw-based EU agency FRONTEX.[4]

These initiatives have thus addressed the development of a common response to unwanted forms of migration, particularly asylum and illegal immigration, and have taken small steps toward a common approach to admissions (CEC, 2004, 2006c; Morrison and Crosland, 2000; Noll, 2000, 2003; Samers, 2004). The point here is that the removal of boundaries within the EU as a result of single-market liberalization has produced new issues of territorial management and population control whose resolution through EU action has taken a particular form in its concern with certain types of migration. These circumstances reflect at the EU level the debates on openness and closure that are central to migration policy. Essentially, the EU is now playing a role in the development of new controls against unwanted forms of migration, which are seen as having potentially damaging consequences for organizational borders of work and welfare and conceptual borders of belonging, entitlement, and identity.

A powerful explanation for these developments concerns the EU as a new arena for the pursuit of control strategies, wherein the executive branches of member state governments face fewer legislative and judicial constraints than they do at the national level. This tends to posit an intergovernmental, state-centered approach to the analysis of EU migration that may not fully capture the new politics of bounded space in the EU and the dilemmas posed by boundary removal, boundary build-up, and boundary shifts as they play out within the context of organizational borders of work and welfare. At the same time, approaches that emphasize supranational leadership may also be deficient because they tend to focus on leadership roles for institutions such as the European Commission, which in the area of migration and asylum has often been a follower of member state agendas rather than the leader of a distinct European agenda. The point is that member state agendas are being tailored to particular arenas and types of cooperation and policy integration within the EU institutional structure. To give an idea of what this means, it is worth reflecting on the kinds of structures that have developed. While the Commission, the Council, and the European Parliament may be the focus for discussions of EU politics, there is actually a more complex reality beneath them (as would be the case in any political system). For example, a key role has been played since the late 1990s by the Strategic Committee on Immigration, Frontiers, and Asylum (SCIFA), a forum for interior ministry representatives whose point of contact within the Commission is the Directorate General of Freedom, Justice, and Security. Interaction between these specific migration-related structures occurs at all stages of the process of developing, elaborating, finalizing, and implementing EU measures on migration and asylum.

In this section I have sought to explain how and why the EU has developed a particular approach to the regional governance of migration. I have related this approach to both the institutional form that the EU has taken and the arena of opportunities it provides for actors to operate at the EU level. These have left little space for action on labor migration by the EU itself, because member states have been reluctant to cede competence to the EU. Eytan Meyers (2002) argues that this is because European states are experiencing an excess of supply relative to their demand for migrant workers—demand that they have been able to meet through national policies—and that they would be less willing to cede competence to the EU if this meant that they were obliged to accept migrant workers at times of both economic growth and slowdown. There are now proposals for more explicit EU-level linkages between admissions policies and anti-immigrant policies (the latter being the main focus of EU action thus far), and there is a broader rationale for EU action in this area that is linked to the economic integration agenda, including its latest manifestation in the Lisbon Agenda for economic reform.

It now seems more likely that the EU will legislate on aspects of admissions policy, as it has via the blue card scheme mentioned earlier, and that this legislation will further demonstrate the centrality of organizational borders of work and welfare in all their diversity across the EU. As we have noted, action thus far has been largely focused on migration into higher-skilled employment by individuals from more economically developed parts of the world. Migration into lower-skilled forms of employment, which is without any doubt a crucial aspect of labor migration into the EU, has largely been neglected. If the EU focuses narrowly on higher-skilled migration and the member states follow suit, then migrants seeking lower-skilled employment may be forced further into the shadows of the informal or illegal economy. In a different context, it has been argued that a focus on border control allows member states to avoid opening the Pandora's box of internal controls. If EU competencies are extended to cover admissions, then this Pandora's box will be opened, with the result that the EU's fight against illegal immigration will no longer suffice (if it ever has), and much tougher efforts would be required to enforce labor market regulations. Stronger EU action might also be taken with regard to the rights of temporary and agency workers. Again, we see how migration issues are nested within a broader discussion about work and welfare in the EU.

Conclusion

In this chapter, I have conceptualized the EU as providing both an institutional setting and a new structure of opportunities. Within this framework, we can see the creation of migration policy competencies (of longer standing for free movement, more recent for extra-EU migration) and the mobilization around migration issues. These mobilizations have thus far tended to be focused on a security-driven understanding of international migration to which the reinforcement of territorial borders is the preferred approach. However, if we make the connection between the international and domestic aspects of the migration issue, then we can also see how organizational borders of work and welfare and conceptual borders of belonging, entitlement, and identity form key sites at which meaning is ascribed to migration within EU states. These are central both to understandings of international migration (as a benefit, a threat, an opportunity, a risk, a danger, an asset, and so on) and to the policy responses that develop therefrom. These policy responses are, however, nested with much bigger debates about, for example, economic reform, security, and the international identity of the EU.

Labor migration in all its complexity is part of these debates. The sheer diversity of migration raises all kinds of regulatory issues at the external and internal borders of the EU and, through migration controls, has important effects on non-member states too. The underlying point that this chapter has made is that these issues need to be seen as an effect of changed border relationships within and between EU member states—relationships that are central to the analysis of migration's place within the contemporary political economy of the EU.

Notes

1. It would be a mistake to describe the migrants themselves as lower or higher skilled, because many migrants, particularly those from developing countries, may possess professional qualifications or skills that are not recognized or certified by EU member states. Thus, the brain drain experienced by sending countries can lead to brain waste in receiving countries (World Bank, 2005).

2. That said, the accession of eight Central and Eastern European countries to the EU in May 2004 constituted a de facto regularization by the UK, as thousands of migrants from the accession states had their status regularized as a consequence of EU membership.

3. The Single Market is defined by Article 8a of the Single European Act of 1986 as an area without internal frontiers within which the free movement of people, services, goods, and capital are ensured.

4. Council Regulation (EC) No 2007/2004 of October 26, 2004, Establishing a European Agency for the Management of Operational Cooperation at the External Borders of the Member States of the European Union, *Official Journal L 349*, November 25, 2004: 1–11.

11

Immigration Reform in the United States

Susan Martin

It is a frequently cited truism that the United States is a nation of immigrants.[1] Certainly, it was settled by successive groups of immigrants, from the first wave of colonization (from the sixteenth to the eighteenth century) through the second (1790–1860) and third (1880–1924) waves of mass European migration to the most recent wave of migration (from 1965 onward), dominated by movements from Latin America, the Caribbean, Asia, and, in smaller numbers, Africa. This contemporary wave is the largest in absolute numbers; although it is not yet the largest as a proportion of the total population, it is approaching the historic levels of immigration at the turn of the nineteenth to twentieth century and may exceed those levels by 2025 (Passel and Cohn, 2008b). Each year, about 1.5 million persons are added to the US population through immigration. According to the demographers Jeffrey Passel and D'Vera Cohn, "From 1960 to 2005, new immigrants and their US-born descendants accounted for 51% of population increase. In the later part of that period, from 1980 to 2005, new immigration accounted for 58% of the 68 million additional people" (2008b: 2). Most immigrants are of working age, which means that immigration is a strong contributor to growth in the US labor force.

Strong growth in the US economy in the 1990s contributed to the arrival of record numbers of immigrants, but, significantly, by the mid-2000s more people were arriving without authorization than through legal channels (Passel, 2005). The disconnect between the rules and regulations of legal admission to the United States and the economic forces that attract foreign workers to the country helps explain the trend toward unauthorized migration. This is not to say that the state is irrelevant in managing migration (see Hunt and Hollifield, 2006). My own interviews in Mexico confirm that many would-be migrants ultimately decide to remain at home either because they are unwilling or afraid to break US law or because they understand the dangers they may face in crossing the border without authorization. In effect, US policies do have a deterrent effect on many who would like to migrate but do not qualify for admission. Yet the point is that a very complex and expensive system of immigration enforcement has been insufficient to curb unauthorized migration, largely because US immigration policies do not reflect the economic realities of the US labor market.

Not only are the laws that regulate immigration complex, but so too are the institutional arrangements to implement the statutory requirements. Major responsibilities are divided between four cabinet-level departments: the Department of Homeland Security (DHS), the State Department, the Justice Department, and the Labor Department. Within the department with the strongest powers, the DHS, there are three major bureaus with immigration-related authorities: US Citizenship and Immigration Services, which is responsible for adjudicating applications for admission and citizenship; Immigration and Customs Enforcement, which is responsible for the interior enforcement of immigration laws; and Customs and Border Protection, which is responsible for enforcement at the borders of the country.

Each year, the US Congress appropriates billions of dollars to these agencies, and each year more migrants arrive beyond the reach of the regulated system. Scholars, employers, and advocates for immigrants have pointed out the disconnect between policy and economics. For instance, Benjamin Johnson, director of the Immigration Policy Center, told the Senate Judiciary Committee in 2006 that "the root of the current crisis of undocumented immigration is a fundamental disconnect between today's economic and labor market realities and an outdated system of legal immigration" (Johnson, 2006). Similarly, the Independent Taskforce on Immigration and America's Future, which included former members of Congress and the executive branch, concluded in 2006 that "illegal immigration occurs within the bounds of a broader immigration system that is over-burdened and no longer serves the nation's needs" (2006: xv–xvi). Yet multiple efforts to reform US immigration law—supposedly to make it more congruent with economic forces—have failed in Congress. In the interim, the number of unauthorized migrants in the United States has continued to grow, reaching an estimated 12 million in 2007, and immigration has become a hot-button issue in American politics. States and especially localities have tried to take actions of their own, citing the failure of the federal government to curb illegal migration. Talk radio programs, particularly those catering to grassroots conservatives, have filled the airwaves with denunciations of the bipartisan agreement on the need for regularization of the millions in the country without authorization. At the same time, immigrants have organized themselves in mass rallies to oppose more restrictive policies, and business has lobbied for additional visas for both temporary and permanent workers at the high and low ends of the skill spectrum.

The political and economic interests that influence immigration policy often join together in support of specific provisions in the law but diverge over others, making the type of comprehensive reform that was proposed most recently by the administration of President George W. Bush very difficult to enact (see Freeman, 1995; Gimpel and Edwards, 1998; Tichenor, 2002). Moreover, as has been the case throughout US history, the public is highly ambivalent about newcomers; seeing their own immigrant forebears through rose-colored glasses, some are nonetheless fearful that today's immigrants will fail to adopt American norms and values. That ambivalence makes immigration reform all the more difficult because there is seldom a strong constituency behind any set of policy changes. The public tends to favor restriction when asked their preferences in opinion polls, but immigration is rarely a key factor in elections (see Schuck, 2007).

In this chapter, I seek to explain the apparent paralysis that affected the Bush administration's ability to address the very real immigration problems that the United States faces. The answer appears to lie in the international political economy of immigration reform, which has prevented Congress from adopting comprehensive reforms that would rationalize an immigration system riddled with contradictions and continuing tolerance for large-scale illegal migration. The chapter takes as its starting point the tension between structure and agency discussed by Nicola Phillips in the introduction to this volume. If US immigration policy were formulated purely on economic principles and the key economic actors shaping the global political economy had greater influence in the policy process, legal admissions would be considerably higher than is the case at the time of this writing in 2011. Then again, if it were formulated purely on the basis of politics, as represented by consistent public opinion polls showing concern that the level of immigration is too high, admission numbers would be considerably lower than is presently the case (Facchini and Mayda, 2008). Not surprisingly given this tension, Congress finds it exceedingly difficult to address immigration policy, debating the details of immigration reform long past the time when a globalized economy would argue for significant change in US policies and practices. More interesting, the economic, political, and social actors on both sides of the immigration reform debate are often themselves ambivalent about reform, disliking current policies but fearing the changes that reform might bring.

I begin the chapter with a discussion of current immigration policies. I then present the debate over immigration reform that took place in the United States following the announcement by President Bush in the early 2000s of his intention to seek a migration agreement with the Mexican government. In the final section, I examine in greater detail the various and shifting interests that have influenced the debate over immigration reform, concluding that the seeming paralysis over immigration reform is consistent with both historical patterns and the contradictions between a global economy that pushes for greater labor mobility and a domestic political dynamic that prefers the status quo to the risk of untested policy reform.

US Immigration Policies

Much of US legal admissions policy was formulated in the 1960s, though some changes were made in 1990 to reflect the political and economic realities of a newly globalized economy. At the core of US policy is the system for permanent admissions. Permanent immigrants—"green carders"—are persons who are entitled to live and work permanently in the United States and, after five years, to become naturalized US citizens. During the 2000s, the four principal bases or doors for admission were family reunification (sponsored either by green carders or naturalized citizens), skills, diversity, and humanitarian interests. By far the largest admissions door has opened for relatives of US residents.

The 1990s saw a large increase in the demand for foreign workers as the US economy grew sharply, but even as US businesses recruited increasingly from a global labor force, no increases after the 1990 legislation were made in the permanent admission categories for employer-sponsored workers. Instead, temporary-worker categories are increasingly important as the vehicles for admission of foreign workers, particularly professionals, executives, and managers. Over time, a large number of temporary-admission visa categories have emerged, each referred to by the letter of the alphabet under which it is described in the Immigration and Nationality Act. The most commonly used categories are H1-B for specialty workers, H2-A for agricultural workers, H2-B for other seasonal workers, and L for intracompany transfers. Professionals, managers, and executives may also enter under the North American Free Trade Agreement (NAFTA). To some extent, the growth in temporary-worker programs reflects changes in the global economy, as seen in the hiring of foreign workers in the information technology (IT) sector, in which product development cycles are short. Yet, the large and increasing backlogs of temporary workers sponsored by employers for permanent admission indicates that market forces alone are not at stake. Rather, the inadequacy of the permanent admissions system to respond in a timely way to business demands has led to the expanded use of temporary visas as a stopgap measure.[2]

Although the United States continues to admit large numbers of legal immigrants and temporary workers, the fastest growth in immigration is now among those without authorization to be in the country. As we have noted, an estimated 12 million unauthorized migrants were in the United States in 2007, and net new entries prior to the economic recession were estimated at 500,000 each year.[3] This net figure reflects the difference between new entries and those who return home or adjust their status and become legal immigrants.

Efforts to prevent unauthorized migration largely failed in the 1990s and early 2000s. The Immigration Reform and Control Act (IRCA) of 1986 tried a three-track approach that introduced new border enforcement measures, sanctions against employers who hired unauthorized workers, and a legalization program for those who were already illegally in the country. The provisions did not succeed in slowing down unauthorized migration. In fact, the mechanisms for determining work authorization that were necessary to an enforceable system of employer sanctions were so faulty that it was no more difficult for irregular migrants to find jobs post-IRCA than it had been before its passage. A proliferation of fraudulent documents allowed employers to hire unauthorized workers with little risk of sanction. Employers were not expected to weed out the counterfeits if the documents looked valid. In fact, if an employer requested additional documentation, he or she faced penalties imposed to ensure that employers did not discriminate against foreign-looking or -sounding workers. Calls for new employment verification systems to strengthen the employer sanctions regime were largely ignored, although Congress passed legislation in 1996 to pilot-test electronic verification.[4] During the second half of the 1990s, in the midst of an economic boom that produced record numbers of new jobs, unauthorized migration increased still further. Throughout the boom period, little was done to curb the growth in irregular migration.

"Fair and Secure Immigration Reform"

George W. Bush campaigned for the presidency in 2000 with a pledge to make immigration reform a top priority of his administration. Many groups had high hopes that the newly elected president would deliver on his campaign promise. President Bush had served as governor of a border state with close ties to Mexico, namely Texas, where more than one-third of the population is of Hispanic origin. Texas has also long depended on cross-border trade with Mexico for its economic livelihood, especially since the launch of NAFTA in 1994. Familiarity with US-Mexico issues thus predisposed the new Bush administration to place immigration at the forefront of the political agenda.

Although it was by no means certain that such legislation would have passed Congress, the events of September 11, 2001, displaced immigration reform from the national agenda. US politics became dominated by the debate over how to combat terrorism, protect homeland security, and neutralize the threat posed by anti-Western, fundamentalist regimes. Serious discussion of immigration reform languished in the United States during the next two years, although some progress was made in achieving agreements with Canada and Mexico on border security strategies.

Immigration reform returned to the US political agenda in 2004. The outlines of the president's proposal to reform the immigration system and create a temporary-worker program were as follows. The Fair and Secure Immigration Reform provided temporary-worker status to those who were in the United States without authorization; it would not lead directly to citizenship. Temporary workers would be eligible to apply for permanent residency, but only through the existing application process and without any preferences over other applicants for citizenship. The Bush administration announced plans to increase the number of people who could obtain a green card and thus lawful permanent residency. However, the number of additional green cards was not disclosed. It should be noted that only 10,000 slots are available each year for less skilled workers, which would be the category by which most of the temporary workers would adjust their status.

Delinkage of the temporary-worker program from citizenship status was designed to deflect criticism of President Bush's proposal from conservative political groups that opposed amnesty for immigrants illegally in the country. Instead, program participants would be eligible to work in the United States for an initial period of three years, at which point they could renew their temporary-worker visas for an unspecified number of three-year periods. Return to the country of origin otherwise would be required after three years.

The primary incentive for individuals to come forward and participate in a guest-worker program is that it would make their presence in the United States legal. Possession of a temporary-worker card would guarantee the right to live and work in the United States and would eliminate the risk of deportation for three years. This would both improve the quality of everyday life and permit individuals to pursue employment opportunities that require proof of legal status. A related benefit of the temporary-worker program, according to the proposal, was that it would assure "circularity," or freedom of travel between the United States and the temporary worker's country of origin. Program participants would no longer have to fear being barred from reentry to the United States after a visit to their home community. The promotion of close ties between guest workers and their countries of origin was intended to encourage their eventual return home, not least because the maintenance of such ties would strengthen the likelihood of finding employment or starting businesses upon return (Aguirre, 2004). Interestingly, however, the Bush proposal weakened some of these incentives to return home by allowing spouses and minor children to live in the United States with the temporary worker. These dependents, however, would not be authorized to work unless they too participated in the program.

Harsh public criticism of Bush's plan emanated from both liberal and conservative camps, effectively blocking passage of any legislation based thereon. At the conservative end of the political spectrum, critics voiced concern that the temporary-worker proposal amounted to amnesty for unauthorized migrants. Concerns about amnesty stemmed from the fact that the 1986 legalization program, which provided a route to eventual citizenship, did not reduce illegal immigration. On the contrary, the population of unauthorized aliens in the US tripled between the mid-1980s and the time when the administration's proposal was made (Antle, 2004). This fact caused opponents of illegal immigration to view with great trepidation any proposal that appeared to absolve persons for having entered the United States illegally. Lawmakers feared such measures simply would encourage migrants to cross the border and would thus necessitate additional amnesties down the road. Alternative proposals to the president's plan consequently tended to stress the need for more thorough border enforcement, increased deportations, and even stiffer penalties for employers that hired unauthorized workers.

Criticism of President Bush's proposal emanated equally from the liberal side of the political aisle. After the plan was unveiled in January

2004, Senator Ted Kennedy disparaged the temporary-worker proposal for being grossly inadequate to resolve the nation's broken immigration system, and he and Senator John McCain subsequently introduced their own version of comprehensive immigration reform. Senators Tom Daschle and Joe Lieberman specifically criticized the proposal for failing to offer guest workers a direct path to citizenship, such as through an earned legalization process (CNN, 2004).

Certain details and basic assumptions of the president's proposal also elicited criticism from nonpolitical groups. Experts in the migration field questioned whether the guarantee of circularity—the ability to return freely to one's home country—provided a sufficient incentive to encourage unauthorized immigrants to enroll in the temporary-worker program. Increased job opportunities, higher standards of living, better access to health care and education—all these aspects of life in the United States offer a compelling reason for immigrants to wish to remain. The fact that the Bush proposal did not provide a clear path to permanent residence, much less actual citizenship status, would tend to undermine the attractiveness of the program to many potential participants. It consequently could prove ineffective for reducing the number of unauthorized immigrants who entered the United States.

It also seemed unlikely to expect that unauthorized immigrants already working in the United States would choose to register for the temporary-worker program if it did not improve their chances of staying in the country permanently. As Demetrios Papademetriou (2004) of the Migration Policy Institute noted in testimony before Congress, a program that allows only for temporary stays is unlikely to provide sufficient inducement for immigrants to come forward. Certain organizations such as the National Immigration Law Center claimed that unauthorized immigrants might even view the temporary-worker program as an enforcement trap (NILC, 2004). The registration process could be interpreted as a ruse to bring undocumented aliens into contact with authorities who would facilitate their deportation.

An additional concern was that most of the onus of immigration reform was placed on the guest worker, not his or her employer. The Bush proposal placed very little emphasis on interior enforcement to control unauthorized migration, at least as compared to border enforcement. Despite calls for increased workplace enforcement and verification of compliance with other labor laws, the proposal earmarked very little funding to verify that employers were hiring only those individuals with temporary-worker cards and were complying with fair labor standards. Whereas the president's proposal designated US$2.7 billion for border security inspections in the budget for the fiscal year 2005, the funding for worksite enforcement was raised to a mere US$25 million (US DHS, 2004).

Notable criticism of the president's proposal was also levied by major legal and labor organizations. For instance, the American Bar Association (ABA) criticized the proposal for providing insufficient mechanisms to guarantee worker rights, including the ability to change employers without threat of deportation. Similarly, the American Federation of Labor–Congress of Industrial Organizations (AFL-CIO), the main US trade union body, asserted that the president's proposal did nothing to strengthen protection of wages, benefits, and other rights for either immigrant or domestic workers. Instead, the proposal would create a permanent, and larger, underclass of workers in the US economy. According to the AFL-CIO, the plan would reward large corporations and employers with a steady stream of vulnerable and underpaid workers while weakening the rights of workers and exacerbating disrespect for individual rights within the immigration system (Sweeney, 2004).

In light of the low priority placed on employer compliance with immigration law and labor rights standards, advocates for the rights of immigrants argued that persons in the United States illegally might be encouraged to come forward to obtain the temporary-worker card but then would have little recourse to demand safe and fair working conditions from their employers. Without adequate workplace enforcement, employers easily could turn to illegal immigrants to replace guest workers who criticized unfair work conditions. For those concerned with immigration enforcement, the president's proposal lacked an essential means to reform effectively the immigration system. Strong incentives would remain for immigrants to enter this country illegally, above all the continued prevalence of employers willing to offer jobs to undocumented workers.

A final concern, articulated by both the ABA and the National Immigration Forum (NIF), was that the president's proposal left out necessary reforms to allow for family reunification. Under US immigration law, it takes many years for permanent residents or US citizens to be reunited with family members. As a result, many choose to enter the country illegally or to overstay their visas. The absence of a plan to widen the legal channel for family reunification through the temporary-worker program meant that reform would do little to correct existing abuses of the immigration system. Individuals wishing to reunite with family members in the United States would likely continue to enter the country without proper documents. The alternative for spouses and children of guest workers was little better. Immediate dependents could apply for temporary legal status under the president's plan. Yet the fact that they were prohibited from working under the proposal meant that many would likely continue to circumvent the law and enter the workforce under the table (Insight, 2004).

Legislative Initiatives in the US Congress

Several legislative alternatives to President Bush's temporary-worker proposal were introduced but not enacted by Congress. In the 109th Congress (2005–2006), the Republican-led Senate and House of Representatives took very different approaches to immigration reform. The House focused primarily on enhanced enforcement while the Senate tried for comprehensive reform. The Border Protection, Antiterrorism, and Illegal Immigration Control Act of 2005 was introduced by James Sensenbrenner, the chair of the Judiciary Committee. It passed the House in December 2005. The bill addressed a number of enforcement issues, but it was roundly criticized because it included what were widely seen in immigration circles as draconian measures and did not include any legal alternatives to unauthorized migration. The bill's border security provisions included increased staffing and training for the Border Patrol, technology for deployment along the border, and physical infrastructure to deter unauthorized crossings. The bill also required the development of a national strategy for border security and it expanded the scope of and enhanced penalties for smuggling and trafficking offenses.

In a particularly criticized provision, the bill increased the penalties for harboring an unauthorized migrant in a manner that increased the likelihood of imprisonment for the staff of religious and social-services organizations that assisted immigrants. As described by the American Immigration Lawyers Association,

> this incredibly overbroad definition of smuggling would criminalize the work of social service organizations, refugee agencies, churches, attorneys, and other groups that counsel immigrants, treating them the same as smuggling organizations. In addition, family members and employers could be fined and imprisoned for "harboring", "shielding" or "transporting" undocumented family members or employees, filling our prisons with people who have done nothing more than try to reunite their families or help a worker, friend or client. (AILA, 2005: 3)

In an equally criticized provision, the bill created a new felony offense of unlawful presence in the United States. Traditionally, simple violations of immigration law have been treated as civil offenses, not criminal ones. Other provisions enhanced the use of mandatory detention, expanded the definition of aggravated felonies that would result in mandatory removal, put into place new terrorism-related reasons for inadmissibility and removal, and eliminated or reduced access to the courts to hear certain immigration-related cases. It also made changes in the burden of proof for an asylum seeker, requiring him or her to establish that "his or her life or freedom would be threatened in the country in question, and that race, religion, nationality, membership in a particular social group, or political opinion would be at least *one central reason* for such threat" (AILA, 2005: 14). A number of these provisions overturned federal court rulings.

The bill also addressed the work magnet for unauthorized migration. It required the Secretary of Homeland Security to implement an employment eligibility verification system, building on the basic pilot program already in use in verifying work authorization. The system would become mandatory for employers, who would need to verify not only new hires but also their existing workforce.

The legislation passed by the House caused an uproar among immigrant-advocacy organizations, businesses, and civil-rights and civil-liberties groups. Opponents argued that enforcement-only approaches would not solve the immigration problem but rather simply further criminalize individuals whose main purpose in violating immigration law was to work. Demonstrations across the country showed the depth of concern among ethnic communities with large immigrant populations. These demonstrations, along with the concerns of business that immigration reform must address their legitimate need for foreign workers, paved the way for a radically different approach in the Senate.

As an alternative, the Secure America and Orderly Immigration Act was introduced by Senators McCain and Kennedy and Representatives Jim Kolbe, Jeff Flake, and Luis Gutiérrez. The bill addressed a wide range of issues, from earned regularization and temporary-work programs to increased border security and new employment verification provisions. It attempted to provide answers to three questions of reform: (1) what to do about existing unauthorized migrants, (2) how to meet the legitimate needs of employers for foreign labor and families for reunification, and (3) how to deter future unauthorized migration. A competing bill, the Comprehensive Enforcement and Immigration Reform Act of 2005, was introduced by Senators John Cornyn and Jon Kyl. It too provided a mechanism for regularization of unauthorized migrants in the United States, but it was far more restrictive than the McCain-Kennedy proposal. A compromise was then negotiated by Senators Chuck Hagel and Mel Martínez that paved the way for passage of the legislation by the Senate. There was no prospect for agreement with the House enforcement-only approach, and the bills died with the elections and the turnover of the Congress to Democratic Party leadership.

In the 110th Congress (2007–2008), immigration reform once more appeared on the political agenda, but with little chance that comprehensive reform would be enacted. The Senate and the House once more took different approaches, although both bodies were now under the control of the Democratic Party. In the Senate, closed-door discussions between senators from both parties and the administration led to the introduction of a bill that lifted elements from each of the previous legislative attempts and introduced new policies not previously encompassed in any of the legislative packages. The bill was comprehensive in scope and radical in many of its strategies for curbing unauthorized migration and reforming legal admissions. The House, by contrast, held numerous hearings on immigration reform issues, but the leadership decided to take a wait-and-see attitude and defer action until the Senate debated its legislation. When the Senate failed to end debate on the bipartisan bill supported by the president, the House deferred action as well.

Before discussing the reasons why comprehensive reform failed, we would do well to examine the specifics of the proposed Senate bill. Its most controversial element was its legalization provisions. The legislation included an earned regularization program (the Z visa) that was at the same time more generous and more restrictive than previous versions. It was more generous in that it provided a route to legal status for all unauthorized migrants in the country as of January 2007. Eliminating the tiered system used in previous legislation, the provision would treat all unauthorized migrants similarly. They would regularize upon the acquisition of a new nonimmigrant visa that could be renewed every four years, when new fees and English- and civics-testing requirements applied. At the same time, the Senate bill was more restrictive in terms of eligibility for eventual permanent residence and citizenship. The regularized would be at the back of a long waiting list, estimated to take about eight years to clear. Moreover, the Senate bill would require what is known as a "touch back," whereby the heads of all regularized families would have to return home to reenter as permanent residents. They would also have to meet the requirements of a points system. Although unauthorized migrants would find immediate relief from deportation, the full regularization program would only go into effect when certain benchmarks were met in the enforcement of immigration laws.

The Senate bill included a new temporary worker program (the Y visa) that would introduce a rotational requirement. Workers would be granted an initial two-year visa, renewable twice more. What made the Senate version of the temporary-worker program a radical departure from earlier versions is the requirement that workers return home for one year between each renewal. After three rotations, they would not be eligible to reenter. A limit of 200,000 Y workers was approved by amendment on the floor of the Senate, but a mechanism remained to permit increases in the case of high demand. Also included in the Senate legislative initiative were major changes in the program for permanent admission. After clearing the backlogs of current applicants, the legislation would eliminate the extended family, employer-petitioned, and diversity visa categories for admission. While immediate family (spouses, minors, and parents) of US citizens and permanent residents would still be eligible, all other immigrants would be admitted on the basis of a points system that would reward education, English language ability, and qualifications in shortage occupations. A small number of points would be awarded for family ties if the applicants amassed a minimum number of points in these other areas.

Most of the enforcement provisions were lifted in their entirety from previous bills or represented a variation on the themes of already negotiated provisions. The legislation emphasized both border security and interior enforcement. With regard to worksite enforcement, the bill included provisions for mandatory electronic employment verification, as well as increased penalties for the illegal hiring of unauthorized workers.

As negotiations over the Senate bill continued, provisions were added that troubled the proponents of comprehensive reform without satisfying the opponents. The agreement began to unravel in its own bipartisan way, with some Democrats peeling off because of concerns about the open-endedness of the temporary-worker programs and their lack of labor protections as well as about the new enforcement measures and the elimination of many family categories. Joined by some newly elected Democrats from usually Republican-leaning districts, many Republicans remained opposed to what they and their supporters considered an amnesty program that signified a reward for illegal activity. When the Senate leadership tried to end debate over the legislation, it failed to garner the sixty votes needed to bring the legislation to a vote. With the 2008 elections looming, few members expected immigration reform to regain any momentum.

Interestingly, neither the executive branch nor Congress considered liberalizing legal immigration through the various bilateral, regional, or global trade agreements under negotiation during this period. The two major agreements ratified during the administration of Bill Clinton—NAFTA and the General Agreement on Trade in Services (GATS)—and the bilateral agreements the George W. Bush administration negotiated with Chile and Singapore had all addressed migration issues, but only in the context of admission for highly skilled professionals, including the managers and executives of multinational corporations, for temporary work purposes. After the Chile and Singapore accords, however, the Senate adopted a nonbinding resolution stating that "trade agreements are not the appropriate vehicle for enacting immigration-related laws or modifying current immigration policy; and future trade agreements to which the United States is a party and the legislation implementing the agreements should not contain immigration-related provisions" (US Senate, 2003: 10691). The opposition to negotiating immigration agreements in trade accords met with bipartisan support from proponents and opponents of free trade and liberalized immigration.

Why Did Immigration Reform Fail?

Comprehensive immigration reform is the exception, not the rule, in US politics. Until 1875, there were few laws regulating immigration to the United States. From then until 1921, Congress put into effect a series of rules that restricted the entry of immigrants (primarily from Asian countries) on the basis of nationality and race, as well as their health and morals, the likelihood that they would become public charges, and other similar factors. During the late nineteenth century and the early twentieth century, debate on immigration heated up as the numbers of southern and Eastern European immigrants increased dramatically. At first the debate focused on a literacy test that proponents thought would restrict immigration to those with higher levels of education. After passage of the literacy requirements in 1917 failed to shift immigration origins and numbers as expected, opponents of mass migration turned to a more comprehensive approach that resulted in the National Origins quota system, passed in 1921 and refined in 1924.

The National Origins laws placed overall numerical restrictions on immigration from the Eastern Hemisphere and set per-country quotas based on the percentage of US residents in the 1890 census who originated from specific countries. As the 1890 census preceded the mass migration from southern and Eastern Europe, higher quotas went to the United Kingdom and northwestern Europe. The quotas for Italy, Poland,

and Russia, by contrast, were much lower than the actual immigration from these countries in the late nineteenth and early twentieth centuries.

The National Origins laws stayed in place until 1965 despite great criticism in the period after World War II and the passage of a series of bills that enabled admission of refugees and displaced persons outside of the quotas. President Harry Truman established a commission that issued a report titled *Whom Shall We Welcome?*, which recommended the elimination of National Origins quotas and the establishment of criteria based on broader US interests. The commission concluded that the National Origins quotas "flout fundamental American traditions and ideals, display a lack of faith in America's future, damage American prestige and position among other nations, [and] ignore the lessons of the American way of life" (President's Commission, 1953: xv). Nevertheless, Congress, over Truman's veto, renewed the National Origins quotas in the 1952 McCarran-Walter Act.

It was not until 1965 that a comprehensive overhaul of US immigration policy took place. Triumphed as a civil-rights initiative, the 1965 amendments eliminated National Origins quotas and rescinded the various Asian-exclusion acts of the nineteenth century. In their place were overall hemispheric caps on visas. At first, there were different caps for the Eastern and Western Hemispheres—170,000 and 120,000, respectively—but in 1978 a global cap of 290,000 was established. To ensure that no one country dominated, a per-country limit of 20,000 visas was instituted. Eligibility criteria broadly mirrored the 1952 law in giving priority to those sponsored by family members and employers, but the 1965 amendments changed the employment categories and opened the door for a sizable increase in family reunification visas. The 1952 legislation included a provision for the admission of highly skilled immigrants whose services are urgently needed in the United States; the 1965 law, however, permitted skilled and unskilled workers in occupations with labor shortages.

Similar delays in enacting legislation for admission of refugees can be seen. During the 1930s and early 1940s, many refugees were rejected for admission to the United States. The most extreme case concerned the *St. Louis*, the ship of Jewish refugees that was turned back by the United States and forced to return to Nazi-controlled Germany, where many passengers died in the Holocaust. After the war, the United States admitted thousands of displaced persons via a series of presidential rulings and laws that, in effect, mortgaged the National Origins quotas. In 1951, the UN Convention Relating to the Status of Refugees was adopted, but the United States did not ratify the convention despite its participation in the drafting. Only in 1969 did the United States ratify the 1967 Protocol to the Refugee Convention. It was not until 1980, however, that the country passed legislation that adopted the UN definition of a refugee and put in place a permanent system for refugee resettlement and asylum proceedings. Previously, refugees from Hungary, Cuba, Indochina, and the Soviet Union had been admitted through the parole authority of the attorney general, because those emergency programs far exceeded the 17,000 refugee visas included in the regular immigration legislation.

When unauthorized migration grew in the 1970s, Congress considered legislation but failed to reach consensus. Instead, it formed the bipartisan Select Commission on Immigration and Refugee Policy (SCIRP), a time-honored way to navigate the complexities and emotions in immigration policy. SCIRP included four cabinet officers, four senators, four representatives, and four public members. The final report, issued in 1981, recommended a three-legged stool that included enhanced enforcement, particularly in the form of sanctions against employers who hired illegal workers; legalization for the estimated 3 to 6 million unauthorized migrants already in the country; and reforms in legal admissions programs that would increase dramatically the number of immigrants to be admitted on the basis of their skills. The basics of the SCIRP proposals were taken up by successive Congresses. The employer sanctions and legalization recommendations were finally enacted in the 1986 IRCA by a narrow vote in the lame-duck Congress. The legal-admission reforms were not enacted until the 1990 Immigration Act.

In the context of these historical trends, the failure of Congress to enact comprehensive reform during the Bush administration, despite strong bipartisan agreement on many points, is not surprising. Major changes in immigration policy generally require years of preparation and negotiation. Even the imprimatur of blue-ribbon panels helps but does not ensure quick passage of new approaches.

An understanding of the political economy of US immigration policy helps explain the difficult nature of reform. Political coalitions form around immigration, representing political, economic, and social interests that are often at odds with each other. These interests can be divided into four categories, organizing groups by their attitudes toward immigration numbers, on the one hand, and immigrant rights, on the other (see Martin, 1998, 2003; Tichenor 2002). The first group, the advocates, includes those who are favorable to high levels of immigration as measured by numbers of admissions and profess a commitment to the protection of the rights of immigrants; their preference is for permanent admissions that provide access to citizenship. The second group, the free-marketers, also supports high levels of immigration, but is willing to restrict the rights of those admitted; its preference is for large-scale temporary-worker programs, limitations on access to public welfare programs, and measures that permit the quick removal of any migrants that commit criminal or other offenses. The third group, the restrictionists, supports limits on the rights of migrants and the numbers to be admitted. The fourth group, the integrationists, sees rights as paramount and is comfortable with numerical limits on admissions, especially on categories that inherently limit the capacity of migrants to exercise their rights (such as temporary-worker programs and unauthorized migration).

In debates over immigration reform, groups within these four categories often form coalitions in support of specific provisions. For example, the supporters of high levels of immigration will often join together to defeat efforts to restrict movements. Nevertheless, they break apart when issues at the core of their differences come up for votes. The shifting interests end up creating strange bedfellows who find it difficult to gain consensus on comprehensive reforms, even if they are able to agree on many elements of policy.

Conclusion

The failure to enact comprehensive immigration reform in the presence of large-scale unauthorized migration reflects fundamental ambivalence about the role of immigration in US society and the US economy. As mentioned in the introduction, most US citizens speak fondly and nostalgically about their own immigrant forebears who, in their minds, created the nation of immigrants. At the same time, they are fearful that today's immigrants are somehow different and less likely to contribute and assimilate—that is, to become true Americans. This ambivalence is by no means new: Benjamin Franklin worried that the Germans immigrating to Pennsylvania in the eighteenth century would never learn English. The result of this ambivalence is the absence of any strong consensus among the public about changes in immigration policy. A small group that knows what it opposes can often preempt action (as witnessed in both the immigrant rallies that derailed the House Republican enforcement measures and the talk radio shows that derailed the Senate regularization measures), but pressure for positive changes is too often lacking. The safe decision for politicians is no decision—at least until there is no choice but to act.

In fact, the status quo surrounding tolerance of unauthorized migration serves many political and economic interests at both the domestic and international levels, whereas reform might usher in changes that could be more harmful than helpful. Much of the research on the impact of immigration on the US economy demonstrates that the principal beneficiaries are employers and consumers (Smith and Edmonston, 1997). Immigrants to the United States tend to fall into two educational categories: most are either worse- or better-educated than the average American. They thereby fill positions that most US workers either do not want because of low pay and poor working conditions or do not have the skills to undertake. Unauthorized migrants tend to fall into the first category, and those admitted under the employment-based permanent and temporary programs fall into the second. The presence of both groups is attractive to the businesses that demand their labor and to consumers who benefit from lower prices.

At present, the networks that provide unauthorized workers in a globalized economy are far more efficient than the bureaucratic processes that approve applications for the admission of foreign workers. In other words, the regulatory structures for responding to demand for immigrants are notably weaker than the agency of key actors who influence actual immigration patterns. Typically, unauthorized migrants get jobs at the referral of family or friends. As long as they have documents—counterfeit or real—that pass muster with government requirements to demonstrate work authorization, they are able to obtain jobs in a wide array of businesses. These businesses in turn risk few penalties for hiring the unauthorized workers so long as they fill out the proper paperwork. Although there have been efforts since the mid-2000s to step up enforcement at worksites and impose greater penalties on the unauthorized workers, they have been largely ineffective.

Although employers and immigrant advocates have pressed for the legal admission of low-wage foreign workers and the regularization of those already in the country, it is far from clear that new admission programs would function with the same efficiency as the system already in place. There are large backlogs and long waiting times for the admission even of high-skilled workers, and the same would likely be true in the event of any large-scale enlargement of low-skilled programs. Moreover, businesses and immigrant advocates have been reluctant to endorse the proposals that have been made to deter new flows of unauthorized workers, particularly those involving new mechanisms for the verification of work authorization, even though tougher enforcement is a likely trade-off for regularization and new legal-admission programs.

Businesses have expressed concern about additional administrative burdens and immigrant advocates worry that legally authorized foreign workers will be targeted and harassed in a context in which employers risk higher penalties when they hire unauthorized immigrants. Given their dependence on unauthorized workers, many low-wage industries are hopeful that Congress will enact legislation to regularize the flow of workers but fearful that the changes will restrict their access to what they see as a needed supply of labor.

Even those who favor restrictions on immigration often question the advisability of new enforcement measures that would have to apply to all US citizens to be effective. While there is broad consensus in Congress regarding border enforcement, there is far less agreement on the steps that would need to be taken to verify work authorization or enforce labor standards. The specter of a national identification system is often raised when discussion turns to mandatory employment verification, whereby all workers would be required to prove their work authorization through some type of biometric identifier. Many political figures who speak loudly in favor of curbing unauthorized migration reject an expansion in government activities, particularly in areas that may violate privacy or interfere with business. Yet, border enforcement alone cannot solve the unauthorized migration problem, given that about 40 percent of those who work without authorization entered through legal channels but overstayed their visas or work in violation of the provisions of their visas (see Lowell et al., 2007).

As long as the status quo continues to serve economic, political, and social interests, comprehensive reform of the immigration system is unlikely to occur. However, there appear to be signs of fray. After reform failed in the Senate in the later stages of the Bush administration, the executive branch began to enforce provisions of the law that had long been dormant, for instance prosecuting unauthorized migrants for using counterfeit or borrowed/stolen documents. Large-scale worksite raids received substantial publicity, apparently as part of an effort by the DHS to demonstrate that the failure to enact comprehensive reform also has a cost. A number of states and localities also passed new enforcement measures, including requirements that businesses and landlords verify work authorization through a voluntary program operated by the DHS, citing the failure of the federal government to control illegal immigration as the reason that they were taking unprecedented action. Reports indicated that some immigrants were leaving such jurisdictions, although it is unclear if they were reacting to xenophobia or loss of employment resulting from the economic downturn of the late 2000s, particularly in the construction industry. As of this writing in 2011, in the aftermath of the passage of legislation in Arizona that requires law enforcement personnel to detain persons whom they have "reasonable suspicion" to believe are in the country illegally, debate about federal immigration reform has once more galvanized attention. Whether Congress will act is another story, particularly with the change in leadership in the House of Representatives as a result of the mid-term elections in November 2010, and the failure to pass the so-called DREAM Act during the lame duck session.[5]

While prospects for immigration reform in the 112th Congress are dubious given what is likely to be political gridlock on the issue, recovery from the global economic crisis and growth in employment could shift the dynamics. Should pressures for enforcement continue to grow even as economic recovery generates increased demand for foreign workers, Congress may find it difficult to do nothing. Whether it adopts meaningful reform is another issue. As long as the economics of immigration to the United States favor easy access to low-wage foreign workers but the politics of reform preclude regularization and the legal admission of large numbers of low-skilled immigrants, as has been the case, enacting comprehensive, effective legislation will likely remain elusive. That is not to say that the actual number of immigrants will necessarily be lower as a result of legislative inactivity; rather, the resumption of large-scale unauthorized migration, growing temporary-worker programs, and ever-lengthier backlogs of those awaiting permanent residence may well remain the reality of US immigration.

Notes

1. In one of the most quoted uses of the term, John F. Kennedy's *A Nation of Immigrants* made the case for repealing the National Origins quota system.

2. The other countries of permanent immigration, Canada and Australia, underwent similar shifts toward the admission of temporary workers during this period. In their cases, the point systems used for admission for permanent residence did not necessarily meet the demand of employers for workers with specific skills.

3. The most authoritative analysis of the numbers and characteristics of unauthorized migrants comes from Jeffrey Passel at the Pew Hispanic Center. Passel estimates that new arrivals of unauthorized migrants have been down significantly since the economic crisis began.

4. The US Commission on Immigration Reform recommended the adoption of an electronic verification system in its 1994 report to Congress. The author of this chapter served as the executive director of the Commission.

5. The Development, Relief, and Education for Alien Minors Act (DREAM Act) would have provided legal status to those who came illegally to the United States as minors if they completed two years of college or military service. Although it had bipartisan support, the legislation failed to garner enough votes in the Senate when considered in the postelection session of the 111th Congress.

12

The Governance of Immigration in Australia

Jock Collins

Australia is an immigration nation, a settler immigration society whose immigrants comprise a greater proportion of the population than they do in any other Western nation (OECD, 2008). One in four Australians today are first-generation immigrants, while first- and second-generation immigrants comprise the majority (between 50 and 60 percent) of the populations of Australia's cosmopolitan cities, including Sydney, Melbourne, Brisbane, and Perth (Burnley, 2001). Australia's sixty-year history of post–World War II immigration is characterized by change, continuity, contradiction, and controversy. Immigration and multiculturalism have been and are very controversial issues in Australia (Castles et al., 1988; Castles et al., 1998) precisely because they have been so central to shaping the economic, social, political, religious, and cultural contours of the Australian cosmopolitan nation. Critics of both immigration and multiculturalism point to the negative economic, social, and environmental consequences of immigration (Collins, 2000a).

In this chapter I investigate the changing political economy of Australian immigration. I take as a point of departure Stephen Castles and Godula Kosack's classic 1973 study of the political economy of western European immigration, which emphasized that economic, political, and social dimensions of immigration required systematic investigation via interdisciplinary methodologies, rooted initially in Marxist analysis of the labor market, class, and the international economy. My main arguments are that the dynamics of Australian immigration have changed since the 1970s in response to the global economy and Australia's place therein. However, while these economic and labor market–based determinants of immigration are important, immigration is a unique aspect of globalization because it brings in people, not capital or goods and services. Immigration fills labor market shortages, but it also adds to and changes neighborhoods and has an impact on social relations, voting patterns, and political discourses and debates. Indeed, the social presence of immigrants, often experienced through a racialized prism, is as much a constraint on the dynamics of immigration as the state of the labor market. It is for this reason that the global movement of people has lagged behind the global movement of capital, goods, and services. In other words, immigration is a fundamentally contradictory phenomenon, constrained as much by social, political, and cultural concerns as by the demands of the economy. In this chapter, I thus aim to explore some of the key changes, continuities, contradictions, and controversies on the economic, social, political, and cultural fronts of the contemporary Australian immigration experience.

One continuity in post–World War II Australian immigration policy is that it has been primarily driven by the labor market. Migrants served as an imported reserve army of labor to fill labor market shortages in specific occupations and areas, although, as a settler immigration country like the United States, Canada, and New Zealand, immigrant families rather than individual workers were sought. Australian immigration intakes peaked with the business cycle, and thus at the end of the first (1947–late 1960s) and second (1992–2008) postwar economic booms. However, the era of globalization that has accompanied the second Australian postwar economic boom and changed the structure of the Australian economy has led to significant changes to the composition of immigration intakes, one being increased emphasis on skilled and professional migration relative to family migration, another being the unprecedented intake of temporary migrant workers (Collins, 2008).

Although immigrants from the United Kingdom, Ireland, and, more recently, New Zealand have always dominated annual flows, there has been considerable change in the ethnic composition of the Australian immigration intake. Immigrant minorities arriving from Asia, Africa, and Latin America have increased significantly, particularly since Australia introduced a nondiscriminatory immigration policy in the early 1970s.[1] With globalization, the characteristics of this minority-immigrant intake have also changed considerably, with increasing emphasis on those with highly skilled and professional qualifications and high levels of English language fluency. Another constant backdrop in Australia's immigration history has been racism. Since the 1950s, minority immigrants have been clearly racialized in the Australian labor market and Australian society (Markus, 2001), although the dynamics of racialization have changed considerably, particularly for immigrants from the Middle East since the events of September 11, 2001 (Poynting et al., 2004).

Contemporary immigration has important social dimensions. Immigrant settlement policy has also changed considerably in postwar Australia. Multiculturalism replaced assimilation as the prevailing philosophical and policy framework for immigrant settlement in Australia in the early 1970s, and it survives despite a strong history of critique from the right (Blainey, 1984; Rimmer, 1991; Sheehan, 1998, 2006) and left (Hage, 1998) as well as a decade spent under the Conservative government of John Howard (1996–2007).[2] The riots at Sydney's Cronulla Beach in December 2005, when thousands of mainly drunk white males, many draped in the Australian flag, chased and bashed isolated men and women of supposed Middle Eastern appearance, led to significant debate about the social impact of Australian immigration policy and the viability of multiculturalism (Collins, 2007).

Social class is an important dynamic underlying international migration. In Australia, immigrants are spread across all social classes, from billionaire business leaders to new and old middle classes through to the working class and the undocumented (Collins, 1991, 2008). Class relations are at once produced and reproduced—and sometimes transformed—in the dynamic of Australia's immigration history. The changing class dynamics of immigration have, over time, reflected the changing dynamics of global capitalism. In the first postwar decades, most immigrants were working-class, manual workers—factory fodder for the growth of manufacturing that characterized Western nations at the time. Today, as manufacturing jobs have been moved offshore, Australia's immigrants mainly fill labor shortages in skilled and professional service-sector jobs.

Although Australian immigration and settlement policy was largely politically bipartisan until the late 1980s, this has not been the case since that time. The Howard government successfully played the so-called race card at the federal level by politicizing issues such as the undocumented arrivals of "boat people" (Marr and Wilkinson, 2003), citizenship, national identity, and multiculturalism. Issues of ethnic crime and ethnic gangs, particularly associated with immigrants from the Middle East, has also played a major role in New South Wales state politics since the 1990s (Collins et al., 2000; Manning, 2006), while the issue of development applications for new Islamic schools and mosques has been a key political issue at the local government level, particularly in Sydney, where most of Australia's Middle Eastern immigrants live (Dunn, 2003).

The structure of the chapter is as follows. The next section provides an overview of immigration in contemporary Australian society in order to provide the context for the sections that follow. The third section reviews the way that globalization has impacted Australian immigration policy. The fourth section considers the socioeconomic aspects of immigrant settlement in Australian cities and towns. The fifth section looks at political debates over immigration and immigrant settlement, while the sixth section speculates on the impact that the global economic crisis that began in 2008 may have on the political economy of Australian immigration. The final section provides an opportunity to apply the conclusions made reached via the Australian situation to that of other Western nations.

An Overview of Contemporary Australian Immigration

Australia, along with the United States, Canada, and New Zealand, is one of the few Western countries to have actively pursued a settler immigration policy over the six decades following the end of World War II. About 1 million migrants arrived in each of the four decades following 1950: 1.6 million between October 1945 and June 1960, about 1.3 million in the 1960s, about 960,000 in the 1970s, about 1.1 million in the 1980s, and 900,000 in the 1990s. The immigration policy was established partly to fill labor shortages and partly to add to Australia's population (Collins, 1991: 77–92). Following the economic recessions of 1974–1975, 1982–1983, and 1990–1991, immigration intakes were cut considerably as unemployment rose. The famous Australian demographer Charles Price used the metaphor of a boa constrictor to generate the image of a hungry snake with a great appetite for immigrants during the boom period, when the migration cycle was closely synchronized with the Australian business cycle. The high-water mark in annual Australian immigration intakes was the peak of the long boom in the late 1960s: the highest number of settlers to arrive in any one year was 185,099 in 1969–1970. The lowest number in any one year was 52,752 in 1975–1976.

As Table 12.1 shows, the 1990s were years of relatively low annual immigration intakes to Australia, following the decline immediately after the 1990–1991 Australian economic recession. In the 2000s, the permanent component of the migration intake increased significantly, reaching a peak of 184,837 in 2008–2009, fueled by strong economic growth and shortages of skilled labor as national unemployment rates fell to 4.1 percent. However, these figures do not include the temporary-migration intake, which will be considered in detail in the next section. When the permanent- and temporary-migration intakes are added, 2008 becomes the new high-water mark of postwar immigration. Following the onset of the global financial crisis of the late 2000s, which resulted in a severe economic downturn but not economic recession in Australia, permanent immigration numbers were cut slightly and a number of occupations removed from the Migrant Occupations in Demand List (MODL). The planned intake for the Australian migration program for 2009–2010 and 2010–2011 was 182,450.

The 2005 data from the Organization for Economic Cooperation and Development (OECD) in Table 12.2 demonstrates that this sustained immigration program led to the highest stock of immigrants relative to the population (23.8 percent) in any Western county with the exceptions of Luxembourg (33.4 percent) and Switzerland (23.8 percent). It was higher than the proportions of the other traditional settler immigration countries of the United States (12.9 percent), Canada (19.1 percent), and

Table 12.1 Australian Immigration Intakes, 1991–1992 to 2010–2011 (settler arrivals under permanent immigration program)

Years	Settler Arrivals
1991–1992	107,400
1992–1993	76,300
1993–1994	69,800
1994–1995	87,400
1995–1996	99,100
1996–1997	85,800
1997–1998	77,300
1998–1999	84,100
1999–2000	92,300
2000–2001	107,400
2001–2002	88,900
2002–2003	93,900
2003–2004	111,600
2004–2005	123,400
2005–2006	157,084
2006–2007	161,217
2007–2008	171,284
2008–2009	184,837
2009–2010[a]	182,450
2010–2011[a]	182,450

Source: Australian Government Department of Immigration and Citizenship, http://www.immi.gov.au (accessed September 15, 2007); Hugo (2010).

Note: a. Indicates planning levels.

New Zealand (19.4 percent), and considerably higher than those of most other European countries.

Despite the promise by Arthur Caldwell, the first postwar Australian immigration minister, that nine out of every ten postwar migrants would be British (Collins, 1991: 20–23), the Australian immigration net has been cast widely, such that today immigrants from most countries in the world call Australia home. Migrants from southern European countries

Table 12.2 Stocks of Foreign-born Population in Selected OECD Countries (percentage)

	1996	2000	2001	2005
Australia	23.3	23.0	23.1	23.8
Austria	n.a.	10.5	11.1	13.5
Belgium	*9.8*	10.3	10.8	12.1
Canada	17.4	*18.1*	*18.4*	*19.1*
Czech Republic	n.a.	*4.2*	4.4	*5.1*
Denmark	5.1	5.8	6.0	6.5
Finland	*2.1*	2.6	2.7	3.4
France	n.a.	n.a.	n.a.	8.1
Germany	*11.9*	12.5	12.6	n.a.
Greece	n.a.	n.a.	10.3	n.a.
Hungary	2.8	2.9	3.0	3.3
Ireland	6.9	*8.7*	*9.3*	*11.0*
Italy	n.a.	n.a.	2.5	n.a.
Luxembourg	*31.5*	*33.2*	32.8	*33.4*
Mexico	n.a.	0.5	n.a.	0.4
Netherlands	9.2	10.1	10.4	10.6
New Zealand	16.2	17.2	18.0	19.4
Norway	5.6	6.8	6.9	8.2
Portugal	*5.4*	*5.1*	6.3	*6.3*
Slovak Republic	n.a.	n.a.	2.5	n.a.
Spain	n.a.	n.a.	5.3	n.a.
Sweden	10.7	11.3	11.5	12.4
Switzerland	*21.3*	21.9	*22.3*	*23.8*
Turkey	n.a.	1.9	n.a.	n.a.
United Kingdom	*7.1*	*7.9*	8.2	*9.7*
United States	*10.3*	*11.0*	*11.3*	*12.9*

Source: Adapted from Organization for Economic Cooperation and Development, http://www.oecd.org (accessed July 29, 2008).

Note: Estimated figures are in *italics*. Data for Canada, France, Ireland, New Zealand, the Slovak Republic, the United Kingdom, and the United States are estimated using the parametric method. Data for Belgium (1995–1999), Czech Republic, Germany, Luxembourg, Portugal, and Switzerland are estimated using the component method. For details, see Organization for Economic Cooperation and Development, http://www.oecd.org.

n.a. indicates data is not available.

(particularly Greece, Italy, and the former Yugoslavia) arrived in large numbers in the 1950s and 1960s. After Australia abandoned the 1901 White Australia policy that excluded "coloured" immigrants, and introduced a nondiscriminatory immigration policy in the 1970s, the Australian immigration net has also been cast to include immigrants born in Asia, the Middle East, and (in smaller numbers) Africa and Latin America. Australian census data records nearly 200 birthplace groups among the Australian resident population. As Table 12.3 shows, those born in England and New Zealand rank at the top of the fifteen major countries of foreign birth of the Australian population in 1996 and 2006.

Table 12.3 Top Fifteen Countries of Birth of Foreign-born Population in Australia, 1996 and 2006

	1996			2006		
Rank	Country of Birth	Persons (thousands)	Percentage of All Overseas Born	Country of Birth	Persons (thousands)	Percentage of All Overseas Born
1	England	872.1	22.3	England	856.9	19.4
2	New Zealand	291.4	7.5	New Zealand	389.5	8.8
3	Italy	238.2	6.1	China (excluding SARs and Taiwan Province)	206.6	4.7
4	Vietnam	151.1	3.9	Italy	199.1	4.5
5	Scotland	146.3	3.7	Vietnam	159.8	3.6
6	Greece	126.5	3.2	India	147.1	3.3
7	China (excluding Taiwan Province)	111.0	2.8	Scotland	130.2	2.9
8	Germany	110.3	2.8	Philippines	120.5	2.7
9	Philippines	92.9	2.4	Greece	110.0	2.5
10	Netherlands	87.9	2.2	Germany	106.5	2.4
11	India	77.6	2.0	South Africa	104.1	2.4
12	Malaysia	76.3	2.0	Malaysia	92.3	2.1
13	Lebanon	70.2	1.8	Netherlands	78.9	1.8
14	Hong Kong	68.4	1.8	Lebanon	74.9	1.7
15	Poland	65.1	1.7	Hong Kong (SAR of China)	71.8	1.6

Source: ABS (2007).

It also indicates a strong growth in the number of Australians who were born in Asia (mainly China, India, Vietnam, the Philippines, Malaysia, and Hong Kong). The number of South African immigrants in Australia has increased significantly, while those born in Italy, Greece, Germany, and the Netherlands—the nations that dominated the non-British and non-Irish intakes of the first decades of postwar immigration—remain as significant populations in contemporary Australia.

It is important to note that these figures on the ethnic composition of the Australian population today do not include second and later generations who are by definition Australian born. Ancestry data can assist in estimating the combined impact of migrant generations on Australia's population today. In the post-1945 period, about 6.4 million immigrants arrived in Australia, representing a major component of the Australian population increase from 7 million to over 22 million. Immigration contributed about half of Australia's postwar population growth (Productivity Commission, 2006: xv–xvi). As Table 12.4 shows, just over one-third of the Australian population (37.1 percent) claims to have Australian ancestry, once again highlighting the degree to which Australia is a migration

Table 12.4 Top Fifteen Ancestries in Australia, 2006 Census

	Persons (thousands)	Percentage of Total Population[a]
Australian	7,371.8	37.1
English	6,283.6	31.6
Irish	1,803.7	9.1
Scottish	1,501.2	7.6
Italian	852.4	4.3
German	811.5	4.1
Chinese	669.9	3.4
Greek	365.2	1.8
Dutch	310.1	1.6
Indian	234.7	1.2
Lebanese	181.8	0.9
Vietnamese	173.7	0.9
Polish	163.8	0.8
New Zealander	160.7	0.8
Filipino	160.4	0.8

Source: ABS (2007).

Note: a. As respondents can identify with up to two ancestries, proportions for all ancestries do not add up to 100 percent.

nation significant not only in terms of the relative size, but also of the diversity in the immigration intake.

Australian Globalization and Immigration Policy

Australia has enthusiastically embraced globalization since the 1980s; indeed, the Australian economy and polity has always been embedded in the international, with ties ranging from colonial Britain and the post-colonial United States to Japan and now China and India. The Labor governments of Bob Hawke (1983–1991) and Paul Keating (1991–1996) were quick to deregulate the Australian finance system, introducing floating exchange rates, reducing tariff protection, and opening up more to foreign capital. Engagement with the international economy, and particularly Australia's Asian neighbors, became a cornerstone of Labor's economic strategy. The Conservative Howard government continued in like manner (Collins, 2000b). The result was a restructuring of the Australian economy, often with international capital, that mirrored that of North American and European economies as manufacturing employment declined and service-sector employment increased—particularly in the finance, media, and telecommunications centers of Australia's global cities, including Sydney and Melbourne, traditionally the major sites of new immigrant settlement (Connell, 2000). In addition, the rise of China and India led to a strong appetite for Australian iron ore, coal, and other minerals and energy sources from the late 1990s onward, further stimulating Australian economic growth and leading to regional labor shortages, particularly in the mining states of Western Australia and Queensland.

Globalization was accompanied by the reduction of protection barriers to international investment and trade, although the failure of the World Trade Organization's round of trade liberalization talks in Doha (Stiglitz, 2006) highlights the contradictions of the massive primary-sector subsidies retained in Europe and the United States. Globalization was also accompanied by increasing international migration (Castles and Miller, 2009). The number of long-term international migrants increased from 84 million people in 1975 to 105 million in 1985, 120 million in 1990, and 150 million in 2000 (McVeigh, 2008: 2). By 2007, estimates had put the number of international migrants at nearly 200 million (Castles and Miller, 2009: 5). As indicated earlier, the global financial crisis of 2008–2009, a consequence of the contradictions of free-market capitalism (Cassidy, 2009; Stiglitz, 2010), interrupted the economic boom fueled by globalization and led to slight reductions in immigration intakes for most Western nations, including Australia, although the trend line of increasing immigration is expected to return as Western economies recover.

Despite this pattern, one contradiction of globalization is that although governments are making it easier for goods and capital to circulate around the globe, they continue to restrict the free movement of people (Legrain, 2006: 15). This is largely because, unlike capital, goods, and services, the internationalization of labor involves the movement and settlement of people, increasingly of religious- and ethnic-minority background, in Western societies. Immigration raises controversial matters related to security, national identity, and the social impact of foreign settlement, which are addressed in later sections of this chapter, in a way that the movement of capital, goods, and services does not.

In Australia, the response to globalization centered on progressively fine-tuning immigration policy in order to ensure that immigration intakes corresponded better to the new, restructured, globalized Australian labor market. First, permanent immigration intakes have been increased over the past decade, responding to the business cycle. Second, the permanent immigration program has been fine-tuned to better respond to new labor market shortages. Third, temporary migration was increased dramatically. The fourth major change is related to the geopolitical shifts that followed the events of September 11, 2001, raising the importance of the security aspects of immigration, particularly in relation to undocumented immigrant arrivals.

Responding to the restructured labor market, the Australian government has swung the balance of the permanent annual intake away from family reunion to skilled, independent immigration. At the same time, it has attempted to improve the way that skilled-immigration selection procedures are synchronized with labor market shortfalls (Birrell et al., 2006). It also revamped the business immigration program to encourage better economic outcomes in Australia. Table 12.5 shows immigration intakes for the period from 1998–1999 to 2008–2009, indicating the increase in the skilled-labor intake relative to the family intake over that period. According to the Productivity Commission, whereas 29 percent of permanent immigrants arrived on skilled visas in 1995–1996, skilled migrants comprised 66 percent of the 2005–2006 intake (2006: xxiii). The planned skilled intake for 2007–2008 was further increased to 69,456, a 250 percent increase on the skilled intake of a decade earlier. In addition to increasing both the proportion and the absolute numbers of skilled permanent entrants, the Immigration Department has consistently linked skilled immigration to revised MODLs in an attempt to ensure that immigrants with the right skills are recruited to Australia. While most of these skilled vacancies are in Australian cities, regional and rural areas also faced severe skill shortages during the second postwar boom. New visa pathways were introduced in the 2000s to attract skilled immigrants to fill labor shortages in regional and rural Australia (National Farmers Federation, 2008).

Many of these new skilled immigrants are immigrant minorities, often from Asia. This has led to changes in the patterns of labor market segmentation and the racialized dynamics of migrant labor in Australia. Up until the 1980s, most immigrant minorities were employed in the secondary labor market, mostly in dirty, dangerous, and low-paying jobs that Australians and Anglo-Celtic immigrants did not want to take. Today many skilled minority migrants enter the primary labor market (Collins, 2000b), although an "accent ceiling" often restrains their upward mobility (Collins, 1996). The term "accent ceiling" describes a situation in which the accent of an immigrant man or woman is construed negatively by the gatekeepers of employment and promotion as an inability to communicate rather than as a positive sign of multilingual abilities and multicultural knowledge. This is particularly the case of minority immigrant women, who face a "double-glazed ceiling" as gender combines with ethnicity to restrict their labor market achievements.

Table 12.5 Australian Immigration Intakes, 1998–1999 to 2008–2009, by Category of Entry

Category	1998–1999	2000–2001	2002–2003	2004–2005	2006–2007	2008–2009
Family	21,501	20,145	28,000	33,182	37,138	37,156
Skilled	27,031	35,715	38,504	53,133	60,755	69,456
Humanitarian/special[a]	8,996	7,767	9,676	13,397	12,356	11,645
Nonprogram migration[b]	25,740	43,739	17,579	23,712	29,899	36,640
Total	84,143	107,366	93,314	123,424	140,148	154,897
Resident permanent departure	36,970	35,133	105,200	41,332	39,686	

Source: Australian Government Department of Immigration and Citizenship, http://www.immi.gov.au (accessed November 20, 2007); Hugo (2010).

Notes: a. Special Eligibility.

b. Mainly New Zealand intakes.

However, with increasing skilled-migrant intakes comes the problem of the failure to recognize education and employment qualifications not obtained in Australia—a problem highlighted in several other chapters in this volume. Critics argue that overseas qualifications are often undervalued in Australia and that assessment criteria are outdated, not sufficiently flexible, and too complex, often leading to racial discrimination (Productivity Commission, 2006: 176–186). This is one of the enduring contradictions of Australian immigration policy (Hawthorne, 1994; Iredale and Nivison-Smith, 1995). As a result, many of those who arrive with skilled-migrant visas cannot find work in Australia commensurate with their skills, a scenario that often results in downward mobility for them, hardship for their families, and a decline in the performance of the Australian economy. It is a cruel irony that these immigrants are often scapegoats for dips in Australia's economic performance (Castles et al., 1998).

While much of the debate about Australian immigration has centered on permanent or settler immigration, the growth in long-term temporary immigration has gone relatively unnoticed. As Graeme Hugo (2003) has noted, in 2001, the number of people who were granted long-term visas to work in Australia—that is, temporary immigrants—exceeded the number granted permanent immigration entry for the first time. The increasing importance of long-term temporary immigration can be gleaned from the fact that, between 1982 and 2000, the growth in permanent immigration to Australia was 11 percent, while temporary intakes soared: long-term residents increased by 65 percent and long-term visitors increased from 30,000 to 133,000 (Macken, 2003). A range of new visa categories was introduced to assist with this explosion of temporary migration and to link temporary migrants to skilled labor shortages. These visas fall under three classes: economic; social and cultural; and international relations. As Table 12.6 shows, 125,705 temporary-resident visas were issued in 1997–1998. By 2005–2006, 224,962 temporary-resident visas had been issued—74,666 in the skilled stream, 27,782 in the social/cultural stream, and 122,514 in the international relations stream.

The impact of this increase in temporary migration to Australia can be seen in the increasing proportion of temporary migrants in the Australian population: in 1992 they comprised 0.23 percent of the total population; in 1997, 0.44 percent; and in 2002, 0.65 percent. This gave Australia a smaller proportion of temporary migrants than New Zealand had (1.61 percent), but a higher proportion than that estimated by Germany (0.42 percent), Canada (0.28 percent), the United States (0.23 percent), the United Kingdom (0.25 percent), Japan (0.16 percent), and France (0.04 percent)

Table 12.6 Temporary Resident Visa Grants in Australia (onshore and offshore), 1997–1998 to 2005–2006

	1997–1998	1999–2000	2001–2002	2003–2004	2005–2006
Economic stream	37,298	39,180	43,303	48,652	74,666
Social/cultural stream	17,165	23,405	20,817	26,400	27,782
International relations stream	71,242	88,929	99,557	104,925	122,514
Total	125,705	151,514	163,677	179,977	224,962

Source: Australian Government Department of Immigration and Citizenship, http://www.immi.gov.au (accessed November 11, 2007).

(Australia Productivity Commission, 2006: 208). Temporary migrants have helped Australia fill vacancies for skilled employment generated by the second postwar boom. However, temporary migration has been accompanied by abuse and exploitation on the part of employers, particularly for those who enter under the 457 visa. This visa category has grown dramatically since the mid-1990s. In 1997–1998, just over 30,000 subclass 457 visas were granted. By 2007–2008, 110,570 subclass 457 visas had been granted, with over 58,000 going to primary applicants (DIAC, 2008a). Reports began to proliferate in the media of unsafe working conditions (leading to a number of migrant deaths) and the exploitation of workers on 457 visas in terms of low wages and long hours of work. This led to strong trade-union opposition and, eventually, a review of the temporary-migration program by the immigration minister under the Labor government of Kevin Rudd (2007–2010). The review recommended that 457-visa workers have the same wages and conditions of employment as other workers, that a "salary floor" be introduced to reduce the exploitation of these temporary workers (DIAC, 2008b: 7–8), and that the operation of the 457-visa temporary-worker category be severely tightened.

Socioeconomic Aspects of Australian Immigrant Settlement

In contrast with the internationalization of trade and finance, international migration impacts the social landscape of the cities and towns of host countries in which immigrants settle. Given the international trend of immigrant minorities to increase their share of migration intakes in most Western nations (Castles and Miller, 2009: 2–7), the social impact of immigration has been the subject of great debate and controversy. Australia is no exception in this regard. This section provides three recent examples of this controversy: refugee and Muslim unemployment rates, ethnic crime and ethnic gangs; and the Sydney Cronulla beach riots of December 2005.

The rate of immigrant unemployment is an important measure of social inclusion, since employment impacts income and well-being. On average, unemployment rates for immigrants are only slightly higher than those for non-immigrants (Australian Productivity Commission, 2006). But it is important to disaggregate this data. Unemployment data for 2004 show that immigrants on skilled visas in Australia had lower unemployment rates (4.3 percent) than did the Australian born (4.9 percent). Those on temporary visas had a higher unemployment rate (6.4 percent), but not as high as that of permanent entrants under the family stream (8.8 percent). Both these immigrant categories suffered less unemployment than the humanitarian intake, whose unemployment rate was 16.9 percent, more than three times that of the Australian born and about two-and-a-half times greater than the average unemployment rate for immigrants in all categories of entry (Australian Productivity Commission, 2006: 64).

Furthermore, immigrants of Muslim background (alongside humanitarian entrants in general) experience significantly higher unemployment rates in Australia than do either other immigrants or the Australian born. Census data from 2006 also show that at a time when national unemployment rates were around 5 percent, unemployment rates for male Muslim immigrants was 13.6 percent, much higher than those for immigrants of other religious backgrounds. Moreover, Australian-born, second-generation Muslim males experienced even higher rates of unemployment (18.1 percent) than did their overseas-born fathers. During the economic downturn of 2008–2009, Muslim and other immigrants from non-English-speaking countries in the Middle East and Africa experienced significantly higher increases in unemployment than did other immigrants or the Australian born (Collins, forthcoming).

This unemployment burden fell particularly heavily on minority-immigrant youth. Labor-force survey data show that male youth born in North Africa and the Middle East experience the highest unemployment rates and the highest increase in unemployment of all male immigrant youth in Australia, reaching a height of about 18 percent in February–March 2009 and falling back to more than 12 percent by October 2009

(Collins, forthcoming). There is also a spatial dimension to Muslim and minority-immigrant unemployment rates. Most immigrants to Australia settle in the large cities of Sydney, Melbourne, Perth, and Brisbane. It is the working-class areas of these cities, particularly the western suburbs of Sydney and Melbourne, where unemployment has been highest and where the long-term unemployed are likely to live.

Since the late 1990s, the link between immigration, ethnicity, and crime has been a preoccupation of the sensationalist media, particularly in Sydney. The ethnic crime debate has been specifically linked to Lebanese and Middle Eastern immigrants (Collins et al., 2000). The resulting moral panic about "Middle Eastern crime" was amplified by the events of September 11, 2001, which escalated anti-Muslim feelings in Australia (Hage, 2002). This debate is not new for multicultural societies; similar debates—particularly about policing in multicultural societies and police racism—occur in the United States, Canada, and the United Kingdom (Tonry, 1997; Hawkins, 1995; Bowling and Phillips, 2002; Wortley, 2002). The contemporary Australian discourse about ethnic crime has shifted from the criminality of a few immigrants to the supposed criminality of an entire, specifically Middle Eastern, culture. Police in New South Wales use racial descriptors such as "Middle Eastern appearance" when reporting crimes.

But the concern about the relationship between minority immigrants and crime is not new in Australia either, occurring regularly throughout Australian history (Francis, 1981; Hazelhurst, 1987). Although some immigrants are involved in criminal gangs, the criminological evidence does not support the view that immigrant groups per se are overrepresented in criminal activity. Data from the 1990s on rates of incarceration by birthplace confirm that there is no clear-cut relationship between ethnic minorities and criminality. The data do show that immigrants born in Lebanon, Vietnam, Turkey, and New Zealand are overrepresented in prisons compared to the Australian born, but they also show that immigrants born in Greece and Italy are underrepresented (Mukherjee, 1999). Moreover, the higher rates of incarceration of immigrants from Lebanon, Vietnam, Turkey, and New Zealand seem to be better explained by their inferior socioeconomic circumstances—particularly their very high unemployment rates—than by cultural factors.

Extra caution is thus required in using these statistics to draw any firm conclusions about the relationship between ethnicity and crime in Australia. To make a claim about the criminality of different ethnic groups in Australia from data on the rates of incarceration of different immigrant groups is valid only if it can be assumed that the foreign born have an equal probability of apprehension and are treated equally by the judicial system. Police attitudes influence how far individuals who are apprehended in alleged criminal acts go in the criminal justice system. In Australia, as in other culturally diverse societies like Canada, the United States, and the United Kingdom, there is a long history of police racism and corruption (Chan, 1996).

This discourse about ethnic or immigrant crime robs first- and second-generation immigrants of their Australian nationality—they are always "immigrants" or "ethnics" and never "Australians"—despite the fact that most were either born in Australia or have Australian citizenship (Poynting et al., 2004). Moreover, by emphasizing the cultural causes of crime, this discourse directs attention away from the socioeconomic roots of crime. Policy responses to immigrant crime constructed in this way lead to cultural or religious solutions such as strong intervention from ethnic minority religious and community leaders: it is "their" problem to solve, not "ours." At the same time, the construction of (some) immigrant cultures as cultures of criminality can lead policymakers to ignore issues such as inequality, unemployment, education, and neighborhood renewal. In this sense, immigrant minorities are again victimized and conceptualized as being from outside the Sydney community rather than a central part of it. The discourse of immigrant criminality leaves little space for a more sympathetic discourse about immigrant victims of crime. It has led to a criminalization of the Arab Other in Australia (Poynting et al., 2004).

The events on Cronulla Beach in Sydney on Sunday, December 11, 2005, sent a tremor through Australian community relations. Images of the violence perpetrated by thousands of white males against men and women of supposed Middle Eastern appearance made for compelling viewing by media audiences in Sydney, the rest of Australia, and the international community. A few days after the riots, a gang of males of, yes, Middle Eastern appearance sought retaliatory revenge in a so-called smash, bash, and flee raid on the suburbs surrounding Cronulla. For months afterward, an unprecedented police presence dominated the sandscape of Sydney's famous beaches, successfully preventing further reverberations and escalation of racial conflict.

To some international commentators (Huntington 1997, 2004), the clash of ethnicities and religions, mostly a product of immigration policies, threatens Western societies in fundamental ways, particularly since September 11. Events around the world and in Australia have led many to associate immigration and ethnic diversity with conflict and violence. To the critics of Australian immigration and multiculturalism (Sheehan,

1998, 2006), immigrant minorities inevitably bring conflict to their host country, threatening social cohesion and dividing the nation, particularly when they come from Asia, the Middle East, and Africa.

The events at Cronulla Beach can only be understood within the broader lens of the changing, uneven processes of the racialization of immigrant minorities in Australia and the international, national, and local contexts that shape this racialization (see Miles, 1989, 1993). The Cronulla riots provided a caution against complacency, a reminder of the challenges and benefits that cosmopolitan societies generate, and a reminder of the responsibilities that political leaders have to manage ethnic diversity and the dangers of political opportunism that flow from attempts to exploit racist undercurrents for short-term electoral ambition. However, these events must be set against the history of racial violence in Australia in order to gain perspective. No one died in the Cronulla riots, although there were instances of personal injury and property damage, and a great deal of damage was done to Sydney's international reputation as a tolerant, cosmopolitan city. Despite the facts that Australia has one of the largest and most diverse immigration programs of Western nations and that Sydney is one of the world's most cosmopolitan cities, home to the majority of Australia's Middle Eastern community, most evidence suggests that social cohesion is the norm and moments of ethnic conflict such as those evident at Cronulla beach are the exception (Collins, 2005, 2007).

Political Debates over Immigration and Immigrant Settlement

Immigration and immigrant-settlement policy were treated as bipartisan issues by the two major national political parties (the Liberal/National Party conservative coalition and the Labor Party) until the late 1980s, when the Liberal/National Party Opposition leader, John Howard, campaigned on ending multiculturalism and significantly reducing Asian immigration (Collins, 2000a). Although this backfired on Howard—he lost leadership of the federal opposition party prior to the federal election—his anti-immigration sentiments resurfaced after he won the 1996 election. The Howard government's attitude to multiculturalism has been at best lukewarm. The prime minister hardly used the term "multiculturalism" in his term of office from 1996 to 2007, and under his government two of the main institutional embodiments of multiculturalism (the Bureau of Immigration, Multicultural, and Population Research and the Office of Multicultural Affairs) were axed. A two-year waiting period for new non-humanitarian immigrants to access welfare benefits, unemployment benefits, and other social services was introduced, while pragmatic funding for immigrant agencies, employment programs, and language services such as the Adult Migrant English Service was cut severely. The policy of mandatory detention of undocumented migrants and their children upon arrival in Australia, originally introduced by Labor, was entrenched under the Howard government, and new detention centers were built in inhospitable areas of regional and rural Australia (Mares, 2002).

The politicization of the immigration issue reached new heights in late August 2001, when the Howard government refused to allow a boatload of 433 asylum seekers aboard the KM *Palapa 1*—rescued by the Norwegian cargo ship MS *Tampa* in Indonesian waters—to enter Australia and land on Christmas Island, the northwestern-most landing post for those seeking asylum on Australian shores. The KM *Palapa 1* had lost power, lacked navigation equipment (other than an old box compass), and was drifting slowly with little food and water. Its passengers—twenty-six females (two pregnant), forty-three children, and 369 men—were thirsty, hungry, and scared for their lives (Marr and Wilkinson, 2003: 19). Most could not swim. The captain of the MS *Tampa*, Arne Rinnan, had responded to calls from Australian rescue authorities to pick up the asylum seekers aboard the KM *Palapa 1*, carrying "the biggest load of asylum seekers ever to set out for Christmas Island" (Marr and Wilkinson, 2003: 3). Most of the adults on board had paid an average of US$10,000 to the so-called snakeheads who arranged the trip, though children were charged less.

The boat people of the MS *Tampa* never made it to the Australian shore. Like all other boats subsequently attempting to enter Australian waters illegally, theirs was intercepted by the Australian Navy and taken to Pacific Island states as part of the Howard government's so-called "Pacific solution." The Howard government paid large sums of money to persuade Pacific Island states to take undocumented immigrants intent on seeking asylum in Australia. David Marr and Marian Wilkinson suggest that it cost the government at least US$500 million to keep 2,390 boat people from landing in Australia (2003: 287–278). This stance gave an imprimatur to intolerance of asylum seekers, particularly those from the Middle East.

The MS *Tampa* was not the first boat carrying asylum seekers to the Australian shores in the past two decades, but it was the first one to be turned away and refused permission to land on Australian territory.

Howard maintained up to the day of the election itself that there was evidence that children from the KM *Palapa 1* were thrown overboard by boat people and Defense Minister Peter Reith claimed that the Navy had photographic proof. Everyone could see that such an act was "un-Australian" and, despite the fact that it was subsequently revealed that the incident did not happen, any public sympathy that there may have been for the MS *Tampa* boat people was undermined. Howard successfully played the race card and enjoyed a resounding victory in the 2001 national election, with most political pundits agreeing that his hard-line stance on the boat people and on refugees in general was a decisive factor (Marr and Wilkinson, 2003: 274).

The Howard government was defeated by Kevin Rudd's Labor government in late 2007. The Rudd government quickly ended the mandatory detention of undocumented arrivals and their children, along with the "Pacific solution." Although immigration issues were not as prominent in the 2007 election as they were in 2001, the hard-line political opportunism of the Howard government in playing the race card helped to define the Howard government in the eyes of the Australian electorate. Howard's dog-whistle politics set the scene for the Cronulla Beach riots and other anti-Muslim political stances, such as opposition to the construction of new Muslim schools or mosques. Other political parties, including fringe right-wing parties, continue to campaign against immigration on the racist basis of the religious, cultural, or linguistic backgrounds of new immigrants. Concerns about excessive ethnic crime and growing illegal migration are key arguments of these parties, though crude racism is never far from the surface. Other political parties, such as pro-environmental groups, want to limit immigration because of the environmental damage that population growth induces.

Just prior to the national election of August 2010, Julia Gillard replaced Kevin Rudd as Australia's Labor prime minister. Gillard differentiated herself from Rudd on the conservative side of the boat-people issue and the population growth/immigration issue, arguing that, unlike Rudd, she was not in favor of a "big Australia"—a code phrase for her willingness to reduce immigration intakes because of the environmental consequences of immigration-led population growth in Australian cities. Gillard also announced that if reelected as prime minister, she would negotiate with East Timor leaders about using that country as a place where boat people could be diverted from Australian shores. The boat-people issue became a key election issue, with the Liberal National party leader, Tony Abbott, promising to "stop the boats" if elected (Megalogenis, 2010: 1, 23). Once again, the immigration issue became a political football in Australia, as both political parties attempted to woo the anti-immigration, xenophobic vote.

These political concerns about immigration, population growth, multiculturalism, immigrant minorities, and undocumented arrivals claiming refugee status constrain the freedom of globalized labor movements in nations like Australia. In this way, racism becomes a dysfunctional ideology for capitalism, leading to opposition to new immigrant-minority settlers regardless of their human or investment capital or their humanitarian claims.

Contemporary Cosmopolitan Contradictions in Australia

Hosting more immigrants of greater ethnic diversity than do other major Western countries, Australia's postwar immigration history has shaped the nation, contributing more than half of the workforce growth and half of the population growth in this period. In this chapter the key changes, continuities, contradictions, and controversies in the economic, social, political, and cultural fields of immigration have been explored. The continuities are the continued reliance on immigration as a major source of Australian population and workforce growth; the procyclical character of immigration, driven by changing labor market conditions and changing patterns of economic growth; and the contentious nature of immigration, as evidenced by contemporary debates about the economic, social, and political merits of such a large and ethnically diverse immigration program. The changes are evident in the way that globalization has encouraged shifts in immigrant selection, with an increasing emphasis on permanent skilled and temporary migration in the 2000s as immigration reached new heights.

But contradictions emerge as well, including those related to the way that the racialization of immigrant minorities acts as a form of market failure. For instance, as we have seen, the accent ceiling prevents many skilled immigrants from achieving labor market outcomes commensurate with their ability, and exploitation of vulnerable temporary immigrants, such as those on 457 visas, by unscrupulous employers is common. Moreover, it is not easy to fine-tune a policy like immigration insofar as the lead time between an individual's decision to emigrate and the moment of immigration is often many years, whereas economic and other conditions often change quite quickly.

The other major contradiction is that the internationalization of labor has not kept pace with the internationalization of capital and trade;

globalization is indirectly constrained by the fact that immigrants have a social presence in their host societies that can become contentious, particularly when they are viewed through a racialized prism. Conflict, crime, and other social contradictions constrain attempts to make labor as mobile as capital; post–September 11 globalization is characterized by both increasing immigration flows (formal and informal) and increasing attempts by nation-states to restrict immigration, largely because of security concerns but also because of the contentious reaction of resident populations to new minority-immigrant neighbors. The ultimate contradiction is of course the crisis of contemporary capitalism, from which no country appears to be immune. The Australian economy, like all its Western counterparts, fell into recession in 2009, ending the second postwar Australian boom. Australian immigration history shows that immigration levels increase during periods of economic boom and reduce during periods of economic recession (Collins, 1991: 19–32).

A final contradiction is that just as it took until the late 1990s for the Australian immigration machine to begin to crank up annual intakes, so it will take some time to decrease them. Time lags suggest that immigration policy is not a very responsive or appropriate macroeconomic policy lever. In early 2009, the Australian immigration minister, Chris Evans, announced a slight reduction of 14 percent, from 135,000 to 115,000, in the planned skilled-immigration intake for 2008–2009. The minister also removed some building and manufacturing trades—such as bricklaying, plumbing, welding, carpentry, and metal fitting—from the critical skills list that the Immigration Department uses to match skilled immigration intakes to labor shortages. The list is now comprised of mainly health and medical, engineering, and information technology (IT) professions. Since temporary immigrants must leave the country if they lose their jobs, it is possible that the Australian immigration intake will have fallen more quickly by the end of the recession that began in 2008 than it had during the previous one, when the number of temporary immigrants was considerably lower. However, there is already evidence that some temporary immigrants who lost their jobs have disappeared into the twilight world of the informal, undocumented immigrant community that exists wherever there are large immigrant populations. Australia may well repeat the experience of Europe after the recession of the mid-1970s, when many temporary migrants stayed to become permanent minorities, the case of the Turkish community in Germany being a prime example (Castles et al., 1984).

Although social cohesion has been the norm in postwar Australia, there are severe tests ahead for one of the world's most cosmopolitan societies. As unemployment rises in Australia and other countries, increasing social conflict related to immigration appears to be inevitable. In uncertain economic climates, scapegoats are sought. Pauline Hanson's One Nation party, which had a dramatic rise to political influence following the 1996 federal election, drew from this insecurity to fuel support for anti-immigration and anti-Aboriginal policies. It is also not a coincidence that the first major national debate on immigration and multiculturalism was ignited by Geoffrey Blainey in 1984 immediately following the 1982–1983 recession, when unemployment rates reached double figures in Australia for the first time since the 1930s. One key anti-immigration argument of both Blainey and Hanson was that immigrants take Australian jobs. This argument gets greater purchase when unemployment levels are rising and the reality of unemployment is immediate and raw. The nations most dependent on immigrants will also face severe social challenges as far-right groups and anti-immigration politicians attempt to play the race card in future national elections, attempting to emulate the previous success of John Howard.

Immigrant minorities in countries like Australia were adversely affected in a number of ways. First of all, they shouldered a disproportionate share of the burden of unemployment. In all Australia's postwar recessions, the unemployment rate of immigrant minorities has been much larger than that of the Australian born, with second-generation immigrant workers doing much better than the first generation. Although Australia escaped economic recession following the global financial crisis, unemployment rates rose for immigrant minorities, particularly those born in Africa and the Middle East. Second, the recession was accompanied by an increase in the racialization of minority-immigrant workers and their families in many Western countries, though this was minimal in Australia because the economy avoided economic recession and, while unemployment levels rose in Australia, they did not reach the high levels experienced in Europe and the United States. Debates about ethnic crime and ethnic criminal gangs as well as illegal immigrants have escalated, as has opposition to Muslim schools and mosques and the institutions of other religious or cultural minorities, in local government areas in Western societies. Third, migrant remittances to dependent family members were reduced as the costs of unemployment due to the economic crisis spread globally. In other words, the crisis of global capitalism has become, in Australia and other countries, a crisis for immigrant workers and multicultural societies alike. However, the extent of the anti-immigrant backlash was proportionate to the severity of the economic downturn induced by the global financial crisis. For this reason, immigrants in Australia have fared better than immigrants in most Western societies.

Conclusion

In this chapter I have argued that, unlike the globalization of trade and capital, international migration involves the settlement of people, increasingly from minority backgrounds, in Western host countries. Immigrants become neighbors, voters, trade unionists, commuters, and school chums; they are the most immediate face of globalization. Immigration therefore carries social and political consequences that, when evaluated through racialized eyes, reduce popular support for immigration and constrain the economic advantages that might be achieved through an open-door or larger-scale immigration policy. When viewed through this lens of racism and xenophobia, increasing numbers of immigrants from minority backgrounds who are allowed or even encouraged to bring their cultural traditions to Australia with them threaten to divide the nation into tribes that could or do undermine the social cohesion of the Christian, white majority. Local campaigns to oppose Muslim schools, provincial campaigns to confront ethnic crime, and national campaigns to send the undocumented boat people back to sea are lumped together with concerns that immigration destroys the environment, leading to an unholy political alliance of unlikely bedfellows in the anti-immigration camp. Tabloid newspapers are eager to run sensationalist anti-immigrant headlines, and political opportunists at all levels of government are eager to exploit the race card to oppose immigration, multiculturalism, or some combination of both. The contradiction is that needed immigrants are not wanted. This constrains immigration policy in a way that applies to no other government policy.

Of course, this story of the changes, continuities, contradictions, and controversies that characterize the political economy of Australian immigration is not uniquely Australian. In all the major countries of immigration, the global movement of people—however much it may be increasing in the contemporary phase of globalization—is severely constrained in comparison with the freedom that is accorded to the international flow of capital and goods. Indeed, the dominant image of this period is that of the walls that are literally being built to stop immigration, whether they be the fences that stretch for 216 miles, supplemented by another 154 miles of vehicle barriers, along the US-Mexico border or the 85-kilometer fence along the Israeli border. At the same time, the barriers to the global movement of trade and capital have been falling.

In most Western countries, the global financial crisis has been accompanied by a rise of anti-immigrant and anti-immigration politics, particularly in relation to claims about the incompatibility of minority immigrants in Western Christian societies and concerns about ethnic crime and illegal migration. This is the case in Europe, where, in the 2009 European parliamentary elections, far-right politicians gained unprecedented representation. The British National Party (BNP), which won its first two seats at the 2009 European Parliament elections, got nearly 1 million votes, or 6.2 percent of the total. Nick Griffin, the leader of the BNP, summarized its political message: "This is a Christian country, and Islam is not welcome because Islam and Christianity, Islam and democracy, Islam and women's rights do not mix" (*Economist*, 2009: 13). At the same election, the Finnish nationalist True Finns Party won its first EU parliament seat, while in the Netherlands, the anti-Islam campaigner Geert Wilders won an EU seat for the Party for Freedom (PVV). In Belgium, the right-wing parties pushing for greater autonomy in Flanders received an increasing vote, while in Slovakia an ultranationalist party won an EU seat. In Hungary, the center-right opposition Fidesz Party carried the majority (56.37 percent) of the vote, and in Bulgaria the ultranationalist Ataka Party won over 10 percent of the vote. These gains in the European Parliament have been matched by the success of many anti-immigrant parties and candidates in local, provincial, and national elections across Europe. This has not been the case in Australia, however, as the mainstream Labor Party government and Liberal-National Party Coalition opposition both moved to the right on immigration policy, squeezing out minority right-wing parties in the process.

The contradictory nature of the political economy of immigration is evident. As the global financial crisis gives way to recovery, the demand for more immigrants—from unskilled dishwashers to doctors and finance specialists—will increase. But the economic advantages of this increasing globalization will be severely constrained by perceptions of the social presence of immigrants, particularly those from minority backgrounds, as neighbors. Immigrant settlement policies such as Australian multiculturalism, designed to respond to the increasing cultural, ethnic, and religious diversity of a society in such a way as to minimize immigrant economic disadvantage, political disenfranchisement, and social exclusion—which, if successful, would themselves produce a greater "diversity dividend" at the economic level—become targets of opposition for the Right and Left, though for different reasons. The

Right sees multiculturalism as accommodating the needs of immigrant minorities too much and the Left too little. The cruel irony is that immigrants have become scapegoats for any economic downturn—including the global financial crisis—while bearing the greatest part of the burden it generates. Similarly, racial discrimination tends to restrain the economic performance of new immigrants, who are often employed at levels below their capability—whether because their skills are not recognized in their host country or because they experience informal racial discrimination—only to become scapegoats for the poor productivity or economic performance of the nations into which they settle.

In this chapter I have explored the contradictions inherent in the political economy of Australian immigration, arguing that although globalization has demanded greater and more diverse immigration, the social, political, and cultural aspects of immigrant settlement in Australia constrain the economic contribution that these newcomers can make and also generate social and political controversy and political opportunism around immigration policy. But local differences are at play, modifying global trends and commonalities. The facts that Australia avoided economic recession following the global financial crisis and that the rise in unemployment rates was less in Australia has meant that the anti-immigrant backlash has been less severe and that the anti-immigrant political right has not gained the traction witnessed in most other Western countries.

Notes

1. There is considerable debate as to when exactly the White Australia policy ended, because it eroded over time and was finally abandoned as one of the first acts of the new Labor government of Gough Whitlam in 1972.

2. There is also considerable debate as to when exactly multiculturalism was introduced into Australia. The groundwork for multiculturalism was laid by Al Grassby, immigration minister in the Whitlam Labor government (1972–1975), though it was the conservative government of Malcolm Fraser that set the major policy framework for multiculturalism by enacting most of the recommendations of the *Galbally Report* that the Fraser government (1975–1983) commissioned (Castles et al., 1988; Collins, 1991).

Part 4

Conclusion

13

Migration and the Global Economic Crisis

Nicola Phillips

It is fitting to conclude this volume by turning our attention to the global economic crisis that emerged in the late 2000s and considering its implications for migration and migrant workers. The task is hazardous in that, at the time that this volume is going to press, we are still in the midst of the fallout from the crisis. The trajectory of the recovery is as yet unclear—indeed, it is not possible to say with confidence that we have even embarked on a sustained recovery—and the longer-term consequences of the crisis for the global political economy remain highly uncertain. But let us put excessive caution to one side and consider what we can and do know about the crisis, its implications for people, especially workers, across the world, and the patterns of migration that have emerged in its wake and are likely to prevail in the near future.

The big political economy picture of the crisis indicates that the impact has thus far been felt most in the arenas in which it originated—that is, the richer economies of the world, first the United States and the United Kingdom and then Europe—in ways that have fueled a burgeoning debt crisis. These economies are of course characterized by high levels of labor immigration, and thus the question of the official and social politics that surround immigration become particularly pertinent, as the chapters in Part 3 of this book all note. Outside the epicenter of the world's financial markets, the impact of the crisis is transmitted primarily through trends in global production, trade, and investment networks. It is widely accepted that the economies, sectors, producers, and workers that are integrated into these global networks are most affected by the crisis in the short term and most likely to feel its long-term consequences. The high levels of orientation to export production and the pronounced dependence on trade in both Latin America and East Asia have made these regions particularly vulnerable to falling demand across export sectors, and the social consequences of falling growth and output are likely to be most profound in parts of those regions. By contrast, economies, sectors, workers, and producers that are most reliant on aid, remittances, and foreign direct investment (FDI) are thought likely to be much less affected by the global trends associated with the crisis. These economies are clustered predominantly in sub-Saharan Africa and South Asia—precisely where the "bottom billion" of the world's poorest people, to use Paul Collier's term, are predominantly concentrated (Sen, 2009; Collier, 2007).

There are a large number of "buts" to this general picture (Phillips, 2010b), but the one that is relevant here emerges when we focus less on the geographical dimensions of the crisis and more on its social profile. In the first place, there is a distinction to be made between the rural and urban poor: rural poor populations are likely to be the least affected by the crisis, particularly when livelihoods do not depend on work within the productive economy but rather on a combination of agricultural self-sufficiency and/or remittances from migrant family members, whereas the urban working poor have been, and are likely to remain, severely affected (Sen, 2009). At the same time, there is a distinction to be made between poor and vulnerable workers in formal and informal sectors of economic activity, exacerbating a general trend toward a widening of the gap between formal and informal economic activity in terms of wages, conditions, and rights. These dynamics contribute to a reinforcement of the social hierarchies explored in the chapters in Part 1 of this volume, reinforcing and deepening the various forms of polarization and inequality that characterize contemporary labor markets.

The large numbers of people working in conditions of precarious employment, particularly in the urban informal sector, are thus disproportionately vulnerable to the impact of the crisis, particularly when those forms of employment are concentrated in the external sector. There is a strong association in this respect with migrant workers, often constituted, as we have seen throughout the volume, as an ultra-flexible "parallel" or "invisible" workforce in the secondary segments of economies and labor markets. The migrant labor force across the world represents the most easily "disposable" part of the workforce, particularly the unauthorized sections thereof, and therefore is especially vulnerable to the impacts of economic downturns, along with native-born, less skilled workers, nonwhites, and younger workers. In some contexts, the impact of the crisis among these workers is felt in terms of unemployment; in others it is felt in wage and price decreases, which may act to cushion the impact on firms and producers of declining domestic demand (Sen, 2009) but also exacerbate vulnerability among the urban poor to transient and chronic forms of poverty as well as to long-term forms of precarious and insecure employment. The vulnerability of migrant workers is also shaped by the politics surrounding their status as migrants, not least in terms of the social resentments among native or local populations that invariably become stronger in situations of economic hardship. These dynamics have been documented insightfully throughout this volume.

Apart from these general observations, what can we say about the concrete mechanisms through which the crisis has made (or is likely to make) itself felt for patterns of global migration and the world's migrant labor force? Philip Martin (2009) has offered an interesting framework for thinking about these issues, which (here in adapted form) serves as a useful starting point. First, the fact that the recession began in industrialized countries and spread outward means that migrants no longer have the ability to move from lagging parts of the world economy to booming parts. In other words, many of the main and secondary destinations for migrants are affected by the crisis to the extent that they no longer offer the sort of plentiful opportunities for employment that attract migrant workers. Furthermore, as we have noted, much of the recession is concentrated in sectors that are sensitive to both economic cycles and trade and traditionally dominated by high numbers of migrant workers. These include construction and manufacturing in economies like those of Spain or the United Kingdom and China or Bangladesh. Unemployment in the US construction sector, for example—in which two-thirds of workers are foreign born—rose from 7.5 million to 13.2 million between the autumn of 2007 and the spring of 2009, representing an unemployment rate among immigrants of more than 17 percent in the first half of 2009 (Martin, 2009: 676; Orrenius and Zavodny, 2009: 4). Unauthorized workers, as the most economically motivated migrants, have been particularly affected by these patterns. The other sectors in which job losses have been concentrated are financial and travel-related services, which have tended to affect different groups of migrant workers. As Martin observes, "This means that migrants laid off in boom areas such as Dubai and Singapore include both financial specialists and construction laborers" (2009: 674).

The particular vulnerability of poorer migrant workers to these trends has been noted above: both internal and international migrants represent the most easily disposable parts of the workforce, particularly when they are undocumented or working in precarious conditions without employment contracts or long-term job security. They are thus likely to be strongly represented among the workers who bear the brunt of layoffs and redundancies or, indeed, the sudden disappearance of insecure jobs. They are even more vulnerable to conditions of underemployment, whereby employers reduce working hours or cut wages rather than lay off workers; these are strongly associated with transient forms of poverty. Finally, undocumented workers are rarely entitled to any kind of welfare benefits, to the extent that they are likely to suffer particular hardships during the recession (Papademetriou et al., 2009).

Second, immigration policies in the primary migrant-receiving countries have changed quite significantly since the 1990s. As Andrew Geddes shows in Chapter 10, in countries across Europe in particular, there has been a shift in emphasis from family reunification to a points-based system designed to attract highly skilled migrants and meet the needs of the economy at a given point in time. While the United States is also moving in this direction, it still gives higher priority to family reunification—a form of immigration that is "less sensitive to recession than economically motivated migration to countries that select newcomers based primarily on economic criteria" (Martin, 2009: 689; Papademetriou and Terrazas, 2009). The emerging, generalized trend in the wake of the crisis is toward reducing the number of visas available to temporary migrant workers.

We should also emphasize again, as many of the authors here have done, the long-standing patterns in popular sentiment surrounding immigration, whereby levels of public tolerance of immigration vary according to prevailing economic conditions. In many parts of the world, both public opinion and public policy have favored dispensing with migrant workers in order to reserve jobs for native-born populations. The Malaysian government implemented a policy known as "foreign workers first out" in early 2009 as demand for electronics goods shrank sharply, attracting criticism particularly from nongovernmental organizations (NGOs) in view of the requirement that migrant workers should leave the country without delay. The government also canceled visas for migrants scheduled to arrive in Malaysia after protests from trade unions about the admission of workers in times of rising unemployment (Martin, 2009: 684–685). Likewise, the government of Singapore announced in September 2009 a decision to "rein in immigration" in view of concerns about social friction between native-born and migrant workers, the latter consisting primarily of low-skilled migrants from Indonesia and mainland China (*Financial Times*, 2009). These represent examples of governments' attempts to restrict inward flows of migration, at least partly in response to public antagonism toward immigration and migrant workers in times of relative economic difficulty.

The situation in the United Kingdom, Ireland, and even Sweden is rather different, as intraregional migration accounts for a large part of the numbers of people flowing into these economies. Arrivals from Eastern European (A8) countries are overwhelmingly economic migrants motivated by employment opportunities and do not encounter the aforementioned concerns about their freedom to move or the costs thereof. As such, these flows are likely to be more responsive to the economic cycle (Papademetriou et al., 2009: 5). Yet the trends are unclear. Some preliminary evidence from the United Kingdom suggests a decline in the numbers of applications approved under the Worker Registration Scheme between 2008 and 2009 (21,275 compared with 46,645) and falling levels of inward migration; still, it offers only scant support for the notion that we are seeing a significant outflow of migrant workers (Dobson et al., 2009). Other research suggests a peak in outflows of migrants (both onward and return migration) even as it emphasizes that remigration is not a new trend. In 2006, 194,000 non-British citizens left the United Kingdom, and 200,000 are thought to have left in 2008 (Finch et al., 2009). Similarly, anecdotal evidence suggests an increase in return migration from the United States to Mexico and some other countries, but data do not yet substantiate these reports in any definitive manner. There is, however, much more solid evidence of a slowing in the growth of the foreign-born population in the United States since late 2007 (Papademetriou and Terrazas, 2009).

Generally, in addition, the available evidence indicates that many low-skilled workers are in fact preferring to remain in their host countries due to a combination of the absence of economic opportunities and the costs of returning to their home countries (Ratha et al., 2009; Castles and Miller, 2010). In Spain, for instance, the fact that migrant workers are eligible for state benefits meant that, in 2008–2009, fewer than 1,400 of 100,000 eligible immigrants signed up for a government scheme that paid unemployed workers to return to their countries of origin (Papademetriou et al., 2009: 4). Similarly, undocumented workers have traditionally been averse to returning to their home countries even for visits, as they would not easily be able to return to the country and the location of their employment. In short, the available evidence indicates that the impact of the economic crisis on flows of migrant workers has been felt at the level of inward migration but not necessarily at the level of outflow. The consequently very slight decline in migrant stocks in destination countries is consistent with trends during other major economic crises over the nineteenth and twentieth centuries (Green and Winters, 2010), but it nevertheless clearly represents an interruption of contemporary trends in the 1990s and early 2000s toward "rapid increases in migrant flows and steady increases in migrant stocks in many regions" (Castles and Miller, 2010: 10).

Put together, these conditions point to significant shifts in the panorama of migration and its developmental impact. As we have seen, migration clearly offers a significant enhancement of earning capacity for vast parts of the world's population, such that much attention is justifiably being devoted to the potential developmental gains of allowing greater labor mobility (World Bank, 2005; Pritchett, 2005). If we accept this view that migration is potentially very positive in developmental terms, then we must also agree that the drying up of available jobs in the primary territorial and sectoral destinations and the hardening of immigration policies to further restrict these opportunities become significant impediments to development through mobility for poor and low- or unskilled migrants. At the same time, the often severe economic hardships that compel people to migrate for work in the first place and then go to considerable lengths to retain employment invite the danger that these migrants will be more vulnerable to exploitative forms of employment in times of recession, when decent jobs become harder to locate. As we have noted, the gap between formal and informal work is likely to widen, and more people are likely to take employment in the informal sector where their rights and well-being are less—or not at all—protected.

We should emphasize that these comments apply as much to internal migration as to international migration. While the issues of immigration law and policy are clearly not relevant, internal migration serves much the same purpose in countries like China, Brazil, or Mexico as migration across national borders. The contraction of employment opportunities in construction and manufacturing in the principal urban areas of China, for instance, has potentially devastating consequences for the millions of migrant workers who have either already moved to these areas or those who saw such jobs as opportunities for employment. Estimates indicate that somewhere between 10 and 20 million Chinese workers will have returned to rural areas from the coastal industrial centers as a result of the decline in manufacturing activity (Skeldon, 2010: 10), itself the result of interrupted demand in the major consumer economies of the United States and Europe.

The third channel through which the developmental impact of the crisis has been transmitted relates to remittances. Their importance was explored in the chapters in Part 2 of this volume. The generalized excitement about remittances and their development potential looks increasingly likely to have been specific to the global economic environment of the earlier part of the 2000s; until 2008, we had not had an opportunity to observe the behavior of remittances under conditions of severe global crisis. Indeed, we are beginning to see a much more volatile picture than the one that is often shown in claims about the stability of remittances as a form of developmental financing. More to the point, patterns appear to have been very mixed across regions and countries. Although remittance flows to countries like Nepal or Bangladesh have not thus far been visibly affected (Sen, 2009), we have seen both declining growth and absolute falls in remittances to many other parts of the world, including the Philippines, Mexico, and other economies to which they have become central. In my own chapter, I present some early data on these trends in the Latin American and Caribbean context, where the fall in remittances has been more severe than in other regions, probably due to the early onset and severity of the crisis in the major destination countries for Latin American migrants (namely the United States and Spain) as well as the marked contraction of particular sectors like construction (Ratha et al., 2009; Castles and Miller, 2010: 11–12). In the middle of the crisis, the World Bank was predicting a decline in remittance volumes of 10 percent in Europe but only 4 percent in Asia (Martin, 2009: 674).

So the picture is mixed and the trajectories remain difficult to discern. It may well be that remittances will prove to have fallen less sharply than FDI over the period of the crisis (Martin, 2009; Ratha and Mohaptra, 2009) and that the most devastating developmental impact of the crisis will have been transmitted through FDI rather than remittances. Furthermore, remittances have been predicted to show gradual recovery as of 2010 (World Bank, 2008; Ratha et al., 2009: 14; Castles and Miller, 2010: 12). Nevertheless, despite a more resilient aggregate picture than many were predicting in the midst of the crisis, we have seen clear evidence in a number of countries and regions of quite sharp alterations to trends in remittances, particularly from workers in the economies or sectors that have been hardest hit by slowdowns in economic activity. The developmental impact of these alterations may well be significant. Even though we are tentatively beginning to talk about emergence from crisis in many of these economies, it is for the most part proving to be a jobless recovery and is therefore unlikely to express itself in the short term as a significantly improved employment and development panorama for many of the world's migrant workers. It is also still too early to rule out the possibility of a "double-dip" recession in many of the most affected economies, such as the United Kingdom, and the debt crisis in a number of European economies is still very much in full flow.

It feels unsatisfactory to conclude a volume on such an uncertain and speculative note, but this is rather beside the point: the importance of the discussion rests much more with the ways in which the crisis has underscored and indeed reinforced many of the trends, processes, and patterns that have been identified in the chapters of this volume. They relate above all to the patterns of social and labor market polarization identified in the contributions to Part 1 and the ways in which the consequent forms of inequality have been exacerbated by the global economic downturn. The position of poor migrant workers, among the most vulnerable members of the global labor force, is thrown into even sharper relief by the uneven geographical and social impact of the crisis, as are the structural forces that perpetuate the polarization between the primary and secondary segments of global and local labor markets. The intimate nexus between migration and development we explored in Part 2 is similarly thrown into the spotlight by the uneven impact of the crisis, and many of the repercussions of the crisis for various dimensions of global human development are being transmitted precisely through the channels associated with migration. Finally, the patterns of the social and political governance of migration discussed in Part 3 are visibly conditioned by the circumstances of the crisis, resulting in increased tensions within and between the social hierarchies built around migration. In this dispiriting context, the kind of IPE perspective we have developed here seems to be more relevant than ever to understanding the global political economy of migration.

Acronyms

ABA	American Bar Association
ABS	Australian Bureau of Statistics
ACP	African, Caribbean, Pacific
ADB	Asian Development Bank
AFFORD	African Foundation for Development
AFL-CIO	Federation of Labor–Congress of Industrial Organizations (US)
AILA	American Immigration Lawyers Association
BNP	British National Party
CCFA	Canada-Chile Free Trade Agreement
CEC	Commission of the European Communities
CoRMSA	Consortium for Refugees and Migrants in South Africa
CRE	Commission for Racial Equality (UK)
DfID	Department for International Development (UK)
DHS	Department of Homeland Security (US)
EC	European Community
ECLAC	United Nations Economic Commission for Latin America and the Caribbean
EIPE	everyday international political economy
EPA	economic partnership agreement
EPZ	export-processing zone
EU	European Union
FARMS	Foreign Agricultural Resource Management Services (Canada)
FDI	foreign direct investment
G-8	Group of Eight Industrialized Nations
GATS	General Agreement on Trade in Services

GCC	global commodity chain
GCIM	Global Commission on International Migration
GDP	gross domestic product
GPN	global production network
GVC	global value chain
ILO	International Labour Organization
IOM	International Organization for Migration
IPE	international political economy
IRCA	Immigration Reform and Control Act (US)
ISPE	international social and political economy
IT	information technology
JMOJ	Japan Ministry of Justice
LAC	Latin America and the Caribbean
MBA	Masters in Business Administration
MDG	Millennium Development Goal
MIDA	Migration for Development in Africa (IOM program)
MODL	migrant occupations in demand list (Australia)
NAFTA	North American Free Trade Agreement
NGO	nongovernmental organization
NIC	newly industrializing country
NIF	National Immigration Forum
NILC	National Immigration Law Center (US)
OCW	overseas contract worker
OECD	Organization for Economic Cooperation and Development
OIM	Organización Internacional para las Migraciones (International Organization for Migration)
OPEC	Organization of Petroleum-exporting Countries
PVV	Party for Freedom (the Netherlands)
RIPE	regulatory international political economy
SCIFA	Strategic Committee on Immigration, Frontiers, and Asylum (EU)
SCIRP	Select Commission on Immigration and Refugee Policy (US)
TIPR	*Trafficking in Persons Report* (US Department of State)
TLWG	Temporary Labour Working Group (UK)
TOKTEN	Transfer of Knowledge through Expatriate Nationals (UNDP program)
TUC	Trade Union Congress (UK)
UN	United Nations

UN DESA	United Nations Department of Economic and Social Affairs
UNDP	United Nations Development Programme
UNFPA	United Nations Population Fund
UNHCR	United Nations High Commissioner for Refugees
UNRISD	United Nations Research Institute for Social Development
USDOS	United States Department of State
WHO	World Health Organization
WTO	World Trade Organization

References

Abella, M. I. (ed.) (1994), "Turning Points in Labor Migration," *Asian and Pacific Migration Journal* 3 (1): 1–7.

ABS (Australian Bureau of Statistics) (2007), "Media Fact Sheet: More than One in Five Australians Born Overseas—Census," http://www.abs.gov.au.

Acosta, P., C. Calderón, P. Fajnzylber, and J. H. López (2006), "Remittances and Development in Latin America," *The World Economy* 29 (7): 957–987.

Acosta, P., P. Fajnzylber, and J. H. López (2007), "The Impact of Remittances on Poverty and Human Capital: Evidence from Latin American Household Surveys," in Ç. Özden and M. Schiff (eds.), *International Migration, Economic Development, and Policy* (Washington, DC: World Bank), 59–98.

Adams, K., and S. Dickey (eds.) (2000), *Home and Hegemony: Domestic Service and Identity in South and Southeast Asia* (Ann Arbor: Michigan University Press).

Adams, R. H. (2006), "Remittances, Poverty, and Investment in Guatemala," in Ç. Özden and M. Schiff (eds.), *International Migration, Remittances, and the Brain Drain* (Washington, DC: World Bank), 53–80.

Adams, R. H., and J. Page (2005), "Do International Migration and Remittances Reduce Poverty in Developing Countries?" *World Development* 33 (10): 1645–1699.

Adams, R. N. (1959), *A Community in the Andes: Problems and Progress in Muquiyauyo* (Seattle: University of Washington Press).

ADB (Asian Development Bank) (2004), *Enhancing the Efficiency of Overseas Filipino Workers Remittances: Final Report*, ADB TA-4185-PHI (Manila: Asian Development Bank).

Adepoju, A. (2006), "Leading Issues in International Migration in Sub-Saharan Africa," in C. Cross, D. Gelderblom, N. Roux, and J. Mafukidze (eds.), *Views on Migration in Sub-Saharan Africa: Proceedings of an African Migration Alliance Workshop* (Cape Town: HSRC Press).

——— (2008a), "Migration in Sub-Saharan Africa," Current African Issues Background Paper 37, Nordiska Afrikainstitutet, Uppsala, Sweden.

——— (2008b), "Perspectives on International Migration and National Development in Sub-Saharan Africa," in A. Adepoju, T. van Naerssen, and

A. Zoomers (eds.), *International Migration and National Development in Sub-Saharan Africa: Viewpoints and Policy Initiatives in Countries of Origin* (Leiden: Brill), 21–48.

African Union (2006), "Draft African Common Position on Migration and Development," MIGR/EXP/Draft/Common Position (I), Experts' Meeting on Migration and Development, April 3–5, Algiers.

Aguirre, E., Jr. (2004), "US and Mexico: Immigration Policy and the Bilateral Relationship," testimony before the US Senate Foreign Relations Committee, Washington, DC, March 23.

Ahmad, A. N. (2008), "Dead Men Working: Time and Space in London's ('Illegal') Migrant Economy," *Work, Employment, and Society* 22 (2): 301–318.

AILA (American Immigration Lawyers Association) (2005), The Border Protection, Antiterrorism, and Illegal Immigration Control Act of 2005 (H.R. 4437), as Amended and Passed by the House on 12/16/05, Section-by-Section Analysis, http://www.aila.org.

Akokpari, J. K. (2000), "Globalisation and Migration in Africa," *African Sociological Review/Revue Africaine de Sociologie* 4 (2): 72–92.

Akyeampong, E. K. (2006), "Race, Identity, and Citizenship in Black Africa: The Case of the Lebanese in Ghana," *Africa* 76 (3): 297–323.

Alesina, A., and E. L. Glaeser (2004), *Fighting Poverty in the US and Europe: A World of Difference* (Oxford: Oxford University Press).

Alesina, A., E. L. Glaeser, and B. Sacerdote, (2001), "Why Doesn't the United States Have a European-style Welfare State?" *Brookings Papers on Economic Activity* 2001 (2): 187–254.

Ålund, A. (1985), *Skyddsmurar: Etnicitet och klass in invandrarsammanhang* (Stockholm: Liber).

Ålund, A., and C.-U. Schierup (1991), *Paradoxes of Multiculturalism: Essays on Swedish Society* (Aldershot: Avebury).

Amin, S. (1995), "Migrations in Contemporary Africa: A Retrospective View," in J. Baker and T. A. Aina (eds.), *The Migration Experience in Africa* (Uppsala: Nordika Afrikainstitutet), 29–40.

Amjad, R. (1996), "Philippines and Indonesia: On the Way to a Migration Transition," *Asian and Pacific Migration Journal* 5 (2–3): 346–349.

Amuedo-Dorantes, C., and S. Pozo (2006), "Remittance Receipt and Business Ownership in the Dominican Republic," *The World Economy* 29 (7): 939–956.

Anarfi, J., and S. Kwankye (2003), "Migration from and to Ghana: A Background Paper," Working Paper C4, Development Research Centre on Migration, Globalisation, and Poverty, University of Sussex, UK.

Andall, J. (2003), "Hierarchy and Interdependence: The Emergence of a Service Caste in Europe," in J. Andall (ed.), *Gender and Ethnicity in Contemporary Europe* (Oxford and New York: Berg), 39–60.

Anderson, B. (1997), "Servants and Slaves: Europe's Domestic Workers," *Race and Class* 39 (1): 37–49.

Anderson, M. (1998), "European Frontiers at the End of the Twentieth Century: An Introduction," in M. Anderson and E. Bort (eds.), *The Frontiers of Europe* (London: Pinter), 1–10.

Andreas, P. (1998–1999), "The Escalation of US Immigration Control in the Post-NAFTA Era," *Political Science Quarterly* 113 (4): 591–615.

——— (1999), "Smuggling Wars: Law Enforcement and Law Evasion in a Changing World," in T. Farer (ed.), *Transnational Crime in the Americas* (London: Routledge), 85–98.

——— (2001), "The Transformation of Migrant Smuggling across the U.S.-Mexican Border," in D. Kyle and R. Koslowski (eds.), *Global Human Smuggling: Comparative Perspectives* (Baltimore, MD, and London: Johns Hopkins University Press), 107–125.

——— (2004), "Illicit International Political Economy: The Clandestine Side of Globalization," *Review of International Political Economy* 11 (3): 641–652.

Andreas, P., and E. Nadelmann (2006), *Policing the Globe: Criminalization and Crime Control in International Relations* (Oxford and New York: Oxford University Press).

Ansell, C. (2004), "Restructuring Authority and Territoriality," in C. Ansell and G. DiPalma (eds.), *Restructuring Territoriality: Europe and the United States Compared* (Cambridge: Cambridge University Press).

Antle, W. J., III (2004), "Amnesty by Another Name Is Still Amnesty: Bush Compounds an Immigration Disaster," January 12, http://www.intellectualconservative.com.

Ardila, G. (2006), *Colombia: Migraciones, Transnacionalismo y Desplazamiento* (Bogotá: Universidad Nacional de Colombia).

Arthur, J. A. (1991), "International Labor Migration Patterns in West Africa," *African Studies Review* 34 (3): 65–87.

Asis, M. M. B. (2004), "Borders, Globalization, and Irregular Migration in Southeast Asia," in A. Ananta and E. N. Arifin (eds.), *International Migration in Southeast Asia* (Singapore: Institute for Southeast Asian Studies), 199–227.

——— (2005), "Caring for the World: Filipino Domestic Workers Gone Global," in S. Huang, B. S. A. Yeoh, and N. A. Rahman (eds.), *Asian Women as Transnational Domestic Workers* (Singapore: Marshall Cavendish Academic), 21–53.

Australian Productivity Commission (2006), *Economic Impacts of Migration and Population Growth: Final Report*, Canberra, April.

Awumbila, M., T. Manuh, P. Quartey, C. A. Tagoe, and T. A. Bosiakoh (2009), "Ghana Migration Country Paper: Trends, Issues, and Emerging Research Gaps," working paper, Centre for Migration Studies, University of Ghana, Legon.

Azam, J. P., and F. Gubert (2006), "Migrants' Remittances and the Household in Africa: A Review of Evidence," *Journal of African Economies* 15: 426–462.

Bade, K. (2003), *Migration in European History* (Oxford: Blackwell).

Badie, B. (1995), *La Fin des Territoires: Essai sur le Désordre International et Sur: Ultilité Social de Respect* (Paris: Fayard).

Bair, J., and G. Gereffi (2003), "Upgrading, Uneven Development, and Jobs in the North American Apparel Industry," *Global Networks* 3 (2): 143–169.

Bakewell, O. (2008a), "Keeping Them in Their Place: The Ambivalent Relationship between Development and Migration in Africa," *Third World Quarterly* 29 (7): 1341–1358.

——— (2008b), "In Search of the Diasporas Within Africa," *African Diaspora* 1 (1): 5–27.

Bakker, I. (2007), "Social Reproduction and the Constitution of a Gendered Political Economy," *New Political Economy* 12 (4): 541–556.

Bales, K. (1999), *Disposable People: New Slavery in the Global Economy* (Berkeley: University of California Press).

——— (2007), *Ending Slavery: How We Free Today's Slaves* (Berkeley: University of California Press).

Balibar, E. (2004), *We, the People of Europe? Reflections on Transnational Citizenship* (Princeton, NJ: Princeton University Press).

Ball, R., and N. Piper (2006), "Trading Labour-Trading Rights: The Regional Dynamics of Rights Recognition for Migrant Workers in the Asia-Pacific," in K. Hewison and K. Young (eds.), *Transnational Migration and Work in Asia* (London: Routledge), 213–233.

Ball, R. E. (2004), "Divergent Development, Racialised Rights: Globalised Labour Markets and the Trade of Nurses—The Case of the Philippines," *Women's Studies International Forum* 27: 119–133.

Ballard, R. (2003), *Migration, Remittances, Economic Growth, and Poverty Reduction: Reflections on the Basis of the South Asian Experience*, report prepared for the Department for International Development (DfID), Centre for Applied South Asian Studies, University of Manchester.

Banting, K. G. (2000), "Looking in Three Directions: Migration and the European Welfare State in Comparative Perspective," in M. Bommes and A. Geddes (eds.), *Immigration and Welfare: Challenging the Borders of the Welfare State* (London and New York: Routledge), 13–33.

Banting, K. G., R. Johnston, W. Kymlicka, and S. Soroka (2006), "Do Multiculturalism Policies Erode the Welfare State? An Empirical Analysis," in K. G. Banting and W. Kymlicka (eds.), *Multiculturalism and the Welfare State: Recognition and Redistribution in Contemporary Democracies* (Oxford and New York: Oxford University Press), 49–91.

Banting, K. G., and W. Kymlicka (2006), "Introduction: Multiculturalism and the Welfare State: Setting the Context," in K. G. Banting and W. Kymlicka (eds.), *Multiculturalism and the Welfare State: Recognition and Redistribution in Contemporary Democracies* (Oxford and New York: Oxford University Press), 1–45.

Barker, J. (1998), "State of Fear: Controlling the Criminal Contagion in Suharto's New Order," *Indonesia* 66: 42–47.

Barrientos, S., A. Bee, A. Matear, and I. Vogel (1999), *Women and Agribusiness: Working Miracles in the Chilean Fruit Export Sector* (Basingstoke, UK: Macmillan).

Barrientos, S., G. Gereffi, and A. Rossi (2008), "What Are the Challenges and Opportunities for Economic and Social Upgrading?" concept note for the workshop on Capturing the Gains, University of Manchester, UK, December.

Bartolini, S. (1998), "Exit Options, Boundary Building, Political Restructuring," SPS Working Paper No.1, European University Institute, Florence.

Basok, T. (1999), "Free to Be Unfree: Mexican Guest Workers in Canada," *Labour, Capital, and Society* 32 (2): 192–221.

——— (2002), *Tortillas and Tomatoes: Transmigrant Mexican Harvesters in*

Canada (Montreal and Kingston, UK: McGill-Queens's University Press).

Bastia, T. (2007), "From Mining to Garment Workshops: Bolivian Migrants in Buenos Aires," *Journal of Ethnic and Migration Studies* 33 (4): 655–669.

Battistella, G. (2004), "Return Migration in the Philippines: Issues and Policies," in D. S. Massey and T. J. Edward (eds.), *International Migration: Prospects and Policies in a Global Market* (Oxford: Oxford University Press), 212–229.

Battistella, G., and M. M. B. Asis (eds.) (2003), *Unauthorized Migration in Southeast Asia* (Quezon City, the Philippines: Scalabrini Migration Center).

Bauböck, R., A. Heller, and A. R. Zolberg (eds.) (1996), *The Challenge of Diversity: Integration and Pluralism in Societies of Immigration* (Aldershot, UK: Avebury).

Bauder, H. (2003a), "'Brain Abuse,' or the Devaluation of Immigrant Labour in Canada," *Antipode* 35 (4): 699–717.

——— (2003b), "Cultural Representations of Immigrant Workers by Service Providers and Employers," *Journal of International Migration and Integration* 4 (3): 415–438.

——— (2005a), "Zuwanderung drückt soziale Standards," *Süddeutsche Zeitung*, July 26, 2.

——— (2005b), "Habitus, Rules of the Labour Market, and Employment Strategies of Immigrants in Vancouver, Canada," *Social and Cultural Geography* 6 (1): 81–97.

——— (2006), *Labor Movement: How Migration Regulates Labor Markets* (New York: Oxford University Press).

——— (2008a), "The Economic Case for Immigration: Neoliberal and Regulatory Paradigms in Canada's Press," *Studies in Political Economy* 82: 131–152.

——— (2008b), "Neoliberalism and the Utility of Immigration: Media Perspectives of Germany's Immigration Law," *Antipode* 40 (1): 55–78.

——— (forthcoming), *Immigration Dialectic: Imagining Community, Economy, and Nation* (Toronto: University of Toronto Press).

Bearak, B. (2008), "Immigrants Fleeing Fury of South African Mobs," *New York Times*, May 23.

Beeks, K., and D. Amir (eds.) (2006), *Trafficking and the Global Sex Industry* (Lanham and Oxford: Lexington Books).

Benería, L. (1979), "Reproduction, Production, and the Sexual Division of Labor," *Cambridge Journal of Economics* 3 (3): 203–225.

——— (2003), *Gender, Development, and Globalization: Economics As If All People Mattered* (New York: Routledge).

Bhagwati, J. (2003), "Borders Beyond Control," *Foreign Affairs* 81 (2), online version, http://www.foreignaffairs.com.

Bicchi, F. (2007), *European Union Foreign Policy-Making Towards the Mediterranean* (New York: Palgrave).

Bigo, D. (2001), "Migration and Security," in C. Joppke and V. Guiraudon (eds.), *Controlling a New Migration World* (London: Routledge), 121–149.

——— (2002), "Security and Immigration: Toward a Critique of the Governmentality of Unease," *Alternatives* 27 (11): 63–92.

Bilefsky, D. (2007), "To Combat Illegal Workers, EU Targets the Employers," *International Herald Tribune*, May 16.

Bilger, V., and A. Kraler (2005), "Introduction: African Migrations: Historical Perspectives and Contemporary Dynamics," *Wiener Zeitschrift für kritische Afrikastudien* 8: 5–21.

Binford, L. (2009), "From Fields of Power to Fields of Sweat: The Dual Process of Constructing Temporary Migrant Labour in Mexico and Canada," *Third World Quarterly* 30 (3): 503–517.

Biofuels Watch Center (2009), "Brazil of Biofuels: Sugarcane 2009: Impacts of Crops Over Land, Environment and Society," NGO Repórter Brasil, São Paulo.

Birrell, R., L. Hawthorne, and S. Richardson (2006), *Evaluation of the General Skilled Migration Categories Report* (Canberra: Commonwealth of Australia).

Black, R., J. Crush, S. Peberdy, S. Ammassari, L. M. Hilker, S. Mouillesseaux, C. Pooley, and R. Rajkotia (2006), "Migration and Development in Africa: An Overview," Southern African Migration Project, Queens University, Kingston, Ontario.

Black, R., L. M. Hilker, and C. Pooley (2004), "Migration and Pro-Poor Policy in East Africa," Development Research Centre on Migration, Globalisation, and Poverty, University of Sussex, UK.

Blainey, G. (1984), *All For Australia* (North Ryde: Methuen Haynes).

Boccagni, P. (2008), "Migrants' Social Protection as a Multi-actor Process: Public Policies and Emigrants' Own Initiatives in the Case of Ecuador," paper presented at the Conference on Migration and Social Protection: Exploring Issues of Portability and Access, University of Sussex, UK, November.

Bolt, P. (2000), *China and Southeast Asia's Ethnic Chinese: State and Diaspora in Contemporary Asia* (Westport: Praeger).

Bommes, M., and A. Geddes (eds.) (2000), *Immigration and Welfare: Challenging the Borders of the Welfare State* (London: Routledge).

Bonacich, E., and R. P. Appelbaum (2000), *Behind the Label: Inequality in the Los Angeles Apparel Industry* (Berkeley: University of California Press).

Bonnett, A. (2006), "The Americanisation of Anti-Racism? Global Power and Hegemony in Ethnic Equity," *Journal of Ethnic and Migration Studies*, 32 (7): 1083–1103.

Boswell, C., A. Geddes, and P. Scholten (2011), "The Role of Narratives in Migration Policy-Making: A Research Agenda," *British Journal of Politics and International Relations* 13 (1): 1–11.

Bourdieu, P. (1984), *Distinction: A Social Critique of the Judgement of Taste* (Cambridge, MA: Harvard University Press).

——— (1986), "The Forms of Capital," in J. G. Richardson (ed.), *Handbook of Theory and Research for the Sociology of Education* (New York: Greenwood Press), 241–258.

——— (2002a), "Against the Policy of Depoliticization," *Studies in Political Economy* 69, 31–41.

——— (2002b), "Habitus," in J. Hillier and E. Rooksby (eds.), *Habitus: Sense of Place* (Aldershot, UK: Ashgate), 28–34.

Bourdieu, P., and J.-C. Passeron (1977), *Reproduction in Education, Society, and Culture* (London: Sage).

Bowcott, O. (2010), "EU Border Agency Says Third Fewer Illegal Immigrants Spotted in Past Year," *The Guardian*, May 25.

Bowling, B., and C. Phillips (2002), *Racism, Crime, and Justice* (Harrow, UK: Longman Press).

Boyd, M., and D. Pikkov (2008), "Finding a Place in Stratified Structures: Migrant Women in North America," in N. Piper (ed.), *New Perspectives on Gender and Migration–Livelihood, Rights, and Entitlements* (London: Routledge), 19–58.

Boyer, R., and J. R. Hollingsworth (1997), *Contemporary Capitalism: The Embeddedness of Institutions* (New York: Cambridge University Press).

Briones, L. (2009), "Reconsidering the Migrant-Development Link: Capability and Livelihood in Filipina Experiences of Domestic Work in Paris," *Population, Space, and Place* 15 (2): 119–132.

Brown, R. P. C., and E. Jimenez (2008), "Estimating the Net Effects of Migration and Remittances on Poverty and Inequality: Comparison of Fiji and Tonga," *Journal of International Development* 20 (4): 547–571.

Brown, S. S. (2006), "Can Remittances Spur Development? A Critical Survey," *International Studies Review* 8 (1): 55–75.

Buchan, J., and L. Calman (2004), *The Global Shortage of Registered Nurses: An Overview of Issues and Actions* (Geneva: International Council of Nurses).

Bulmer, M., and J. Solomos (eds.) (2004), *Researching Race and Racism* (London: Routledge).

Bulut, T., and C. Lane (2011), "The Private Regulation of Labour Standards and Rights in the Global Clothing Industry," *New Political Economy* 16 (1), 41–72.

Bump, M. (2006), "Ghana: Searching for Opportunities at Home and Abroad," Migration Information Source, March.

Bundesamt für Migration und Flüchtlinge (2008), *Migrationsbericht 2008* (Berlin: Bundesministerium des Innern).

Bundesministerium des Innern (2007), "Zuwanderung," http://www.zuwanderung.de.

Bundesverwaltungsamt (2003), *Jahresstatistik Aussiedler und deren Angehörige, 2002*, report by Bunderverwaltungsamt, http://www.bundesverwaltungsamt.de.

Burawoy, M. (1976), "The Functions and Reproduction of Migrant Labour: Comparative Material from Southern Africa and the United States," *American Journal of Sociology* 81 (5): 1050–1087.

Butterworth, D., and J. K. Chance (1981), *Latin American Urbanization* (Cambridge: Cambridge University Press).

Byrne, R., G. Noll, and J. Vedsted-Hansen (2002), *New Asylum Countries? Migration Control and Refugee Protection in an Enlarged European Union* (The Hague: Kluwer Law International).

Cai, F., and D. Wang (2008), "Impacts of Internal Migration on Economic Growth and Urban Development in China," in J. DeWind and J. Holdaway (eds.), *Migration and Development Within and Across Borders: Research and Policy Perspectives on Internal and International Migration* (Geneva: International Organization for Migration and the Social Science Council of New York), 245–271.

Calavita, K. (2005), *Immigrants at the Margins: Law, Race, and Exclusion in Southern Europe* (Cambridge: Cambridge University Press).

Camarota, S. A. (2007), *Immigration Is Hurting the US Worker: Low-Paid American Workers Have Borne the Heaviest Impact of Immigration*, report of the Centre for Immigration Studies, Washington, DC, http://www.cis.org.

Canales, A. I. (2007), "Inclusion and Segregation: The Incorporation of Latin American Immigrants into the US Labor Market," *Latin American Perspectives* 34 (1): 73–82.

Caporaso, J. (1996), "Forms of State in the European Union: Westphalian, Regulatory, and Post-modern," *Journal of Common Market Studies* 34 (1): 29–52.

Cárdenas, M., and C. Mejía (2006), "Migraciones Internacionales en Colombia: ¿Qué Sabemos?," Working Paper No. 20, Fedesarrollo, Bogotá, Colombia, September.

Carnoy, M. (1994), *Faded Dreams: The Politics and Economics of Race in America* (New York: Cambridge University Press).

Carr, M., M. A. Chen, and J. Tate (2000), "Globalization and Its Intimate Other: Filipina Domestic Workers in Hong Kong," in M. Marquand and A. Sisson Runyan (eds.), *Gender and Global Restructuring: Sightings, Sites, and Resistances* (London: Routledge), 27–43.

Cassidy, J. (2009), *How Markets Fail: The Logic of Economic Calamities* (New York: Farrar, Strauss, and Giroux).

Castells, M. (1975), "Immigrant Workers and Class Struggles in Advanced Capitalism: The Western European Experience," *Politics and Society*, 5 (1): 32–66.

——— (1996), *The Rise of the Network Society* (Oxford: Basil Blackwell).

——— (1998), *End of Millennium* (Oxford: Basil Blackwell).

Castells, M., and L. Benton (eds.) (1989), *The Informal Economy: Studies in Advanced and Less Developed Countries* (Baltimore, MD: Johns Hopkins University Press), 11–37.

Castells, M., and A. Portes (1989), "World Underneath: The Origins, Dynamics and Effects of the Informal Economy," in A. Portes, M. Castells, and L. A. Benton (eds.), *The Informal Economy: Studies in Advanced and Less Developed Countries* (Baltimore, MD: John Hopkins University Press), 11–37.

Castles, S. (2000), "International Migration at the Beginning of the Twenty-first Century: Global Trends and Issues," *International Social Science Journal* 52 (165): 269–281.

——— (2003), "Towards a Sociology of Forced Migration and Social Transformation," *Sociology* 37 (1): 13–34.

——— (2006), "Guestworkers in Europe: A Resurrection?" *International Migration Review* 40 (4): 741–766.

Castles, S., with H. Booth and T. Wallace (1984), *Here for Good: Western Europe's New Ethnic Minorities* (London: Pluto Press).

Castles, S., and R. Delgado Wise (2008), "Introduction," in S. Castles and R. Delgado Wise (eds.), *Migration and Development: Perspectives from the South* (Geneva: International Organization for Migration): 1–13.

Castles, S., W. Foster, R. Iredale, and G. Withers (1998), *Australia and Immigration: A Partnership—A Review of Research and Issues* (Sydney: Allen and Unwin).

Castles, S., M. Kalantzis, B. Cope, and M. Morrissey (1988), *Mistaken Identity: Multiculturalism and the Demise of Nationalism in Australia* (Sydney: Pluto Press).

Castles, S., and G. Kosack (1973), *Immigrant Workers and Class Structure in Western Europe* (London: Oxford University Press).

Castles, S., and M. J. Miller (1998), *The Age of Migration: International Population Movements in the Modern World*, 2nd ed. (Basingstoke, UK: Palgrave).

——— (2009), *The Age of Migration: International Population Movements in the Modern World*, 4th ed. (Basingstoke, UK: Palgrave).

——— (2010), "Migration and the Global Economic Crisis: One Year On," update 1L, April, http://www.age-of-migration.com.

Castles, S., and E. Vasta (eds.) (1996), *The Teeth are Smiling: The Persistence of Racism in Multicultural Australia* (Sydney: Allen and Unwin).

CEC (Commission of the European Communities) (1997), *An Action Plan for Free Movement of Workers*, COM(97)586, Brussels.

——— (2002), *Policy Priorities in the Fight Against Illegal Immigration: Impact Assessment*, SEC(2006)964, Brussels.

——— (2004), *Green Paper: A Common Approach to Managing Economic Migration*, COM(2004)811 final, Brussels.

——— (2005a), *Migration and Development: Some Concrete Orientations*, COM(2005)390 final, Brussels.

——— (2005b), *Policy Plan on Legal Migration*, Brussels, December 21.

——— (2006a), *The Global Approach to Migration One Year On: Towards a Comprehensive European Migration Policy*, Brussels.

——— (2006b), *Annual Report on the Development of a Common Policy on Illegal Immigration, Smuggling and Trafficking of Human Beings, External Border Controls, and the Return of Illegal Residents*, SEC(2006)1010, Brussels.

——— (2006c) *Policy Priorities in the Fight Against Illegal Immigration*, COM(2006)402 final, Brussels.

Ch'ng, D. (1993), *Overseas Chinese Entrepreneurs in East Asia: Background, Business Practices and International Networks* (Melbourne: CEDA).

Chafetz, J. S. (1988), "The Gender Division of Labor and the Reproduction of Female Disadvantage: Toward an Integrated Theory," *Journal of Family Issues* 9 (1):108–131.

Chaib, S. (2003), "Women, Migration, and the Labour Market: The Case of France," in J. Freedman (ed.), *Gender and Insecurity: Migrant Women in Europe* (Aldershot, UK: Ashgate), 107–118.

Chamberlayne, P. (1997), "Social Exclusion: Sociological Traditions and National Contexts," Sostris Working Paper 1, Centre for Biography in Social Policy, University of East London.

Chamie, J., and L. Dall'Oglio (eds.) (2008), *International Migration and Development—Continuing the Dialogue: Legal and Policy Perspectives* (New York and Geneva: Center for Migration Studies and International Organization for Migration).

Chan, J. (1997), *Changing Police Culture: Policing in a Multicultural Society* (Cambridge: Cambridge University Press).

Chant, S. (2008), "The 'Feminisation of Poverty' and the 'Feminisation' of Anti-Poverty Programmes: Room for Revision?" *Journal of Development Studies* 44 (2): 165–197.

Chin, C. B. N. (1998), *In Service and Servitude: Foreign Female Domestic Workers and the Malaysian "Modernity" Project* (New York: Columbia University Press).

Chin, K.-l. (1999), *Smuggled Chinese: Clandestine Immigration to the United States* (Philadelphia, PA: Temple University Press).

——— (2001), "The Social Organization of Chinese Human Smuggling," in D. Kyle and R. Koslowski (eds.), *Global Human Smuggling: Comparative Perspectives* (Baltimore, MD: Johns Hopkins University Press), 216–234.

Chiuri, M. C., G. de Arcangelis, and G. Ferri (2005), "Crisis in Countries of Origin and Illegal Immigration into Europe via Italy," *Global Migration Perspectives* 53, online version, http://www.gcim.org.

Chung, S. P. (1998), *Chinese Business Groups in Hong Kong and Political Change in Southern China* (London: St. Martin's Press).

Citizenship and Immigration Canada (2007), "Working Temporarily in Canada: Special Categories—Business People," http://www.cic.gc.ca.

——— (2009), "Facts and Figures 2008: Immigration Overview," Ottawa, http://www.cic.gc.ca.

Clemens, M. (2007), "Do Visas Kill? Health Effects of African Health Professional Emigration," Working Paper No. 114, Center for Global Development, Washington, DC.

CNN News (2004), "Democrats: Bush Immigration Plan Not Enough," January 7.

Coe, N. M., and H. W. C. Yeung (2001), "Geographical Perspectives on Mapping Globalisation," *Journal of Economic Geography* 1 (4): 367–380.

Cohen, B. J. (2008), *International Political Economy: An Intellectual History* (Princeton, NJ: Princeton University Press).

Cohen, J. H. (2005), "Remittance Outcomes and Migration: Theoretical Contests, Real Opportunities," *Studies in Comparative International Development*, 40 (1): 88–112.

Cohen, R. (1987), *The New Helots: Migrants in the International Division of Labour* (London: Gower).

Colectivo Ioé (2003), "The Integration of Immigrant Women into the Spanish Labour Market," in J. Freedman (ed.), *Gender and Insecurity—Migrant Women in Europe* (Aldershot, UK: Ashgate), 91–106.

Collier, P. (2007), *The Bottom Billion: Why the Poorest Countries Are Failing and What Can Be Done About It* (Oxford: Oxford University Press).

Collins, J. (1991), *Migrant Hands in a Distant Land: Australia's Post-war Immigration* (Sydney and London: Pluto Press).

——— (1996), "The Accent Ceiling," *Education Links* 51: 20–23.

——— (2000a), "Immigration and Immigrants: Ethnic Inequality and Social Cohesion," in P. Boreham, G. Stokes, and R. Hall (eds.), *The Politics of Australian Society: Political Issues for the New Century* (Sydney: Longman), 302–316.

——— (2000b), "Globalisation, Deregulation, and the Changing Australian Labour Market," in S. Bertone and H. Casey (eds.), *Migrants in the New Economy* (Melbourne: Workplace Studies Centre, Victoria University), 13–45.

——— (2005), "From Beirut to Bankstown: The Lebanese Diaspora in Multicultural Australia," in P. Tabar (ed.), *Lebanese Diaspora: History, Racism, and Belonging* (Beirut: Lebanese American University), 187–211.

——— (2007), "The Landmark of Cronulla," in J. Jupp and J. Nieuwenhuysen (eds.), *Social Cohesion in Australia* (Cambridge: Cambridge University Press), 61–69.

——— (2008), "Globalisation, Immigration, and the Second Long Post-war Boom in Australia," *Journal of Australian Political Economy* 61: 244–266.

——— (forthcoming), "The Global Financial Crisis, Immigration and Immigrant Unemployment, and Social Inclusion in Australia," in J. Higley and J. Nieuwenhuysen (eds.), *Immigration in Harder Times: The United States and Australia Compared* (Northampton, MA: Edward Elgar).

Collins, J., G. Noble, S. Poynting, and P. Tabar (2000), *Kebabs, Kids, Cops, and Crime: Youth Ethnicity and Crime* (Sydney: Pluto Press).

Connell, J. (ed.) (2000), *Sydney: The Emergence of a World City* (New York: Oxford University Press).

Connell, J., B. Dasgupta, R. Laishley, and M. Lipton (1976), *Migration from Rural Areas: The Evidence from Village Studies* (Delhi: Oxford University Press).

Conradson, D., and A. Latham (2007), "The Affective Possibilities of London: Antipodean Transnationals and the Overseas Experience," *Mobilities* 2 (2): 231–254.

Constable, N. (1997), *Maid to Order in Hong Kong: Stories of Filipina Workers* (Ithaca: Cornell University Press).

Conti, G., and C. Perelli (2005), "Traditional Mass Tourism Destinations: The Decline of Fordist Tourism Facing the Rise of Vocational Diversification," *Planum: The European Journal of Planning* XI: 1–22.

Cook, J., and J. Roberts (2000), "Towards a Gendered Political Economy," in J. Cook, J. Roberts, and G. Waylen (eds.), *Towards a Gendered Political Economy* (Basingstoke, UK: Macmillan), 3–13.

Cooper, M. (1997), "When Push Comes to Shove: Who Is Welfare Reform Really Helping?," *The Nation*, June 2.

CoRMSA (Consortium for Refugees and Migrants in South Africa) (2008), "Protecting Refugees, Asylum Seekers, and Immigrants in South Africa," Johannesburg, June 18, http://migration.org.za.

Cornelius, W. (2001), "Death at the Border: Efficacy and Unintended Consequences of US Immigration Control Policy," *Population and Development Review* 27 (4): 661–685.

Cornelius, W. A., and T. Tsuda (2004), "Controlling Immigration: The Limits of Government Intervention," in W. A. Cornelius, T. Tsuda, P. L. Martin, and

J. F. Hollifield (eds.), *Controlling Immigration: A Global Perspective* (Stanford, CA: Stanford University Press), 3–48.

Cornelius, W. A., T. Tsuda, P. L. Martin, and J. F. Hollifield (eds.) (1994), *Controlling Immigration: A Global Perspective* (Stanford, CA: Stanford University Press).

Council of the European Union (2004), *The Hague Programme: Strengthening Freedom, Security and Justice in the European Union*, 16054/04 JAI559, Brussels.

Cox, R. (1987), *Production, Power, and World Order: Social Forces in the Making of History* (New York: Columbia University Press).

Crepaz, M. (2006), "'If You Are My Brother, I May Give You a Dime!' Public Opinion on Multiculturalism, Trust, and the Welfare State," in K. G. Banting and W. Kymlicka (eds.), *Multiculturalism and the Welfare State: Recognition and Redistribution in Contemporary Democracies* (Oxford: Oxford University Press), 92–117.

Crisp, J. (2003), "No Solutions in Sight: The Problem of Protracted Refugee Situations in Africa," *New Issues in Refugee Research* (Geneva: UNHCR).

Cross, M., and R. Moore (2002), "Globalization and the New City," in M. Cross and R. Moore (eds.), *Globalization and the New City: Migrants, Minorities, and Urban Transformations in Comparative Perspective* (Basingstoke, UK: Macmillan), 1–15.

Crush, J. (2000), *Borderline Farming: Foreign Migrants in South African Commercial Agriculture* (Cape Town, South Africa: SAMP).

——— (2003), "South Africa: New Nation, New Migration Policy?" Migration Information Source, Washington, DC.

Cushman, J. W., and G. Wang (eds.) (1988), *Changing Identities of the Southeast Asian Chinese Since World War II* (Hong Kong: Hong Kong University Press).

Dannecker, P. (2009), "Migrant Visions of Development: A Gendered Approach," *Population, Space, and Place*, 15 (2): 103–118.

Davies, R. (2007), "Reconceptualising the Migration-Development Nexus: Diasporas, Globalisation, and the Politics of Exclusion," *Third World Quarterly* 28 (1); 59–76.

Davis, N. (2009), "Bahamas Outlook Clouds for Haitians," *BBC News*, September 20.

de Bruijn, M., R. van Dijk, and D. Foeken (eds.) (2001), *Mobile Africa: Changing Patterns of Movement in Africa and Beyond* (Leiden, the Netherlands: Brill).

de Haan, A. (1999), "Livelihoods and Poverty: The Role of Migration—A Critical Review of the Migration Literature," *Journal of Development Studies* 36 (2): 1–47.

de Haan, A., and B. Rogaly (2002), "Introduction: Migrant Workers and Their Role in Rural Change," *Journal of Development Studies* 38 (5): 1–14.

de Haas, H. (2006), "Engaging Diasporas: How Governments and Development Agencies Can Support Diaspora Involvement in the Development of Origin Countries," Oxfam Novib, The Hague.

——— (2007), "Turning the Tide? Why Development Will Not Stop Migration," *Development and Change* 38 (5): 819–841.

——— (2008), "The Myth of Invasion: The Inconvenient Realities of African Migration to Europe," *Third World Quarterly* 29 (7): 1305–1322.

——— (2010), "Migration and Development: A Theoretical Perspective," *International Migration Review* 44 (1): 227–264.

de Waal, A. (2010), "The Political Marketplace," *London Review of Books* 32 (12): 38–41.

Delgado Wise, R., and H. Márquez Covarrubias (2007a), "The Reshaping of Mexican Labor Exports Under NAFTA: Paradoxes and Challenges," *International Migration Review* 41 (3): 656–679.

——— (2007b), "Migration and Development in Mexico: Toward a New Analytical Approach," *Journal of Latino-Latin American Studies* 2: 101–119.

——— (2008), "Capitalist Restructuring, Development, and Labour Migration: The Mexico-US Case," *Third World Quarterly* 29 (7): 1359–1374.

Deshingkar, P., and C. Natali (2008), "Internal Migration," in International Organization for Migration, *World Migration 2008* (Geneva: IOM), 173–199.

Development Research Centre on Migration, Globalisation, and Poverty (2007), "Global Migrant Origin Database," version IV, University of Sussex, UK, March, http://www.migrationdrc.org.

DfID (UK Department for International Development) (2007), *Moving Out of Poverty: Making Migration Work Better for Poor People* (London: DfID).

DIAC (Department of Immigration and Citizenship, Australia) (2008a), "Visa SubClass 457 Integrity Review: Issue Paper No. 3 Integrity/Exploitation," http://www.immi.gov.au.

——— (2008b), *Visa SubClass 457 Integrity Review: Final Report*, October 2008, http://www.immi.gov.au.

Diamond, J. (2005), *Collapse: How Societies Choose to Fail or Survive* (London: Allen Lane).

Dias, M., and L. Wanasundera (2002), "Sri Lankan Migrant Garment Factory Workers: Mauritius and Sultanate of Oman," Study Series No. 27, Centre for Women's Research (CENWOR), Colombo, Sri Lanka.

Dicken, P. (2007), *Global Shift: Mapping the Changing Contours of the World Economy*, 5th ed. (New York: Guilford Press).

Dobbin, C. (1996), *Asian Entrepreneurial Minorities: Conjoint Communities in the Making of the World Economy* (Richmond, UK: Curzon).

Dobson, J., A. Latham, and J. Salt (2009), "On the Move? Labour Migration in Times of Recession: What Can We Learn From the Past?," Policy Network Paper, London, July.

Docquier, F., and A. Marfouk (2006), "International Migration by Educational Attainment, 1990–2000," in Ç. Özden and M. Schiff (eds.), *International Migration, Remittances, and the Brain Drain* (Washington, DC: World Bank), 151–199.

Dodson, B. (1998), "Women on the Move: Gender and Cross-Border Migration to South Africa," Migration Policy Series No. 9, The Southern African Migration Project, Cape Town, South Africa, http://www.queensu.ca.

——— (2008), "Gender, Migration, and Livelihoods: Migrant Women in Southern Africa," in N. Piper (ed.), *New Perspectives on Gender and*

Migration—Rights, Entitlements, and Livelihoods (London: Routledge), 137–158.

Dodson, B., H. Simelane, D. Tevera, T. Green, A. Chikanda, and F. de Vletter (2008), "Gender, Migration, and Remittances in Southern Africa," Migration Policy Paper Series No. 49, Southern African Migration Project, Cape Town.

Donato, K. M., and D. S. Massey (1993), "Effect of the Immigration Reform and Control Act on the Wages of Mexican Migrants," *Social Science Quarterly* 74 (3): 523–541.

Donato, K. M., M. Aguilera, and C. Wakabayashi (2005), "Immigration Policy and Employment Conditions of US Immigrants from Mexico, Nicaragua, and the Dominican Republic," *International Migration* 43 (5): 5–29.

Dörr, S., and T. Faist (1997), "Institutional Conditions for the Integration of Immigrants in Welfare States: A Comparison of the Literature on Germany, France, Great Britain, and the Netherlands," *European Journal of Political Research* 31 (4): 401–426.

Ducanes, G., and M. Abella (2008), "Overseas Filipino Workers and Their Impact on Poverty," Working Paper No. 5, ILO Asian Regional Programme on Governance of Labour Migration, International Labour Organization, Bangkok.

Dunn, K. (2003), "Representations of Islam in the Politics of Mosque Development in Sydney," *Tidjschrift* 92 (3): 291–308.

Dunn, L. (1999), "Export Processing Zones: A Caribbean Development Dilemma," *Development in Practice* 9 (5): 601–605.

East Asia Analytical Unit (1995), *Overseas Chinese Business Networks in Asia* (Canberra: Department of Foreign Affairs and Trade).

ECLAC (United Nations Economic Commission for Latin America and the Caribbean) (2006), *International Migration, Human Rights, and Development in Latin America and the Caribbean: Summary and Conclusions*, LC/G.2303(SES.31/11), Montevideo, March 12.

——— (2008), *Social Panorama of Latin America: Briefing Paper* (Santiago: ECLAC).

Economist (2007a), "Asia's Skills Shortage," August 16.

——— (2007b), "Special Report: Technology in India and China," November 10.

——— (2007c), "Information Technology in India," December 15.

——— (2008), "Where Is Everybody?" March 13.

——— (2009), "The BNP's Breakthrough," June 13.

——— (2010), "The Next China — Briefing: China's Labour Market," July 31.

Ehrenreich, B., and A. R. Hochschild (eds.) (2003), *Global Woman: Nannies, Maids, and Sex Workers in the New Economy* (New York: Metropolitan Books).

Ehrlich, P. (1968), *The Population Bomb* (New York: Ballantine Books).

Einaudi, L. (2007), *Le Politiche dell'Immigrazione in Italia dall'Unità a Oggi* (Rome: Laterza).

Ellison, N. (2006), *The Transformation of Welfare States* (London and New York: Routledge).

Elson, D. (1998), "The Economic, the Political, and the Domestic: Businesses, States, and Households in the Organisation of Production," *New Political Economy* 3 (2): 189–208.

Elson, D., and J. Gideon (2006), "Organising for Women's Economic and Social Rights: How Useful is the International Covenant on Economic, Social, and Cultural Rights?" *Journal of International Gender Studies* 8 (1–2): 135–152.

Elson, D., and R. Pearson (1981), "Nimble Fingers Make Cheap Workers: An Analysis of Women's Employment in Third World Export Manufacturing," *Feminist Review* 7: 87–107.

England, Kim (ed.) (1996), *Who Will Mind the Baby? Geographies of Child-Care and Working Mothers* (London: Routledge).

Epstein, T. S., and D. Jezeph (2001), "Development—There Is Another Way: A Rural-Urban Partnership Development Paradigm," *World Development* 29 (8): 1443–1454.

Esbenshade, J. (2004), *Monitoring Sweatshops: Workers, Consumers, and the Global Apparel Industry* (Philadelphia, PA: Temple University Press).

Escobar Latapí, A. (2009), "Can Migration Foster Development in Mexico? The Case of Poverty and Inequality," *International Migration* 47 (5): 75–113.

Esim, S., and M. Smith (eds.) (2004), *Gender and Migration in Arab States—The Case of Domestic Workers* (Geneva: International Labour Organization).

Esping-Andersen, G. (1985), "Power and Distributional Regimes," *Politics and Society* 14 (2): 223–256.

——— (1990), *The Three Worlds of Welfare Capitalism* (Cambridge: Polity Press).

European Council (1999), "Tampere European Council Presidency Conclusions," Tampere, Finland, October 15–16.

European Industrial Relations Observatory (1999), "Temporary Agency Work in Europe," European Foundation for the Improvement of Living and Working Conditions, Dublin, http://www.eurofound.europa.eu.

European Migration Network (2007), *Illegally Resident Third Country Nationals in EU Member States: State Approaches Towards Them, Their Profile, and Social Situation 2005,* Synthesis Report, January, http://emn.sarenet.es.

Evans-Pritchard, E. E. (1940), *The Nuer: A Description of the Modes of Livelihood and Political Institutions of a Nilotic People* (Oxford: Oxford University Press).

Facchini, G., and A. M. Mayda (2008), "From Individual Attitudes Towards Migrants to Migration Policy Outcomes: Theory and Evidence," *Economic Policy* 23 (56): 651–713.

Faist, T. (2008), "Migrants as Transnational Development Agents: An Inquiry into the Newest Round of the Migration-Development Nexus," *Population, Space, and Place* 14 (1): 21–42.

Fajnzlber, P., and J. H. López (2007), *Close to Home: The Development Impact of Remittances in Latin America* (Washington, DC: IBRD).

Farah, I. H., and G. C. Sánchez (2002), "Bolivia: An Assessment of the International Labour Migration Situation—The Case of Female Labour Migrants," GENPROM Working Paper No. 1, International Labour Organization, Geneva.

Faret, L. (2007), *Migrations, Espaces de Mobilité, et Recompositions Territoriales,* Mémoire de Synthèse, Travaux presentés en vue de l'habilitacion à diriger des recherches en géographie, Université Paris Diderot, Paris.

FARMS (Foreign Agricultural Resource Management Services) (2007), "Statistics," http://www.farmsontario.ca.

——— (2010), "Statistics," http://www.farmsontario.ca.

Favell, A. (1998), "The Europeanisation of Immigration Politics," European Integration On-Line Papers 2 (10), http://eiop.or.at.

Favell, A., and R. Hansen, (2002), "Markets Against Politics: Migration, Enlargement, and the Idea of Europe," *Journal of Ethnic and Migration Studies* 28 (4): 581–601.

Ferguson, J. (1999), *Expectations of Modernity: Myths and Meaning of Urban Life on the Zambian Copperbelt* (Berkeley: University of California Press).

Ferguson, L. (2010), "Tourism Development and the Restructuring of Social Reproduction in Central America," *Review of International Political Economy* 17 (5): 860–888.

Ferrera, M. (2005), *The Boundaries of Welfare: European Integration and the New Spatial Politics of Social Protection* (Oxford: Oxford University Press).

Financial Times (2009), "Singapore to Rein In Immigration," September 16.

Finch, T., M. Latorre, N. Pollard, and J. Rutter (2009), *Shall We Stay or Shall We Go? Re-migration Trends Among Britain's Immigrants*, Institute for Public Policy Research, London, August.

Findlay, A. M., and F. L. N. Li (1998), "A Migration Channels Approach to the Study of Professionals Moving to and from Hong Kong," *International Migration Review* 32 (3): 683–703.

Findlay, A. M., P. J. N. Li, A. J. Jowett, M. Brown, and R. Skeldon (1994), "Doctors Diagnose Their Destinations: An Analysis of the Length of Employment Abroad for Hong Kong Doctors," *Environment and Planning A* 26 (10): 1605–1624.

Fitzgerald, D. (2006), "Inside the Sending State: The Politics of Mexican Emigration Control," *International Migration Review* 40 (2): 259–293.

——— (2009), *A Nation of Emigrants: How Mexico Manages Its Migration* (Berkeley: University of California Press).

Flórez, C. E. (2003), "Migration and the Urban Informal Sector in Colombia," paper presented to the Conference on African Migration in Comparative Perspective, Johannesburg, June 4–7.

Forde, C. (2001), "Temporary Arrangements: The Activities of Employment Agencies in the UK," *Work, Employment, and Society*, 15 (3): 631–644.

Fox Piven, F. (1998), "Welfare and Work," *Social Justice* 25 (1): 67–81.

Fox Piven, F., and R. A. Cloward (1993), *Regulating the Poor: The Functions of Public Welfare* (New York: Vintage Books).

Francis, R. D. (1981), *Migrant Crime in Australia* (St. Lucia: University of Queensland Press).

Frankfurter Allgemeine Zeitung (2010), "EU will fremde Fachkräfte schneller aufnehmen," July 14, 9.

Freeman, G. P. (1986), "Migration and the Political Economy of the Welfare State," *Annals AAPSS* 485: 51–63.

——— (1995), "Modes of Immigration Politics in Liberal Democratic States," *International Migration Review* 29 (4): 881–902.

——— (1998), "The Decline of Sovereignty: Politics and Immigration Restriction in Liberal States," in C. Joppke (ed.), *Challenge to the Nation*

State: Immigration in Western Europe and the United States (Oxford: Oxford University Press), 86–108.

——— (2006), "National Models, Policy Types, and the Politics of Immigration in Liberal Democracies," *West European Politics* 29 (2): 227–247.

Frieden, J. A. (2006), *Global Capitalism: Its Fall and Rise in the Twentieth Century* (New York: W. W. Norton).

Friman, H. R. (2001), "Snakeheads in the Garden of Eden: Immigrants, Smuggling, and Threats to Social Order in Japan," in D. Kyle and R. Koslowski (eds.), *Global Human Smuggling: Comparative Perspectives* (Baltimore, MD: Johns Hopkins University Press), 294–317.

——— (2004), "The Great Escape? Globalization, Immigrant Entrepreneurship, and the Criminal Economy," *Review of International Political Economy* 11 (1): 98–131.

Friman, H. R., and P. Andreas (1999), *The Illicit Global Economy and State Power* (Lanham, MD, and Boulder, CO: Rowman and Littlefield).

Friman, H. R., and S. Reich (2007a), "Human Trafficking and the Balkans," in H. R. Friman and S. Reich (eds.), *Human Trafficking, Human Security, and the Balkans* (Pittsburgh: University of Pittsburgh Press), 1–19.

——— (eds.) (2007b), *Human Trafficking, Human Security, and the Balkans* (Pittsburgh: University of Pittsburgh Press).

Frost, S. (2006), "Building Hong Kong: Nepalese Labour in the Construction Sector," in K. Hewison and K. Young (eds.), *Transnational Migration and Work in Asia* (London: Routledge), 110–125.

Fuchs, L. S. (1990), *The American Kaleidoscope: Race, Ethnicity, and the Civic Culture* (Middletown, CT: Wesleyan University Press).

Gamble, A. (1995), "The New Political Economy," *Political Studies* 43 (3): 516–530.

García, A. I., M. Barahona, C. Castro, and E. Gomariz (2002), "Costa Rica: Female Labour Migrants and Trafficking in Women and Children," GEN-PROM Working Paper No. 2, International Labour Organization, Geneva.

Gardner, K. (1995), *Global Migrants, Local Lives: Travel and Transformation in Rural Bangladesh* (Oxford: Clarendon Press).

Gayathri, V. (2002), "Rethinking High-Skilled International Migration: Research and Policy Issues for India's Information Economy," in OECD, *International Mobility of the Highly Skilled* (Paris: OECD), 201–212.

GCIM (Global Commission on International Migration) (2005), *Migration in an Interconnected World: New Directions for Action* (Geneva: GCIM).

Geddes, A. (2005), "Getting the Best of Both Worlds: Britain, the EU, and Migration Policy," *International Affairs* 81 (4): 723–740.

——— (2006), "Europe's Borders and International Migration Relations," *Journal of Common Market Studies* 43 (4): 787–806.

——— (2008a), *Immigration and European Integration: Beyond Fortress Europe?* 2nd ed. (Manchester, UK: Manchester University Press).

——— (2008b), "Il Rombo dei Cannoni? Immigration and the Centre-right in Italy," *Journal of European Public Policy* 15 (3): 349–356.

——— (2008c), "Staff Shortages and Immigration in Food Processing," paper prepared for the Migration Advisory Committee, HM Treasury, London.

Geddes, A., S. Scott, K. Nielsen, and P. Brindley (2007), *Gangmasters*

Licensing Authority: Annual Review (Nottingham, UK: Gangmasters Licensing Authority).

Gereffi, G. (1996), "Global Commodity Chains: New Forms of Coordination and Control Among Nations and Firms in International Industries," *Competition and Change* 1 (4): 427–439.

——— (2006), *The New Offshoring of Jobs and Global Development*, ILO Social Policy Lectures, International Labour Organization, Geneva.

Gereffi, G., and R. Kaplinsky (eds.) (2001), *The Value of Value Chains: Spreading the Gains from Globalisation*, special issue of *IDS Bulletin* 32 (3).

Ghosh, B. (2000), "Return Migration: Reshaping Policy Approaches," in B. Ghosh (ed.), *Return Migration: Journey of Hope or Despair?* (Geneva: International Organization for Migration), 181–225.

Gibbon, P., J. Bair, and S. Ponte (2008), "Governing Global Value Chains: An Introduction," *Economy and Society* 37 (3): 315–338.

Gilpin, R. (1987), *The Political Economy of International Economic Relations* (Princeton, NJ: Princeton University Press).

Gimpel, J. G., and J. R. Edwards Jr. (1998), *The Congressional Politics of Immigration Reform* (Boston: Allyn and Bacon).

Ginsborg, P. (2001), *Italy and Its Discontents 1980–2001* (Allen Lane: Penguin Books).

Girard, E., and H. Bauder (2007a), "Assimilation and Exclusion of Foreign Trained Engineers in Canada: Inside a Canadian Professional Regulatory Organization," *Antipode* 39 (1): 35–53.

——— (2007b), "The Making of an 'Arcane' Infrastructure: Professional Engineering Regulation in Canada, 1867–1937," *The Canadian Geographer* 51 (2): 233–246.

Glebe, G., and P. While (2001), "Hochqualifizierte Migranten im Prozess der Globalisierung," *Geographische Rundschau* 53: 38–44.

Gonzales, G. G. (2006), *Guest Workers or Colonized Labor? Mexican Labor Migration to the United States* (Boulder, CO: Paradigm Publishers).

Goswami, N. (2010), "Bangladeshi Illegal Migration into Assam: Issues and Concerns from the Field," IDSA Issue Brief, Institute for Defense Studies and Analyses, http://www.idsa.in.

Green, T., and L. A. Winters (2010), "Economic Crises and Migration: Learning from the Past and the Present," Working Paper T-31, Development Research Centre on Migration, Globalisation, and Poverty, University of Sussex, UK, March.

Grieco, E., and M. Boyd (1998), "Women and Migration: Incorporating Gender into International Migration Theory," Working Paper 98–139, Center for the Study of Population, University of Florida, Gainesville.

Grieco, J. M., and J. G. Ikenberry (2003), *State Power and World Markets* (New York: W. W. Norton).

Griffiths, I. (1996), "Permeable Boundaries in Africa," in P. Nugent and A. I. Asiwaju (eds.), *African Boundaries: Borders, Conduits, and Opportunities* (London: Pinter), 68–83.

Groth, A. (2008), "Migration and Trade Policy in Europe," http://www.rosaluxemburgstiftung.de.

Grove, D. J. (2007), "Global Cultural Fragmentation: A Bourdieuan Perspective," *Globalizations* 4 (2): 157–169.

Grugel, J. B., and N. Piper (2007), *Critical Perspectives on Global Governance: Rights and Regulation in Governing Regimes* (London: Routledge).

Guarnizo, L. E., and L. M. Díaz (1999), "Transnational Migration: A View from Colombia," *Ethnic and Racial Studies* 22 (2): 397–421.

Guild, E. (ed.) (1998), *The Legal Framework and Social Consequences of Free Movement of Persons in the European Union* (The Hague: Kluwer Law International).

——— (2001), "Moving the Borders of Europe," inaugural lecture, Catholic University of Nijmegen, the Netherlands, May 8.

Guiraudon, V. (2000), "The Marshallian Triptych Reordered: The Role of Courts and Bureacracies in Furthering Migrants' Social Rights," in M. Bommes and A. Geddes (eds.), *Immigration and Welfare. Challenging the Borders of the Welfare State* (London: Routledge), 72–89.

——— (2001), "European Integration and Migration Policy: Vertical Policy-Making As Venue Shopping," *Journal of Common Market Studies* 27 (2): 334–353.

Guldin, G. E. (1997), "Hong Kong Ethnicity: Of Folk Models and Change," in G. Evans and M. Tam (eds.), *Hong Kong: The Anthropology of a Chinese Metropolis* (Honolulu: University of Hawaii Press), 25–50.

Guochu, Z., and W. Li (2002), "International Mobility of China's Resources in Science and Technology and Its Impact," in OECD (ed.), *International Mobility of the Highly Skilled* (Paris: OECD), 189–190.

Hage, G. (1998), *White Nation: Fantasies of White Supremacy in a Multicultural Society* (Sydney: Pluto Press).

——— (2002), "Postcript: Arab-Australians Belonging After September 11," in G. Hage (ed.), *Arab-Australians Today: Citizenship and Belonging* (Carlton: South Melbourne University Press), 241–248.

Hale, A., and J. Wills (2007), "Women Working Worldwide: Transnational Networks, Corporate Social Responsibility, and Action Research," *Global Networks* 7 (4): 453–476.

Hall, P., and D. Soskice (eds.) (2001), *Varieties of Capitalism: The Institutional Foundations of Comparative Advantage* (Oxford: Oxford University Press).

Hamilton, G. G. (1998), "Culture and Organisation in Taiwan's Market Economy," in R. W. Hefner (ed.), *Market Cultures: Society and Values in the New Asian Capitalisms* (Singapore: Institute of Southeast Asian Studies), 41–77.

Hammar, T. (ed.) (1985), *European Immigration Policy: A Comparative Study* (Cambridge: Cambridge University Press).

Hampshire, K. (2002), "Fulani on the Move: Seasonal Economic Migration in the Sahel as a Social Process," *Journal of Development Studies* 38 (5): 15–36.

Handler, J. F. (2003), "US Welfare Reform: The Big Experiment," in J. Zeitlin and D. M. Trubek (eds.), *Governing Work and Welfare in a New Economy: European and American Experiments* (Oxford: Oxford University Press), 215–239.

Hankivsky, O. (2009), "The Live-In Caregiver Program: Exploiting Care Work in Canada," paper presented at the Annual Meeting of the American Political Science Association, Philadelphia, May 24.

Haque, M. S. (2006), "Ambiguities and Confusions in Migration-Trafficking Nexus: A Development Challenge," in K. Beeks and D. Amir (eds.), *Trafficking and the Global Sex Industry* (Lanham and Oxford: Lexington Books), 3–20.

Hardjosudarmo, S. (1965), *Kebijaksanaan Transmigrasi dalam rangka Pembangunan Masyarakat Desa di Indonesia* (Jakarta: Bhratara).

Harris, N. (1995), *The New Untouchables: Immigration and the New World Worker* (London: Penguin).

Hartmann, M. (1999), "Auf dem Weg zur transnationalen Bourgeoisie?," *Leviathan* 27: 113–141.

——— (2000), "Class-Specific Habitus and the Social Reproduction of the Business Elite in Germany and France," *The Sociological Review* 48 (2): 241–261.

Hawkins, D. F. (ed.) (1995), *Ethnicity, Race, and Crime: Perspectives Across Time and Place* (Albany: State University Press of New York).

Hawthorne, L. (1994), "Labour Market Barriers for Immigrant Engineers in Australia," Bureau of Immigration and Population Research, Australian Government Publishing Service.

Hazlehurst, K. M. (1987), *Migration, Ethnicity, and Crime in Australian Society* (Canberra: Australian Institute of Criminology).

Heeren, H. J. (1979), *Transmigrasi di Indonesia* (Yogyakarta, Indonesia: Universitas Gadjah Mada Press).

Hefner, R. W. (ed.) (1998), *Market Cultures: Society and Values in the New Asian Capitalisms* (Singapore: Institute of Southeast Asian Studies).

Heisler, M. (1992), "Migration, International Relations, and the New Europe: Theoretical Perspectives from Institutional Political Sociology," *International Migration Review* 26 (2): 596–622.

Henderson, L. W. (1978), *Angola: Five Centuries of Conflict* (Ithaca, NY: Cornell University Press).

Henry, L., and G. Mohan (2003), "Making Homes: The Ghanaian Diaspora, Institutions and Development," *Journal of International Development* 15 (5): 611–622.

Herbert, U. (2001), *Geschichte der Ausländerpolitik in Deutschlan: Saisonarbeiter, Zwangsarbeiter, Gastarbeiter, Flüchtlinge* (Munich: C. H. Beck).

Hernández, E., and S. B. Coutin (2006), "Remitting Subjects: Migrants, Money, and States," *Economy and Society* 35 (2): 185–208.

Hernández-León, R. (2005), "The Migration Industry in the Mexico-US Migratory System," On-Line Working Paper Series, California Center for Population Research, University of California at Los Angeles, http://repositories.cdlib.org.

Heron, T. (2004), "Export Processing Zones and Policy Competition for Foreign Direct Investment: The Caribbean 'Offshore' Development Model," in G. Harrison (ed.), *Global Encounters: International Political Economy, Development, and Globalization* (Basingstoke, UK: Palgrave Macmillan), 213–228.

Hewison, K. (2006), "Thai Workers in Hong Kong," in K. Hewison and K. Young (eds.), *Transnational Migration and Work in Asia* (London: Routledge), 90–109.

Hickey, S., and A. du Toit (2007), "Adverse Incorporation, Social Exclusion, and Chronic Poverty," Working Paper No. 81, Chronic Poverty Research Centre, University of Manchester, UK, June.

Hiebert, D. (2006), "Beyond the Polemic: The Economic Outcomes of Canadian Immigration," Research on Immigration and Integration in the Metropolis Working Paper Series 6 (15), http://www.riim.metropolis.net.

Hiebert, D., J. Collins, and P. Spoonley (2003), "Uneven Globalization: Neoliberal Regimes, Immigration, and Multiculturalism in Australia, Canada, and New Zealand," Research on Immigration and Integration in the Metropolis Working Paper Series No. 03–05, February.

Highham, J. (1993), "Multiculturalism and Universalism: A History and Critique," *American Quarterly* 45 (2): 195–219.

Hilsdon, A.-M. (2000), "The Contemplación Fiasco: The Hanging of a Filipino Domestic Worker in Singapore," in A.-M. Hilsdon, M. McIntyre, V. Mackie, and M. Stivens (eds.), *Human Rights and Gender Politics* (London: Routledge), 172–192.

Hirai, K. (2002), "Exhibition of Power: Factory Women's Use of the House-warming Ceremony in a Northern Thai Village," in S. Tanabe and C. F. Keyes (eds.), *Cultural Crisis and Social Memory: Modernity and Identity in Thailand and Laos* (London: Routledge), 185–201.

Hix, S. (2005), *The Political System of the European Union* (Basingstoke, UK: Palgrave Macmillan).

Hjarnø, J. (2003), *Illegal Immigrants and Developments in Employment in the Labour Markets of the EU* (Aldershot, UK: Ashgate).

Hobson, J. M., and L. Seabrooke (2007), "Everyday IPE: Revealing Everyday Forms of Change in the World Economy," in J. M. Hobson and L. Seabrooke (eds.), *Everyday Politics of the World Economy* (Cambridge: Cambridge University Press), 1–24.

Hochschild, A. R. (2000), "Global Care Chains and Emotional Surplus Value," in W. Hutton and A. Giddens (eds.), *On the Edge: Living with Global Capitalism* (London: Jonathan Cape), 130–146.

Hochschild, J. L. (1984), *The New American Dilemma: Liberal Democracy and School Desegregation* (New Haven, CT: Yale University Press).

Hoefer, M., N. Rytina, and C. Campbell (2006), "Estimates of the Unauthorized Immigrant Population Residing in the United States: January 2005," Department of Homeland Security, Office of Immigration Statistics.

Hollifield, J. F. (2000), "The Politics of International Migration: How Can We 'Bring the State Back In'?" in C. B. Brettell and J. F. Hollifield (eds.), *Migration Theory: Talking Across the Disciplines* (New York and London: Routledge), 137–186.

——— (2004), "The Emerging Migration State," *International Migration Review* 38 (3): 885–911.

Horst, C. (2006), *Transnational Nomads: How Somalis Cope with Refugee Life in the Dadaab Camps of Kenya* (Oxford: Berghahn Books).

Hoskyns, C., and S. M. Rai (2007), "Recasting the Global Political Economy:

Counting Women's Unpaid Work," *New Political Economy* 12 (3): 297–317.

Huang, S., B. S. A. Yeoh, and N. A. Rahman (eds.) (2005), *Asian Women as Transnational Domestic Workers* (Singapore: Marshall Cavendish Academic).

Hughes, D. (2000), "The 'Natasha' Trade: The Transnational Shadow Market of Trafficking in Women," *Journal of International Affairs*, 53 (2): 625–651.

Hugo, G. (2003), "A New Paradigm of International Migration Between the European Union and Australia: Patterns and Implications," paper prepared for the Conference on The Challenges of Immigration and Integration in the European Union and Australia," University of Sydney, February 18–20.

——— (2004), "International Migration in the Asia-Pacific Region: Emerging Trends and Issues," in D. S. Massey and J. E. Taylor (eds.), *International Migration: Prospects and Policies in a Global Market* (Oxford: Oxford University Press), 77–103.

——— (2005a), "The New International Migration in Asia: Challenges for Population Research," *Asian Population Studies* 1 (1): 93–120.

——— (2005b), "Indonesian International Domestic Workers: Contemporary Developments and Issues," in S. Huang, B. S. A. Yeoh, and N. A. Rahman (eds.), *Asian Women as Transnational Domestic Workers* (Singapore: Marshall Cavendish Academic), 54–91.

——— (2009), "Care Worker Migration, Australia, and Development," *Population, Space, and Place*, 15 (2): 189–203.

——— (2010), "International Migration in Australia and the Global Financial Crisis," paper presented at the Conference on Immigration in Harder Times: The United States and Australia, Monash University, Prato Centre, Prato, Italy, May 23–25.

Hujo, K., and N. Piper (2007), "South-South Migration: Challenges for Development and Social Policy," *Development* 50 (4): 19–25.

——— (2010), "Linking Migration, Social Development, and Policy in the South: An Introduction," in K. Hujo and N. Piper (eds.), *South-South Migration: Implications for Social Policy and Development* (Basingstoke, UK: Palgrave Macmillan), 1–45.

Hunt, V., and J. Hollifield (2006), "Immigrants, Markets, and the American State: The Political Economy of US Immigration," paper presented at the Annual Meeting of the International Studies Association, San Diego, CA, March 22.

Huntington, S. P. (1997), *The Clash of Civilisations and the Remaking of the World Order* (New York: Simon and Schuster).

——— (2004), *Who Are We? The Challenges to America's National Identity* (New York: Simon and Schuster).

Huysmans, J. (2006), *The Politics of Insecurity: Fear, Migration, and Asylum in the European Union* (London: Routledge).

ILO (International Labour Organization) (2003), *Preventing Discrimination, Exploitation, and Abuse of Women Migrant Workers: An Information Guide—Booklet 1: Why the Focus on Women International Migrant Workers* (Geneva: ILO).

——— (2009), "Tackling the Global Jobs Crisis—Recovery Through Decent

Work Policies," International Labour Conference, 98th Session, Report I (A), Geneva.

Independent Taskforce on Immigration and America's Future (2006), *Immigration and America's Future: A New Chapter* (Washington, DC: Migration Policy Institute).

India (n.d.), "Internal Migration and Regional Disparities in India," http://community.eldis.org.

Insight on the News (2004), "Should the White House Do More to Legalize America's Undocumented Aliens?," April 27–May 10, 46–50.

Inter-American Dialogue (2004), *All in the Family: Latin America's Most Important International Financial Flow*, report of the Inter-American Dialogue Task Force on Remittances, Washington, DC, January.

International Herald Tribune (2007), "Russia Cracking Down on Illegal Migrants," January 15.

IOM (International Organization for Migration) (2005), *World Migration 2005: Costs and Benefits of International Migration* (Geneva: IOM).

——— (2008), *World Migration 2008: Managing Labour Mobility in the Evolving Global Economy* (Geneva: IOM).

Ionescu, D. (2006), "Engaging Diasporas as Development Partners for Home and Destination Countries: Challenges for Policymakers," Migration Research Series, International Organisation for Migration, Geneva.

Iredale, R. (2001), "The Migration of Professionals: Theories and Typologies," *International Migration* 39 (5): 7–24.

——— (2004), "Gender, Immigration Policies, and Accreditation: Valuing the Skills of Professional Women Migrants," *Geoforum* 36: 155–166.

Iredale, R., and I. Nivison-Smith (1995), *Immigrants' Experiences of Qualifications Recognition and Employment: Results from the Prototype Longitudinal Survey of Immigrants to Australia (LSIA)* (Canberra: Australian Government Publishing Service).

IRENE and IUF (2008), "Respect and Rights—Protection for Domestic/Household Workers!" www.domesticworkerrights.org.

Irewanti, A. (2003), *Kebijakan luar Negeri Indonesian terhadap masalah TKI illegal di negara-negara ASEAN* (Jakarta, Indonesia: Pusat Penelitian Politik, LIPI).

ISTAT (2006), *La popolazione straniera residente in Italia* (Rome: ISTAT).

ITU (International Telecommunication Union) (2008), "Measuring Information and Communication Technology Availability in Villages and Rural Areas," Geneva.

Jacka, T. (2008), "The Impact of Gender on Rural-to-Urban Migration in China," in IOM (ed.), *Gender and Labour Migration in Asia* (Geneva: IOM).

Jayaram, N. (ed.) (2004), *The Indian Diaspora: Dynamics of Migration* (New Delhi: Sage Publications).

Jessop, B. (2002), *The Future of the Capitalist State* (Cambridge: Polity Press).

JMOJ (Japan, Ministry of Justice) (2009), *Immigration Control in Recent Years*, Immigration Control Report 2009, http://www.moj.go.jp.

Johnson, B. (2006), "Written Testimony of Benjamin Johnson, Director, Immigration Policy Center, American Immigration Law Foundation, Before the Committee on the Judiciary," United States Senate, July 12, http://www.immigrationpolicy.org.

Johnston, R. (2001), "Out of the Moribund Backwater: Territory and Territoriality in Political Geography," *Political Geography* 20 (6): 677–693.

Jokisch, B. (2007), "Ecuador: Diversidad en Migración," Migration Information Source, February, http://www.migrationinformation.org.

Jones, C., and T. Novak (1999), *Poverty, Welfare, and the Disciplinary State* (London: Routledge).

Jongkond, F. (1974), "A Reappraisal of the Role of Regional Associations in Lima, Peru," *Comparative Studies in Society and History* 14: 471–482.

Joppke, C. (1998), "Why Liberal States Accept Unwanted Immigration," *World Politics* 50 (2): 266–293.

——— (1999), "How Immigration Is Changing Citizenship: A Comparative View," *Ethnic and Racial Studies* 22 (4): 629–652.

Jordan, B., and P. Brown (2007), "Migration and Work in the United Kingdom: Mobility and the Social Order," *Mobilities* 2 (2): 255–276.

Junestav, M. (2004), "Arbetslinjer i svensk socialpolitisk debatt och lagstiftning 1930-2001," mimeo, Department of Economic History, Uppsala University, Sweden.

Kahmann, M. (2002), "Trade Unions and Migrant Workers: Examples from the United States, South Africa, and Spain," Discussion and Working Paper 2002.02.03, International Confederation of Free Trade Unions (ICFTU), Brussels.

Kahn, J. S. (2006), *Other Malays: Nationalism and Cosmopolitanism in the Modern Malay World* (Singapore: Singapore University Press).

Kalm, S. (2008), "Governing Global Migration," Lund Political Studies Paper 158, Lund University, Sweden.

Kaplinsky, R. (1993), "Export Processing Zones in the Dominican Republic: Transforming Manufactures into Commodities," *World Development* 21 (11): 1851–1865.

——— (2005), *Globalization, Poverty, and Inequality* (Cambridge: Polity).

Kapur, D. (2004), "Remittances: The New Development Mantra?" G-24 Discussion Paper Series, United Nations Conference on Trade and Development, New York.

——— (2007), "The Janus Face of Diasporas," in B. J. Merz, L. C. Chen, and P. F. Geithner (eds.), *Diasporas and Development* (Cambridge, MA: Harvard University Press), 89–118.

Kapur, D., and J. McHale (2005), *Give Us Your Best and Brightest: The Global Hunt for Talent and Its Impact on the Developing World* (Washington, DC: Center for Global Development).

Kara, S. (2008), *Sex Trafficking: Inside the Business of Modern Slavery* (New York: Columbia University Press).

Katseli, L. T., R. E. B. Lucas, and T. Xenogiani (2006) "Effects of Migration on Sending Countries: What Do We Know?," OECD, Paris.

Kelly, P., and T. Lusis (2006), "Migration and the Transnational Habitus: Evidence from Canada and the Philippines," *Environment and Planning A* 38 (5): 831–847.

Kennedy, J. F. (1964), *A Nation of Immigrants* (New York: Harper and Collins).

Kgosana, C., and C. de Plessis (2010), "End of the Line for Illegal Zim Nationals," Timeslive, September 2, http://www.timeslive.co.za.

Khadria, B. (1999), *The Migration of Knowledge Workers: Second-Generation Effects on India's Brain Drain* (New Delhi: Sage).

——— (2001), "Shifting Paradigms of Globalization: The Twenty-first Century Transition Towards Generics in Skilled Migration from India," *International Migration* 39 (5): 45–71.

Khoudour-Cásteras, D. (2007), "Migraciones Internacionales y Desarrollo: El Impacto Socioeconómico de las Remesas en Colombia," *Revista de la CEPAL* 92: 143–161.

Kim, E. M. (ed.) (1998), *The Four Asian Tigers: Economic Development and the Global Political Economy* (New York: The Academic Press).

King, D. (1999), *In the Name of Liberalism: Illiberal Social Policy in the United States and Britain* (Oxford: Oxford University Press).

King, R., and R. Skeldon (2010), "Mind the Gap: Integrating Approaches to Internal and International Migration," *Journal of Ethnic and Migration Studies* 36 (10): 1619–1646.

Kingma, M. (2005), *Nurses on the Move* (Ithaca, NY: Cornell University Press).

Kitschelt, H. P., with A. McGann (1995), *The Radical Right in Western Europe: A Comparative Analysis* (Ann Arbor: University of Michigan Press).

Kleist, N. (2007), "Somali-Scandinavian A Dreaming: When 'the Diaspora' Returns to the Desert," in N. Nyberg-Sørensen (ed.), *Living Across Worlds: Diaspora, Development, and Transnational Engagement* (Geneva: International Organization for Migration).

——— (2008), "Mobilising 'the Diaspora': Somali Transnational Political Engagement," *Journal of Ethnic and Migration Studies* 34 (2): 307–323.

Kloosterman, R. (1999), "The Institutional Context: Theoretical Exploration," in J. Rath (ed.), *Immigrant Businesses: The Economic, Political, and Social Environment* (Houndmills, UK: Macmillan), 90–106.

Kofman, E. (2004), "Gendered Global Migration," *International Feminist Journal of Politics* 6 (4): 643–665.

——— (2008), "Gendered Migrations, Livelihoods, and Entitlements in European Welfare Regimes," in N. Piper (ed.), *New Perspectives on Gender and Migration: Rights, Entitlements, and Livelihoods* (London: Routledge), 59–100.

Kofman, E., and P. Raghuram (2006), "Gender and Global Labour Migrations: Incorporating Skilled Workers," *Antipode* 38 (2): 282–303.

Kolb, H. (2005), "Die deutsche 'Green Card,'" *Focus Migration* 3: 1–3.

Kong Liyun, M. (2008), "Economic Globalization and Transnationalizing Labour: Thai Construction Workers in Singapore," masters' thesis, Department of Sociology, National University of Singapore.

Korovkin, T., and O. Sanmiguel-Valderrama (2007), "Labour Standards, Global Markets, and Non-State Initiatives: Colombia's and Ecuador's Flower Industries in Comparative Perspective," *Third World Quarterly* 28 (1): 117–135.

Koslowski, R. (2001), "Economic Globalization, Human Smuggling, and Global Governance," in D. Kyle and R. Koslowski (eds.), *Global Human Smuggling: Comparative Perspectives* (Baltimore, MD: Johns Hopkins), 337–358.

Kratochwil, F. (1994), "Citizenship: On the Border of Order," *Alternatives* 19 (4): 485–506.

Kratoska, P. (1985), "The Peripatetic Peasant in British Malaya," *Journal of Southeast Asian Studies* 26 (1): 16–45.

Kritz, M. M. (2006), "Globalization and Internationalization of Tertiary Education," paper presented at the International Symposium on International Migration and Development, United Nations Population Division, Turin, June 28–30.

Kritzinger, A., S. Barrientos, and H. Rossouw (2004), "Global Production and Flexible Employment in South African Horticulture: Experiences of Contract Workers in Fruit Exports," *Sociologia Ruralis* 44 (1): 17–39.

Kuznetsov, Y. (ed.) (2006), *International Migration of Skills and Diaspora Networks: How Countries Can Draw on Their Talent Abroad* (Washington, DC: World Bank).

Kwong, P. (1987), *The New Chinatown* (New York: Hill and Wang).

——— (1997), "Chinese Staff and Workers' Association: A Model for Organizing in the Changing Economy," in D. Y. Hamamoto and R. D. Torres (eds.), *New American Destinies: A Reader in Contemporary Asian and Latino Immigration* (New York: Routledge), 183–192.

Kyle, D., and J. Dale (2001), "Smuggling the State Back In: Agents of Human Smuggling Reconsidered," in D. Kyle and R. Koslowski (eds.), *Global Human Smuggling: Comparative Perspectives* (Baltimore, MD: Johns Hopkins University Press), 29–57.

Kyle, D., and R. Koslowski (2001), "Introduction," in D. Kyle and R. Koslowski (eds.), *Global Human Smuggling: Comparative Perspectives* (Baltimore, MD: Johns Hopkins University Press), 1–25.

Kyle, D., and C. A. Siracusa (2005), "Seeing the State Like a Migrant: Why So Many Non-criminals Break Immigration Laws," in W. van Schendel and I. Abraham (eds.), *Illicit Flows and Criminal Things: States, Borders, and the Other Side of Globalization* (Bloomington: Indiana University Press), 153–176.

Lacey, M. (2007), "New Routes and New Risk, as More Haitians Flee," *New York Times*, May 19.

Laczko, F. (2005), "Introduction," in F. Laczko and E. Gozdziak (eds.), *Data and Research on Human Trafficking: A Global Survey* (Geneva: International Organization for Migration), 5–17.

Laffan, M. F. (2003), *Islamic Nationhood and Colonial Indonesia: The Umma Beneath the Winds* (London: Routledge Curzon).

Lakha, S. (2005), "Negotiating the Transnational Workplace: Indian Computer Professionals in Australia," *Journal of Intercultural Studies* 26 (4): 337–359.

Lampert, B. (2009), "Diaspora and Development? Nigerian Organizations in London and the Transnational Politics of Belonging," *Global Networks* 9 (2): 162–184.

Lavenex, S. (1999), *Safe Third Countries: Extending the EU Asylum and Immigration Policies to Central and Eastern Europe* (Budapest: Central European University Press).

——— (2001), "Migration and the EU's New Eastern Border: Between Realism and Liberalism," *Journal of European Public Policy* 8 (1): 24–42.

Lavenex, S., and E. Uçarer (2002), *Migration and the Externalities of European Integration* (Lanham, MD: Lexington Books).

Legrain, P. (2006), *Immigrants: Your Country Needs Them* (London: Little Brown Book Group).
Leibfried, S. (1992), "Towards a European Welfare State? On Integrating Poverty Regimes into the European Community," in Z. Ferge and J. E. Kolberg (eds.), *Social Policy in a Changing Europe* (Frankfurt am Main and Boulder, CO: Campus Verlag and Westview Press), 227–259.
Levitt, P. (1999), "Social Remittances: A Local-level, Migration-driven Form of Cultural Diffusion," *International Migration Review* 32 (124): 926–949.
Levitt, P., and N. N. Sorenson (2004), "Global Migration Perspectives: The Transnational Turn in Migration Studies," *Global Migration Perspectives* 6, online version.
Ley, D. (2003), "Seeking Homo Economicus: The Canadian State and the Strange Story of the Business Immigration Program," *Annals of the Association of American Geographers* 93: 426–441.
——— (2010), *Millionaire Migrants: Trans-Pacific Life Lines* (Malden, MA: Wiley-Blackwell).
Lie, J. (2000), *Multiethnic Japan* (Cambridge, MA: Harvard University Press).
Lim, L., and N. Oishi (1996), "International Migration of Asian Women: Distinctive Characteristics and Policy Concerns," in G. Battistella and A. Paganon (eds.), *Asian Women in Migration* (Quezon City, the Philippines: Scalabrini Migration Centre), 106–121.
Lindley, A. (2007), "Protracted Displacement and Remittances: The View from Eastleigh, Nairobi," *New Issues in Refugee Research*, Policy Development and Evaluation Service, United Nations High Commissioner for Refugees, Geneva.
Lipton, M. (1980), "Migration from Rural Areas of Poor Countries: The Impact on Rural Productivity and Income Distribution," *World Development* 8 (1): 1–24.
Litt, J. S., and M. K. Zimmerman (2003), "Guest Editors' Introduction—Global Perspectives on Gender and Carework: An Introduction," *Gender and Society* 17 (2): 156–165.
Little, K. (1957), "The Role of Voluntary Associations in West African Urbanization," *American Anthropologist* 59: 579–596.
Loescher, G., and J. Milner (2005), "Protracted Refugee Situations: Domestic and International Security Implications," *The Adelphi Papers* 45 (375).
Loveband, A. (2006), "Positioning the Product: Indonesian Migrant Women Workers in Taiwan," in K. Hewison and K. Young (eds.), *Transnational Migration and Work in Asia* (London: Routledge), 75–89.
Low, L., M. H. Toh, and T. W. Soon (1991), *Economics of Education and Manpower Development, Issues and Policies in Singapore* (Singapore: McGraw-Hill).
Lowell, B. L., S. F. Martin, and M. N. Bump (2007), *Worksite Solutions to Unauthorized Migration* (Washington, DC: Institute for the Study of International Migration).
Lucassen, L., D. Feldman, and J. Oltmer (eds.) (2006), *Paths of Integration: Migrants in Western Europe (1880–2004)* (Amsterdam: Amsterdam University Press).
Lycklama, G. (1994), "The Changing International Division of Labour and Domestic Workers: A Macro Overview," in N. Heyzer, G. Lycklama, and N. Weerakoon (eds.), *Trade in Domestic Helpers: Causes, Mechanisms,*

and Consequences of International Migration (Kuala Lumpur: Asian and Pacific Development Centre), 3–29.

McCormick, D., and H. Schmitz (2001), *Manual for Value Chain Research on Homeworkers in the Garment Industry* (Cambridge, MA: WIEGO/Harvard University).

McDowell, L. (1997), *Capital Culture: Gender at Work in the City* (Oxford: Blackwell).

McKay, D. (2003), "Filipinas in Canada—De-skilling as a Push towards Marriage," in N. Piper and M. Roces (eds.), *Wife or Worker? Asian Women and Migration* (Lanham, MD: Rowman and Littlefield), 23–52.

McKeown, A. (2004), "Global Migration, 1846-1940," *Journal of World History* 15 (2): 155–189.

McVeigh, T. (2008), "'Your Huddled Masses Yearning to Breathe Free': A Global Quest for Home," *Guardian Weekly*, January 25–31, 2–3.

McVey, R. (1992a), "The Materialization of the Southeast Asian Entrepreneur," in R. McVey (ed.), *Southeast Asian Capitalists* (Ithaca: Cornell University Southeast Asia Program), 7–34.

——— (ed.) (1992b), *Southeast Asian Capitalists* (Ithaca: Cornell University Southeast Asia Program).

Mabogunje, A. L. (1970), "Systems Approach to a Theory of Rural-Urban Migration," *Geographical Analysis* 2 (1): 1–18.

Macken, D. (2003), "Talent in Transit: The New Migratory Pattern," *Weekend Australian Financial Review*, March 22–23, 26–27.

Mackie, J. (1992a), "Overseas Chinese Entrepreneurship," *Asian-Pacific Economic Literature* 61 (1): 41–65.

——— (1992b), "Changing Patterns of Chinese Big Business in Southeast Asia," in R. McVey (ed.), *Southeast Asian Capitalists* (Ithaca, NY: Cornell University Southeast Asia Program), 161–190.

——— (1998), "Business Success Among Southeast Asian Chinese: The Role of Culture, Values, and Social Structures," in R. W. Hefner (ed.), *Market Cultures: Society and Values in the New Asian Capitalisms* (Singapore: Institute of Southeast Asian Studies), 129–146.

Maingot, A. (1999), "Emigration Dynamics in the Caribbean: The Cases of Haiti and the Dominican Republic," in R. Appleyard (ed.), *Emigration Dynamics in Developing Countries*, vol. 3 (Brookfield, VT: Ashgate), 178–231.

Malarek, V. (2004), *The Natashas: Inside the New Global Sex Trade* (New York: Arcade Publishing).

Mangin, W. (1959), "The Role of Regional Associations in the Adaptation of Rural Population in Peru," *Sociologus* 9: 23–36.

Mann, M. (1987), "Ruling Class Strategies and Citizenship," *Sociology* 21 (3): 339–354.

Manning, P. (2006), *Us and Them* (Milsons Point: Random House Australia).

Manning, R. (2000), "Five Years After NAFTA: Rhetoric and Reality of Mexican Immigration in the 21st Century," Center for Immigration Studies, March, http://www.cis.org.

Mares, P. (2002), *Borderline: Australia's Treatment of Refugees and Asylum Seekers* (Sydney: University of New South Wales Press).

Markova, E., and R. Black (2007), *East European Immigration and Community Cohesion* (York, UK: Joseph Rowntree Foundation).

Markus, A. (2001), *Race: John Howard and the Remaking of Australia* (Crows Nest: Allen and Unwin).

Mármora, L. (1979), "Labor Migration Policy in Colombia," *International Migration Review* 13 (3): 440–454.

Marr, D., and M. Wilkinson (2003), *Dark Victory* (Sydney: Allen and Unwin).

Marshall, T. H. (1950), *Citizenship and Social Class* (Cambridge: Cambridge University Press).

Martin, P. L. (1994), "The United States: Benign Neglect Toward Immigration," in W. A. Cornelius, P. L. Martin, and J. F. Hollifield (eds.), *Controlling Immigration: A Global Perspective* (Stanford, CA: Stanford University Press), 83–100.

——— (1998), "The Endless Debate: Immigration and US Agriculture," in P. Duignan and L. Gann (eds.), *The Debate in the United States over Immigration* (Stanford, CA: Hoover Institution), 79–101.

——— (2006), "Immigration Reform: Implications for Agriculture," *Update—Agricultural and Resource Economics* 9 (4): 1–4.

——— (2009), "Recession and Migration: A New Era for Labor Migration?" *International Migration Review* 43 (3): 671–691.

Martin, P. L., M. Abella, and C. Kuptsch (2006), *Managing Labor Migration in the Twenty-first Century* (New Haven, CT: Yale University Press).

Martin, P. L., S. F. Martin, and P. Weil (2006), *Managing Migration: The Promise of Cooperation* (Lanham, MD: Lexington Books).

Martin, P. L., A. Mason, and T. Nagayama (1996), "Introduction to the Special Issue on the Dynamics of Labour Migration in Asia," *Asian and Pacific Migration Journal* 5 (2–3): 163–173.

Martin, P. L., E. Midgley, and M. S. Teitelbaum (2002), "Migration and Development: Whither the Dominican Republic and Haiti?" *International Migration Review* 36 (2): 570–592.

Martin, S. (1998), "Politics and Policy Responses to Illegal Migration in the US," paper presented at the Conference on Managing Migration in the 21st Century, Hamburg, June 21–23, http://isim.georgetown.edu/.

——— (2003), "The Politics of US Immigration Reform," *The Political Quarterly* 74 (1): 132–149.

Martin, S., and B. L. Lowell (2005), "'Competing for Skills: US Immigration Policy Since 1990," *Law and Business Review of the Americas* 11 (3–4): 387–407.

Martin, S., B. L. Lowell, and P. Martin (2002), "US Immigration Policy: Admission of High Skilled Workers," *Georgetown Immigration Law Journal* 16 (3): 619–636.

Martínez Pizarro, J., with V. Cano and M. Soffia (2009), "Notas sobre las Características de la Fuerza Laboral Migrante en las Américas," paper presented at the workshop Programas para Trabajadores Migratorios Temporales, San Salvador, April 23–24.

Marx, K. ([1867] 2001), *Das Kapital: Kritik der politischen Ökonomi— Erstes Buch, der Produktionsprozeß des Kapitals*, in *Karl Marx, Friedrich Engels: Werke*, No. 23, 20th ed. (Berlin: Karl Dietz Verlag).

Massey, D. S., and J. E. Taylor (eds.) (2004), *International Migration: Prospects and Policies in a Global Market* (Oxford: Oxford University Press).

Massey, D. S., J. Arango, G. Hugo, A. Kouaouchi, A. Pellegrino, and J. E. Taylor (1993), "Theories of International Migration: A Review and Appraisal," *Population and Development Review* 19 (3): 431–466.

——— (1998), *Worlds in Motion: Understanding International Migration at the End of the Millennium* (Oxford: Oxford University Press).

Matsas, R. (2008), "The Global Forum on Migration and Development: A New Path for Global Governance?" paper presented at the 2008 ACUNS Annual Meeting on The United Nations and Global Development Architecture, Bonn, June 5–7.

Mathews, O. (2009), "The Kremlin Vigilantes," *Newsweek*, February 14.

Maxton, G. (2008), "Not Enough People in China," in *The Economist* (ed.), *The World in 2008*, http://www.economist.com.

Mazzucato, V., and M. Kabki (2009), "Small Is Beautiful: The Micro-Politics of Transnational Relationships Between Ghanaian Hometown Associations and Communities Back Home," *Global Networks*, 9 (2): 227–251.

Meadows, D. H., D. L. Meadows, J. Randers, and W. W. Behrens (1972), *The Limits to Growth* (New York: Universe Books).

Megalogenis, G. (2010), "Trivial Pursuit: Leadership and the End of the Reform Era," *Quarterly Essay* (1): 1–84.

Messina, A.M., and G. Lahav (eds.) (2006), *The Migration Reader: Exploring Politics and Policies* (Boulder, CO: Lynne Rienner).

Meyers, E. (2002), "Multilateral Co-operation in International Labor Migration," Working Paper 61, Centre for Comparative Immigration Studies, University of California at San Diego.

Michon, F. (2006), "Temporary Agency Work in Europe," in S. Gleason (ed.), *The Shadow Workforce: Perspectives on Contingent Employment in the United States, Japan and Europe* (Kalamazoo, MI: W.E. Upjohn Institute for Employment Research), 271–309.

Migration News (1995), "Illegal Immigration to South Africa," August, http://migration.ucdavis.edu.

Milanovic, B. (2003), "The Two Faces of Globalization: Against Globalization as We Know It," *World Development* 31 (4): 667–683.

——— (2007), "Globalization and Inequality," in D. Held and A. Kaya (eds.), *Global Inequality: Patterns and Explanations* (Cambridge: Polity).

Milberg, W. (2007), "Export Processing Zones, Industrial Upgrading, and Economic Development: A Survey," background paper for ILO Governing Board Discussion of Export Processing Zones, October 28.

Miles, R. (1982), *Racism and Migrant Labour* (London: Routledge and Kegan Paul).

——— (1989), *Racism* (London: Routledge).

——— (1993), *Racism After Race Relations* (London: Routledge).

Miles, W. F. S. (2005), "Development, Not Division: Local Versus External Perceptions of the Niger-Nigeria Boundary," *Journal of Modern African Studies* 43 (2): 297–320.

Milkman, R. (2006), *L.A. Story: Immigrant Workers and the Future of the US Labor Movement* (New York: Russell Sage Foundation).

Mingione, E. (1996), "Conclusion," in E. Mingione (ed.), *Urban Poverty and the Underclass: A Reader* (Oxford: Blackwell), 372–383.

Mittelman, J. H. (2000), *The Globalization Syndrome: Transformation and Resistance* (Princeton, NJ: Princeton University Press).

Mobrand, E. (2007), "What If Remittances Are Requited? Evidence from South Korean Internal Migration," paper presented at the International Conference on Migration and Development, Korea Research Foundation, Korea University, Seoul, June 1–2.

Mohan, G. (2008), "Making Neoliberal States of Development: The Ghanaian Diaspora and the Politics of Homelands," *Environment and Planning D: Society and Space* 26 (3): 464–479.

Mohan, G., and A. B. Zack-Williams (2002), "Globalisation from Below: Conceptualising the Role of the African Diasporas in Africa's Development," *Review of African Political Economy* 29 (92): 211–236.

Monar, J. (2001), "The Dynamics of Justice and Home Affairs: Laboratories, Driving Factors, and Costs," *Journal of Common Market Studies* 39 (4): 747–764.

Montclos, M.-A.P.D. (2005), *Diasporas, Remittances, and Africa South of the Sahara: A Strategic Assessment* (Pretoria: Institute for Security Studies).

Morrison, J., and B. Crosland (2000), "The Trafficking and Smuggling of Refugees: The End Game of European Asylum Policies," Working Paper No. 39, United Nations High Commission for Refugees, Geneva.

Morokvasic, M. (2003), "Transnational Mobility and Gender: A View from Post-wall Europe," in M. Morokvasic-Müller, U. Erel, and K. Shinozaki (eds.), *Crossing Borders and Shifting Boundaries, Vol. 1: Gender on the Move* (Opladen: Leske and Budrich), 101–136.

Mountford, A. (1997), "Can a Brain Drain Be Good for Growth in the Source Economy?" *Journal of Development Economics* 52 (2): 287–303.

Mukherjee, S. (1999), "Ethnicity and Crime," paper presented to the 3rd National Outlook Symposium of Crime in Australia, Australian Institute of Criminology, Canberra, March 22–23.

Münz, R., T. Straubhaar, F. Vadean, and N. Vadean (2007), "What Are the Migrants' Contributions to Employment and Growth? A European Approach," HWWI Policy Papers 3–3, Hamburg Institute of International Economics.

Murphy, C. N., and D. R. Nelson (2001), "International Political Economy: A Tale of Two Heterodoxies," *British Journal of Politics and International Relations* 3 (3): 393–412.

Murray, C. (1981), *Families Divided: The Impact of Migrant Labour in Lesotho* (Cambridge: Cambridge University Press).

Murray, D. H. (1994), *The Origins of the Truandihui: The Chinese Triads in Legend and History* (Stanford, CA: Stanford University Press).

Myrdal, G., and S. Bok (1996), *An American Dilemma: The Negro Problem and Modern Democracy* (New Brunswick, NJ: Transaction Publishers).

Naik, A., J. Koehler, and F. Laczko (2008), "Migration and Development:

Achieving Policy Coherence," IOM Migration Research Series, International Organization for Migration, Geneva.

Naím, M. (2005), *Illicit: How Smugglers, Traffickers, and Copycats Are Hijacking the Global Economy* (New York: Doubleday).

Nair, P. R. G. (1989), "Incidence, Impact, and Implications of Migration to the Middle East from Kerala (India)," in R. Amjad (ed.), *To the Gulf and Back: Studies on the Economic Impact of Asian Labour Migration* (New Delhi: International Labour Organization), 344–364.

Nandy, C. (2005), "Illegal Immigration from Bangladesh to India: The Emerging Conflicts," Mellon Foundation on NGOs and Forced Migration, November 30, http://web.mit.edu.

Narushima, Y. (2009), "Sacked Workers on 457 Visas Stay Illegally," *Sydney Morning Herald*, January 23.

National Farmers Federation (2008), "2008 Labour Shortage Action Plan: An Ongoing Plan Investigating New and Existing Solutions to Agricultural Labour Shortages, Their Practical Implementation and Policy Solutions," March, http://www.innovation.gov.au.

National Immigration Law Center (2004), "NILC Reflections on President Bush's Immigration Reform Proposal," January 9, http://www.nilc.org.

Naylor, R. T. (2002), *Wages of Crime: Black Markets, Illegal Finance, and the Underworld Economy* (Ithaca, NY: Cornell University Press).

Noll, G. (2000), *Negotiating Asylum: The EU Acquis, Extra-Territorial Protection and the Common Market of Deflection* (Leiden, the Netherlands: Martinus Nijhoff).

——— (2003), "Visions of the Exceptional: Legal and Theoretical Issues Raised by Transit Processing Centres and Protection Zones," *European Journal of Migration and Law* 5 (3): 303–341.

Nugent, P., and A. I. Asiwaju (eds.) (1996), *African Boundaries: Borders, Conduits, and Opportunities* (London: Pinter).

Nyberg-Sørensen, N., N. Van Hear, and P. Engberg-Pedersen (2002), "The Migration-Development Nexus: Evidence and Policy Options: State-of-the-art Overview," *International Migration* 40 (5): 3–47.

Nyíri, P., and I. R. Savelev (2002), *Globalizing Chinese Migration: Trends in Europe and Asia* (Aldershot, UK: Ashgate).

OECD (Organization for Economic Cooperation and Development) (1997), *Trends in International Migration: Annual Report 1996* (Paris: OECD).

——— (2002), "International Mobility of the Highly Skilled," OECD Policy Brief, Paris.

——— (2004), "The International Mobility of Health Professionals: An Evaluation and Analysis Based on the Case of South Africa," in *Trends in International Migration*, SOPEMI 2003 (Paris: OECD), 116–151.

——— (2006), *International Migration Outlook*, SOPEMI 2006 (Paris: OECD).

——— (2007a), *Policy Coherence for Development: Migration and Developing Countries* (Paris: OECD).

——— (2007b), *International Migration Outlook: Annual Report 2007* (Paris: OECD).

——— (2007c), "Editorial – The Medical Brain Drain: Myths and Realities," in *International Migration Outlook*, SOPEMI 2007 (Paris: OECD).

Offe, C. (1984), *Contradictions of the Welfare State* (London: Hutchinson Education).

Office for National Statistics (2004), "Focus on Ethnicity and Identity," http://www.statistics.gov.uk.

OIM (Organización Internacional para las Migraciones/International Organization for Migration) (2008), *Perú: Características de los migrantes internacionales, hogares de origen y receptores de remesas* (Lima: OIM).

Oishi, N. (2005), *Women in Motion: Globalization, State Policies, and Labor Migration in Asia* (Stanford, CA: Stanford University Press).

Okano, K., and M. Tsuchiya (1999), *Education in Contemporary Japan: Inequality and Diversity* (Cambridge: Cambridge University Press).

Ong, A. (1999), *Flexible Citizenship: The Cultural Logics of Transnationality* (Durham, NC: Duke University Press).

Onuki, H. (2009), "Care, Social (Re)production, and Global Labour Migration: Japan's 'Special Gift' Toward 'Innately Gifted' Filipino Workers," *New Political Economy* 14 (4): 489–516.

Oppenheimer, A. (2008), "Brain Exports Are Chile's Big Bet for the Future," *Miami Herald*, June 5.

Orrenius, P. M., and M. Zavodny (2009), "Tied to the Business Cycle: How Immigrants Fare in Good and Bad Economic Times," Migration Policy Institute, November.

Oucho, J. O. (2006), "Migration and Refugees in Eastern Africa: A Challenge for the East African Community," in C. Cross, D. Gelderblom, N. Roux, and J. Mafukidze (eds.), *Views on Migration in Sub-Saharan Africa: Proceedings of an African Migration Alliance Workshop* (Cape Town: HSRC Press).

Pan, L. (ed.) (1998), *The Encyclopaedia of the Chinese Overseas* (Singapore: Archipelago Press).

Papademetriou, D. G. (2004), testimony before the Senate Foreign Relations Committee, March 23.

Papademetriou, D. G., and A. Terrazas (2009), "Immigrants and the Current Economic Crisis: Research Evidence, Policy Challenges, and Implications," Migration Policy Institute, January.

Papademetriou, D. G., M. Sumption, and W. Somerville (2009), "Migration and the Economic Downturn: What to Expect in the European Union," Transatlantic Council on Migration, Migration Policy Institute, January.

Papadopoulos, T. (2005), "The Recommodification of European Labour: Theoretical and Empirical Explorations," Working Paper Series WP-05-03, European Research Institute, University of Bath, UK.

Parreñas, R. S. (2001), *Servants of Globalization: Women, Migration, and Domestic Work* (Stanford, CA: Stanford University Press).

Passel, J. S. (2005), *Unauthorized Migrants: Numbers and Characteristics* (Washington, DC: Pew Hispanic Center).

——— (2006), *The Size and Characteristics of the Unauthorized Migrant Population in the U.S.: Estimates Based on the March 2005 Current Population Survey*, Pew Hispanic Center, Washington, DC, http://pewhispanic.org.

Passel, J. S., and D. Cohn (2008a), *Trends in Unauthorized Immigration:*

Undocumented Inflow Now Trails Legal Inflow, Pew Hispanic Center Report, Washington, DC, October, http://pewhispanic.org/.

——— (2008b), *US Population Projections: 2005–2050* (Washington, DC: Pew Hispanic Center).

——— (2010), *US Unauthorized Immigration Flows Are Down Sharply Since Mid-Decade*, Pew Hispanic Center Report, September, http://pewhispanic.org.

Payne, A. (1998), "The New Political Economy of Area Studies," *Millennium: Journal of International Studies* 27 (2): 253–273.

Payne, A., and N. Phillips (2010), *Development* (Cambridge: Polity).

Pearson, R. (2004), "Organising Home-Based Workers in the Global Economy: An Action-Research Approach," *Development in Practice* 14 (1–2): 136–148.

Peck, J. (2004), *Workfare States* (New York: Guilford Press).

Pendleton, W., J. Crush, E. Campbell, T. Green, H. Simelane, D. Tevera, and F. De Vletter (2006), "Migration, Remittances, and Development in Southern Africa," Migration Policy Paper Series, No. 44, Southern African Migration Project, Cape Town.

Penninx, R., M. Berger, and K. Kraal (eds.) (2006), *The Dynamics of International Migration and Settlement in Europe* (Amsterdam: Amsterdam University Press).

Pérez Vichich, N. (2005), *El Mercosur y la migración internacional*, Document UN/POP/EGM-MIG/2005/05, Expert Group Meeting on International Migration and Development in Latin America and the Caribbean, Population Division, Department of Economic and Social Affairs, United Nations Secretariat, Mexico City, November 30–December 2.

Persson, G. (1972), "Invandrarna och arbetarklassen i Sverige," *Zenit* 27.

Peterson, J., and E. Bomberg (1999), *Decision-Making in the European Union* (Basingstoke, UK: Palgrave).

Peterson, V. S. (2003), *A Critical Rewriting of Global Political Economy: Integrating Reproductive, Productive, and Virtual Economies* (London: Routledge).

Petras, J. (2006), "MesoAmerica Comes to North America: The Rise of the Migrant Workers' Movement," *Counterpunch*, May 3.

Petrillo, A. (1999), "Italy: Farewell to the 'Bel Paese,'" in M. Cole and G. Dale (eds.), *The European Union and Migrant Labour* (Oxford: Berg), 231–264.

Phillips, N. (2004), *The Southern Cone Model: The Political Economy of Regional Capitalist Development in Latin America* (London: Routledge).

——— (2005a), "Globalizing the Study of International Political Economy," in N. Phillips (ed.), *Globalizing International Political Economy* (Basingstoke, UK: Palgrave), 1–19.

——— (2005b), "Whither IPE?," in N. Phillips (ed.), *Globalizing International Political Economy* (Basingstoke, UK: Palgrave), 246–269.

——— (2009a), "The Slow Death of Pluralism," *Review of International Political Economy* 16 (1): 85–94.

——— (2009b), "Migration as Development Strategy? The New Political Economy of Dispossession and Inequality in the Americas," *Review of International Political Economy* 16 (2): 231–259.

——— (2010a), "Poverty Reduction and the Role of Regional Institutions," in G. Mace, A. F. Cooper, and T. M. Shaw (eds.), *Inter-American Cooperation at a Crossroads* (Basingstoke, UK: Palgrave).

——— (2010b), "Global Economic Crisis and Global Development: Reflections on the Emerging Panorama," *Irish Studies in International Affairs* 21: 179–190.

——— (forthcoming), "Formality, Informality, and the Constitution of Global Production Networks," *Global Networks*.

Phillips, N., and G. C. Prieto (2011), "The Demise of New Regionalism: Reframing the Study of Contemporary Regional Integration in Latin America," in A. Warleigh-Lack, N. Robinson, and B. Rosamond (eds.), *New Regionalisms and EU Studies: Dialogues, Comparisons and New Research Directions* (London: Routledge).

Phillips, N., and L. Sakamoto (2010), "Poverty, Marginalisation, and 'Slave Labour' in Brazil: The Dynamics of Adverse Incorporation in Global Production Networks," presented at the Conference of the Chronic Poverty Research Centre, University of Manchester, September 8–10.

Phillips, N., and C. E. Weaver (eds.) (2010), *International Political Economy: Debating the Past, Present, and Future* (London: Routledge).

Pierson, C. (1998), *Beyond the Welfare State* (University Park: Pennsylvania State University Press).

Pimpawan, B., P. Guest, A. Marddent, and S. Sanders (2003), "From Trafficking to Sex Work: Burmese Migrants in Thailand," in M. Darwin, A. Wattie, and S. Yuarsi (eds.), *Living on the Edges: Cross-Border Mobility and Sexual Exploitation in the Greater Southeast Asia Sub-Region* (Yogyakarta: Center for Population and Policy Studies, Universitas Gadjah Mada), 87–103.

Pinder, S. O. (2007), *From Welfare to Workfare: How Capitalist States Create a Pool of Unskilled Cheap Labour (A Marxist-Feminist Social Analysis)* (Lewiston, Queenston, Lampeter: Edwin Mellen Press).

Piore, M. J. (1979), *Birds of Passage: Migrant Labor and Industrial Societies* (Cambridge: Cambridge University Press).

Piper, N. (2000), "Globalisation, Gender, and Migration: International Marriage in Japan," in J. Roberts, G. Waylen, and H. Cook (eds.), *Towards a Gendered Political Economy* (Basingstoke, UK: Macmillan), 205–225.

——— (ed.) (2008a), *New Perspectives on Gender and Migration: Rights, Entitlements, and Livelihoods* (London: Routledge).

——— (2008b), "Political Participation and Empowerment of Foreign Workers: Gendered Advocacy and Migrant Labour Organising in Southeast and East Asia," in N. Piper (ed.), *New Perspectives on Gender and Migration: Rights, Entitlements, and Livelihoods* (London: Routledge), 249–275.

——— (2009) "Editorial Introduction: The Complex Interconnections of the Migration-Development Nexus—A Social Perspective," *Population, Space, and Place* 15 (2): 93–102.

Polanyi, K. (1944), *The Great Transformation* (Boston, MA: Beacon Press).

Ponte, S. (2008), "Developing a 'Vertical' Dimension to Chronic Poverty Research: Some Lessons from Global Value Chain Analysis," Working Paper No. 111, Chronic Poverty Research Centre, University of Manchester, UK, June.

Ponte, S., and P. Gibbon (2005), "Quality Standards, Conventions, and the Governance of Global Value Chains," *Economy and Society* 34 (1): 1–31.

Portes, A. (2009), "Migration and Development: Reconciling Opposite Views," *Ethnic and Racial Studies* 32 (1): 5–22.

Portes, A., and R. E. Rumbaut (2001), *Legacies: The Story of the Immigrant Second Generation* (Berkeley: University of California Press).

Potts, D. (2005), "Counter-urbanisation on the Zambian Copperbelt? Interpretations and Implications," *Urban Studies* 42 (4): 583–609.

Poynting, S. (2006), "What Caused the Cronulla Riot?" *Race and Class* 48 (1): 85–92.

Poynting, S., G. Noble, P. Tabar, and J. Collins (2004), *Bin Laden in the Suburbs: Criminalizing the Arab Other* (Sydney: Federation Press).

Pratt, G. (2004), *Working Feminism* (Edinburgh: Edinburgh University Press).

President's Commission on Immigration and Naturalization (1953), *Whom Shall We Welcome?* (Washington, DC: US Government Printing Office).

Preston, V. (2003), "Gender, Inequality, and Borders," *ACME* 2 (2): 183–187.

Prieto, M., and C. Quinteros (2004), "Never The Twain Shall Meet? Women's Organisations and Trade Unions in the Maquila Industry in Central America," *Development in Practice* 14 (1): 149–157.

Pritchett, J. A. (1990), *Continuity and Change in an African Society: The Kanongesha Lunda of Mwinilunga, Zambia* (Cambridge, MA: Harvard University Press).

Pritchett, L. (2004), "Boom Towns and Ghost Countries: Geography, Agglomeration, and Population Mobility," Working Paper 36, Center for Global Development, February.

——— (2005), *Let Their People Come: Breaking the Gridlock on Global Labor Mobility* (Washington, DC: Center for Global Development).

Prügl, E. (2002), "Towards a Feminist Political Economics," *International Feminist Journal of Politics* 4 (1): 31–36.

Purcell, M., and J. Nevins (2005), "Pushing The Boundary: State Restructuring, State Theory, and the Case of US-Mexico Border Enforcement in the 1990s," *Political Geography* 24 (2): 211–235.

Radcliffe-Brown, A. R. (1952), *Structure and Function in Primitive Society: Essays and Addresses* (London: Cohen and West).

Rafael, V. (ed.) (1999), *Figures of Criminality in Indonesia, the Philippines, and Colonial Vietnam* (Ithaca, NY: Cornell University Southeast Asian Program).

Rahman, N. A., B. S. A. Yeoh, and S. Huang (2005), "'Dignity Overdue': Transnational Domestic Workers in Singapore," in S. Huang, B. S. A. Yeoh, and N. A. Rahman (eds.), *Asian Women as Transnational Domestic Workers* (Singapore: Marshall Cavendish Academic) 233–261.

Rakodi, C. (1997a), "Global Forces, Urban Change, and Urban Management in Africa," in C. Rakodi (ed.), *The Urban Challenge in Africa: Growth and Management of Its Large Cities* (Tokyo: United Nations University Press), 17–73.

——— (1997b), "'Conclusion," in C. Rakodi (ed.), *The Urban Challenge in Africa: Growth and Management of Its Large Cities* (Tokyo: United Nations University Press).

——— (ed.) (1997c), *The Urban Challenge in Africa: Growth and Management of Its Large Cities* (Tokyo: United Nations University Press).

Ratha, D. (2003), "Workers' Remittances: An Important and Stable Source of External Development Finance," in World Bank (ed.), *Global Development Finance 2003* (Washington, DC: World Bank).

Ratha, D., and S. Mohapatra (2009), *Revised Outlook for Remittance Flows, 2009–2011*, World Bank, March.

Ratha, D., S. Mohapatra, and A. Silwal (2009), "Migration and Remittance Trends 2009," Migration and Development Brief, World Bank, November 3.

Ratha, D., and W. Shaw (2007), "South-South Migration and Remittances," World Bank Working Paper, Development Prospects Group, World Bank, Washington, DC.

Ratha, D., and Z. Xu (2008), *Migration and Remittances Factbook 2008* (Washington, DC: World Bank).

Ravenstein, E. (1885), "The Laws of Migration," *Journal of the Statistical Society* 48: 167–227.

Redding, S. G. (1990), *The Spirit of Chinese Capitalism* (New York: De Gruyter).

Rees, M. (2003), *Our Final Century: Will the Human Race Survive the Twenty-first Century?* (London: Heinemann).

Reid, A. (1988), *Southeast Asia in the Age of Commerce, 1450–1680* (New Haven, CT: Yale University Press).

——— (ed.) (1993), *Southeast Asia in the Early Modern Era: Trade, Power, and Belief* (Ithaca, NY: Cornell University Press).

Riaño, P., and M. Villa (2008), 'Las fronteras del no reconocimiento: Los colombianos en situación de refugio en Ecuador," in P. Riaño and M. Villa (eds), *Poniendo tierra de por medio: Migración forzada de colombianos en Colombia, Ecuador y Canadá* (Medellín: Corporación Región), 222–278.

Richter, K., and H. Napaporn (1995), *Women's Economic Contribution to Households in Thailand: Implications for National Development and Social Welfare* (Bangkok: Gender Press).

Ricklefs, M. C. (1993), *War, Culture, and Economy in Java 1677–1726: Asian and European Imperialism in the Early Kartasura Period* (Sydney: Allen and Unwin).

Rimmer, S. J. (1991), *The Costs of Multiculturalism* (Bedford Park: Flinders Press).

Robinson, K. (1991), "Housemaids: The Effects of Gender and Culture on the Internal and International Migration of Indonesian Women," in G. Bottomley, M. de Lepervanche, and J. Martin (eds.), *Intersexions: Gender/Class/Ethnicity* (Sydney: Allen and Unwin), 33–51.

Robinson, W. I. (2008), *Latin America and Global Capitalism: A Critical Globalization Perspective* (Baltimore, MD: Johns Hopkins University Press).

Rodas, S., and S. Arguello, S. (2004), "'Aquí no pasa nada': El conflicto colombiano en la frontera con Ecuador," *Arcanos* 10, http://www.nuevoarcoiris.org.co.

Rogaly, B. (2006), "Intensification of Work-Place Regimes in British Agriculture: The Role of Migrant Workers," *Population, Space, and Place*, 14 (6): , 497–510.

Rojas Wiesner, M. L., and H. A. Cruz (2008), "Gendered Migrations in the Americas—Mexico as Country of Origin, Destination, and Transit," in N.

Piper (ed.), *New Perspectives on Gender and Migration: Rights, Entitlements, and Livelihoods* (London: Routledge), 191–247.

Rosen, E. I. (2002), *Making Sweatshops: The Globalization of the US Apparel Industry* (Berkeley: University of California Press).

Rosenblum, M. R. (2004), "Moving Beyond the Policy of No Policy: Emigration from Mexico and Central America," *Latin American Politics and Society* 46 (4): 91–125.

Rozental, A. (2004), "Fox's Foreign Policy Agenda: Global and Regional Priorities," in L. Rubio and S. K. Purcell (eds.), *Mexico Under Fox* (Boulder, CO: Lynne Rienner) 87–114.

Ruggie, J. G. (1993), "Territoriality and Beyond: Problematizing Modernity in International Relations," *International Organization* 47 (1): 139–174.

Ruhs, M. (2005), "The Potential of Temporary Migration Programmes in Future International Migration Policy," paper prepared for the Policy Analysis and Research Programme of the Global Commission on International Migration, Geneva.

——— (2006), "The Potential of Temporary Migration Programmes in Future International Migration Policy," *International Labour Review* 145 (1–2): 7–36.

Rybakovsky, L., and S. Ryzantsev (2005), "International Migration in the Russian Federation," United Nations Expert Group Meeting on International Migration and Development, New York, July 6–8, http://www.un.org.

Ryner, M. (2000), "European Welfare State Transformation and Migration," in M. Bommes and A. Geddes (eds.), *Immigration and Welfare: Challenging the Borders of the Welfare State* (London: Routledge), 51–70.

Ryter, L. (1998), "Pemuda Pancasila: The Last Loyalist Free Men of Suharto's Order?" *Indonesia* 66: 73–45.

Sachs, J. D., N. Bajpai, and A. Ramiah (2001), "Understanding Regional Economic Growth in India," paper presented at the Asian Economic Panel, Seoul, October 25–26.

Sack, R. (1986), *Human Territoriality: Its Theory and History* (Cambridge: Cambridge University Press).

Sadiq, K. (2009), *Paper Citizens: How Illegal Immigrants Acquire Citizenship in Developing Countries* (New York: Oxford University Press).

Sahlström, O. (2008), "Migration—A Lever for Union Renewal?" *Eurozine*, http://www.eurozine.com.

Sainsbury, D. (2006), "Immigrants' Social Rights in Comparative Perspective: Welfare Regimes, Forms in Immigration, and Immigration Policy Regimes," *Journal of European Social Policy* 16 (229): 229–243.

Salt, J. (1992), "Migration Processes Among the Highly Skilled in Europe," *International Migration Review* 26 (2): 484-505.

Salt, J., and J. Stein (1997), "Migration as a Business: The Case of Trafficking," *International Migration* 35 (4): 467–494.

Samers, M. (2004), "An Emerging Geo-politics of Illegal Immigration in the EU," *European Journal of Migration and Law* 6 (1): 23–41.

Sander, C., and S. M. Maimbo (2003), "Migrant Labor Remittances in Africa:

Reducing Obstacles to Developmental Contributions," Africa Region Working Paper Series, World Bank, Washington, DC.

Sandholtz, W., and A. Stone Sweet (eds.) (1997), *European Integration and Supranational Governance* (Oxford: Oxford University Press).

Samarn, L. (2000), "Thai Migrant Workers in Taiwan," in S. Chantavanich, A. Germershausen, and A. Beesey (eds.), *Thai Migrant Workers in East and Southeast Asia* (Bangkok: ARCM), 156–172.

Sassen, S. (1996), *Losing Control: Sovereignty in an Age of Globalization* (New York: Columbia University Press).

——— (1998), *Globalization and Its Discontents: Essays on the New Mobility of People and Money* (New York: The New Press).

——— (2000), "Women's Burden: Counter-Geographies of Globalization and the Feminization of Survival," *Journal of International Affairs* 53 (2): 503–524.

——— (2001), *The Global City: New York, London, Tokyo*, 2nd ed. (Princeton: Princeton University Press).

——— (2006a), *Territory, Authority, Rights: From Medieval to Global Assemblages* (Princeton: Princeton University Press).

——— (2006b), *Cities in a World Economy*, 3rd ed. (Thousand Oaks: Pine Forge Press).

——— (2007), *A Sociology of Globalization* (New York: W. W. Norton).

Satzewich, V. (1991), *Racism and the Incorporation of Foreign Labour: Farm Labour Migration to Canada Since 1945* (London: Routledge).

Saucedo, R., and T. Chretien (2007), "Legalization, Not Guest Worker Programs, Is the Solution: The New Challenges Facing the Immigrant Rights Movement," *Counterpunch*, July 6.

Saul, J. S. (2005), *The Collapse of Globalism* (London: Atlantic Books).

"SC to Govt: Stop Infiltration of Bangladeshis" (2009), *The Statesman* (New Delhi), April 16.

Schierup, C.-U., P. Hansen, and S. Castles (2006), *Migration, Citizenship, and the European Welfare State: A European Dilemma* (Oxford: Oxford University Press).

Schierup, C.-U., and S. Paulson (1994), *Arbetets etniska delning: Studier från en svensk bilfabrik* (Stockholm: Carlssons).

Schloenhardt, A. (2003), *Migrant Smuggling: Illegal Migration and Organized Crime in Australia and the Asia Pacific Region* (Dordrecht: Martinus Nijhoff Publishers).

Schmidley, A. D. (2001), *Profile of the Foreign-Born Population in the United States: 2000*, Current Population Reports, Series P23-206, US Census Bureau (Washington, DC: US Government Printing Office).

Schmidt, V. (2006), *Democracy in Europe: The EU and National Polities* (Oxford: Oxford University Press).

Schuck, P. H. (2007), "The Disconnect Between Public Attitudes and Policy Outcomes in Immigration," in C. Swain (ed.), *The Politics of Immigration Reform* (Cambridge: Cambridge University Press), 17–31.

Schuerkens, U. (2003), "Structural Change in Western Africa as a Legacy of European Colonialism: The Labour System in Ghana and the Ivory Coast," *Current Sociology* 51 (3–4): 287–304.

Schwartz, H. M. (2006), "Globalization: The Long View," in R. Stubbs and G. R. D. Underhill (eds.), *Political Economy and the Changing Global Order* (Oxford and Ontario: Oxford University Press), 51–63.

Sciortino, G. (2004), "Immigration in a Mediterranean Welfare State: The Italian Experience in Comparative Perspective," *Journal of Comparative Policy Analysis* 6 (2): 111–129.

Scott, J. C. (2009), *The Art of Not Being Governed: An Anarchist History of Upland Southeast Asia* (New Haven, CT: Yale University Press).

Seddon, D., G. Guring, and J. Adhikari (2000), *Foreign Labour Migration and the Remittance Economy of Nepal: Final Report to DfID* (Norwich: Overseas Development Group).

Sen, K. (2009), "The Financial Crisis and Development," mimeo, University of Manchester, UK.

Sexton, J. J. (2001), *The Feasibility of Providing Statistical Information on the International Mobility of the Highly Skilled for OECD European Countries*, Report of the OECD Directorate for Education, Employment, Labour, and Social Affairs, Paris.

Seymour, C. (1996), *Yakuza Diary: Doing Time in the Japanese Underworld* (New York: Atlantic Monthly Press).

Sharma, N. (2006), *Home Economics: Nationalism and the Making of "Migrant Workers" in Canada* (Toronto: University of Toronto Press).

Sheehan, P. (1998), *Among the Barbarians: The Dividing of Australia* (Sydney: Random House).

——— (2006), *Girls Like You* (Sydney: Macmillan).

Siddiqui, T. (2001), *Transcending Boundaries: Labour Migration of Women from Bangladesh* (Dhaka, Bangladesh: The University Press).

Siegel, J. T. (1998), *A New Criminal Type in Jakarta: Counter-Revolution Today* (Durham, NC: Duke University Press).

Sinha, S. K. (1998), *Report on Illegal Migration into Assam*, submitted to the President of India by the Governor of Assam, November 8, http://www.satp.org.

Skeldon, R. (1976), "Regional Associations and Population Migration in Peru: An Interpretation," *Urban Anthropology* 5 (3): 233–252.

——— (1977), "Regional Associations: A Note on Oposed Interpretations," *Comparative Studies in Society and History* 19 (4): 506–510.

——— (1992), "International Migration Within and from the East and Southeast Asian Region: A Review Essay," *Asian and Pacific Migration Journal* 1 (1): 19–63.

——— (1997), *Migration and Development: A Global Interpretation* (London: Longman).

——— (2000), "Trends in International Migration in the Asian and Pacific Region," *International Social Science Journal* 52 (165): 369–382.

——— (2003), "The Chinese Diaspora or the Migration of the Chinese Peoples?" in L. J. C. Ma and C. Cartier (eds.), *The Chinese Diaspora: Space, Place, Mobility, and Identity* (Lanham, MA: Rowman and Littlefield), 51–66.

——— (2005), "Linkages Between Migration and Poverty: The Millennium Development Goals and Population Mobility," in *International Migration*

and the Millennium Development Goals (New York: United Nations Population Fund), 55–63.
——— (2006), "Interlinkages Between Internal and International Migration and Development in the Asian Region," *Population, Space, and Place* 12 (1): 15–30.
——— (2008a), "International Migration as a Tool in Development Policy: A Passing Phase?" *Population and Development Review* 34 (1): 1–18.
——— (2008b), "Migration Policies and the Millennium Development Goals," Policy Network, London, www.policy-network.net.
——— (2009), "Migration and Development: Contested Consequences," in M. Kremer, P. van Lieshout, and R. Went (eds.), *Doing Good or Doing Better: Development Policies in a Globalizing World* (Amsterdam: Amsterdam University Press), 321–339.
——— (2010), "The Current Global Economic Crisis and Migration: Policies and Practice in Origin and Destination," Working Paper T-32, Development Research Centre on Migration, Globalisation and Poverty, University of Sussex,UK, May.
Skinner, G. W. (1998), "Creolized Chinese Societies in Southeast Asia," in A. Reid (ed.), *Sojourners and Settlers: Histories of Southeast Asia and the Chinese* (Sydney: Allen and Unwin), pp. 51–93.
Sklair, L. (1989), *Assembling for Development: The Maquila Industry in Mexico and the United States* (Winchester, MA: Unwin Hyman).
——— (2001), *The Transnational Capitalist Class* (Oxford: Blackwell).
Slavnic, Z. (2010), "The Political Economy of Informalization," *European Societies* 12 (1): 3–23.
Smith, J. (2006), "Guatemala: Economic Migrants Replace Political Refugees," Migration Information Source, April.
Smith, J. P., and B. Edmonston (1997), *The New Americans: Economic, Demographic, and Fiscal Effects of Immigration* (Washington, DC: National Academies Press).
Smith, M. P., and L. E. Guarnizo (eds.) (1998), *Transnationalism from Below* (New Brunswick, NJ: Transaction Publishers).
Smith, P. J. (ed.) (1997), *Human Smuggling: Chinese Migrant Trafficking and the Challenge to America's Immigration Tradition* (Washington, DC: Center for Strategic and International Studies).
Smith, S. (2006), "Who's Illegal? Shooting to Kill on the Border," *Counterpunch*, May 23.
Social Justice (2001), "In the Aftermath of Welfare 'Reform,'" *Social Justice* 28 (4): 1–128.
Solinger, D. J. (1999), *Contesting Citizenship in Urban China: Peasant Migrants, the State, and the Logic of the Market* (Berkeley: University of California Press).
Solomon, H. (1996), "Strategic Perspectives on Illegal Immigration into South Africa," *African Security Review* 5 (4), http://www.iss.co.za.
Solomos, J. (2003), *Race and Racism in Britain* (Basingstoke, UK: Palgrave).
SOPEMI (2001), *Annual Trends in International Migration 2000* (Paris: OECD).
Sophal, C., and S. Sovannarith (1999), "Cambodian Labour Migration to

Thailand: A Preliminary Assessment," Working Paper No. 11, Cambodia Development Resource Institute, Phnom Penh.

Sørensen, N. N. (ed.) (2007), *Living Across Worlds: Diaspora, Development, and Transnational Engagement* (Geneva: International Organization for Migration).

Sørensen, N. N., N. Van Hear, and P. Engberg-Pedersen (2002), "The Migration-Development Nexus: Evidence and Policy Options State of the Art Review," *International Migration* 40 (5): 3–48.

Soskice, D. (1999), "Divergent Production Regimes: Coordinated and Uncoordinated Market Economies in the 1980s and 1990s," in H. Kitschelt, P. Lange, G. Marks, and J. D. Stephens (eds.), *Continuity and Change in Contemporary Capitalism* (Cambridge: Cambridge University Press), 101–134.

South Africa (2010), "South Africa: Deportation of Zimbabweans to Begin Again," *IRIN*, Humanitarian News and Analysis, September 3, http://www.irinnews.org.

Soysal, Y. N. (1994), *Limits of Citizenship: Migrants and Postnational Membership in Europe* (Chicago: University of Chicago Press).

Srawooth, P. (2002), "The Labour Markets: An Overview," *TDRI Quarterly Review* 17 (1): 6–16.

Standing, G. (1989), "Global Feminization Through Flexible Labor," *World Development* 17 (7): 1077–1095.

——— (1999), "Global Feminization Through Flexible Labor: A Theme Revisited," *World Development* 27 (3): 583–602.

Stark, O. (2004), "Rethinking the Brain Drain," *World Development* 32 (1): 15–22.

Stark, O., and D. Levhari (1982), "On Migration and Risk in LDCs," *Economic Development and Cultural Change* 31 (1): 191–196.

Statistics Canada (2007), "Impact of Immigration on Labour Markets in Canada, Mexico, and the United States," *The Daily*, May 25, http://www.statscan.ca.

Statistisches Bundesamt Deutschland (2006), "Arbeitsmarkt," Statistisches Jahrbuch 2007, http://www.destatis.de.

Stiglitz, J. (2006), *Making Globalisation Work* (New York: Allen and Lane).

——— (2010), *Freefall: America, Free Markets, and the Sinking of the World Economy* (New York: W. W. Norton & Company).

Sugimoto, Y. (2003), *An Introduction to Japanese Society*, 2nd ed. (Cambridge: Cambridge University Press).

Sullivan, T. (2007), "Neighbor India Quietly Fencing Out Bangladesh," *Seattle Times*, June 26.

Sweeney, J. J. (2004), Statement by AFL-CIO President John J. Sweeney on President Bush's Principles for Immigration Reform, American Federation of Labor–Congress of Industrial Organizations, Washington, DC, January 8.

Sydney Morning Herald (2009), "Extremist Parties Appeal to Those Feeling Threatened," June 9, 8.

Taylor, M. (2008), "Introduction: Global Economy Contested," in M. Taylor (ed.), *Global Economy Contested: Power and Conflict Across the International Division of Labour* (London: Routledge), 1–8.

Taylor, P. (1994), "The State as Container: Territoriality in the Modern World-system," *Progress in Human Geography* 18 (2): 151–162.

Taylor-Gooby, P. (2005), "Is the Future American? Or, Can Left Politics Preserve European Welfare States from Erosion through 'Racial' Diversity?," *Journal of Social Policy* 34 (4): 661–672.

Teo, Y., and N. Piper (2009), "Foreigners in Our Homes: Linking Migration and Family Policies in Singapore," *Population, Space, and Place*, 15 (2): 147–159.

Thomas, F. (2008), "Migrants as Transnational Development Agents: An Inquiry into the Newest Round of the Migration-Development Nexus," *Population, Space, and Place* 14 (1): 21–42.

Thuno, M. (2001), "Reaching Out and Incorporating Chinese Overseas: The Trans-territorial Scope of the PRC by the End of the 20th Century," *The China Quarterly* 168: 910–929.

Tichenor, D. (2002), *Dividing Lines: The Politics of Immigration Control in America* (Princeton, NJ: Princeton University Press).

Tirtosudarmo, R. (2004), "Cross-border Migration in Indonesia and the Nunukan Tragedy," in A. Ananta and E. N. Arifin (eds.), *International Migration in Southeast Asia* (Singapore: ISEAS), 310–330.

TLWG (Temporary Labour Working Group) (2007), "The Journey to Licensing," http://dev.ethicaltrade.org.

Tokman, V. (2008), "Movilidad internacional de personas y protección social," CEPAL, Serie Macroeconómica del Desarrollo, 67, LC/L.2913-P, Santiago.

Tonry, M. (ed.) (1997), *Ethnicity, Crime, and Immigration: Comparative and Cross-national Perspective* (Chicago, IL: University of Chicago Press).

Traynor, I. (2010), "EU Keen to Strike Deal with Muammar Gaddafi on Immigration," *The Guardian*, September 1.

Triandafyhllidou, A., and R. Gropas (2007), *European Immigration: A Sourcebook* (Aldershot, UK: Ashgate).

Trifiletti, R. (1999), "Women's Labour Market Participation and the Reconciliation of Work and Family Life in Italy," in L. den Dulk, A. van Doorne-Huiskes, and J. Schippers (eds.), *Work-Family Arrangements in Europe* (Amsterdam: Thela-Thesis).

Trocki, C. (ed.) (1998), *Gangsters, Democracy, and the State in Southeast Asia* (Ithaca, NY: Cornell University).

Tu, W. (ed.) (1994), *China in Transformation* (Cambridge, MA: Harvard University Press).

TUC (Trade Union Congress) (2007), *The Economics of Migration: Managing the Impacts* (London: TUC).

Turner, B. (1992), "Outline of a Theory of Citizenship" in C. Mouffe (ed.), *Dimensions of Radical Democracy: Pluralism, Citizenship, Community* (London and New York: Verso), 33–62.

——— (1997), "Citizenship Studies: A General Theory," *Citizenship Studies*, 1 (1): 5–18.

UNDESA (United Nations Department of Economic and Social Affairs) (2001), *Replacement Migration: Is It a Solution to Declining and Aging Populations?* (New York: United Nations).

UNDP (United Nations Development Programme) (2003), *Human Development*

Report 2003: Millennium Development Goals—A Compact Among Nations to End Human Poverty (New York: Oxford University Press).
——— (2008), *Human Development Report 2007/2008: Fighting Climate Change: Human Solidarity in a Divided World* (New York: Oxford University Press).
——— (2009), *Human Development Report 2009: Overcoming Barriers—Human Mobility and Development* (Basingstoke, UK: Palgrave Macmillan), http://hdr.undp.org/en/media/HDR_2009_Tables_rev.xls.
UNFPA (United Nations Population Fund) (n.d.), "Trafficking in Human Misery," http://www.unfpa.or.
——— (2006), *A Passage to Hope—Women and International Migration* (New York: UNFPA).
UNHCR (United Nations High Commissioner for Refugees) (2008), "Protracted Refugee Situations: Revisiting the Problem," UNHCR Executive Committee Standing Committee—42nd Meeting, Geneva.
United Nations (2000a), "Protocol Against the Smuggling of Migrants by Land, Sea, and Air, Supplementing the United Nations Convention against Transnational Organized Crime," http://www.uncjin.org.
——— (2000b), "Protocol to Prevent, Suppress and Punish Trafficking in Persons, Especially Women and Children, Supplementing the United Nations Convention against Transnational Organized Crime," http://www.uncjin.org.
——— (2002), "Number of World's Migrants Reaches the 175 Million Mark," UN Press Release POP/844, October 28, http://www.un.org.
——— (2004), "UN Habitat Report Celebrates Multicultural Cities," September 14, http://www.unhabitat.org.
——— (2005), *Trends in Total Migrant Stock: The 2005 Revision*, Department of Economic and Social Affairs, Population Division, http://www.un.org.
——— (2006), *World Urbanization Prospects: The 2005 Revision*, Population Division, Economic and Social Affairs, New York.
——— (2008a), *Human Trafficking: An Overview* (New York and Geneva: UN Global Initiative to Fight Human Trafficking), http://www.ungift.org.
——— (2008b), *Toolkit to Combat Trafficking in Persons* (Vienna and New York: UN Global Program Against Trafficking in Human Beings), http://www.unodc.org.
——— (2009), *International Migration 2009*, Population Division, Department of Economic and Social Affairs, New York.
UNRISD (United Nations Research Institute for Social Development) (2005), *Gender Equality—Striving for Justice in an Unequal World* (Geneva: UNRISD).
US DHS (United States Department of Homeland Security) (2004), "Budget in Brief—Fiscal Year 2005," February 2, http://www.dhs.gov.
USDOS (United States Department of State) (2002), *Trafficking in Persons Report 2002*, http://www.state.gov.
——— (2005), *Trafficking in Persons Report 2005*, http://www.state.gov.
——— (2007), *Trafficking in Persons Report 2007*, http://www.state.gov.
——— (2009), *Trafficking in Persons Report 2009*, http://www.state.gov.
——— (2010), *Trafficking in Persons Report 2010*, http://www.state.gov.

US Senate (2003), "Expressing the Sense of the Senate Regarding the Temporary Entry Provisions in the Chile and Singapore Free Trade Agreements," S.RES.211, 108th Congress, 1st Session, Washington, DC.

Van Eyck, K. (2004), *Women and International Migration in the Health Sector* (Ferney-Voltaire Cedex, France: Public Services International).

Van Hear, N. (1998), *New Diasporas: The Mass Exodus, Dispersal, and Regrouping of Migrant Communities* (London: UCL Press).

van Oorschot, W. (2006), "Making the Difference in Social Europe," *Journal of European Social Policy* 16 (1): 23–42.

Väyrynen, R. (2003), "Illegal Immigration, Human Trafficking, and Organized Crime," Discussion Paper No 2003/72, United Nations University World Institute for Development Economics Research (UNU/WIDER).

Verdera V., F. (2007), *La Pobreza en el Perú: Un Análisis de Sus Causas y de las Políticas para Enfrentarla* (Lima: Instituto de Estudios Peruanos).

von Oppen, A. (1995), *Terms of Trade and Terms of Trust: The History and Contexts of Pre-colonial Market Production around the Upper Zambezi and Kasai* (Hamburg: Lit).

Wacquant, Löic J. D. (1996), "Red Belt, Black Belt: Racial Division, Class Inequality, and the State in the French Urban Periphery and the American Ghetto," in E. Mingione (ed.), *Urban Poverty and the Underclass* (Oxford: Blackwell), 234–274.

Waldinger, R., N. Lim, and D. Cort (2007), "Bad Jobs, Good Jobs, No Jobs? The Employment Experience of the Mexican-American Second Generation," *Journal of Ethnic and Migration Studies* 33 (1): 1–35.

Wallace, H. (2005), "An Institutional Anatomy and Five Policy Models," in H. Wallace, W. Wallace, and M. Pollack (eds.), *Policy-Making in the European Union*, 5th ed. (Oxford: Oxford University Press), 49–90.

Wallace, H., W. Wallace, and M. Pollack (eds.) (2005), *Policy-Making in the European Union*, 5th ed. (Oxford: Oxford University Press).

Wang, G. (1992), *Community and Nation: China, Southeast Asia, and Australia* (St. Leonards: Asian Studies Association of Australia/Allen and Unwin).

——— (2003), *Don't Leave Home: Migration and the Chinese* (Singapore: Times Academic Press).

Waters, J. L. (2003), "Flexible Citizens? Transnationalism and Citizenship Amongst Economic Immigrants in Vancouver," *The Canadian Geographer* 47 (3): 219–234.

——— (2006), "Emergent Geographies of International Education and Social Exclusion," *Antipode* 38 (5): 1046–1068.

Waylen, G. (2000), "Gendered Political Economy and Feminist Analysis," in J. Cook, J. Roberts, and G. Waylen (eds), *Towards Gendered Political Economy* (Basingstoke, UK: Macmillan), 14–38.

——— (2004), "Putting Governance into the Gendered Political Economy of Globalization," *International Feminist Journal of Politics* 6 (4): 557–578.

Wee, V., and A. Sim (2005), "Hong Kong as a Destination for Migrant Domestic Workers," in S. Huang, B. S. A. Yeoh, and N. A. Rahman (eds.), *Asian Women as Transnational Domestic Workers* (Singapore: Marshall Cavendish), 155–189.

Weekley, K. (2006), "From Wage Labourers to Investors? Filipina Migrant Domestic Workers and Popular Capitalism," in K. Hewison and K. Young (eds.), *Transnational Migration and Work in Asia* (London: Routledge), 193–212.

Weiner, M. (1997), *Japan's Minorities: The Illusion of Homogeneity* (London: Routledge).

Weiss, A. (2005), "The Transnationalization of Social Inequality: Conceptualizing Social Positions on a World Scale," *Current Sociology* 53 (4): 707–728.

——— (2006), "Hoch qualifizierte MigrantInnen: Der Kern einer transnationalen Mittelklasse?" in F. Kreutzer and S. Roth (eds.), *Transnationale Karrieren: Biografien, Lebensführungen, und Mobilität* (Wiesbaden, Germany: VS Verlag für Sozialwissenschaften), 283–300.

Weiss, L., and J. M. Hobson (1995), *States and Economic Development: A Comparative Historical Analysis* (Cambridge: Polity Press).

WHO (World Health Organization) (2006a), *Working Together for Health* (Geneva: WHO).

——— (2006b), *Human Resources for Health in the WHO European Region* (Geneva: WHO).

Williams, A. (1991), *The European Community* (Oxford: Blackwell).

Williamson, J. G. (1998), "Globalization, Labor Markets, and Policy Backlash in the Past," *Journal of Economic Perspectives* 12 (4): 51–72.

Willmore, L. (2000), "Export Processing Zones in Cuba," UNDESA Discussion Paper 12, United Nations Economic and Social Affairs.

Wilpert, C. (1998), "Migration and Informal Work in the New Berlin: New Forms of Work or New Sources of Labour?" *Journal of Ethnic and Migration Studies* 24 (2): 269–294.

Wilson, W. J. (1987), *The Truly Disadvantaged: The Inner City, the Underclass, and Public Policy* (Chicago: University of Chicago Press).

——— (1999), *The Bridge Over the Racial Divide* (Berkeley: University of California Press).

Winkelman-Gleed, A. (2006), *Migrant Nurses: Motivation, Integration, and Contribution* (Oxford: Radcliffe Publishing).

Winters, L. A., and S. Yusuf (2007), "Dancing with Giants," in L.A. Winters and S. Yusuf (eds.), *Dancing with Giants: China, India, and the Global Economy* (Washington, DC: World Bank), 1–34.

Wolf, D. L. (1992), *Factory Daughters, Gender Household Dynamics, and Rural Industrialisation in Java* (Berkeley: University of California Press).

Wong, S.-L. (1985), "The Chinese Family Firm: A Model," *British Journal of Sociology* 36 (1): 58–72.

——— (1986), "Modernization and Chinese Culture in Hong Kong," *The China Quarterly* 106: 306–325.

——— (1988), *Emigrant Entrepreneurs: Shanghai Industrialists in Hong Kong* (Hong Kong: Oxford University Press).

Wood, Geoffrey (2000), "Concepts and Themes: Landscaping Social Development," *Social Development SCOPE Papers* 9, DfID, London.

——— (2003), "Staying Secure, Staying Poor: The 'Faustian Bargain,'" *World Development* 31 (3): 455–471.

World Bank (2005), *Global Economic Prospects 2006: Economic Implications of Remittances and Migration* (Washington, DC: IBRD).

——— (2008), *World Development Report 2008: Agriculture for Development* (Washington, DC: IBRD).

——— (2009), *World Development Report 2009: Reshaping Economic Geography* (Washington, DC: IBRD).

——— (2011), *Migration and Remittances Factbook 2011,* 2nd ed. (Washington, DC: World Bank).

Wortley, S. (2002), "Misrepresentation or Reality? The Depiction of Race and Crime in the Toronto Print Media," in B. Schissel and C. Brooks (eds.), *Marginality and Condemnation: An Introduction to Critical Criminology* (Halifax, Nova Scotia: Fenwood Publishing), 55–82.

Wouterse, F. S. (2006), *Survival or Accumulation? Migration and Rural Households in Burkina Faso* (Wageningen, the Netherlands: Wageningen University).

——— (2008), "Migration, Poverty, and Inequality: Evidence from Burkina Faso," IFPRI Discussion Paper, International Food Policy Research Institute, Washington, DC.

Wright, M. (2006), *Disposable Women and Other Myths of Global Capitalism* (London: Routledge).

Xiang, B. (2001), "Structuration of Indian Information Technology Professionals' Migration to Australia: An Ethnographic Study," *International Migration*, 39 (5): 73–90.

——— (2004), "Indian Information Technology Professionals' World System: The Nation and the Transnation in Individuals' Migration Strategy," in B. S. A. Yeoh and K. Willis (eds.), *State/Nation/Transnation* (London: Routledge), 161–178.

——— (2005), *Transcending Boundaries: Zhejiangcun: The Story of a Migrant Village in Beijing* (Leiden, the Netherlands: Brill).

Yamanaka, K., and N. Piper (2005), "Feminized Migration in East and Southeast Asia: Policies, Actions, and Empowerment," United Nations Research Institute for Social Development, Geneva.

Yeates, N. (2004), "Global Care Chains: Critical Reflections and Lines of Enquiry," *International Feminist Journal of Politics* 6 (3): 369–391.

Yeoh, B. S. A., S. Huang, and T. Lam, (2005), "Transnationalizing the 'Asian' Family: Imaginaries, Intimacies, and Strategic Intents," *Global Networks* 5 (4): 307–315.

Young, K. (2006), "Globalization and the Changing Management of Migrating Service Workers in the Asia-Pacific," in K. Hewison and K. Young (eds.), *Transnational Migration and Work in Asia* (London: Routledge), 15–36.

Yusuf, S., K. Nabeshima, and D. H. Perkins (2007), "China and India Reshape Global Industrial Geography," in L. A. Winters and S. Yusuf (eds.), *Dancing with Giants: China, India, and the Global Economy* (Washington, DC: World Bank), 35–66.

Zachariah, K. C., K. P. Kannan, and S. I. Rajan (eds.) (2002), *Kerala's Gulf Connection* (Kerala, India: Centre for Development Studies).

Zhang, G., and W. Li (2002), "International Mobility of China's Resources in

Science and Technology and Its Impact," in OECD (ed.), *International Mobility of the Highly Skilled* (Paris: OECD), 189–190.

Zhang, S. X. (2007), *Smuggling and Trafficking in Human Beings: All Roads Lead to America* (Westport: Praeger Publishers).

Zimbabwe Independent (2008), "South Africa: Editor's Memo—Country Must Contain Hate Crimes," May 15.

Zlotnik, H. (2006), "The Dimensions of Migration in Africa," in M. Tienda, S. Findley, S. Tollman, and E. Preston-Whyte (eds.), *Africa on the Move: African Migration and Urbanisation in Comparative Perspective* (Johannesburg: Wittwatersrand University Press).

Zolberg, A. (1989), "The Next Waves: Migration Theory for a Changing World," *International Migration Review* 23 (3): 403–430.

——— (2006), *A Nation by Design: Immigration Policy in the Fashioning of America* (Cambridge, MA: Russell Sage Foundation/Harvard University Press).

The Contributors

Oliver Bakewell is senior research officer at the International Migration Institute (IMI) at the University of Oxford, UK.

Harald Bauder is associate professor in the Graduate Program in Immigration and Settlement Studies (ISS) and the Geography Department at Ryerson University, Canada.

Stephen Castles holds a research chair in sociology at the University of Sydney, Australia, and is associate director of the International Migration Institute (IMI) at the University of Oxford, UK.

Jock Collins is professor in the School of Finance and Economics at the University of Technology, Sydney, Australia.

H. Richard Friman is Eliot Fitch Professor for International Studies and professor of political science at Marquette University, United States.

Andrew Geddes is professor of politics at the University of Sheffield, UK.

Susan Martin is executive director of the Institute for the Study of International Migration and Donald G. Herzberg Chair in International Migration at Georgetown University, United States.

Nicola Phillips is professor of political economy and director of the Political Economy Institute at the University of Manchester, UK.

Nicola Piper is senior lecturer in the School of Environment and Society and associate director of the Centre for Migration Policy Research at Swansea University, UK.

Carl-Ulrik Schierup is professor at the National Institute for Working Life (NIWL) and in the Department of Ethnic Studies at the University of Linköping, Sweden.

Ronald Skeldon is professorial fellow in geography at the University of Sussex, UK.

Ken Young is adjunct professor in sociology at Latrobe University, Australia.

Index

About the Book

How does the evolution of global capitalism shape patterns and processes of migration? How does migration in turn shape and intersect with the forces at work in the global economy? How should we understand the relationship between migration and development, and how is migration connected with patterns of poverty and inequality? How are processes of migration and immigration governed in different parts of the world? The authors of *Migration in the Global Political Economy* tackle these questions in a set of engaging and authoritative chapters.

Mobilizing the core insights of critical IPE scholarship and combining analysis of the big picture with attention to particular regions, countries, and actors, the authors seek to bring the increasingly important processes of migration to the center of enquiries into globalization and its social underpinnings.

Nicola Phillips is professor of political economy at the University of Manchester. She also serves as director of the Political Economy Institute at the University of Manchester and editor in chief of the journal *New Political Economy*. Her recent publications include *Development* (with Anthony Payne) and *The Southern Cone Model: The Political Economy of Regional Capitalist Development in Latin America*.